The Landfill Chronicles

Unearthing Legends of Modern Music

Dan Ouellette

Cymbal Press

Published by Cymbal Press, Torrance, CA USA
cymbalpress.com

This and other Cymbal Press books may be purchased at cymbalpress.com. Volume and education discounts are available.

ISBN
Paperback: 978-1-955604-14-7
Hardcover: 978-1-955604-15-4

MUS025000   MUSIC / Genres & Styles / Jazz
MUS055000   MUSIC / Essays
MUS050000   MUSIC / Individual Composer & Musician
BIO004000   BIOGRAPHY & AUTOBIOGRAPHY / Music

All marks are the property of their respective owners.

Publisher: Gary S. Stager
Editor: Sylvia Martinez
Cover: Yvonne Martinez

While every precaution has been taken, the publisher and author assume no responsibility for errors, omissions, changed information or URLs, or for damages resulting from the use of the information herein.

Table of Contents

Preface   i

John Abercrombie—Six-String Adventures   1

Laurie Anderson—Life on a String   7

Carla Bley—Jumping Jazz Loops   11

Dee Dee Bridgewater—The Mali Adventure   23

David Byrne—Always Makes Sense   33

Regina Carter—Jazz Violin Virtuoso   41

Ornette Coleman—A Celebration   57

Elvis Costello—Musical Omnivore   59

Charlie Haden—Wide World of Wonders   83

John Lee Hooker—King of the Boogie   107

Freddie Hubbard—An Infamous Blindfold Test   115

Bobby Hutcherson—California Dreaming   121

Abdullah Ibrahim—Musical Depth   129

Keith Jarrett—Reinvented   141

Elvin Jones—Ferocious Beatmaster   159

Wynton Marsalis—The Empire at the Crossroads   165

Joni Mitchell—Stranger in the Strange World of Pop Music   175

Jason Moran—Pivots   189

Astor Piazzolla—Nuevo Tango Pioneer   197

Lou Reed—Ecstasy and Poe   203

Saxophone Summit—A Holy Jazz Trinity   213

Wayne Shorter—The Ultimate Jazz Astronaut   219

Jimmy Smith—Basking in the B-3   231

Esperanza Spalding—Sings the Melody, Anchors the Rhythm   237

Henry Threadgill—Explores the Contrary   247

McCoy Tyner—Lyrical Thunder   257

Frank Zappa—The Last Interview   263

About the Author   283

Appendix—Attributions   284

Also from Cymbal Press   287

Preface

In Don DeLillo's epic postmodern novel *Underworld*, the protagonist Nick Shay is an executive for a waste management firm. Early in the book, he says, "We were waste handlers, waste traders, cosmologists of waste...Waste is a religious thing. We entomb contaminated waste with a sense of reverence and dread. It is necessary to respect what we discard."

In this instance, Nick is talking about toxic chemical and radioactive refuse, but he's also reflecting on the big picture of a consumer culture awash in trash. Later in the book, while discussing what course of resolve to take with their ailing mother, Nick and his estranged younger brother Matt talk while they wash and dry dishes. At a pause in their uncomfortable conversation, Matt steers away from the difficult topic at hand to a mundane inquiry. He asks, "How's the waste business?"

Nick sarcastically responds, "Booming. The waste business. Bigger by the minute."

"I'll bet it is."

"We can't build enough landfills, dig enough gaping caverns."

Nick is an alienated expert on the escalation of waste and a detached connoisseur of landfills—the mountains of garbage created by modern society and containing the byproducts of history, waiting to be probed like ancient tells by future excavators seeking for insight into a crazed mass-consumption culture.

Filling the bulk of these bulldozer-compacted sites are common-day, throw-away items like nonrecyclable plastics, glass shards, pulverized concrete and twisted rebar, animal fat and bones, decaying wet vegetable matter fit for the compost pile, and arguably the most notorious toss: paper, which when decomposed by bacteria in the soil accounts for the potent greenhouse gas, methane, which is twenty percent more detrimental to the atmosphere than carbon dioxide.

Some reports estimate that fourteen percent of a typical landfill is newsprint, which if not interred but recycled is generally used to create tissue and cardboard. The EPA in a 2005 recycling report estimated that paper in general accounted for fifty percent of national landfill, at a weight of 42 million tons. Other studies found that municipal waste of paper was more in the range of thirty-five percent. The good news is that 1993 marked the first year that more paper was recycled than was buried in landfills (or burned for the sake of landfill shortages).

Even so, my guess is that the bulk of my career writing about popular music in magazines and newspapers is forever buried in landfills throughout America. Some of my stories—including a 1993 cover story on Frank Zappa shortly before his death for the long-shuttered Tower Records monthly magazine *Pulse!*—had a short shelf life before being bundled up and hauled away to make way for the new issue. Interestingly, since *Pulse!* died before the reign of digital, there's no official web address where you can access what I wrote.

The same holds true for the once-heralded daily, the *San Francisco Chronicle.* I wrote "Special to the Chronicle" stories as a regular contributor when I lived in the Bay Area as well as when I moved to New York City. While some of my stories are available online (it requires being a deep-dive sleuth), the paper versions were added to landfill mountains in Northern California.

Then there's *Spectrum* magazine that I edited and wrote for before its demise in the late '90s and early aughts. A Google search for my two sit-downs with Lou Reed reveals zilch.

A contributor to *DownBeat* magazine since 1987, hardly any of my contributions, including a cover story on John Lee Hooker, are available online. While many people tend to save copies of the "jazz, blues and beyond" bible, far more clean out their cellars and cart off the magazines to the trash, where the pages rot in the garbage dump. Recently *DownBeat* digitized its archives, but only time will tell how easily the stories are accessible.

So, as a nod to posterity, I've compiled a portfolio of articles on pop, blues and jazz legends for magazines and newspapers I have written for since the late '80s that have largely contributed to the landfills. The title? Appropriately, *The Landfill Chronicles.*

There are three "writer's-cut" *DownBeat* jazz travel tales, including two cover stories: Regina Carter going to meet a famous, guard-protected violin in Genoa, Italy, and Dee Dee Bridgewater seeking her African roots in Mali. Then there's another *DownBeat* profile on South African pianist Abdullah Ibrahim (Dollar Brand) who I interviewed in his Cape Town hometown and a decade-plus later on the road at a festival in Austria.

While my Zappa piece is not an exhaustive review of the icon's legendary career, it does serve as a snapshot of his life from our conversation in his home shortly before he died. The original manuscript I turned in to my *Pulse!* editors stretched to 6,000+ words which was shaved down to a manageable 2,000+ word story. For the book, I provide the writer's cut, keeping sections of my original that were lopped off for the print version. A diehard Zappa fan or two has scanned the edited copy, but this is the first time the full interview has been published.

My Lou Reed chapter is a stitching together of conversations in his SoHo office about two of his latter-day studio albums, *Ecstasy* and *The Raven*, a collection inspired by Edgar Allen Poe's writing. My stories appeared as two articles for *Spectrum* and the *San Francisco Chronicle.*

My Astor Piazzolla profile, which originally appeared in the *Berkeley Monthly*, opens a window onto the bandoneón player's fascinating story of how he came to develop and suffer for nuevo tango. It is long gone into the landfill.

The Landfill Chronicles was born as a passionate exploration of artistry during the early dark days of the pandemic. At the time, with a lack of writing assignments,

I reflected on meaningful and ultimately historical conversations I had with a long list of musicians in my writing career. They ranged from such rock artists as Elvis Costello and David Byrne to such jazz maestros as Charlie Haden, Carla Bley, Wynton Marsalis, Keith Jarrett, and more.

Other chapters include profiles on a day in the life of iconoclastic jazz composer Henry Threadgill, a rambling conversation with blues icon John Lee Hooker, and a mystical dialogue with jazz great Wayne Shorter.

There a few stories that did not make it into print. The article on Regina Carter's concert in New York was rejected by a New York publication. I retrieved it to complete the full narrative of her adventure with one of the most famous violins in the world. And the second half of the John Lee Hooker chapter ended up on the *DownBeat* cutting-room floor so never saw the light of day in print.

The most significant story in this book that did not appear in print in a magazine or newspaper is the snapshot of Joni Mitchell in 2007 on the eve of the release of *Shine*, her first album of new material in ten years—and perhaps her finale of original songs. I was asked to come to her house north of Vancouver and help with its launch. Excerpts of what appears here ended up in press kits for the album (long tossed by journalists, but perhaps saved by Joni fanatics), but there is also an unpublished journal-like overview of meeting her and talking with her about topics not related to the album. I felt like I had to include it here because it captures this moment in her life and career that might otherwise be lost forever.

Dating back to 1988, the stories here are based on conversations that were published in magazines, newspapers, and sometimes online as the early days of the digital era took hold. They most often took place during pivotal junctures in the careers of these legends of modern music.

In addition to being archives for future reference, these articles became something more to me as I unearthed the stories and edited them together. They became personal to me again—a memoir of sorts of my deep connections with artists I conversed with.

The majority of my in-print stories are forever gone—largely unavailable or invisible in any digital version. I have retrieved them in *The Landfill Chronicles*, a 27-chapter compilation that was given birth on the writer's platform Medium and is now returned to print through Cymbal Press.

Retrieving these stories from the landfill has been a dumpster-diver's dream.

John Abercrombie— Six-String Adventures

My 2012 trip upstate to John's home is a memorable journey for a conversation with one of jazz's most remarkable guitarists. He had wonderful stories that he shared with wry and humorous reflections. Five years after our hang, John passed way. This is my writer's cut of the article that ran in DownBeat.

THE MOMENT LOOKS FOR YOU
2012

FINDING A NEW HOME

After years living in Boston post-Berklee College and then relocating in 1970 to a loft space in New York, the amiable and self-effacing John Abercrombie today dwells in the country, about an hour from New York by car or train. He's got a deck for barbecuing, a pool that's perfect for a summer day, a yard with tall trees and a disheveled downstairs jam-session room scattered with instruments, most of them guitars.

John seems contently settled yet also ready to pounce onto a new quartet project that's already in the wings (including pianist Marc Copeland, a longtime collaborator).

There were no straight lines, no sudden leaps, no predictable trajectory in John's coming of age as a jazz guitarist. He didn't arrive as a child prodigy nor did he exude an overpowering confidence. He came up listening to Chuck Berry and Scotty Moore on Elvis Presley sides in the '50s. He encountered his first jazz revelation taking in Barney Kessel on the 1957 LP *The Poll Winners* with Shelly Manne and Ray Brown. He experienced his second guitar epiphany hearing Jim Hall's counterpoints to Sonny Rollins on the saxophonist's *The Bridge* and later bowed to Jimi Hendrix, especially 1967's *Axis: Bold As Love*.

In his early days, John was more likely to unplug and retreat to his room when he heard further-evolved musicians—saxophonists, pianists, other guitarists—than to charge full-speed into jam sessions unprepared and unable to keep up.

During John's first year at Berklee School of Music in 1962 (eight years before its name was changed to Berklee College of Music), he heard saxophonist Sadao Watanabe, a fellow classmate, practicing Charlie Parker tunes, which crushed him. "I felt terrible," John says. "I thought, 'I'll never be able to play this music. It's too hard.' But I stuck it out. I didn't know what else to do. If that didn't work, well, I thought I could go home and pump gas. I could give it up and become one of everyone else."

Not a chance. Determined, John dug in, studied heavily, listened intently, practiced vehemently and overcame the urge to retreat. Fifty years after enrolling at Berklee, the 67-year-older is recognized as one of jazz's most identifiable and adventurous six-stringers.

He has enjoyed a profoundly successful career as a leader almost exclusively on ECM Records, including his new album, *Within A Song*, an homage largely to the music of the early '60s that made an impact on his young ears. It features a support team of Joe Lovano on saxophone, Drew Gress on bass and Joey Baron on drums. John pays tribute to Rollins and Hall, Art Farmer, Bill Evans, Miles Davis and Ornette Coleman—artists who were resolute on re-envisioning the tradition.

In the album's liner notes, John writes, "It was this music that spoke to me. When I heard it, it was like finding a new home. The music on this recording is dedicated to all those musicians [who] gave me a place to live."

THE EARLY DAYS

Convinced he wanted to pursue a musical life while still in high school in Greenwich, Connecticut, John started poking around at post-graduation possibilities. Two schools he investigated were Manhattan School of Music and The Juilliard School. "None acknowledged jazz, and none accepted guitar as a major instrument," he says. "Plus, they were looking for students who had super-good grades, which I didn't, so they were out from the beginning."

He heard about Berklee from a friend and sent away for a catalog. When it arrived, there on the cover were various musicians hanging around the front steps of the school. One was Hungarian guitarist Gábor Szabó, who had his instrument with him. John opened the booklet and discovered there were numerous classes for guitarists.

"'That's for me, I'm in,'" he recalls. "The requirements were two years of musical experience. Everybody lied. I had classes with guys who couldn't play at all, and real professional players." He adds, with a laugh, "Keith Jarrett was there my first year. He came and realized there was nothing they could offer him, so he went off to fame and fortune."

After a discouraging first year at Berklee, John gained confidence, especially through the encouragement of such teachers as Herb Pomeroy, John LaPorta and Jack Petersen (the first full-time guitar teacher and inaugural chair of the guitar department). John soon scored a gig with a small band. "It felt good to be a working musician, carrying my guitar down the street," he says. "It was being on a team, where you don't quite know what it is but that you're part of it, you're in this thing called music."

There weren't many opportunities to play in public, so at first John did that more in private. He was hired to play in the Danny White Orchestra R&B/blues

band, whose gigs included playing at Air Force and Army bases. Repertoire included R&B standards as well as arrangements of Horace Silver's and Ray Charles' music. That led to John being enlisted by Hammond B3 player John "Hammond" Smith.

"John was looking for a young guitar player whom he could abuse and pay the least amount of money possible," he says with a laugh. It was a funky, jazz-tinged job in the organ tradition that kept the young guitarist busy for seven nights a week plus a Sunday matinee.

John later made his first recording with Smith in 1968, *The Soulful Blues*, in a band that included saxophonist Houston Person and drummer Grady Tate.

During this time, two seminal events were taking place in the outside world. First was the rise in popularity of rock music, precipitated by The Beatles and enlarged upon by bands that John listened to, including Cream and later Hendrix. But the most immediate backdrop was the Vietnam War. John attended Berklee from 1962–'66, which sheltered him from the draft, then graduated in 1967. If he had pushed to teach, he would have avoided conscription, but he opted not to go that route. "I didn't want to teach," he says. "I was too young. I wanted to play."

Two days after graduation he received his notice to report to the induction center in New Haven, Connecticut, to take his physical. "I flunked," says John with a big smile. "It's a true story. I was born with a short right leg that required me to wear a lift in my shoe. Of course, it was embarrassing as a kid. It looked weird. Kids at school would call me Frankenstein. So I stopped wearing it. But when I got my draft notice, my mother suggested getting new shoes with a lift. And my doctor wrote a letter that said something like, 'Please excuse John from killing and maiming today. He's not feeling well.' So I took the physical and I was rejected."

John soon jumped into the jazz rock fire by joining the pioneering fusion band Dreams, which included Randy and Michael Brecker, Billy Cobham (then Bill Cobham Jr.) and others. "It was an assorted group of maniacs," John says. "That was the beginning of me not playing straightahead jazz for many years."

While the band largely fizzled in the fusion zone, it did help launch Billy's career. The drummer played with Miles, joined up with John McLaughlin's Mahavishnu Orchestra, and into the early-to-mid-'70s helmed his own fusion band. He enlisted John. It was exciting, and John loved his bandmates, but the gig ultimately took him away from his jazz roots.

"I was playing with a wah-wah pedal and other effects," he recalls. "I could play this music and still play a standard like 'Stella By Starlight,' which a lot of the guys couldn't go near. I knew Billy could play with a beautiful swing, but he was playing rock rhythms in odd meters and always funky. The harmonies didn't go very far. The solos were played on a vamp. Something was missing."

When Billy's band went on tour as the opening act for the Doobie Brothers, John's dissatisfaction grew. It climaxed when they played the Spectrum in Philadelphia. "They play football there," he says in mock exasperation. "And I thought, 'What the hell am I doing here? Wait a minute—this isn't what I set out to do.' I needed an out."

3

The big turning point, John says, came when he got a call out of the blue. "The phone rang and it's, 'Hey man, this is Jack DeJohnette. I got your number from a friend, and I've been hearing good things about you. I'm starting a band. Would you like to come to my house with Miroslav Vitous and jam?'"

John agreed. They set up in Jack's backyard (at this time the drummer was living in Flemington, New Jersey) and played free improvisations. "All of sudden," John says, "we hear someone playing a soprano saxophone off in the distance. It was Steve Marcus, who lived across this field. As he got closer and closer, we were playing along with him. It was a mind-blowing hippie experience. That was how I got out of hard-core fusion into something that was way more expansive."

Around this same time, John linked up with ECM label founder Manfred Eicher, who knew the guitarist from his appearance on trumpeter Enrico Rava's 1973 album *Katchapari Rava* (on the Italian label BASF) and invited him to make a recording as a leader. Initially John told Manfred that he was just a sideman and hadn't written much of his own music.

But Manfred persisted. They corresponded by mail, and finally the guitarist said that he was ready. His vision for a trio included Jack and organist/pianist Jan Hammer. "I hired two ridiculous guys who were so good, so wide open, so exploratory, so full of amazing chops, it was all I could do to keep up with them to make the record," he says. The result was John's *Timeless*, which teems with a rare blend of spirited fusion, gripping rhythms and acoustic jazz, including two ballads that John wrote specifically for the session.

In 1975, John, Jack and bassist Dave Holland formed the monster post-fusion band Gateway and recorded its eponymous debut for ECM. "Phew, that was such a great band," John says. "The music was so fresh. I was a crazy kid then. We were all like kids let loose in a toy shop. It was like, 'Take any toy—you won't get in trouble.' I had permission to take all kinds of risks. It was the Wild West. One audience member told us that he heard that record and he shaved his head. There were no guitar trios then playing in that free style." The group recorded two albums, then reconvened nearly 20 years later for two more.

Dave recalls those heady early days. "That band meant a lot in the '70s," he says. "We got to explore music that no one else was doing. We had great tours." As for John's guitar voice, Dave adds, "He has always looked to seek new music. He has great range. And he has such a personal voice on the guitar, which is not easy. Over the years he's come up with his own sound, approach, phrasing. He can straddle a lot of styles, going into the contemporary field with open-form music and contemporary beats."

Beginning with *Timeless* and *Gateway*, with rare exceptions, Abercrombie has been in ECM's stable since, playing with a dizzying array of musicians, including a quartet with pianist Richie Beirach, more sessions with Rava, albums with Ralph Towner as well as Jan Garbarek, a trio with Peter Erskine and Marc Johnson, and for the last four albums before *Within a Song*, a quartet with violinist Mark Feldman.

WITHIN A SONG

John opted to form a new quartet for the *Within a Song* sessions, this time with a saxophonist instead of violin. "I felt like that last quartet had run its course," he says. "I went back and forth with Manfred about this and finally he said, 'Why don't you call Lovano?' I'd played with Joe over the years, but I figured he was just so busy with recordings and touring. Still, I called him up, and he said, 'Absolutely.' I knew he would be the best person because he knows the music."

On the new disc, John creates a compassionate, very personal reflection on the integral music of his awakening years as a jazz guitarist. Rather than paying tribute to one artist, he zeroes in on songs from albums that influenced him, including Miles's *Kind Of Blue*, Rollins' *The Bridge*, Coleman's *This Is Our Music*, Evans' *Interplay* and John Coltrane's *Crescent*—all music that John says makes for "a celebration of an era when the musicians were stretching the forms."

"My favorite record of all time is *The Bridge*," John says. "I first heard it in 1962 at a record store in Port Chester, New York. I saw the picture of Sonny on the cover. He had a strange haircut, jacket and his tenor saxophone. I asked the guy in the shop to play it for me, and the first track was 'Without a Song,' with Sonny playing the melody and Jim Hall playing a little counterpoint. Remember the little girl from *The Exorcist* when her head spins around 360 degrees? That's what happened to me. And I kept thinking, 'What are they doing?' The sound grabbed me, and it was at that point that I knew what I wanted to do more than anything. Those moments, they just happen. You can't look for them. They look for you, and *wham!*"

John knew he needed to pay tribute to that tune, and he complemented it with his own composition "Within a Song," which opens the track with an upbeat, dance-like guitar/tenor sax connection. That transforms into "Without a Song," before returning to the original head.

John also includes the *Bridge* track "Where Are You." He gives further salutation to Hall by including a take on Sergio Mihanovich's lyrical song "Sometime Ago," which was a staple of the quartet Hall and trumpeter Art Farmer co-led (featuring bassist Steve Swallow and drummer Pete La Roca). "Jim was a big influence on me, in the way he played and worked inside of a band," John says. "The Hall-Farmer group was my favorite, especially live."

Also featured on *Within a Song* is a nod to *Kind of Blue* with a reflective-to-ecstatic rendition of "Flamenco Sketches." Abercrombie didn't discover the 1959 album until he was at Berklee: "People were talking about modes while I was still in Barney Kessel-Tal Farlow land and trying to figure out how to play a root-position chord."

John approached the song by taking the form and improvising with it, a lesson he learned when playing with Gil Evans at the Village Vanguard years before. "We were playing 'Summertime' and I didn't state the melody, but improvised around it," he says. "After the set, I apologized to Gil for doing that, and he said, 'Don't apologize. Who cares? Gershwin's dead, so you can make your own melody.'"

On "Flamenco Sketches," Abercrombie and Lovano solo above and below each other. "We're not comping," the guitarist says. "We're playing together without stepping on each other's toes. It's more a commentary. That's the way the entire session worked, which made it such an easy record to do."

Other tracks recorded in homage to classic '60s jazz LPs include "Wise One" (from *Crescent*), the blues-swinging "Interplay" (the title track from the Evans album) and "Blues Connotation" (from *This Is Our Music*).

John contributes two originals that he says have nothing to do with the era: "Easy Reader," a sober waltz with yearning tenor, and the playful "Nick of Time," with intertwining guitar and tenor sax lines.

While *Within a Song* is powered on the front line by John and Joe, the album also trains a spotlight on the rhythm team's prowess. "Joey Baron and Drew Gress can change on a dime," John says. "They can play the most straightahead or go into the outer limits. They are two guys who are adaptable and ready to change."

The guitarist has known Joey for a long time. Originally the default drummer of an Abercrombie quartet when the original drummer jumped ship to tour on the eve of a recording session, Joey became "a blessing in disguise," says John, for "his unusual playing that's so colorful and out of the ordinary. He gets so involved in my music and is full of suggestions and ideas."

Joey returns the compliments. "John is one of those guys who models an aesthetic of making music that's somewhat vanished from the scene," he says. "He's particularly brilliant in the way he carries a foundation of the tradition from a period, like on the new album where we pay tribute to a time without playing like the people then. When he plays, you can hear the connection to the roots of jazz. Even though he's not given due credit, he's opened the door for a lot of people. John doesn't wear it on his sleeve. He doesn't lecture. He makes music in the moment, which is a rare trait."

As for the other half of the rhythm section, Abercrombie appreciates how Drew plays bass in a dependable way that's also very modern. "Drew is linked to the tradition," he says.

Drew in turn, values the freedom that John brings to a session. "John doesn't say much about what happens," he explains. "It's about the conversations we have, not about agendas or judgment. Instead, it's, let's talk with our instruments. It's nice to know that still exists."

Drew feels that John's guitar tone transcends his playing. "He's immediately recognizable," Drew says. "He keeps the group sensibility in mind even when he solos. He can really shred on his instrument. He takes chances to break new territory."

Drew adds, "John's an important musician in the sense that he doesn't want jazz to become calcified. He's game for whatever. It's hard to keep up with the energy he has. I hope I can be like him when I grow up."

Growing up is a notion that John doesn't appear to subscribe to. He's still evolving, still making his way. He vividly recalls those days when he felt behind the times, in skills and style. While not outwardly a rule-breaker, the guitarist has quietly made it his goal to subvert the music from the inside—not with a brash blast such as in the early Gateway days, but from within.

Laurie Anderson—Life on a String

I interviewed Laurie Anderson at her home in August 2001 on her radical new project for a San Francisco Chronicle piece. The avant-garde artist and musician is one of modern music's most esteemed performers. She and Lou Reed were together from 1992 and officially got married in 2008, five years before he died. My writer's cut follows.

LAURIE ANDERSON'S HONESTY

2001

Outside, it's a sweltering day, but Laurie is sitting comfortably in the air-conditioned mixing room of her fifth-floor studio in a lower Manhattan loft.

She has a perky personality and a cute dimply smile. She sports a short, spiky coif, but dresses conservatively—all told, not the kind of look or temperament one usually associates with a person steeped in the avant-artsy New York scene.

One flight up from her work space via a spiral staircase is her spacious former living quarters (she now resides a few minutes by bicycle upriver in the West Village with Lou). There are a couple of vases of peach-colored roses, a bronze baby shoe on a table, binoculars and a telescope for looking out onto the Hudson River.

There are several wall photos including a black-and-white portrait of Lou and a color shot of the Dalai Lama. In the space there's a precious Stickley oak rocker and perched over the TV set is a comic stuffed raccoon holding a straw crucifix. One wall is filled with bookshelves boasting an aquarium and an eclectic array of titles, including *Atlas of Advanced Orthodontics, College Algebra, America and the Sea—A Maritime History,* and *Live at the Fillmore East.*

Downstairs there are wires everywhere in the control room, and listening to Laurie talk, one assumes she knows the function of them all.

She talks about the long process of recording her newest album *Life on a String*—changing its thematic direction, adding and deleting tracks, stripping away multiple layers of instrumentation to get a sparer sound.

She admits that she's meticulous about details. "I know every song file backwards," she says. "Do you want to know how many song files there are? 32,000. Now, that's a real burden, but I know where they are and how to find them if I need to."

She's getting ready to tour *Life on a String* to seven cities with an early stop in San Francisco. The last time Laurie appeared in the Bay Area was two years ago at UC Berkeley's Zellerbach Auditorium showcasing *Songs and Stories from Moby*

Dick. It was her gargantuan, high-tech, multimedia performance piece that remade Melville's classic novel in her own quirky image.

When Laurie slips into town this week for a two-night Thursday and Friday engagement at Bimbo's 365 Club, she'll be toting a much lighter load—her violin, a few electronic keyboards—and traveling with only a support-team trio: bassist Skúli Sverrisson, keyboardist Peter Scherer and drummer Jim Black.

"It's a club tour," says Laurie, who will be performing some songs from *Life on a String.* It's her first recording in seven years and the most personally revealing collection of lyrical songs in her 20-year career. "No movies, no slides, no digital effects," she says. "It's going to be kind of a living room show. The last thing I wanted to do was another gigantic production."

She notes that playing Bimbo's is consistent with her penchant for gravitating toward novel experiences. "It's hilarious. I've got a band, and we're going to play clubs," she says. "I've never done something like this, ever."

She pauses, then makes a minor revision to her theater-only performance past. "Actually, way, way, way back I played in a couple of clubs with my violin and I loved it, especially if they served food," she says. "I love watching people eat. They think they're invisible, and they're looking at you as if you're on T.V. I suppose it makes for a more passive audience because their hands are full, and the music is not too mysterious because they're busy eating and drinking."

She giggles. "It feels very sociable to me, like when I'm sitting with my dog and she is chewing on a bone."

The Hal Willner-produced *Life on a String* CD is her first for the boutique Nonesuch label after a string of artistically triumphant but commercially under-achieving albums for Warner Bros. On it the violinist-vocalist-poet delivers a multitextured collection of originals influenced by pop, new music, storytelling, spoken word and jazz. Originally planned three years ago as the companion recording to *Moby Dick,* Laurie was so tired of working on the production of the performance piece that she decided to "throw 90 percent of it away and work on new material" for her next CD.

The new songs are simpler and more accessible than past recordings. She's notes that she feels more subjectively present on this outing. "I don't think I totally succeeded, but I tried to be as honest as I could," she says. "Sometimes that's hard for me, but that's a way in which Lou was very helpful. I'd play him something ,and he'd say, why don't you really say what you mean? So, I tried to be more direct."

A category defier since her debut 1982 *Big Science* album, Laurie again exhibits her expansive musical purview. She takes a whimsical jaunt through the suite-like Van Dyke Parks arranged "Dark Angel," grooves into the peppy, jazz-curved "The Island Where I Come From," colors a rainy-day feel on the poetic, film-noir-ish "Washington Street," and uses sci-fi-like effects on her peculiar love song, the loopy "My Compensation."

Laurie's most intimate song is "Slip Away," a tune she wrote for her father who passed away at the age of 88 two years ago. "It was his birthday yesterday, and my mother called and thanked me again for writing it," she says. "I was with my dad when he died. He wasn't very prepared when he found out he was ill. He didn't know how to die, so he rented a bunch of cowboy films, I guess to see how to die bravely—like boom-ahhh-whooo, last words in the dust, there you go, goodbye. I was there with him on his last day, sitting close by him and synchronizing my breathing with his."

Laurie attributes much of the introspective moments and at times dark tints on *Life on a String* to the loss of her father. "I am a driven person, but anytime you lose someone close to you, you think, what's really important?" she says. "Around that same time, Lou was on the road, and I was very lonely. Not a painful lonely, but a beautiful lonely where I'd go for three-hour walks with my dog and just look around and let things open up to me."

As for the tour, which will focus on her new songs as well as revisit such classic numbers as "O, Superman," "Strange Angels" and "Beautiful Red Dress." Again, Laurie took Lou's advice: "I was trying to figure out how to make this club date work, and Lou said, 'Why not play some of your old songs too, stuff that people might like to hear,'"

Laurie laughs. "I'm so used to putting on big productions, that had genuinely never occurred to me," she says, then adds, "Hey, I thought, what a concept."

Carla Bley—Jumping Jazz Loops

I was unfamiliar with Carla until, as a DownBeat *rookie, I was assigned her 1991* The Very Big Carla Bley Band *album. I was sent for a jazz loop. An immediate fan!*

Over the years I talked with her, most notably in a duo interview with Charlie Haden as he was ramping up for his newest Liberation Jazz Orchestra's Not In Our Name *album in 2004—arranged by Carla. I talked with them about it for a* DownBeat *feature.*

In 2019 I met up with Carla to talk with her about her new ECM Records album Life Goes On *and the roots of her career.*

Part of our conversation focuses on her masterwork Escalator Over the Hill. *In 1967 at the height of the musical experimentations across the genres, the ambitious 31-year-old Carla began work on her epic jazz opera,* Escalator Over the Hill, *one of the most audacious recordings of the era that took four years to complete. It featured a revolving cast of more than 53 players, ranging from important avant-jazz players she knew from the vibrant New York scene to rock artists who were already stars as well as a pop artist on her rise: Linda Ronstadt.*

Carla's stylistically, unpredictable music of playful mystery, soulful contemplation, humor and grace was praised by heralded jazz scribe Nat Hentoff who wrote that "Her scores for jazz big bands are matched only by those of Duke Ellington and Charles Mingus for yearning lyricism, explosive exultation and other expressions of the human condition."

AT HOME WITH CARLA

2019

This is a writer's edit of an article for ZEALnyc, an online site focused on arts and media in New York City. It ceased to exist shortly after this piece was published. A shorter version also appeared in QWEST, a jazz magazine, also now shuttered. QWEST.tv was a project launched in 2017 by co-founders Quincy Jones and French producer Reza Ackbaraly as the first subscription-based video-on-demand online TV channel for jazz and beyond. I interviewed Ackbaraly for a sidebar in a major Billboard feature on Quincy. Ackbaraly described it as the "Netflix" for jazz. He told me about the accompanying magazine for the service and I wrote a lot for them until its final day in 2019. All magazine copy has disappeared from its archives.

QWEST.tv is still alive for a subscription fee.

In talking to her longtime partner (not husband, mind you) Steve Swallow while he's brewing her a cup of tea, the iconic composer, arranger, bandleader and pianist Carla Bley (born Lovella May Borg) says that she's tired of the kind of encyclopedic interviews that ask the same things over and over. "That's so boring," she moans. "You can find all that kind of stuff on our website."

Even so, in talking to me, she laughs a lot as she sifts through some of her significant historical moments of melody making and free improvisations and even dredges up a memory that she has never talked about before.

She also weighs in on the creation of her youthful magnum opus: *Escalator Over the Hill,* with collaborator poet Paul Haines, a three-LP project that they subtitled *A Chronotransduction.* "It takes a long time to listen to," she says. "It's insane." She pauses with a smile and adds, "Insane is good."

Before our conversation starts rolling, she engages with Steve about how their house in the deep woods in the Woodstock, New York, area is their refuge. Woods surround the wooden structure on a dead-end street in an isolated sector of Willow, and there's a stream down below that is quite active with a steady flow given this winter's snowfall, still evident in pockets of snow near the house where the sun has yet to peek into.

"We're amazed about everything in this place," Carla says.

Steve concurs: "We try to notice how gorgeous it is. This is the last year we'll be heating the house with wood fires. We're switching to profane, doing the anti-eco thing. I can't go another season hauling the wood in here."

Carla pipes in, "It will still be in the stove but with fake logs." She frowns at that move to modernity, even though the pair has yet to adapt to smart phones—which wouldn't work anyway out here without the cell coverage to tap into. Plus, no doorbell. Just loud knocks.

This is where Carla's culture of spontaneity resides—stylistically unpredictable music of playful mystery, soulful contemplation, humor and grace.

Carla sits down at the kitchen table overseeing the brook as Steve takes his exit. "If Steve's with me when I talk to people, I usually ask him everything to make sure I've got it right," she says, to which Steve replies, "I'm going downstairs to practice like a dog just like all good bass players should. I'm seizing the moment. As long as she's occupied, I can go practice."

So, I start our meandering conversation on the same theme.

Do you practice as much as Steve?

Every single day when I'm home. Before a tour, I'll play for a couple of hours, and then I join Steve downstairs and we play for an hour and a half together. I prefer not to play at all when I'm working on a piece. The playing part is not the part that I do best. That's what I have to work on the most. The writing comes out easily. Pencil and paper. No computer. But Steve forces me to play and write every day. He tells me to get to the piano to make us some money. He thinks of me as the cash cow.

You are.

I know that. I give him a lot of gigs. That's my secret with men. Give them gigs, and they're like putty in my hands.

You're on a roll of shows with Steve and saxophonist Andy Shepherd, gearing up to record your third full-fledged recording for ECM this spring. In March you played the first show of your tour at the New York club Jazz Standard. It was a sublime experience.

That was hard when you have to change the audience over completely for each show. It's like starting from scratch. That first set was good because I had the adrenaline, and then the second set sucked. But I'm exaggerating. We went on tour after those two nights and even played in Knoxville, Tennessee at the Big Ears Festival. We finished that part of the tour in Boston [at the Regatta Bar in Cambridge]. That night was the best. All of a sudden, I had an excellent night as far as playing. The music is written, but the playing can go either way—impressive or distasteful, where the solo ends and the tune collapses into disaster.

I've read that you consider yourself a 99 percent composer and a 1 percent pianist.

That's true, but right now I think I'm 2 percent after that last gig in Boston. I love getting better instead of getting worse. If you practice, you can't help but get better. Steve's downstairs, and he's desperate to keep getting better.

Let's dial way back to your childhood. You were born in Oakland, California on May 11, 1936.

I lived on 1642 8th Avenue. Not in the hills. The flatlands. I lived about a mile away from the Oakland Airport, which then was just a little shack. What an improvement now. My father was a pianist and church choir master. He encouraged me to play. It came with the territory. He was a teacher, so he taught me. It was a chore. I became a professional at three. I would go around in the church singing songs like "This Little Light of Mine" with a cup in my hand and people would put coins in. Even then, I knew I wasn't playing for free. Once my mother tried to give me a lesson, and I bit her because I was so angry I couldn't get my fingering correct. She died when I was eight. She was sick. I don't have any unpleasant memories about her. But my father always reminded me that I bit her. Then my own daughter became a biter. She would bite other children at school. I guess it goes with the family.

What did you do when you were a youngster in Oakland?

I left high school in 10th grade. I became a roller skater when I was 14. That was my serious hobby. I was almost a professional. I would skate in competitions, but I didn't place very high. But I loved to listen to music. My excuse was to find music I liked and skate to it. It was very Oakland then. Skating rinks, bowling alleys, 75-cent dinners at the market. Back home, there was a succession of students coming to our house, and there was a curtain between my room and the room where my father gave the lessons. I heard all the scales and all the mistakes of those poor students who were being forced by their parents to learn music. I saved all those mistakes and I used them daily. It's hard to find good mistakes anymore with all the recording machines they have today. The singers get their pitch corrected so they can try to get the hits.

What made you decide to come to New York?

I went to the Oakland Auditorium to hear Lionel Hampton when I was 12. I was changed forever. That's the kind of music I wanted to pursue. The band was marching up and down the aisles, and it was unusual music that I had never heard in church. My father called it the devil's music. Even years later when I worked in the Bay Area clubs, he wouldn't come because he felt it was the devil's music and he was a righteous person. He was kind of like a Baptist evangelical. He wasn't like [Pentecostal evangelist] Aimee Semple McPherson who would stand on a stage in a white gown and preach. My father lived to be 92 or 93, and he never came to see me play. The rest of my family—cousins, aunts, uncles—would come but not him. First, he would say that he made a mistake and had scheduled choir practice for the night, but then he eventually told me. He did not believe in the music I was playing and didn't want to be touched by the devil. That was weird, but the good thing in him not coming is I could smoke at my shows. I wasn't allowed to smoke cigarettes around him.

How did you get to New York from 3,000 miles away?

At 17, I hitchhiked the whole way. It was so romantic. My whole life has been that way. Strange and romantic. The first place I lived in New York was on a bench in Grand Central Station. I guess you could say I was homeless. But then I almost immediately went to Café Bohemia in Greenwich Village and I just listened. My ears were falling off. I heard Miles Davis play my first night there. My life was magical. He was with Paul Chambers and Philly Joe Jones and probably John Coltrane, but I wasn't paying attention to him. I just listened to Miles. I can't explain it in words but only in notes. The notes were perfect.

What happened next?

I kept going to Café Bohemia, but then I got a job at Birdland as a cigarette girl and I got to hear the music all the time. Every band, every night. I don't remember how I got that job. Maybe a wanted ad in the newspaper? But I couldn't quit because I didn't make enough money to go back to Oakland. I had to hand in all my tips. I could never keep them. And if I didn't make enough money in tips, they'd take it out of my salary. At the time, Birdland was a mob-run club. But I was fascinated by it. I'd do anything just to hear that music. I got a hotel room about a block from Birdland where a lot of the musicians stayed. So I also sold stuffed animals and was the photography girl who went to tables and asked if couples would like to commemorate their evening. Some guys would say, no, please, I don't want my wife to see this. Those were my listener years.

Did you catch Bird?

Charlie Parker was still alive. I never saw him, but I would stand outside the clubs and listen. I was smitten like a teenager. There are a lot of people who still adore jazz and I am one of them. It's not just a teenage thing anymore. Your identity is tied in with it even though I did not qualify to be a musician in that world—and I still don't qualify, but they make some exceptions for me now.

But you're a star.

I am a star—and you know that has nothing to do with music. My agent once told me, you're a star, so that's different. He was booking me with someone who wasn't a star. I said, are you kidding? He's so much better than me. My agent looked at me and said, "He's not a star." So I began to notice what that meant, but it never rang true even though I do understand that now.

Did you see Thelonious Monk perform?

You need big ears to hear Thelonious Monk's music. He wrote all these songs in a small room, in a small apartment with his wife and kids screaming. He wrote all these songs and he didn't need any quiet. That's what makes him so great. He had a strong identity. But when I did see him at first, I thought he was mentally ill or strung out, but he could play. I love doing my arrangement of his "Misterioso."

How did you transition from selling cigarettes to being a part of the jazz scene?

That had already started before I was working at Birdland. Anything I heard on the radio would influence me. I wrote an arrangement of "Lullaby at Birdland" in a John Lewis style. It was crazy music. It was all from the radio. I didn't have a phonograph. I got one years later. The first record I bought—and I listened to it again and again— was "Where Did the Love Go" by the Supremes [1964]. That was my favorite and I still quote "baby baby" in many of my songs. That was not the typical thing for a jazz player to like, but when the whole Motown thing came along, I was totally in love with it. Even today, I have a collection of everything Motown recorded, and I studied a lot of different people.

But back in the '50s?

Well, when I was at Birdland, Paul Bley bought a pack of cigarettes from me even though he didn't smoke. Maybe that was 1956. I had been playing gigs at coffeehouses and be paid $5 for an afternoon. And I would hire some other guys, and I used to hire Steve whenever he needed money. Steve was a poor boy too. He lived in a loft. Years earlier I met him when I was a cigarette girl at Basin Street East, and he came to a show with his father because he was underage. He sat in the front row to listen to Clifford Brown. I didn't meet him. I just saw him. He remembers going to that show and seeing me—a gorgeous woman with a primitive dress that looked like she made it herself. I had.

Back to Paul Bley, did he know you were a piano player?

No, I guess he just liked the way I looked or walked. I think that maybe he just picked up women one after the other. I don't know if I was that special. But I was useful as a composer and arranger. Every time he needed a tune, he would ask me for one. One night he needed five tunes and I came up with all five in one night.

Did that open you up to the jazz world?

It was more through Steve Swallow because he'd bring my tunes with him everywhere he went. He worked with Art Farmer and Steve Kuhn and then Gary Burden who adored my "dark opera with words" compositions on *A Genuine Tong Funeral*. I had abandoned getting anyone to record it. It was living on a shelf. But Steve turned Gary on to it, and he recorded it {in 1967].

So you knew Steve almost from the beginning. Did you ever know he would be your romantic partner?

Absolutely not. I thought he was a drip. He even went to Yale University but left midway through his second year. I only married Paul and later Michael Mantler to get them into the country. Paul was from Canada and Michael was from Austria. They needed a green card. I was friends with them, so each asked me to get married and I said, of course. I didn't value marriage or myself, so that's a perfect combination for giving it away.

You didn't value yourself?

No, but I got better a few years later when I started to play piano with Steve. He said, you know how to read, so here's the Real Book. Play the melody with your right hand and with your left hand you have to read symbols—and then have to deal with letters and numbers. Oh my God. So I slowly learned how to play, and when I wanted to play I'd call him up. He was living in Connecticut with his wife and two kids. So he would come over when I told him I needed a lesson. But we had nothing romantic going on. In fact, with Paul and Michael, there was no romance. I never married Steve which shows you I didn't value marriage.

Did Michael influence you to go into the avant-garde world?

Oh no, it was Ornette Coleman. I was married to Paul and he was going to Los Angeles to play at the Hillcrest Club with Charlie Haden, so I went with him. Then Charlie went with Ornette, Don Cherry and Billy Higgins. Pretty soon Ornette came to New York, and I tried to play free. I had lost respect for bebop then—temporarily, I assure you—and started to play free. You don't even have to try to play free, it just sort of happens. Anything you play without knowing what you're doing is freedom to make mistakes. It's like punk rock. Maybe it was punk jazz. Ornette and Donny were totally amazing guys. People are calling me up now to know more about Donny. So I had moved back to New York and I got jobs at clubs and Jazz Gallery just to listen to them. I worked in the cloakroom. I didn't get to know them very well. I was just a fly on the wall.

You founded the Jazz Composers Orchestra in 1965 with Michael.
In 1964, the jazz artists allowed me to be in the Jazz Composers Guild even though I was a woman. Sun Ra objected. He said, any ship with a woman onboard is going to sink. I felt again like a fly on the wall. If I ever said anything, it wasn't taken seriously. But one of my biggest breaks came from Archie Shepp. I've never mentioned this to anyone in my interviews over the years.

Michael and I had formed the Jazz Composers Orchestra in 1965, so Archie knew about me. So he asked me to write a big band piece for his big band. That was a big break to have him ask me to do that.

After that, the biggest break was Charlie Haden who asked me to do his very first album as a leader, *Liberation Music Orchestra*. In 1969 he commissioned me to write all these compositions and then arrange and orchestrate them. He had a couple of tunes in mind, but he didn't write them out. He'd sing them to me on the telephone and I'd write them down and put chords to them. So, I was the arranger. He was the player. He got to play more without writing.

What was Charlie like?
I met him when he played with Paul and then Ornette in Los Angeles. He was definitely a fellow soul who I wanted to keep united with as far as the music goes. We enjoyed each other's company, but we had no romantic relationship. Actually if I was in an interview that I didn't like the direction of where it was going, I'd tell the interviewer that I was the mother of Charlie's three children. In New York, Charlie would sometimes need $5—if you know what I mean— so he would show up at the coffeehouse where I was playing and earning only $5. It was the same sometimes with Bill Evans who'd sit down and play a couple songs when he needed the money.

In the meantime, you had begun working on what some people consider to be your most ambitious and wildly adventurous piece, Escalator Over the Hill, *that took three years to complete, from 1968–1971. How did* Escalator Over the Hill *start?*
Paul was playing with Mingus after Roland Hanna, so I got to get into all the shows at the Five Spot or some club for a couple of months. I came every night as well as this guy Paul Haines. We introduced ourselves. He was a poet and we talked about doing something together. He was a writer of words, and I was a writer of notes. We thought, let's do an opera. It really started without my knowledge or permission. I had a piece I was working on for myself, and I was sitting at the piano. I was stuck. He was living in Paris, and he sent me a poem. It fit exactly, syllable by syllable, into what I was writing. And his poem gave me the next phrase that I was missing. It was called "Detective Writer Daughter." That was the first piece for *Escalator*. I wrote right back, and said the opera is beginning. Meanwhile he was corresponding

to me from India. It wasn't very orderly, and it took a long time. He sent me more writings, and I didn't leave out one word, not even an "and" or "if" or "but." I used every word he sent.

Why call this an opera?

The term opera was used loosely from the start, an overstatement by two people who didn't have to watch their words. We ended up calling it a chronotransduction, which was a word coined by Sherry Speeth, a scientist friend of Paul's, although we still call it opera for short.

I've read you used 53 players, from Linda Ronstadt to Don Cherry.

News traveled fast about what I was doing and people wanted to jump in. I had met Jack Bruce backstage when he was playing with Cream, and he told me he really liked Gary Burton's *A Genuine Tong Funeral.* So he joined in. I said yes to everyone even if they couldn't play or they couldn't sing. I paid union rates which meant that sometimes we ran out of money to continue.

There was never any question about using my main crew: Gato Barbieri, Roswell Rudd, Don Cherry, Charlie Haden, and other long-time friends and accomplices including Michael who I married after divorcing Paul.

Viva from Andy Warhol fame agreed to be the narrator, but the character Ginger was still missing. Drummer Paul Motian suggested that I request the then-unknown Linda Ronstadt whose manager thought it would be good for her to do. I collected other singers like Paul Jones [from Manfred Mann] who had heard about the project and offered his services. I sought out other women voices as jazz singers Jeanne Lee and Sheila Jordan. I got to know Don Preston from Zappa's Mothers of Invention and convinced him to take a singing role. Former NRBQ singer Steve Ferguson agreed to sing a part. As far as other roles and performances I said yes to everyone even if they couldn't play or sing. Even my four-year-old daughter Karen Mantler played a part. During the course of the project, we recorded over 100 hours of music. Only 2 percent made the cut.

What else was so unique?

The record was originally released as a 3-LP box which also contained a booklet with lyrics, photos and profiles of the musicians. Side six of the original LPs ended in a locked groove, the final track "And It's Again" continuing infinitely on manual record players. [For the CD reissue, the hum is allowed to play for almost 20 minutes before slowly fading out.]

How did this massive album get out to the market?

We did it on the label JCOA Records where Michael and I had started to record Jazz Composers Orchestra music. We also invited people like Don Cherry, Leroy Jenkins, Roswell Rudd to make records. Then we formed New Music Distribution Service which is how ECM Records got in the door in the U.S. We had no idea if we were of any value, but we wanted to help get free music out to the world.

Who else besides ECM did you distribute?
There were four or five labels, like Evan Parker's Incus Records, Futura, FMP. We'd drive to Elizabeth, New Jersey, to pick up shiploads of albums, then we'd ship twenty Escalators in return. It was crazy. It didn't pay for us to do it, but we got each other's music out there. It lasted five years.

Another subject: In addition to Motown, you were also a listener of pop music.
I liked the *Sgt. Peppers* album for a while, but that's just something you have to go through. You don't have to be doing that when you're 80. It doesn't match. I don't listen to the music Motown is making now. They should still have Valerie Simpson who wrote some of the greatest Motown tunes. I played in some pop bands like the Golden Palominos as an organ player for a couple of Anton Fier's projects. And I love Terry Adams's NRBQ bands from over the years. He played in my band on my first European tour in 1976

You also had a punk band when that was popping.
Yes, it was 1979 and I put together Penny Cillin and the Burning Sensations with two of my students at Karl Berger's Creative Music Studio in Woodstock: trumpeter Steven Bernstein and saxophonist Peter Apfelbaum—both from Berkeley, California. I had a lot of fun with them. You don't really have to do anything. I wrote songs with lyrics like "You're wervy and swervy." Everybody sang. Nick Mason, the drummer from Pink Floyd, didn't write but was wanting to make his first record, a vanity project. His car mechanic told him about me and I sent him a cassette of the Penny Cillin tunes. And he loved them. In fact, he recorded all the tunes and released them as *Fictitious Sports* [1981].

You have a great sense of humor in your music.
That's the way everyone is in the big band. We're always making each other laugh or doing horribly funny things like filling somebody's trumpet up with water before they play a solo. Once when we played the music live from *Goes to Church* [1996], the whole brass section lowered their pants to their ankles and played the horn parts—naked from the waist down. I approved of that stuff. I encouraged it.

I was just commissioned to write a big band piece for Arturo O'Farrill. He says he's very influenced by me. I think he's being generous because I was influenced by the crazy things he would do like stand onstage without moving. I love it when people laugh. All of my musicians are funny, except for some real sour ones who end up being fodder for our jokes. Charlie and I had wonderful jokes, but he didn't bring it into his music. I did.

I think it's also funny that you recorded one of your most covered songs, "Ida Lupino," backwards as "Oni Puladi."
It sounds pretty good. Jack Bruce wanted Cream to record it. I think the rest of the band was just putting up with me. I went to one of their rehearsals. I sat there all day and Jack couldn't convince them to do it.

It's interesting that you once distributed Manfred Eicher's ECM label and now he's recording you. He's commented that you are in "the tradition of radical originality."
I never heard that. I like it. It sounds like a song lyric.

Would you describe yourself in that way?
No, I'm trying to be normal, to sound totally classical, but I fail. Miserably.

Because that's not who you are.
But I want to be.

But you can't because you're Carla Bley.
I guess I do want to be Carla Bley.

Who would you want to be?
Keith Jarrett. What a piano player. Or Larry Willis. I could go on. People who play one note and it's beautiful. I just hit the notes as hard as I can.

And your relationship with Manfred?
He's not like anyone else. He's a man who had such a strong musical taste to a point where he could make a living out of it. When we first distributed his albums, he wasn't well-known in the U.S. But he believed so hard with what all of us weirdos were doing. He had extreme musical tastes and a great sense of business. He had the solutions on how to make it happen. He's the kind of person who has so much power, even though he has no idea how much power he has.

You're going to be meeting up with Manfred in Switzerland this spring to record your new record with Steve and your longtime saxophonist Andy Shepherd.
I've been working with Andy for 25 years. He's on every album I make, whether as the only soloist on his tenor or playing horn backgrounds in the big band. I need him. For the trio, I need to have someone up there onstage for people to look at while I play. He stands up there and is so handsome and dresses really well. All he has to do is give the gift of one note and you know it's him. He has the most beautiful sound, and I love the way his vibrato goes really slow. The word is beauty. I once transcribed a solo of his, and it didn't appeal to me. But it doesn't matter what he plays, it's how he plays it. He could play "Twinkle Twinkle Little Star" and I would collapse with joy.

What about the tunes?

There are only three songs on the new album, but each tune has three parts, like the piece "Copy Cat" that we did at Jazz Standard. Then there's another three-part piece called "Life Goes On." That composition followed this illness I had and that I survived from. After that, I thought, "Life goes on." It's a simple blues that sounds like real life. It's hard playing these for just a trio and not a big band where I can play a tiny solo every three songs. Now I have to play a lot more. I have to learn how to play a decent solo.

The other three-part piece, "Beautiful Telephones," was inspired by Donald Trump's comment on his first visit to the Oval Office after his election. That's one of the comments he made. That's funny. I don't want to do damage with my music like Charlie might have done with his serious political tone. I'd rather write music that makes fun of the president.

So many of your compositions have three or more movements. Do you deliberately write like that?

I write long because I can't figure out an ending. Seriously, I write until it has an ending. Look at *Escalator Over the Hill*. There was no ending. I kept writing and writing and writing to be perfect. It has to have an ending for it to be perfect. Paul kept sending lyrics from India, and I worked to find melodies to fit them. The possible meaning of their words didn't matter to me. I just thought they were strange and wonderful. Paul told me later, "It falls outside the natural reach of narrative, and this is left to the music to describe."

ESCALATOR OVER THE HILL RECEPTION

- Carla was honored with Jazz Album of the Year 1972 by the Melody Maker Readers Poll, and the Oscar du meilleur disque de jazz moderne (best modern jazz album) in 1972, given by the French Académie du jazz.
- In 1972 Carla was given a Guggenheim award for composition.
- Jonathon Cott's Rolling Stone article stated, "Like an electric transformer, *Escalator Over the Hill* synthesizes and draws on an enormous range of musical materials— raga, jazz, rock, ring modulated piano sounds, all brought together through Carla Bley's extraordinary formal sense and ability to unify individual but diverse musical sections by means of the editing of the record medium... The opera is an international musical encounter of the first order."
- Marcello Carlin, writing for *Stylus* Magazine, considered the album to be "the greatest record ever made." He said: "No protest, no social commentary. No expression of love, of grief, of hope, of despair. It is literally whatever you want to make of it. It is devoid of every quality which you might assume would qualify it to be the greatest of all records. And yet it is that tabula rasa in its heart, the

blank space which may well exist at the very heart of all music, revealing the hard truth that we have to fill in the blanks, we have to interpret what is being played and sung, and our interpretation is the only one which can possibly be valid, as we cannot discern any perspective other than our own."

In Carla's own words from her 2011 biography by Amy C. Beal:

"All dimensions of *Escalator Over the Hill* are extravagant. The long (a triple album, nearly two hours) stylistically eclectic work fuses singers and players from all over the musical map—fifty-three individuals participated in the recording, including some of the most productive and original jazz and rock musicians working at the time…The work as a whole seems simultaneously to assimilate and annihilate rock gestures, jazz harmonies, and classical structures. By nature of its absolute autonomy, *Escalator Over the Hill* also seems to thumb its nose at all musical authorities and institutions, particularly the recording industry. In this sense it is perhaps the quintessential antiestablishment statement of its time."

Due to the enormity of *Escalator Over the Hill* with its sizable cast and the prohibitive cost to perform it live, Carla never planned to take her magnum opus on the road.

However, the extended piece still resonated especially in Europe. Twenty-six years after it first appeared on disc, Carla agreed to present the jazz opera with a truncated band in Cologne, Germany in 1997. She enlisted the harmonic sophistication of her arranger friend Jeff Friedman to re-orchestrate *Escalator Over the Hill* for its premiere live date. Word of its success spread which led to a full-scale tour of Europe in 1998. The final performance to date took place in May 2006 in Essen, Germany.

Escalator Over the Hill has never been performed in the U.S.

Dee Dee Bridgewater—
The Mali Adventure

I first met Dee Dee in San Francisco in 1995 when she was doing press for her inspired new album, Love & Peace: A Tribute to Horace Silver. *We clicked, not only talking about the music but also gushing about our equal love of fresh tomatoes (I wished that I had brought her some of my delicious Berkeley backyard harvest).*

We kept in touch from her shows ranging from Oakland to Bern, Switzerland. We had a connection that resulted in me writing the liner notes for 2000's Live at Yoshi's at the prestigious jazz club in my Berkeley-Oakland neighborhood. (I later wrote the liners in 2009 for her Grammy Award-winning album Eleanora Fagen (1915-1959): To Billie With Love from Dee Dee Bridgewater.)

In between those liners, in 2006 Dee Dee requested that I join her and her management team on a very special journey to Mali. It was my most memorable adventure in the jazz world. Our friendship continued with visits to her Harlem apartment and then to her daughter Tulani's house in Los Angeles.

For an introduction to the hardest-working vocal legend in jazz, one needs only to peruse the opening page of her website: Triple Grammy Winner. Tony Winner. Producer. ASCAP Champion. 2017 NEA Jazz Master. Memphis Music Hall of Fame Inductee. Record Label Founder. Doris Duke Artist Awardee, Bruce Lundvall Visionary Awardee. For 23 Years host of National Public Radio's JazzSet syndicated show. She also serves as a United Nations Goodwill Ambassador for the Food and Agriculture Organization (FAO).

DEE DEE BRIDGEWATER—FINDING HER ROOTS
2007

EXPERIENCING BAMAKO

In the middle of August 2006, the heat is brutal and dust-encrusted in Bamako. The flat, brightly colored metropolis split in two by the serpentine Niger River is the capital of Mali, the seventh largest country in Africa and one of the poorest in the world.

West Africa time is liquid, and the evening air saturated with equatorial humidity. Cotton shirts are drenched with sweat as Dee Dee Bridgewater arrives at one of the best clubs for music in Bamako, Le Hogon Restaurant Espace Cultural. Dressed in a black cotton dress, she weaves her way through a couple of dozen motorcycles parked in front.

The one-story building from the outside looks like a Mississippi Delta juke joint even though the music emanating from inside is distinctively Malian with its scintillating polyrhythms accentuating the bluesy beat. After paying the entrance fee (the equivalent of $3, which includes a free bottle of Castel, the dark lager national beer), the crowd flows through the low-ceilinged entrance toward the large open-air patio where, above, the stars pierce the night sky and the heat lightning flashes.

On stage is a makeshift band of local guitarists, a kora player, a ngoni player and several percussionists, including calabash and talking drum players. They are cooking up a storm of rippling dance music that Dee Dee soon plunges into, catching the sparkling Malian groove and dancing on the tiled floor packed with other likeminded people enraptured by the mesmerizing beats and the undulating, blues-like storytelling sung in Bambara.

In a blue shirt adorned with Malian art motifs, Cheick Tidiane Seck, a Malian keyboardist/producer who has homes in both Bamako and Paris, escorts Dee Dee to the stage, hands her a microphone and encourages her to sing while the band plays. She closes her eyes and immediately scats into the soul of the rhythm.

During a break in the dance floor action, Dee Dee beams. "This is home," she says, as the fluidity of the evening makes her skin glow. "I believe my roots are in Mali."

This faith undergirds her latest project, *Red Earth: A Malian Journey*, a striking mélange of music where Dee Dee's traditional American jazz background converges with her newfound passion for the music of Mali. "It's a whole new musical departure for me," she says. "I've just finally found myself, I've finally found my identity, I've found the African part of who I am."

As an art form, jazz has always promoted the invaluable notion of exploring one's true identity. The study of the elders leads to the incubation of emulation and eventually—and hopefully—the discovery phase of finding one's own voice. But for Dee Dee, who years ago found her voice within the context of the straight-ahead jazz world, Mali has represented a deeper search for identity that she needed to embark upon: unearthing those arcane roots that seek life-affirming aquifers. *Red Earth* goes far beyond a concept album. Indeed, it's a profound homecoming that sonically pleases the ear and spiritually offers deliverance to the singer.

In her liner notes to *Red Earth*, Dee Dee concludes, "This project is my ode to Mali and to Africa; it is the story of a lost child finding her way home. It is my reawakening…[The album] is, simply put, my journey home."

MALIAN ODYSSEY

Dee Dee's Malian odyssey begins in 1999, the year when she was elected as an ambassador of the United Nations' Food and Agricultural Organization. She began to visit several FAO projects in such African countries as Senegal. Meanwhile she began collecting albums of African music. Her husband and producer Jean-Marie

Durand recalls that whenever they played the music at their home in Paris, Dee Dee kept gravitating to Malian traditional tunes.

"Dee Dee was blindfolded," he says. "The music of Mali resonated with her, without her knowing where it came from." She notes, "Whenever I heard the music from Mali, I would get jolted. It was as if I knew it was coming from a deep place within me."

In 2004, Dee Dee went to Mali to test her assumption that the country was the source of her African ancestry. She contacted Cheick to help her explore the music scene and seek his wisdom on her plan to embark upon a jazz-Mali musical voyage. "I loved the musical connection Cheick made with Hank Jones producing the [1995] album, *Sarala*," she says. "I was looking to him to be the musical coordinator, to propose songs, musicians and singers—to come up with new arrangements of traditional Malian songs. He knows this music."

One of their first Bamako stops was a restaurant to see ngoni player Bassékou Kouyaté. "I was so touched by what I was hearing that on Cheick's prodding I went onstage and sang," Dee Dee says. "The music made my spirit soar. I can't explain what happened. It was an unspoken thing; we spoke the same language musically. I was making up lyrics as we jammed. It was like I was in a trance."

But even before that, Dee Dee had already experienced two significant non-musical incidents in Bamako, one upon arrival and the other the next morning. "At the airport an old man kept calling out to me," she recalls. "He was calling me a name, but I didn't understand him and he didn't understand French. He started getting upset because he felt that I was ignoring him. So I asked Cheick to talk with him. As it turned out, the old man was convinced that I was his long-lost niece who was finally returning home."

Later, she says, when she was given an outfit made of Malian cotton fabric and would walk down the street, people talked to her in Bambara and told her she looked like a Peul, the nomadic ethnic group from the north not far from Timbuktu. "I even met the president of Mali and he told me I was Peul," she says.

Dee Dee's growing suspicions that her ancestral roots were in Mali were further confirmed the next day when she opened the curtains of her room at the Sofitel Hotel. "I looked out and there was red earth everywhere," she says. "All my life I have been fascinated by red earth."

Dee Dee says that when she was a young child in Memphis, where she was born, she used to revel in the red earth in her family's driveway. "My mother tells me that I would take off all my clothes and roll in it," she says. "My sandy blond hair would be covered with red earth. I just loved it."

After her 2004 visit, Dee Dee returned to Paris and jumpstarted a jazz-meets-Malian music album that she initially planned to record in France with Malian musicians who had emigrated there. "But I had doubts I could pull that off," says Dee Dee. "I told Jean-Marie that we had to go back to Bamako. I wanted to be there, to smell the land, to touch the people, to feel the country, to be inspired by Mali. I wanted to embrace the culture."

So, in August 2006, Dee Dee arrives in Bamako with a mission: to meet Malian musicians, to jam with them, to find common personal and musical ground, and begin recording at Bogolon, the modest Bamako studio of the late guitar master Ali Farka Touré.

On the second day of her visit, she says, "I want to make this be a heartfelt meeting of two cultures where Malian musicians come into my world and where they come into mine. We're going to throw ourselves into the water and swim. We're all great musicians open to the music. We'll understand when we speak, even if it is in different languages. I want to make this an honest album."

Given that Mali's traditional music sounds like it has a direct link to the Delta-fueled blues of John Lee Hooker, many American acts have comfortably recorded with the country's musicians. Notable collaborations include roots guitarist Ry Cooder hooking up with Ali Farka Touré on the 1994 Grammy Award-winning *Talkin' Timbuktu* CD (Rykodisc), blues artist Taj Mahal linking up with kora master Toumani Diabaté on 1999's *Kulanjan* (Rykodisc) and jazz trombonist Roswell Rudd's meeting with Diabaté on 2004's *MALIcool* (Sunnyside).

But, arguably, Dee Dee's desire to marry the two musical worlds, with their common African ancestry, is the most ambitious recorded undertaking to date. "We'll be doing some jazz standards like Wayne Shorter's 'Footprints,' Mongo Santamaria's 'Afro Blue' and Les McCann's 'Compared to What,'" she says. "But I'm also setting off to discover Malian traditional music."

JAZZ BIRTH

Dee Dee made her New York debut in 1970 as the lead vocalist in Thad Jones/Mel Lewis Orchestra. At the time, she was married to trumpeter Cecil Bridgewater, who was in Horace Silver's band. Even though in 1974 she recorded her first album as a leader, *Afro Blue* on the Japanese Trio Records label, she broke from the jazz camp that year to perform on Broadway, winning a Tony Award in 1975 for her role as Glinda, the Good Witch in *The Wiz.*

A few years later, she jettisoned onto the pop music scene via Elektra Records. "I grew up in jazz, and jazz was second nature to me, but I was a closet rock 'n' roller," she says. "When I got signed to Elektra, I was over the moon to be on the same label as Jackson Browne and the Eagles. Don Henley wanted to produce my first album, but the label said, 'No, you're black. You have to make a soul/disco album, not rock.'"

Finally after battling for creative say, she recorded her label debut in 1978, *Just Family*, produced by Stanley Clarke and George Duke, where she got the chance to cover an Elton John song and enlist rock violinist Scarlet Rivera. "Back then I was living in a make-believe world," she recalls. "I didn't know a thing about record sales, I was treated like a queen, was wined and dined, and treated to L.A. Lakers [basketball] games. I was the darling. But unbeknownst to me, I was paying for all of this from my royalties."

When she moved over to Atlantic Records, her music was "canned because I wouldn't sleep with the VP of the label," Dee Dee says. Meanwhile, she continued to perform in musicals that later led to her portraying the role of Billie Holiday in Stephen Stahl's *Lady Day*, which garnered her a best actress nomination for a Laurence Olivier Award.

When Dee Dee moved to France in 1986, she was immediately heralded as the new Josephine Baker. That's when she says she also "got serious about music and not waiting for a record company to help. I decided to help myself. Before, everything was done for me. All I had to do was sing. But then I realized that I wanted to work on my albums, from beginning to end, from choosing the musicians I wanted to work with to deciding on the arrangements."

In 1993, she met Jean-Philippe Allard, the head of Polygram France at the time. "He believed in me," she says. "So he gave me a producer contract. Since that time, I've had complete control over my music—the songs, the sound, the studio, the image. I've been able to express myself in any way."

In 1997 Dee Dee released her tribute to Ella Fitzgerald, *Dear Ella* (Verve), which scored a Grammy and received critical accolades. But that combined with her Billie role and Josephine image began to take its toll. "I took a five-year walk with Ella," she says. "I was determined to help keep her image alive. But all the while, I felt like I was losing myself. Wonderful things happened to me in France, but I got to a place where I became a person with a serious identity crisis. What am I? Who am I?"

Those questions were amplified by coming to terms with her racial identity. She knows she's part Cherokee, Chickasaw, Irish and German, but she rarely questioned her African heritage, a subject her mother did not encourage her to pursue when she was young.

"It was all about being more white than having African roots so that you could get a better job," says Dee Dee. "When I was young in the '50s and '60s, Africa meant ignorance, savages, loin clothes, spears and bones pierced through the nose. I was into emulating white girls, straightening my hair with a hot comb and trying to fit in as much as possible. I was always in an all-white environment, even as a little girl when I was sent to Catholic school where the kids used to call me nigger-bitch. I used to get in fights over that, so being on the defense is like second nature to me. That continues today, as I recently had to endure a new racism when I grew my hair out and did the African dread thing. People refused to sit next to me on airplanes."

Dee Dee turned a corner after Polygram France unceremoniously dropped her and in 2005 she recorded *J'ai Deux Amours* (recorded by her own DDB Records and released by Sovereign Artists in the U.S.). It's a remarkable album of well-known French chansons given the jazz treatment. However, the French press lambasted her, criticizing her for turning her back on the jazz tradition.

"I'm damned if I do, and damned if I don't," she says, with a tinge of bitterness in her voice. "I've always been about keeping vocal jazz alive in my own way, and I've always set out to emulate Miles Davis by doing something different each time out. I hate repeating myself."

All this paved the way for Dee Dee's musical and spiritual journey to Mali. "Doing the American-African thing is the result of an accumulation of all my life experience," she says. "I'm entering the third phase of my life, and I want to go out as a whole person. I want to accept myself totally. So, let me go to Africa; let me find the country that I believe I'm from; let me embrace its music while at the same time educating people about the motherland."

Ironically, Dee Dee, who at the time had been the host of NPR's JazzSet since October 2001, signed a deal with the international arm of Universal Records, based in England, which is distributing *Red Earth* internationally via its newly resurrected Emarcy imprint. Polygram France may have dumped her, but it's now selling her latest CD that's been supported by the overarching entity of the major label.

MALI CLUBBING

It's Sunday night and again the air is so humid it could be carved with a butter knife, but no one seems to notice at Malian superstar vocalist Oumou Sangaré's Space Cultural Wassulu, an under-the-stars club adjacent to Residence Wassulu, a hotel she also owns. Cheick has organized a jam session that serves as an audition of sorts for Dee Dee's project. The sound check ends and Cheick introduces various Malian musicians to Dee Dee whose small entourage is ordering dinner and drinks. More bottles of Castel help cool the evening. Keep hydrated is the operative demonstrative.

With the ever-smiling Cheick taking on the role of a cultural mayor, gradually more musicians arrive, each getting their pictures taken with Dee Dee. Eventually the music begins and her project starts to take shape. At first, cooling herself with a beige fan, she approaches the stage that's separated from the audience by a pool of water and observes the musicians casually yet confidently delivering the enthralling beat and shimmering kora notes. Then she goes up to the vocalist microphone and the magic begins. As she dances, she sings wordless vocals buoyed by a bluesy sensibility as Cheick makes his electric keyboard sound like marimbas.

After each song, new musicians fill the stage and Dee Dee elevates the energy of the tunes with her gusty vocal scats. The rhythm accelerates with a talking drum solo, then settles as Dee Dee extemporizes about her journey: "I've come a very long way...We're going to let the music take us tonight...Everybody's got the spirit."

After several tunes, Oumou Sangaré arrives with a bouquet of flowers and hugs. With the band playing a funky, hip-hop beat, she enters the action, joining in with Dee Dee and four other female Malian vocalists. Soon the music turns into a traditional Malian tune, and all the singers hug each other again.

As for Sangaré, who has been an out-spoken advocate for women's rights in Mali, Dee Dee says, "Oumou has become like a sister to me. Even though I'm older, she's taken on the responsibility of being an older sister."

The day before Dee Dee and Oumou, who is also a United Nations Goodwill Ambassador for the Food and Agriculture Organization, visited two rural villages outside the city where women run self-sufficiency grassroots projects seeded by the U.N. They stop at a beekeeping collective in Kati and a homespun animal husbandry operation in Fana Fiercoro. The roads are rutted and dusty red and populated by donkey-drawn carts hauling corn and firewood. At each stop, the townspeople welcome the visitors with festive music and dancing. In Fana Fiercoro, the community leader organizes an impromptu meeting, introducing the two ambassadors and asking them to speak.

Dee Dee, speaking in English that was translated into Bambara, says, "I'm so impressed by all the work of the women. I'm here to tell the people of the United States that the people of Mali are not waiting for help, but are helping themselves." She then adds, "I'm proud to be the first and only black American who is a Food and Agriculture Organization ambassador, and I strongly believe my roots are in Mali."

Later Dee Dee, reflecting on her own business prowess, says, "What's so impressive about the Food and Agriculture Organization is that it financially supports women. In Mali, a man can sleep well even if his family his starving. A woman cannot. She will always seek to nourish her family. In that way Mali is a very feminine country. Women are taking the lead."

That theme is accentuated on *Red Earth* by the plaintive tune "No More (Bambo)," written by Tata "Bambo" Kouyaté. She joins Dee Dee on the song critiquing forced marriage. The song proved to be so culturally powerful in the early '60s that the newly born Republic of Mali abolished its practice.

ALI FARKA TOURÉ STUDIO

On Monday morning, Dee Dee arrives at Bogolon, a modest building that in the control room features a wall-of-fame montage of album cover art for recordings made there, by such musicians as Ali Farka Touré, Rokia Traoré, Neba Solo, Boubacar Traoré and Toumani Diabaté.

In the studio several guitars are hung on a brick wall as well as several canvases of hand-painted mud cloth (called bogolon). The room feels simple and rootsy, perfect for the first session of Dee Dee's album, a Malian griot tune given a catchy jazzy update: "Demissènw (Children Go 'Round)," featuring Kouyaté on ngoni and his wife Ami Sacko on vocals, along with Kouyaté's group, Ngoni Ba, and Dee Dee's 14-year-old son, Gabriel Durand, on guitar. Everyone plays in the same studio room, in lieu of separating into isolation booths.

Dee Dee, in a short-sleeved white cotton blouse and jeans, writes down the pronunciation of the song's Bambara words in her journal, which also includes the lyrics in English she wrote to make the cultural connection on importance of children taking charge in the world. The tune starts out with a traditional Malian feel as Kouyaté takes the fluttering, mandolin-like lead, then bursts with a bluesy and jazzy ecstasy as Dee Dee and Sacko sing.

At the end of one take, Dee Dee says, "C'est bien," asks Sacko to be more assertive in her vocals and they all charge back into the piece with an exhilarating rush, with the two vocalists dancing as they sing.

This time, Dee Dee says, "We nailed it!" and the performers retreat to the engineering room to hear the playback. Cheick, who played percussion-like keyboards on the tune, says, "The emotion was so great. My job has been to find the right kind of musicians for Dee Dee to play with. This session had magic in many moments."

Cheick, who has a long history of working with American jazz musicians from Don Cherry to Hank Jones, is pleased with how Dee Dee is following her muse. "She has been so respectful of the Malian music and musicians," he says. "She feels the vibe of the music's roots."

Kouyaté agrees. "We love what Dee Dee is doing," he says. "We practiced this song at our house, structuring it so that it would come out just the right way." Sacko adds: "Dee Dee working with my husband was able to adapt the Malian tradition into any musical situation."

"This is our little gem," says Dee Dee. "We thought about polishing it up in the mixing, but decided to leave it."

Writing in *Red Earth*'s liner notes, Dee Dee says the one-room recording session, the only one on the CD, was organically raw and honest: "That's why it has such a different sound. Mixing it was almost impossible because everyone bled together— voices and instruments melded, but that was the original album concept." But she adds, "It would have been quite an undertaking to do the whole album that way."

As it turns out, the bulk of *Red Earth*, with its mix of traditional jazz and traditional Malian music—all played with Malian instruments and including guest vocalists—was recorded in October at Bogolon. After her longtime U.S. sound engineer James Hate died suddenly in early October, Dee Dee was so distraught that she nearly delayed her return to Bamako. "I almost quit the project," she says. "I didn't know how I'd be able to get through it. But Jean-Marie convinced me to return. Just being there re-inspired me. I wrote two songs in the first day and eventually eight more."

In one of the CD highlights, Dee Dee updates Sangaré's gently lilting "Djarabi" (which means "my love" in Bambara) with a new soulful arrangement and English lyrics and titled "Oh My Love." It's sung as a duet with Sangaré. Another strong number is Dee Dee's skipping version of Ramata Diakité's "Mama Digna Sara Yé (Mama Don't Ever Go Away)," also sung in a vocal exchange with the composer.

Because they couldn't find one playable piano in all of Bamako, Dee Dee's pianist Edsel Gomez recorded all the piano parts in Paris during a week of recording there to finish up the project. Edsel also arranged the Malian-steeped take on "Afro Blue" as well as the haunting tune "Meanwhile" that he and Dee Dee composed. The other key members of her band, bassist Ira Coleman and drummer Minino Garay, arranged the superb Africanized version of "Footprints" with words written by Dee Dee and retitled "Long Time Ago."

MALI ON THE ROAD

Initially released earlier in Europe, Dee Dee took the project on the road in 2007 including a date at the North Sea Jazz Festival in July, with her jazz quartet and a full ensemble of France-based Malian musicians on talking drum, kora, ngoni, balafon and a variety of percussion instruments. The Rotterdam date opens with the Bridgewater band turning "Afro Blue" into a full-blown rhythm blast and includes the accentuate-the-positive "Bad Spirits (Bani)," based on a 12th-century griot tune from Mali and teeming with a Dee Dee scat, and a poignant version of Nina Simone's "Four Women," spiced with percussive swells.

Known throughout her career for shaking up her repertoire, putting new spins on music ranging from Horace Silver to Kurt Weill, Dee Dee seems to have truly found home. Watching her dance deep into the Malian polyrhythms, taking on the mantle of a modern-day storytelling griot, singing with such exhilaration, she appears to have found a true freedom on her Malian journey that will find her touring the U.S. this fall at such venues as the San Francisco Jazz Festival and Kennedy Center.

And who knows, maybe Dee Dee will actually complete the circle. "Being in Mali is the first time I've felt like I belonged somewhere, where I fit in," she says. "I started to have a yearning to live there, to be with beautiful people who live with a beautiful simplicity and honesty. I've had so many accolades, I've realized all my dreams, and I've lived the comfortable life. Being with and helping the people of one of the poorest countries in black Africa…" she pauses, then says, "What a beautiful way to go."

POST NOTE

When Dee Dee was living in Harlem, I visited her and talked about Red Earth and her comment about living there given the 2012 Malian coup d'état and unrest in Bamako. Not in the near future, she told me while in the midst of packing all her belongings to move to New Orleans where she resides when she's not continuously on the road.

David Byrne—Always Makes Sense

David is a genius. He's active in the conceptual arts and just recently took the stage at this year's Academy Awards show singing "This Is the Life," a song he composed for the Oscar-winning best movie Everything Everywhere All at Once. *It was one of the best-song nominations (though it didn't get the award). For the song's live performance, supporting actress nominee Stephanie Hsu filled in for original artist Mitski. Along with David and Son Lux, Hsu put her Broadway-honed theatricality into a performance with David as a vocalist foil. The big production featured martial arts choreography, backup dancers, and from the movie's psychedelic fuel David revealing long hot dog fingers (think way back to his Big Suit in Jonathan Demme's classic concert film* Stop Making Sense*). Like the movie the song was written for,* Everything Everywhere All at Once *must be seen to be believed.*

LOOK INTO THE EYEBALL
2001

I met up with David in 2001 to talk about his new Look Into the Eyeball *album, the Luaka Bop label he founded and of course, Talking Heads—one of my favorite pop bands of all time.*

On a damp, rainy New York day in early June 2001, David sits in the lower level of his Greenwich Village office that houses his boutique Luaka Bop label and serves as an art studio. To get here from the sidewalk, you climb a few stairs then have to pass by a life-size, lightweight black boxer dog statue that stands guard at the front door. Upon entry, you walk down a corridor lined with CD boxes and photos of album covers and head downstairs to a spacious room where various quirky and mildly subversive Byrne art projects are scattered about, including a giant blow-up photo of a George Bush mask turned inside out.

Dressed casually in black jeans and a gray button-down shirt, the 49-year-old David is still as slender as his nerdy-looking Talking Heads days. His close-cropped hair has gone silver with age, and he wears wire-rim glasses that make him look, well, business-like. Nowhere in sight is his restless, quirky big-suit stage persona best captured in *Stop Making Sense*. It was the definitive 1984 concert film directed by Jonathan Demme that documented the Heads in their prime (it was heralded by many as the best rock-oriented film since the Beatles' *A Hard Day's Night*). Sipping a cup of almond tea, David is mild-mannered, even shy, but articulate and funny in a low-key way.

On the eve of releasing his new CD, *Look Into the Eyeball*), he seems fulfilled as an artist—proud of the T-Heads legacy, his various artistic pursuits and his record label that has given voice in the U.S. to an array of musicians from around the world, especially Brazil. His latest disc is his seventh as a solo artist, his first album for Virgin, his first venture since 1997's *Feelings* and arguably the best outing of his post-Heads career. It's a groove-and-strings affair, a catchy classical-tinged pop disc that's also spiked with the percussive funk he and his former bandmates employed for burning down the house in the late '70s through the '80s.

But there's a hint of insecurity in David's voice as he talks about the album. He admits he had doubts about it when he finished it. "But after getting over the initial repulsion, I find that it does what I hoped it would do," he says, then adds, "I just talked with a journalist in Munich who said he and his friends felt the album was too commercial. I don't know exactly what that means. I'm thinking that *Look Into the Eyeball* doesn't sound anything like the latest new thing they're into."

The fact that it doesn't has its pros and cons. As a solo act, David hasn't enjoyed the commercial popularity of his days with the Heads when the band dominated the pop music scene for nearly a decade with a string of hot-wire albums: *Talking Heads '77* (1977), *More Songs About Buildings and Food* (1978), *Fear of Music* (1979), *Remain in Light* (1980), *Speaking in Tongues* (1983), the film soundtrack *Stop Making Sense* (1984) and *Little Creatures* (1985).

Yet David has maintained a vital creative presence by steering clear of the same-as-it-ever-was pop mindset. In addition to scouting new acts for his label, directing videos and films, and delving into photographic art projects, he continues to write oddly whimsical songs that deviate from the norm.

On *Look Into the Eyeball*, David gets high marks for his melodies—catchy enough to sing along to while driving on the open road—and his funky beats. But it's his use of strings that sets the album apart from anything that's on the pop map today. "I wanted to move people to dance and cry at the same time," he says. "These tunes are emotional, warm, but they also have beats." And the strings? "Most of the time in pop music they're added as icing on the cake, to sweeten a tune. But I wanted them to be part of the cake, to replace keyboards and guitars as well as add to the rhythmic drive."

As with his Talking Heads collaborations, the result is a blend of pop accessibility crafted with artistic sensibility. This, in essence, is David Byrne's modus operandi.

THE HISTORY

Born in Dumbarton, Scotland in 1952 and brought up in Baltimore, David revealed his penchant for throwing artsy changeups early. A musical child who played violin and accordion then switched to guitar, he was rejected in his attempts to join his junior high choir because he sang off-key. That didn't deter him from expressing himself musically.

David went on to form a garage band called the Revelation, although he didn't sing lead vocals. However, he did test his singing voice while playing ukulele in solo gigs at a coffeehouse near the University of Maryland (Dylan was his specialty). Then, influenced by Stockhausen and the Beatles, David began exploring musique concrète by making tape collages on a reel-to-reel recorder. One of his early projects was a bizarre version of the Turtles' hit "Happy Together," with multi-track feedback and Tupperware tubs used for the drum parts. During this time his scientist father offered encouragement, helping him with such rudiments of recording technology for electronic effects.

"I grew up listening to the hits of the day by R&B and rock bands," David says. "But back in the '60s, it was cool to be openminded about music, to accept a musician who put a sitar into a song or made a reference to Stockhausen. It wasn't frowned upon as snobbish or world music-y. In fact, it was so cool that it encouraged me to go to the library to check out various Folkways records and albums by contemporary classical composers. Frank Zappa had a quote from Varèse on the early Mothers albums. I thought, who is this guy? So I checked Varèse out and got exposed to his early electronic compositions."

With such eclectic musical tastes percolating within David, it's not surprising that his high school peers considered him an oddball. He sang an old song while accompanying himself on ukulele in his high school talent show. He ran for senior class student council president and got trounced. Upon graduation, fascinated by both science and art, he was accepted at both the tech-oriented MIT and the Rhode Island School of Design. He chose art school, he says, because the graffiti in the hallways was superior.

It was at Rhode Island School of Design that David's artistic vision expanded. It's where he soon met future bandmates Tina Weymouth and Chris Frantz. However, David dropped out and hit the road living for a spell in a hippie commune, making artsy video tapes and playing standards on ukulele and violin in a duo called Bizadi between 1971 and '72 with accordionist friend Marc Kehoe.

Upon returning to Rhode Island, he co-founded the group the Artistics (later renamed the Autistics) with Tina on electric bass and Chris on drums. David dropped out of college and moved to New York. Tina and Chris later followed him to the city where they shared a loft and renamed their act Talking Heads. Already in the repertoire was one of David's early compositions, "Psycho Killer," a circa-1974 pop tune that was part playful, part social commentary.

They created a buzz generated by gigs at CBGB and other hip downtown venues which led to a recording contract. As he notes in his "David Byrne on David Byrne" autobiography that accompanied Look Into the Eyeball press materials: "I continued making art for a while…but soon the band and my day job took all my time. The band became successful too."

Ex-Modern Lover guitarist Jerry Harrison joined the group in its early stages, bringing a beefier guitar and keyboard sound to augment David's rhythm guitar.

SUBVERSIVE ROCKERS

On stage, instead of looking like glam mid-'70s rock stars, the members dressed preppy, especially David, who wore white button-down-collar dress shirts. "In the early Talking Heads days, our appearance on the bandstand made us subversive," says David. "We were being radical by looking conservative. We didn't follow any rock stereotypes."

The same held true with the band's tunes. The Heads, already committed to making music with an artistic flair, linked up with likeminded Brian Eno, who co-produced *More Songs About Buildings and Food*, *Fear of Music* and *Remain in Light*. He helped the band create a minimalistic pop that had oblique lyrics and multi-layers of rhythm. By 1984, when they documented their Big Suit performance piece, *Stop Making Sense*, rhythm ruled. Two years ago in San Francisco, David reflected back, "I look at the film now and think, what a funk show," he said. "We were labeled new wave, but we really were a funk band."

That period proved to be the band's golden age. Even though the Heads made three more fine studio albums—1985's *Little Creatures*, the 1986 soundtrack to the flawed film project *True Stories* (co-written by David, Pulitzer Prize winning playwright Beth Henley; and actor-director Stephen Tobolowsky), and 1988's *Naked*—individual members' side projects intervened, plus personality conflicts within the band caused major fissures. In 1992, the band officially dissolved, though it resurfaced Byrne-less in 1996 to record a flop of an album as the Heads.

However, David wasn't looking in the rear view mirror. By the time he filed the divorce papers, he had already recorded three solo albums—1988's forgettable avant-garde theater score for Robert Wilson's *The Forest*, 1989's cooking, Brazilian-tinged *Rei Momo*, and another upbeat pop gem, 1992's *Uh-Oh*. Subsequent albums include the self-titled 1994 album and 1997's *Feelings*, both of which featured David exploring a range of musical styles from Latin beats to trip-hop.

In the midst of his own recording career, David found the time to launch the Luaka Bop imprint in 1988. The label helped to introduce to North American audiences the deep riches of Brazilian music (far beyond the well-known samba and bossa nova styles). He also helped to break down the cultural barriers the U.S. had erected for all things Cuban by issuing music from the nation island. Currently, Luaka Bop has been riding a wave of success with the Venezuelan band Los Amigos Invisibles and the reissue of Shuggie Otis' 1974 album *Inspiration Information*.

"Well, yes, it's hanging in there," says David politely. He explains that it was an outgrowth of "a weird little blip" in the Talking Heads renegotiated contract with Warner Brothers. The band was allowed to have its own label, which Byrne christened with the name Fly Records (to record various fly-on-the-wall projects, including Harrison's solo debut, *Casual Gods*).

However, Fly was discontinued in 1989 because an indie with the same name was found to have already been in existence. It was then that David inked a solo deal with Warners, which resulted in his own label, Luaka Bop, a hip-sounding four-syllable name that is actually a brand of tea.

"I wanted to have an outlet for projects that weren't Talking Heads," says David, who recorded his 1989 *Rei Momo* album on Luaka Bop. But it wasn't meant to be merely a vanity label. He was hearing too much good music, most of which originated from outside the U.S. "At first we did compilations of tapes I had been collecting which people seemed to enjoy. Eventually we started signing bands, and everyone began taking us more seriously even though the compilations are still what pay the bills."

The label's raison d'être is to fulfill David's desire to expose people to different styles of music and artistry. Sometimes he serves as the talent scout, sometimes others working at the label fill in. "Really, everyone who works here hears the music and decides," he says. "If people aren't enthusiastic about an act, we generally won't sign them. A woman who used to work here brought a tape in from former schoolmates of hers. It was Geggy Tah from Pomona, California. I had never heard anything like it, so we signed them."

As if dealing with Luaka Bop business and supporting his new album weren't enough, Byrne is working on another extracurricular activity: designing a bilingual pictures-and-words book commissioned by an art fair in Valencia, Spain. The book title is *Los Nuevos Pecados (The New Sins)* and will be given out free to people in the streets. "It's going to look like a little religious book," he says, while holding a worn red copy of the devotional *Imitation of Christ* by Thomas à Kempis that he's using as a model.

As for his fascination with the religious—from his spastic onstage T-Heads portrayals of a Bible-slapping Pentecostal minister to several allusions on *Look Into the Eyeball*—David says, "Well, it's powerful stuff. It definitely strikes a nerve in me and others. It's connected to something else and adds another layer to life that makes it even more confusing."

Creatively restless, David even put a whimsical artistic touch on the packaging of *Look Into the Eyeball*. It comes with a plastic sleeve filter that works like one of those toy gadgets in Cracker Jack boxes. Tilt the CD slightly and the image of Byrne on the CD cover changes: his eyes close. Tilt it again and the eyes open. It's eerie and comic at the same time.

As for the music, David came up with the concept of writing songs with strings in mind after working with the Balanesçu Quartet at the Expo in Lisbon in 1998. "The idea was to curate an evening by inviting different musicians to collaborate," he says. "I was curious to hear how the driving music of a drummer, sampler, bassist and singer would sound with a string quartet that would provide the harmonic fullness."

The experiment worked. David then made a reference tape of music that he felt achieved a similar effect: tunes by Björk, Brazilian singer Caetano Veloso, the O'Jays and Isaac Hayes' "Theme from Shaft." He wrote songs on his guitar, programmed grooves and used a keyboard sequencer to make loops and fake string parts. He then sought out a simpatico producer in Mike Mangini, whose work he admired on the first Digible Planets' CD and Imani Coppola's album.

"Mike also got a Grammy for 'Who Let the Dogs Out,'" David says with a laugh. "He doesn't like to boast about it, but that song sure pays the bills. He came to my project with an objective ear, which was great. He gave me the harshest criticism of anyone when I played him my demos." For example, Mangini recommended that David write a chorus to the '70s-soul-vibed "Neighborhood," which now features an indelible, singalong refrain. And the buoyant "U.B. Jesus," though still an unconventionally constructed pop song, benefits from a tighter structure thanks to Mangini's input.

For the lyrics—more personal, less ironic, still clever, witty and obscure enough to make you think—David fit the words to pre-existing melodies. "It's kind of like solving a crossword puzzle, but making a crossword puzzle that has something to say," he says. "There are curve balls that I throw into tunes, especially if they're melancholic or romantic, to keep them from sounding too sentimental."

Case in point: the schmaltzy-sounding love song, "Everyone's in Love with You," with the lines: "I want to kill and kiss you too." David laughs. "That's it exactly, isn't it? It's real. Love and jealousy mix together."

David is on the record as saying that he isn't quite sure where his lyrics come from and what they mean exactly. He's said: "Those things aren't known to me often until at least a year later, when the whole thing is behind me and I can listen to [a song] as if it's someone else's record."

The exception to this is "The Accident," a number with ominous-sounding kettle drums and bassoon—and one of the most compelling tunes on *Look Into the Eyeball*.

"I can clearly tell you the inspiration," David says about the song that on the surface is an eyewitness account of a car wreck. The inspirational sources? A combination of Kurt Weill and George Jones. "The opening chord is from a Brazilian tune," David says. "When I heard that chord I knew I could write something that sounded like a Kurt Weill song. It went through three different sets of words. It's a short song, but it took a lot of work."

The key that unlocked the tune's lyrics was David's recollection of a Jones country song called "The Grand Tour," in which the narrator acts like a guide giving a tour of his house. He says, "He's singing about the chair where she used to sit, the table where they used to have dinner, and your heart is just breaking even though all he's doing is describing furniture."

David has been closing his live shows with "The Accident." It seems a strange choice after a set with plenty of raucous moments, but you leave the gig with a lingering sense of mystery and reflection. He's pleased with the results. Does he like touring? "Yes, I love performing, and I like going to different cities," he says. "I bring a folding mountain bike with me. Sometimes it's just a thrill to buzz around when there are no other bicycles. You beat the traffic, cut down side streets and get to where you want to go twice as fast as the cars. You feel on top of the world."

Has he ever been recognized in mid-pedal? "Not really," David says then laughs. "I guess people don't expect to see me."

That sums up David's art pop: expect the unexpected. When he appeared at Irving Plaza in New York on Mother's Day, he announced he would play "new stuff, old stuff, and maybe have a surprise." Well, he treated the crowd to such catchy Heads' tunes as "And She Was" and "Once in a Lifetime" and turned in a surprisingly effective rendition of Whitney Houston's hit "I Wanna Dance with Somebody." But the surprise David alluded to turned out to be a full string section performing the new songs from *Look Into the Eyeball*.

Perhaps some fans in attendance were hoping that a Talking Head or two might show up. But those well-versed in the band's history knew better—the acrimonious break-up, the accusations that David had become uppity, a court case over using the group's name: all described in detail in David Bowman's band biography, *This Must Be the Place: The Adventures of Talking Heads in the 20th Century*. It was obvious that wouldn't happen. The show had T-Heads energy and whimsy, but it was David's charisma that carried the day.

But there's still speculation: Will the Heads reunite some day?

At a screening of *Stop Making Sense* in 1999 at Dolby Studios in San Francisco (the newly remixed film was going to be shown for the first time at the San Francisco Film Festival where the original premiered 15 years earlier), all four band members made a tense appearance together. When asked about a reunion, Weymouth and Frantz expressed interest, Harrison dodged the question and David was conspicuously silent on the matter.

And today? David takes a breath and responds: "To be honest, it's hard to seriously consider that after various people have been criticizing you, bad-mouthing you, writing you nasty letters for years. For them to say, 'Gee, let's get together and make some beautiful music,' you wonder which side of the mouth is talking."

He's not flustered, not outwardly angry. He talks like someone who only wants to creatively move on.

"So, I figure, I don't need to deal with that," he says. "I can get on with my life."

DANCE PARTY WITH HUMAN HOPE

2017

In 2017 the Umbria Jazz Festival in Perugia, Italy celebrated its 45th anniversary. In the ancient central Italy town, the party atmosphere was omnipresent. It was hot in temperature and songs through the different venues were broiling. But outside at the festival's large-scale Arena, the star of the gala event proved to be not jazz but transcendently beyond—the brilliant David Byrne performing decidedly non-jazz,

Afro-punk-funk and rock-fueled new music from his latest album *American Utopia* augmented by dance-crazed Talking Heads hits.

His *American Utopia* showcase toured Europe before its North American shows and over a year before its celebrated runs on Broadway stages. That alone was a rare treat. But David's ambitious part-theater, part-dance, part-rock, part-funk show proved to be the best pop concert I've ever seen.

At 66, he was in amazingly terrific physical shape as he energetically delivered with his 11-piece band—all dressed in matching gray suits and with the exception of one player playing in barefoot—a constant dancing motion choreographed to perfection. His setup was radical, at once making the traditional rock setup (all band members standing in place) obsolete. No wires or amps visible. Even the six drummers were a part of the funky procession for each song.

David and co. played killer tunes from the new album—his first solo recording in 14 years—including the lyrical "Every Day Is a Miracle," the stomping "I Dance Like This" and the fun but poignant singalong chorus, "Everybody's Coming to My House."

Mindful of how influential his Afro-punk-funk band Talking Heads still are, he delivered dance-frenzied tunes "Slippery People," "This Must Be the Place (Naïve Melody)," and "Once in a Lifetime." Right in the middle of the latter, David halted the song, called for security and told them to get rid of the barriers and "let the people dance." The crowd flooded the stage for the rest of the show.

David also added in "Like Humans Do" from his 2001 solo album *Look Into the Eyeball* and two tunes he collaborated on with British rapper Fatboy Slim ("Toe Jam" and "Here Lies Love"). Of course (about as predictable as he can be) the show ended with a torrid run through the T. Head's dance floor hit, "Burning Down the House."

There's a political vein in David's music, especially on the latest album, but it's not stated as politics. It's more, as he says in his liner notes, a reflection on the "utter collapse" of the American experiment in dreaming for a better, more hopeful life. In a profound end to the 90-minute show in the second encore, David and his band stood at the edge of the stage and soberly rendered Janelle Monáe's powerful tune "Hell You Talmbout," the chanted list of black Americans killed by police. As David writes in the album's liners: "It's not easy, but music helps. Music is kind of a model—it often tells us or points us toward how we can be."

The show was an entrancing dance party with a strong beam of human hope. And it took a jazz festival to bring this light to a small town in Italy.

Regina Carter—Jazz Violin Virtuoso

My relationship with Regina Carter began in her early days, writing a mini-feature in 1995 for Strings *magazine on her self-titled first album for Atlantic Records that previewed her status as an important rising star of the jazz violin. Around the same time, I pitched a full-blown feature to a magazine that I won't mention, and the editor said that he didn't think she was worthy.*

Really? Look at her today: a winner of the prestigious MacArthur Fellowship Award in 2006, granted a 2018 Doris Duke Award, and in 2023 honored as an NEA Jazz Master.

Over the years, I touched base with Regina a lot, including more features for Strings *magazine and* Schwann Spectrum, *a quarterly publication that catalogued all available non-classical recordings with features and reviews. It ceased publication in 1997 when I was editor. In 2019, I produced an interview and video with colleague Bob Danziger regarding her starring appearance at the Monterey Jazz Festival.[1]*

On the verge of becoming a renowned jazz star in America, Regina finds an overseas welcome in Italy when she defies the odds and plays/records the most famous of all violins—the Cannon owned by Niccolò Paganini, the most celebrated virtuoso of the 19th century.

Unfortunately, the story of Regina's dream project story from 2002 seems to get lost in the shuffle. It comes back to life here.

TAMING THE GHOST: REGINA'S COURTSHIP WITH PAGANINI'S VIOLIN

2003

On the Tuesday before Thanksgiving in 2002, I arrive at noon in Genoa, the genteel Mediterranean seaside resort in the crook of northwestern Italy. I am greeted by a torrential rainstorm that deluges the highway from Cristoforo Columbo International Airport. My espresso-fueled taxi driver who speeds through foot-deep ponds is finally forced off the expressway by traffic police because of the flooding and rerouted through narrow, winding streets crammed with honking vehicles.

This gives me a chance to admire the old district of the city—the ancient stone buildings and churches, some of which date back to the 12th century—and to peer

---

1   Listen to the interview at the California State University Monterey Bay's Jazz Interviews archive: digitalcommons.csumb.edu/jazz-interviews/31

down dark, curving alleyways that mysteriously descend toward the port. I make mental notes of intriguing pathways where I can wander when the clouds part, but I know full well that any in-depth exploration will have to wait until another visit.

I have only 48 hours in Genoa—renowned for its pesto and hometown hero Christopher Columbus—and my time will be dominated by a different kind of sightseeing experience associated with another historical figure. I travel to observe the celebrated New York jazz violinist Regina Carter record an album with the holy Giuseppe Guarneri del Gesú-made violin that renowned virtuoso Niccolò Paganini possessed, literally and as some of his contemporaries claimed, figuratively.

After a short nap and a late pasta lunch in the hotel restaurant, I join Regina and her support team—including her manager Michelle Taylor, producer Ettore Stratta, pianist/musical director Werner "Vana" Gierig, recording engineer Joe Ferla and a video crew documenting the event—to walk two blocks to Carlo Felice Opera House where an auditorium would serve as the recording studio. We stop at a café for cappuccinos and then enter the building with Regina leading the way.

Dressed in casual black slacks and black turtleneck sweater, the dreadlock-haired, nose-ringed, gap-toothed Regina is nervous. She navigates the labyrinth of corridors of Carlo Felice into an underground dressing room to rendezvous with an old Italian acquaintance.

Actually, she jokes, it is more like an old lover: Paganini's violin, nicknamed the Cannon by the maestro for its booming sound.

In the classical music world, his violin—the sonorous, dark-toned instrument he bequeathed to the city of Genoa upon his death in 1840—is almost as famous as the virtuoso himself. In fact, the last time the Cannon came to America, it was greeted as a celebrity at Lincoln Center. It was carried on stage and given a standing ovation even before anyone played it.

The violin (according to some estimates in 2003, is insured for $30 million to $40 million) has a celebrity of its own and travels from its resting place in a vault inside Palazzo Tursi, Genoa's city hall, with an entourage that includes two armed guards, a violin maker responsible for its care and a representative of the committee in charge of its well-being.

As daunting an experience as this is, playing a priceless violin under watchful eyes, Regina is up for the challenge. She is, after all, jazz's most celebrated contemporary violinist who has been breaking down barriers ever since she picked up a pint-sized instrument as a child. She was originally groomed to play classical music, so why shouldn't she re-enter that world bowing one of its most renowned violins?

In December 2001, Regina was invited to headline a concert in Carlo Felice playing Paganini's violin—the first time in history a nonclassical violinist and African American had been allowed such a privilege. She warmed up to the Cannon by thinking of her mother Grace and her favorite hymn, "Amazing Grace." She closed her eyes and bowed a soulful rendition.

The 2001 event, a success on many levels, was not without controversy. Detractors vehemently protested that "jazz itself is not suited" to the Paganini violin and that Regina's music would "debase the image of the instrument."

So why, nearly a year later, is she so intent on having another Paganini encounter? Plain and simple: to make a recording using the Cannon. Easier said than done. But after miles of red tape and dozens of emails, the recording sessions were scheduled, and Regina prepared for another meet-and-greet with the ghost of Paganini.

In 2002, the encounter takes place at Genoa's Carlo Felice. The violin procession marches into the dressing room. Stern-faced violin maker Pio Montanari carries the case that is escorted by two stoic police officers, clad in blue uniforms, high black boots with pistols in white holsters hung from their white belts. Pio asks the video crew documenting the scene to leave the room while the Cannon is lifted from its case and placed on a blood-red velvet cloth spread out on the make-up table.

Regina smiles anxiously and waits for her partner. Pio walks the violin to her and then adjusts her shoulder pad onto the instrument.

"If only they saw how I put the shoulder rest on my own violin," Regina jokes.

Everyone in the room laughs except the violin guardians. Finally, with one guard in the hallway and the other a few feet away from her, the courtship resumes.

At first, Regina is tentative, but she quickly relaxes with the instrument, practicing riffs and lines for several minutes in front of the make-up mirror. With dreadlocks dangling, she interrupts one classical excursion with the chorus from the pop tune "Louie, Louie." It's another tension-breaking moment.

Regina gently places the violin on the velvet cloth and kneads her biceps. "Playing this is like a workout," she says, noting that the Cannon is so much heavier than her violin, which was resting in its case on the floor. She picks it up and bows it softly to demonstrate the sonic contrast: a lighter, feminine tone compared to the Cannon's dark-roast voice.

"Pio must have been playing the Cannon lately," she says. "Still, it won't really wake up until tomorrow. It acts like when you get up in the morning and you try to talk. You've got froggy voice. By tomorrow it'll be wide awake."

The first time Regina ever played the Cannon in the previous year, she compared it to a wild beast with a mind of its own. "It took me an hour to make peace with it," she says. "I finally told it, 'I'm going to be playing you the next couple of days, so let's get with it!'"

Regina so frequently personifies the cherished instrument it's almost as if she believes it's alive. When tell her that, her eyes get big and she laughs. "It is." She points to the violin. "Paganini's living in there."

THE SECOND MEETING

Since Regina had been on her best behavior with the violin during their first convergence in 2001, she requested another meeting, this time to document her relationship with the Cannon.

"Right off, the people in charge of the violin wanted to know what we'd be recording," Regina says, prior to her second Genoa trip, while relaxing in her small Central Park West apartment. "They said the music has to match the instrument. So, to me that said classical. I decided that since so many musicians were going back to their roots that I'd do the same. I started out as a classical player, so why not make an album of classical-oriented pieces."

Regina's request to continue her courtship with the ghost of Paganini was granted.

Two weeks before Genoa, Carter tracked nine numbers with her band at Right Track Studios in New York. It was a jovial session in preparation for the real deal.

The playlist for the sessions included four classical works (by Maurice Ravel, Claude Debussy and two by Gabriel Fauré), two pieces written for film (Luiz Bonfá's "Black Orpheus" and Ennio Morricone's "Cinema Paradiso"), the Astor Piazzolla composition "Oblivion," a Vana original ("Healing in a Foreign Land") and an excerpt from Regina's four-movement work, "Alexandra," commissioned by the Kennedy Center in Washington, D.C.

With her support team, Carter flew to Genoa to overdub the violin parts in three days with the Cannon.

Paganini: After a Dream, Carter's third Verve release and fifth as a leader, features her genial touring band: Vana, bassist Chris Lightcap, drummer Alvester Garnett and percussionist Mayra Casales. Cellist Borislav Strulev guests on two tracks ("Black Orpheus" and Fauré's "Après un Rêve"), and a string orchestra conducted by Stratta and recorded after the trip to Genoa colors the pieces by Piazzolla, Morricone and Ravel ("Pavane Pour une Infante Défunte").

As suggested by the title, the album captures a dreamscape, characterized by both melancholy and joy. The Ravel work is a somber ballad. "Black Orpheus" opens slow and blue before awakening into a Brazilian rhythmic flow. Likewise "Pavane" swings with an uptempo feel. And "Oblivion" lushly settles into a sober muse. Debussy's "Reverie" is arranged for whimsy and even finds Regina getting a little sassy with the violin, while she and Vana dance through the jocund take on "Cinema Paradiso."

The most compelling of the covers is Fauré's "Après un Rêve," where violin and cello converse then embrace. But the strongest numbers of the collection are the originals: Vana's pensive, lyrical "Healing in a Foreign Land" and Regina's poignant and sunny "Alexandra," which features a cadenza of quiet ecstasy and a glide into bossa glee.

As for Regina's violin contributions, you can hear the inspired passion in her virtuosity on the treasured instrument. The Cannon sound is full-bodied, solid, ruby in color, a soul mate of Strulev's cello. There's nothing brittle about it, especially its high notes which pierce. Regina carries the emotion of the recording with the instrument, offering whimpers, sighs and flutters on "Black Orpheus," clarion soliloquies on "Alexandra."

In the New York session while first recording "Alexandra," Regina played the wistful notated intro that has an edgy, dive-off-a-precipice feel. She said that it was the hardest piece of the pack to perform. She worried about hitting the high notes on the large-sized Cannon. "It's like a viola, so I have to move my arm more," she says. "I'm hoping I'll be able to hit the notes in Genoa. I don't know. I'm not banking on it."

Regina dubs the Paganini touch into "Alexandra" on the second day of recording in a small auditorium in the Genoa opera house. The day before she had been jetlagged but exhilarated. The takes were strong even though the guards nearby made her tense.

While a more congenial pair of security guards shows up on day two, a deeper sense of fatigue sets in and the morning session proves difficult. With earphones on, Regina listens to what had already been recorded and attempts to duplicate with the Cannon the same spirit and space of the original session.

Frustrated, she takes a break and talks about why she likes Paganini so much. "He was an improviser," she says. "That gets lost in the mix when the small-minded people get so upset about a jazz musician playing the Cannon. Improvisation disappeared in classical music after the baroque period. If Paganini knew what I what doing with his instrument he'd say, 'It's about time. Now I can sleep.'"

After lunch, Regina and company visit the second-term mayor Giuseppe Pericu at City Hall. Local reporters cover the event and quiz him about Regina's return. He rehashes the original resistance to her visit, then jokes that the concert's success actually helped him get re-elected. He also notes that he's been a jazz fan for a long time.

Returning to the studio auditorium, Regina again launches into "Alexandra," nailing the cadenza's high notes she feared she couldn't and gently swinging into the bossa beat. She's more relaxed and even adds an impromptu pizzicato part. She smiles, consults with everyone at the board and finally proclaims, "Alexandra's dirty diaper has been changed."

Regina laughs and talks about a dream she had the night before. "There was something funny about how the violin sounded, and I wondered if they had switched violins and not given me the real Cannon," she says. She woke, studied photographs of the real McCoy and felt relieved.

She admits this was nothing compared to the nightmares she had before her performance the year before. "I was petrified," she says. "In one dream I dropped the violin and then fell through the floor after it. Then I dreamed I played and people hated it and started booing. Audiences in Italy are honest. If they don't like something, they'll let you know. They'll throw things at you. But then I thought, they won't throw a thing at me because I have the violin for protection."

THE GAME PLAN

The genesis of Regina's involvement with the Paganini violin began over a casual dinner conversation in the summer of 2001. She and Vana were at an East Village sushi bar with his longtime friend, Andrea Liberovici, an electronic music composer and mover-and-shaker in Genoa.

"Andrea was visiting New York and Vana played him a rehearsal tape of charts I had John Clayton arrange to help me get orchestral dates," Regina says. "Andrea was so impressed he offered to take the tape to the community in Genoa and propose that I play the Paganini violin. Of course, as a violinist I had heard about it and how it was God, how no one can figure out why its sound is so dark and loud. It's a spectacular instrument. It's like the crown jewels."

Regina became intrigued by the possibilities. She was fascinated with Paganini himself: a rebel musician who purportedly made a pact with the devil long before blues guitarist Robert Johnson allegedly did the same in the Mississippi Delta.

"People thought Paganini was possessed because of the way he played," Regina explains. "He was imprisoned; people tried to hang and burn him. People thought he had some disease that made him double- and triple-jointed. He could play like no one else. He was so amazing, he could break all his strings except one and still play a concerto."

Over coffee in Genoa, Andrea Liberovici says, "I saw Regina as a great violinist, and I knew Genoa had a great violin." As luck would have it, when he returned to Genoa, he ran into a person who was involved in the cultural politics of the city. He said the committee in charge of the Cannon had been thinking about getting someone new to play the instrument that year.

"It was an incredible coincidence," Andrea says. "I went to the mayor the next day. He loved the idea. Two days later was September 11."

Instead of derailing the plan, the aftermath of the disaster made the proposal more sensible. Regina could perform the Cannon at a benefit concert as an expression of Italian solidarity with the United States.

Even then, the wheels moved slowly—so slowly that Regina was convinced that the proposal would fail. Sensing her frustration, Vana took the lead. He says, "The commission wanted to know what kind of chin rest, shoulder rest and strings Regina used. They made her fill out an application and asked for a song list. It looked good until someone in Genoa saw a photo of her on the Internet with a pickup on her violin."

The plan went back to zero. Regina had to assure them she would play acoustic. They responded with more questions: What was her classical background? Who were her teachers? She grew pessimistic and felt she was being disrespected.

"It was difficult for me," Regina says. "I didn't understand why they were doing this. Several times I thought, 'Screw them. They can keep their violin. I'm not going to do this.' But Vana kept telling me that everyone goes through the same thing. It's the way they do things."

Finally, two weeks before the December 30 concert, Regina got the green light. But then the Italian press caught wind of the event, interviewed some disgruntled members of the Institute of Paganini Studies and ruffled feathers in the community with such headlines as "Regina, Queen of Scandal."

A week before the benefit concert, only 100 tickets for the 2,000-seat house had been sold. A press conference was hastily called and Regina's spunk and charisma won out. With a flurry of last-minute ticket sales, the show sold out, and the violinist, after channeling Paganini via his instrument for half the show, received a standing ovation.

Overnight, Regina became the darling of Genoa and immediately got Vana and Andrea thinking ahead to the next stage: making a recording with the Cannon. Regina recalls her initial response: "I told them, leave me out of this mess. I'm done. I've had enough. But they wouldn't let it go. So here I am."

After a Dream is just that: the gift after a dream fulfilled. Regina says that playing Paganini's violin once was a thrill beyond belief. "That was the most exciting thing that's happened in my musical life," she says.

She pauses, then adds, "Maybe even in my entire life. For me, that's my Grammy. I made history. It was a huge deal and very personal."

With the release of the CD, perhaps more dreams will soon be realized.

PAGANINI COMES TO NEW YORK
2004

I pitched this article to an editor at The New Yorker. *It was rejected but I feel it completes the story of Regina and Paganini's violin.*

Genoa was tabbed as Europe's City of Culture in 2004, and there are rumors that the organizers of municipal events were thinking of asking Regina to do an encore performance. There were also negotiations underway to have Paganini's prized possession make another trip to the U.S. this year so that Regina can perform After a Dream *dates with the real deal.*

The last time the Cannon came to America, it was greeted as a celebrity by those conversant in classical music. When it was carried on stage at Lincoln Center, it received a standing ovation even before anyone played it.

It seems almost comic to the American mindset that a mere fiddle gets so pampered, heralded and protected in Italy. But then again, such concern speaks volumes on cultural values. Regina agrees. "Even with all the hassles I had to go through just to play it, it's comforting to know there are still places that hold such high respect for music and art," she says. "It would be lovely if we had more of that here."

THE ARRIVAL
Since its founding in 1932, the Columbia Association, the New York Police Department's fraternity of officers of Italian descent, has been providing volunteer security guards for numerous events, from patrolling the annual Columbus Day parade to escorting visiting dignitaries. But until this past week, it had never been

called upon to safeguard a musical instrument, specifically a priceless two-hundred-and-sixty-year-old violin.

Built in 1743 by Bartolomeo Giuseppe Guarneri del Gesù, owned by the free-spirited virtuoso Niccolò Paganini, and bequeathed to the city of Genoa upon his death in 1840, the violin, a celebrity of sorts, arrives in New York from Italy on Halloween for a starring role: jazz artist Regina Carter would be playing it at Alice Tully Hall the following Monday.

It was a daunting task of transit, beginning in Genoa with its removal from safekeeping—its vault inside Palazzo Tursi in the city's town hall.

It commands an entourage: a local violin maker responsible for its upkeep, a municipal representative overseeing its well-being, and two pistol-packing guards flanking its every movement.

In New York, officers of the Columbia Association were asked to fill in for their Italian brethren who I saw in action last fall when Regina was in Genoa preparing to record with the Cannon. Two severe guards scrutinized her every move as if she might pull a Pete Townshend. In a word, she summed up her experience with one particularly impassive pair keeping close watch: oppressive.

The day before the violin's arrival stateside—its fourth visit to New York including a Guernari exhibit at the Metropolitan Museum of Art in 1994 and an Avery Fisher Hall performance by Salvatore Accardo in 2000—Columbia Association officer Manny Rossi is mum about the stratagem he and his partners would employ to thwart potential fiddle snatchers. Citing security, he says, "I can't comment on how many of us there'll be or how we'll transport the violin to the city."

The president of the Columbia Association, Giovanni Porcelli, is equally circumspect when asked if the violin required any special security precautions. "We'll employ the same tactics we use when guarding a head of state," he says. "But I won't go into specifics. Let's just say we're proud as Italian police officers to be guarding something from Italy that's so highly regarded."

All this attention for a mere violin? Maybe there's more, suggests Regina, who once half-jokingly told me while pointing to the violin, "Paganini's living in there."

When the Cannon flies into JFK on Alitalia flight 610 from Rome, Rossi, a trim man with close-cropped black and gray hair and a black-gray caterpillar moustache, and fellow Columbia Association officer R.J. Coleman, with short dark hair and a stout build, position themselves at the gate with representatives from the Italian Cultural Institute of New York. They meet Anna Rita Certo from the Municipality of Genoa toting the violin in its gray-canvas waterproof case and commence the Columbia Association's five-day shield of supervision.

Outside, in the Arrivals area of the International Terminal, Regina, along with her manager Michelle Taylor and publicist Helene Greece, anxiously await the violin she intimately encountered in Genoa twice before—at the groundbreaking and controversial 2001 concert and the 2002 recording session that yielded *Paganini: After a Dream.*

The keepers of the Cannon stroll through the security doors with Rossi and Coleman, dressed inconspicuously in suits and ties. After a quick greeting, the violin is whisked away into one of the two curbside black town cars with red beacons on the dash and driven through Friday rush hour traffic to Machold Rare Violins on West Seventy-Second Street.

Inside, after a quick inspection of the Cannon's health, Ditemar H. Machold, president of the establishment, walks under Rossi and Coleman's watchful eyes down a hallway of propped-up cellos and deposits the instrument in a walk-in safe that also houses other collectibles built by Guarneri and Stradivari. Machold smiles and says, "It will be spending the weekend with friends."

As for the violin's protectors, Regina says, "They're a whole lot friendlier and relaxed than Italy." When told about the guards in Genoa, Rossi, obviously packing a pistol under his double-breasted brown suit, grins. "We're the friendly police."

Early on Saturday the Cannon is taken from Machold to the Italian Cultural Institute on Park Avenue for Regina to practice. Another Columbia Association officer, Robert Haley, fills in for Rossi who is celebrating his daughter's birthday. A classically trained violinist well versed in the Cannon's history and value, Haley, tall and sturdy, eagerly volunteered for guard duty. "It's an honor to be in the same room and not have to travel to Italy to see it," he says while admiring the violin at rest on a blood-red velvet cloth. "I usually see these kind of violins behind a piece of glass. If I died tonight, I'd be happy."

When asked if he worried about a heist of the crown jewel of Genoa, Haley shakes his head. "People I work with are more afraid of me." He laughs. "If the violin disappears under my watch, they'll know." What about any temptation to pick up the Cannon and bow a few notes? "No way. I'm not worthy to even touch it."

After Regina and the violin take Sunday off, Rossi and Coleman are back at their posts at the Institute on the Monday morning of the concert when the press is invited to get an up-close view of the Cannon. The room is packed with reporters and photographers as Regina cradles the instrument like a newborn and demonstrates its dark tonality. When it was time for a photo op, most of the photographers, who had been swapping tales of snapping shots of P. Diddy at the New York City Marathon the day before, edge toward Regina with paparazzi-like fervor.

Later, the two Columbia Association cops shrug off concerns that the swarm of photographers might have harmed the instrument. "I was more worried about the bottles of Pellegrino getting spilled onto the violin when it was displayed on the table," says Coleman. "But the hardest thing for me is to not be seduced by its sound when Regina plays it."

As people file out of the room, Rossi lets Coleman stand guard alone while he got in line with a copy of Regina's CD to get her autograph. "I'm not much of a jazz or classical music fan, but maybe I will be now," he says, while uncapping the top of a thick-tipped red Sharpie. "This is my favorite pen. It's the same one I used to get Derek Jeter to sign a baseball at a parade."

THE CONCERT

On November 3, in part three of Regina's trilogy of musical encounters with Paganini's priceless violin, she performs at a triumphant, sold-out concert at Alice Tully Hall. While the concert was billed as a spotlight for her quintet, clearly many in the audience are here to witness a spectacle: the jazz violinist playing the quarter-millennium-old instrument.

The Alice Tully crowd has to wait until the second half of the show to hear the booming voice of the treasured violin. However, perhaps because of the big-production ramp-up to the show, the performance itself feels anti-climactic and restrained.

The first set of the concert which Regina performed on her own smaller and thinner-voiced violin exhibited a swinging, burning and grooving exuberance. In contrast, the Cannon showcase, with the quintet embellished by a large string orchestra conducted by Ettore Stratta (co-producer of the CD), came off sounding almost dreamy.

Perhaps it was telling four days earlier en route to the airport with the Regina camp to meet the Cannon's escorts flying in from Rome when she sighed when asked if she was excited about being reunited with the Paganini. "It's like planning a wedding," she said jokingly, in reference to how monumental a production the instrument's visit had become—including jumping through the hoops of gaining permission from Genoa, securing police protection on U.S. soil, finding a vault where the violin could safely be stored, coming up with a guest list, planning pre- and post-concert events, then dealing with the wildfire of media attention including mainstream press and a CBS Sunday Morning camera crew. So, even before the big event, Regina was already feeling a bit fatigued.

While fully engaged with the violin at warm-up rehearsals leading up to the show, Regina seems a bit tentative with it in concert. She plays the Cannon with little zest until she launches into a fiery section of Astor Piazzolla's "Oblivion" toward the end of the second set. It is most obvious how protectively Regina is playing the violin when she duets with animated classical cellist Borislav Strulev on two pieces, "Black Orpheus" and Fauré's "Après un Reve." He digs in while it feels like Regina is holding back. The best demonstration of the Guarneri's power comes on Regina's jazz rendition of Debussy's "Reverie." Conspicuously missing from the show are two of the CD's highlights: pianist Gierig's "Healing in a Foreign Land" and Regina's original "Alexandra," both of which would have spiced up the mix.

Even so, it exhibits Regina's joy in once again taming the ghost. A triumph and celebration.

REGINA SINGS ELLA

2017

Fifteen years and a world away from the Cannon, Regina sings Ella Fitzgerald B-sides on Ella: Accentuate the Positive, *on SonyMusic Masterwork's imprint OKeh. It's not only a tribute to Ella in the centennial of her birth, but it's also a personal homage to the First Lady of Song.*

"I love Ella," says Regina in an afternoon conversation at Lincoln Center's Atrium. "I've always loved her since I was a child. We had lots of music around the house. My brothers were listening to Motown, the Beatles and there was lots of jazz. But the first time I put on an Ella record, I felt that motherly love wrap around me. I loved the music because I could go to another place. When I was a teenager, I would daydream about going out on a date and dancing to Ella's music."

After her youthful elation over Ella, Regina continues to be magically connected to her and her music. "When I became an adult, I realized how incredible her voice, her instrument, was," she says. "She's another—more like she's the other—with a spirituality that no one else had. Playing her music is my connection to her. Her music has always made me happy, upbeat. In the mornings, I would put on a pot of coffee and listen to Ella. That was how I started my day."

In the album's liner notes, she expresses her marvel in the iconic legend by singling out a quote from one of the singer's accompanists: "Perhaps Jimmy Rowles said it best. Music comes out of her…When Ella walks down the street, she leaves notes."

Those dazzling notes along the pathway impacted the violinist. Previously Regina had occasionally covered the song stylist's tunes in her nearly two-decade career, including most famously the 1938 Chick Webb Orchestra hit "A-Tisket, A-Tasket" (on her 2006 *I'll Be Seeing You—A Sentimental Journey* tribute to her mother Grace who had passed away). Ella treated the 19th century nursery rhyme with resonant new lyrics.

Regina also recorded her interpretation of Ella's 1947 hit with the George and Ira Gershwin-composed tune "Oh, Lady Be Good" on her 1999 *Rhythms of the Heart* album. In addition, in concert, especially with orchestras, Regina renders the vocalist's beauty, "Imagine My Frustration," written by Billy Strayhorn, Duke Ellington and Gerald Wilson for her 1965 album *Ella at Duke's Place.*

However, the thought of recording an entire album of Ella's music was daunting, especially during this historic year. A MacArthur Foundation Award fellow in 2006, Regina didn't want to be in step with the Ella tribute circuit. "I knew people were going to be celebrating her," she tells me. "I see people performing Ella's songs all over the place. All you have to do is look at the flurry on the internet. But I know that what I've done is so much different."

Regina credits vocalist Carla Cook—a close friend from Detroit's renowned music program at Cass Technical School when they both attended the Center for Creative Studies, then called the Detroit Community Music School)—for the inspiration.

"Carla is the person who said I had to do this album," Regina says. "So I agreed but decided not to do the tunes people think of when they think about Ella. There are so many songs to explore beyond the obvious ones. Ella gave us such a wealth of music from R&B to swing, from country and western to soul. Everything. She just loved the music. One of the things that most attracted me to her was that she didn't create boundaries in her music. She just sang because that's what she loved to do. Most of the songs I discovered I had never heard, so I listened to them and then found the stories behind the songs. So I decided to showcase songs that weren't as popular like 'Crying in the Chapel' and 'I'll Chase the Blues Away.' I call them the B-sides."

In looking at this year's Verve's 4-CD compilation, *Ella 100—Ella Fitzgerald 100 Songs for a Centennial*, there's only one of Regina's chosen tunes, "Undecided," that's in the package.

She laughs at this, thinking that a more likely double might have occurred with her buoyant take on "Ac-Cent-Tchu-Ate the Positive," written in 1944 by Harold Arlen and Johnny Mercer. Regina showcases the tune, saying that given the troubled times we're living in, "we need some positive vibes."

As for "Undecided" (Ella first recorded it with the Chick Webb Orchestra in 1939), she commissioned vocalist Charenee Wade to write an arrangement because simply she just loved the melody. "Charenee sang the tune in her arrangement," Regina says. "I thought that would be cool to play that melody on my violin. Originally the album was going to be all vocals, but then I decided not to have any vocals at all. At the last minute, I decided to do two vocal songs."

The songs on *Ella: Accentuate the Positive* are arranged by a team of artists that Regina feels simpatico with. "It's been a long time since I've arranged or even written new music," she says with a laugh. "I got out of the habit. I wrote the music on my first two records, and over the years I've been commissioned to write some pieces. But I'm my biggest critic. When I get something down, my first reaction is, 'It's horrible,' and I throw it away. When I moved from Atlantic Records to Verve [in 1999], the A&R person there said he didn't like my music because it sounded like smooth jazz. So with all these voices, I kept thinking I'm not going to be good enough. Even now, I'm more apt to send the music I want to do off to other people to do the arranging."

Her arranger friends on the album include soul pianist/producer Ray Angry ("Ac-Cent-Tchu-Ate the Positive" and "Reach for Tomorrow") and bassist Ben Williams ("Crying in the Chapel") in addition to bassist Chris Lightcap and guitar master Marvin Sewell.

"I told everyone the same thing," says Regina. "When I listened to these songs, I didn't want them to be straightahead. I wanted an old-school, R&B vibe like Otis Redding and Mavis Staples. That's what I told everyone. I'd send three or four songs to each person and told them it was important that they feel a connection. Anyone can arrange a tune, but if they don't have a personalized connection and really dig it to ask for another song."

That's what happened when Regina sent Marvin, who has been performing with her since 2014's *Southern Comfort*, a couple of tunes, one of which he declined. In a phone conversation with him, he says he can't remember what the song was, but he said it didn't hit him. "So then Regina sent me a Hoagy Carmichael recording of 'Judy,' and I thought I can work with this," Marvin says. "I liked the way the harmony and melody moved, and I knew Regina liked the standards from the '20s and '30s. The tune had a movement. I could hear a different harmony that still respected the melody. I didn't do reharms with stacks of chords that sometimes get in the way of the melody. Complex chords and rhythms may not serve the melody. The way Regina plays is like a singer in that she uses only a mic and doesn't use a monitor. She plays with a certain sensitivity like the singers I often play with."

The song ends up on the album as a gently grooving Carter-Sewell duo. "I choose any tune where the melody gets me," Regina says. "I love this melody, and I love the story around it that gave me a lot of insight into Ella's life and what could have been different. Plus, this song really lays well on my instrument."

The backstory on "Judy" is that the swinging jazz harmony group The Boswell Sisters made this song a hit in the early '30s and was a favorite of Ella's mother. When the 17-year-old youngster took the stage as a dancer at the Apollo Theater's Amateur Night on November 21, 1934, she got the jitters after an earlier dance act had gotten booed off the stage. So she asked the band to play the tune. She sang it and became the winner.

"That whole story is remarkable," says Regina. "Just think, Ella could have been a dancer and not a singer. And the fact that the Apollo paid her the $25 award but didn't let her back that week because of how disheveled her clothes looked. When you think about her life growing up, with her father dying and her mother remarrying and her stepfather abusing her. She ran away, ended up in an orphanage then ran away again. When you think of that, somehow her music was always so full of love and joy. It could have been the exact opposite. She could have been a real dark singer."

Another interesting note: Marvin was in a youth group as a child in Chicago and a bus driver picked up the kids and drove them to the youth center every day. "I must have heard 'Judy' because this guy was constantly listening to Boswell Sisters music," he says. "Here we were, listening to funk, the Isley Brothers, Parliament Funkadelic, and this was a whole different world of music I experienced that probably helped me with this arrangement."

Chris Lightcap contributed an arrangement of the Ella song "I'll Never Be Free" as well as a bonus track "I Fell in Love With a Dream." He has been working on and off with Carter since 2000 touring in support of her *Rhythms of the Heart* Verve debut. He discovered the breadth of Regina's range of music from working with such players as Muhal Richard Abrams, Mark Helias and the String Trio of New York.

"Regina has such a rhythmic ability," he says, "and a great ear for melody and melodic improvisation. We toured almost constantly and she was crushing it, whether we were in Cancun or Thailand. Out of about a half dozen tracks she sent me for the Ella project, I chose 'I'll Never Be Free' based on hearing Ella perform it with Louis Prima. I love the song and the arrangement, so I thought, what more can I do to improve it? I also heard Etta James sing it and Zooey Deschanel from *She & Him*. So I did it based on a '50s slow jam, a 12/8 ballad, added a couple of chords, speeded it up, left space for Marvin and treated Regina's violin like a singer."

The one tune on the recording that does not have an arrangement credit is the funky end song "I'll Chase the Blues Away," that Ella sang with the Chick Webb Orchestra in 1935 and that was the first song credited to her on the 78 RPM single. "That song happened at a rehearsal one day," Regina explains. "Chris started playing an electric bass line from Parliament Funkadelic. We were all just goofing around, then all of sudden we're playing 'I'll Chase the Blues Away' with Marvin doing that old blues slide thing on his guitar like he had done on *Southern Comfort*. We stopped, and wow, it worked." She laughs, then adds, "But I told everybody we can't use that bass line."

REGINA AS EDUCATOR

Having worked with Regina for such a long period of time, does Chris see her as a role model for younger musicians? "I can't think of a better person," he says. "I wouldn't want to put that kind of pressure on her, but she lives her life with a lot of grace, is kind, generous, open. She's one of the least judgmental people I know. She asserts her leadership in a subtle way, but when she needs to, she'll take the reins."

Regina's response to the same question: "Yeah, I think we all are. People are watching us and checking us out. So I think I am, and I'm hoping that I'm a positive role model. But young kids are impressionable and sometimes they see this bad behavior and they see in jazz these personalities and vibe and the way of treating others in a negative way. So they try to emulate. And they think it's OK. So that's the bad role model."

Regina makes her good-model appearance in classes and clinics she's asked to participate in, including earlier this year a violin workshop at the Instituto Superior de Arte as a part of the educational activities of the Thelonious Monk Institute of Jazz-sponsored International Jazz Day in Havana. "The clinic was at the university, but they also brought in some of the younger students from other schools—all string players," she says. "It was amazing. They were so excited to be there and so excited to learn. We worked on call-and-response and phrasing. When I work with a large group, I have the students stand in a circle and then I find the shyer students and pair them with someone who is catching on really fast, and get them to help each other. That's the best way to learn—from our peers. They were so enthusiastic about learning. They wanted this knowledge. They were ready. It inspired me."

Back home Regina serves as the artist in residence at her alma mater, Oakland University in Rochester, Michigan, where twice a year she works with students and performs a concert once a year with students and faculty. This year she'll also be co-teaching an improvisational class for strings players at the Manhattan School of Music. In addition, when she plays in certain cities like St. Louis at the club Jazz at the Bistro, she spends her days performing for students at the Children's Hospital as well as at hospice facilities.

So, with the Ella project gaining speed on the touring circuit (including a headline show on the Jimmy Lyons Stage at the Monterey Jazz Festival where she is this year's featured artist), does the New Jersey-based Regina have any ideas for her next project? She calmly says, "No."

Is that a good thing? "Yeah, that's OK. It's like that for the first time,'" she says. "Actually there are some other things I'm focusing on now. It's my hospice work. I enjoy doing that. I spent the last month of my mother's life at the hospital, and I saw a lot of elderly people who don't have anybody in their lives and are alone. And I felt sad. When you're dying, you shouldn't have to be alone. So I became a hospice volunteer, and it took me a long time to be OK with that."

It was the first time in her life since she was four and first learning her instrument that she wasn't "eating, sleeping, breathing the violin," Regina says. "That's all I had ever known, all that I'd ever done, all that I ever wanted to do. But then I found this other passion. I'm realizing that we are not one-dimensional. I need to follow that. I've been in this business for a long time, and I need some balance. The music I love; the business I'm not that crazy about."

Ornette Coleman—A Celebration

It was special to be invited to the studio opening and then being in a small space where Ornette played with such ferocity. While I never interviewed him, we did cross paths over the next few years at festivals. Ornette even invited me to come visit him at his loft. Biggest regret: I never took up his offer.

JOIN UPPER MANHATTAN EMPOWERMENT ZONE AND THE HARLEM CHAMBER OF COMMERCE
As we celebrate
Black Music Month 2003
with
Ornette Coleman
and
The Grand Opening of
Harmolodic Recording Studios
Harlem, USA

Opening Reception Thursday, June 12th
Featuring a live performance by Ornette Coleman previewing his upcoming Carnegie Hall Concert

Harmolodic Recording Studios has opened the *only* world-class recording environment in Harlem. Founded by legendary musician and composer Ornette Coleman, Harmolodic opens its doors to the recording and entertainment industries in June of 2003. The best-kept secret in the Big Apple has arrived. The music and entertainment industry is invited to track and mix their projects in the historic community where music for the world has always been created.

"In the twenty-first century, music and language will become homogenous in sound where the ethnical tongues remain the same." —Ornette Coleman

Date: June 12th, 2003
Time: 6pm – 9pm
Address: 103 East 125th Street @ Park Avenue, Suite 609

HARMOLODIC RECORDING STUDIO LIFT-OFF

2003

In his 1966 book *Black Music—Four Lives*, author A.B. Spellman quoted Ornette Coleman's proactive advice to aspiring musicians: "If you've got to do something and you feel it's just a matter of being tired of waiting for someone to come along and give you the chance to do it, don't wait for that. Go out and do it for yourself." This DIY philosophy undergirds Orenette's latest project: opening his Harmolodic Recording Studios to the public for tracking and mixing albums. It's Ornette's invitation to the musical community to use his refurbished house of song to let their voices be heard.

The studio's opening ceremony took place on June 12. It was staged as a coming-out party at the Harlem facility and featured several guest speakers, including members of the Harlem empowerment zone and chamber of commerce. Ornette shyly uttered a few brief remarks too soft to be deciphered by most attendees crowded into the Live Room of the studio.

Ornette has used the studio for the past decade to track his own recording projects. It was recently remodeled and is decked out in the latest technology, including a Neve-VR 72-channel Mad Labs modified recording console with Flying Faders and 48-channel Pro Tools. Designed by Ornette and his son/business partner Denardo Coleman, the studio has several hard-wood floored rooms and was called that evening "the best kept secret in the Big Apple."

The highlight of the evening was a trio performance by Ornette, Denardo on drums and Tony Falanga on bass. Originally the brief set in the Live Room was scheduled to be a preview of new material Ornette was going to play two weeks later at his JVC Festival Carnegie Hall date. But, as Denardo explained later, his dad made a last-minute change. "Ornette decided to write new music that afternoon for the occasion," he said. The titles? "No titles. At least, none as far as I know."

In front of a crowd of a couple dozen people, Ornette and company played two tunes, one short, the other expansive. The first number sped out the gate. Dressed in a dark three-piece suit and a black porkpie hat, Ornette charged into a squiggly and sweet melody that ended almost as quickly as it started.

On the second tune, the alto saxophonist dug in and played layers of melodies that had pockets of almost child-like ditties. He embarked on a search through the music that was sunny, skipping and meandering. At one point Ornette alluded to a New Orleans brass band; at another juncture he accelerated the tempo and wailed and fluttered. It was yelp and song throughout the musical journey as Ornette blew geometric figures while rhythmically bobbing in place.

Remarkably many partygoers could be heard in the other rooms chattering in conversation. Like the naysayers of Ornette's early years who talked through or walked out on his sets, many Harmolodic Studios guests never knew how much they were missing.

Elvis Costello—Musical Omnivore

Elvis Costello may be a rock music star, but he has deep roots in jazz and roots music. My first meet-up with Elvis came in 1994 when he agreed to be Blindfold tested for DownBeat *magazine. I fed him a sampling of jazz and blues in our backstage sit-down before his sell-out show at the Concord Pavilion in Concord, California.*

This chapter is an inverted chronology, beginning with a 2006 conversation with him and Allen Toussaint on their collaboration in the aftermath of Hurricane Katrina.

All were originally written for DownBeat. *These are the writer's cuts before editing for print space.*

ELVIS COSTELLO & ALLEN TOUSSAINT SEEK THE INDESTRUCTIBLE BEAT OF NEW ORLEANS

DownBeat cover story 2006

FLOWING COLLABORATION

Post Hurricane Katrina, Allen Toussaint's house still stands, but remains inhabitable. His recording studio is gone, swept away. The diaspora to which he belongs persists. And his city's music endures, even if its musicians have been scattered by last fall's maelstrom. But New Orleans, presently a hint of its former glory, will be fine in the future, says Allen, the city's 68-year-old maestro of popular music.

The soft-spoken, refined Crescent City native—who's temporarily residing in New York while waiting for his house to be refurbished—has a positive outlook. "I've heard people worry about the city becoming a Disneyland when it's rebuilt," he says. "That'll never happen. New Orleans has something about it that says, 'I'm this.' That will prevail. The baptism of Katrina didn't kill that."

Allen smiles and nods across the hotel suite at the W in Union Square to Elvis Costello, the pop music omnivore who shares his passion—and optimism—in restoring the New Orleans soul that sired the heart of American music. Elvis also served as the catalyst to their collaborative CD project, *The River in Reverse*, which was the first major recording project tracked in New Orleans after Hurricane Katrina and the subsequent floods. It serves as a poignant and joyful testament to the city's cultural legacy.

"Popular music wouldn't be what it is today if New Orleans was only about Louis Armstrong," Elvis says. "People think I'm exaggerating when I say something like this, but it's true. The music there is so deep, wide, rich and beautiful."

As for *The River in Reverse*, Elvis says, "I don't want people to think of this as a grandstand statement. This album began as a way to celebrate Allen's songbook and his voices—as a piano player, arranger and singer—that have been underestimated."

But Elvis acknowledges that the recording of the album became something bigger. It's a symbol of hope that the spirit of New Orleans will again shine vibrantly in its homeland. As for his role in the recording, Elvis says, "I can't adopt the legends of the Mardi Gras and be credible. I had to find my own way to express how all the music that has come from that city has affected me over the years."

Both looking dapper in suits and sipping cups of licorice tea, Allen and London-born, New York-based Elvis are preparing to perform a showcase of music from *The River in Reverse*—a mix of obscure Toussaint tunes, collaboratively written new songs and a fresh Elvis number written in the aftermath of Katrina—in the intimate Joe's Pub later this evening. It's mid-February, a few months after the plethora of benefit concerts for hurricane relief and fundraising CDs, when the attention to the cause has waned.

It's no surprise then that the Elvis link up with Allen has been suspect in some camps and chastised by detractors who question the former's motivation. In its capsule preview to the show at Joe's Pub, *TimeOut New York* wrote that "Costello's late-breaking buddy-buddyship with …Toussaint to us smacks of opportunism. Moreover, the pairing just doesn't make sense."

On the surface, the Costello-Toussaint team does seem like an odd partnership. Personality-wise, the two couldn't be more different. Elvis, 51, talks fast and beams in boyish enthusiasm as if he were living his wildest dream every day as a musician exploring beyond pop music constraints. The jovial Brit is a classic outgoing bloke.

In contrast, Allen is reserved with a gentlemanly manner who speaks slowly and quietly in a slight Southern drawl. He's steeped in the A-through-Z of New Orleans music, and comes from the Big Easy piano school of Professor Longhair. "I'm a Fess disciple," he says. "He's my patron saint, my Bach."

While Elvis and Allen come from different planets, they're both on the same page when it comes to music. Each admires the other for his sensitivity to song craft.

As for Elvis seeking out a "late-breaking" friendship with Allen, the criticizing lacks substance. In fact, the two worked together twice before, dating back to 1983 when Elvis sought out Allen to produce his rendition of Yoko Ono's song, "Walking on Thin Ice," for an album of interpretations of her own compositions she was releasing.

"I heard Allen's songs before I knew his name," says Elvis, who remembers well the fondness of the Merseybeat bands of his youth for Allen's song "Fortune Teller." He was also a fan of R&B singer Lee Dorsey, who was a hit-maker with many of Allen's tunes, including "Ride Your Pony" and "Working in the Coal Mine."

"Lee Dorsey's music was when I started to pay attention to who was behind the songs," Elvis says. "It was like a good secret. Little by little I got the story that Allen wrote or arranged this and that and that."

When he was becoming established as a rising-star pop artist, Elvis was also seeking out his heroes in vital outposts of American music such as Memphis and New Orleans. "When we'd tour, on our days off I always tried to plot out a way to get to those towns that I wanted to visit," he says. "For Yoko's song, I knew I could only record it on the road. I thought of making the impossible request—getting either Willie Mitchell or Allen to produce the track. I called Allen up and he said, 'Let's do it.' We went to New Orleans and spent three days at his Sea-Saint Studio. It was difficult interpreting a song as unusual as Yoko's, but we did a good job. Plus, it was magical working with Allen. It was like a dream."

In 1988, a couple of years following his 1986 *King of America* album, Elvis began working on *Spike* with his co-producer T Bone Burnett. Recording sessions took place in Dublin, London, Hollywood and—because Elvis was hearing different sounds in his new songs—New Orleans, where he enlisted Allen. "I felt completely comfortable working with him again," he says.

In the liner notes to the expanded version of *Spike*, Elvis wrote about recording with the Dirty Dozen Brass Band and Allen at Southlake Studio: "He pretty much set the scene for 'Deep Dark Truthful Mirror' with his colossal piano part [while] the Dozen played off his performance....It was like seeing a sketch turn into a painting."

Allen didn't know much about Elvis before they met. "I just knew there was an Elvis Costello," he says. "But I was stationary in New Orleans. New Orleans was cut off from the rest of the world in many ways. What was common knowledge to other folks, well, you'd have to leave New Orleans to check that out. I didn't know his music."

Elvis regrets that he lost contact with Allen, but was pleased to run into him when they both performed on the same stage at the 2005 New Orleans Jazz & Heritage Festival.

THE KATRINA CATASTROPHE

Their next encounter came in the wake of the Katrina catastrophe. Elvis was on holiday on Vancouver Island with his wife, Diana Krall, when Katrina hit New Orleans and the levees were breached. One of his first concerns was for the wellbeing of Allen. He contacted his friend Joe Henry, who told Elvis that he heard Allen was fine, but that he had vacated New Orleans for New York at the urging of Joshua Feigenbaum, who co-founded NYNO Records in 1996 with Allen to record music from the Crescent City.

The next day, Sept. 4, Elvis played the Bumbershoot Seattle Arts Festival main stage as a solo act. "I wanted to sing what was in my head and heart," he says, "so I closed the show with Allen's 'Freedom for the Stallion.' I sang it to remind people of what was happening in New Orleans."

As Katrina approached the Crescent City, Allen figured he'd weather the storm. "I had been through hurricanes, and I thought I knew the nature of them," he says. "They come and wreak a little havoc, then you take your boards [on your windows] back down and put 'em behind the garage. I've had 12 inches of water in my house more than once. I knew how to handle that. I wanted to stick it out. But this was quite different."

Allen checked into the Astor Crowne Plaza Hotel on Bourbon Street, but as the city's plight worsened, he took a bus to Baton Rouge and caught a flight to New York. Joshua called him the day before the storm hit. "Allen refused to leave, but then came here when he could get out of the city," Joshua says. "He stayed up here, but got depressed every day watching CNN. So I asked him if he wanted to work, and he said sure."

Joshua contacted Bill Bragin, who programs Joe's Pub and had been the founding general manager of NYNO Records. "I asked Bill if maybe Allen could open up some shows on the piano, and he said, 'We can do better than that,'" he says.

Bill recalls a conversation he had with Danny Melnick, the artistic director of Festival Productions, about what the music community could do to help in the aftermath of Katrina. "Our conclusion was that [since] we produce concerts, we should produce concerts," Bill says. "The best way to help New Orleans musicians was to let them do what they do—make a living and support their city by making music."

Since Joe's Pub's evening shows were booked, Bill inserted into the schedule a couple of solo piano weekend matinees featuring Allen. Remarkably this was the first time he had ever performed solo. They were immediate sellouts. Meanwhile, Wynton Marsalis had asked Elvis to perform at the Jazz at Lincoln Center Frederick P. Rose Hall benefit to raise hurricane relief funds. Elvis told Wynton about his Bumbershoot tribute, that Allen was in New York and that he wanted to perform the song with him. Elvis and Allen met up and rehearsed.

"We followed McCoy Tyner and Harry Belafonte," Elvis says about the tribute. "McCoy played this mind-bending music, then Harry came on and it's like hearing Moses speak. All I could do was sing the best I could."

The performance was not only moving, but it also planted a seed.

RIVER IN REVERSE

With the wheels turning inside his head about putting together an Allen Toussaint songbook album, the next day Elvis caught his Joe's Pub matinee. "I didn't know what the album would look like, if I could produce it or maybe sing on it," he told me. "But I knew that Allen's songs and the traditions he comes from are so central to jazz and popular music."

Around the same time, Elvis and Allen performed together again at the Madison Square Garden "From the Big Apple to the Big Easy" benefit. Verve Music Group A&R exec John McEwen contacted Elvis with a similar recording concept. "Allen and I started discussing what this record would look like," Elvis says. "We agreed to record selections from his songbook that were not the obvious ones that everyone knew—songs that were close to the heart. And we discussed the possibilities that we could write some songs together."

For Allen, everything in his musical life was suddenly converging at a whirlwind tempo. "I always make the distinction between the pace of New Orleans and everywhere else in America," he tells me. "We sort of mosey along in New Orleans. I've been coming to New York for years—for business and I have family in the Bronx—so I know the pace here. You have to hold your hand out and catch it. That's what I understood about Elvis' exhilaration. As fast as the pace of New York is, the pace of Elvis is even faster. There's a lot going on with Elvis."

After a tour in Europe, Elvis returned to New York in early November, and the pair met up in Joshua Feigenbaum's Central Park West apartment. "It was a comfortable place for them," Joshua says. "I got the piano tuned up and made sure they had plenty of tea. Then I got out of the apartment and let the two professionals work."

Nothing jelled at first. "It seemed like the piano was antimagnetic," Elvis says. "We couldn't touch it for a long time. It was like we had never heard music before."

The icebreaker was Allen's minor-key version of Professor Longhair's classic, "Tipitina," which he had played at Joe's Pub. "A door opened with that onto a whole musical history that never gets talked about," Elvis says. "I wanted to catch something of the feeling of what Allen was playing, to write lyrics that fit the melancholy and reflection of this piece. It's a presumptuous thing to add new lyrics to something as indelible as 'Tipitina,' but I wanted to adopt the signature of Allen's music, like the hymnal cadence in the chorus."

The next day Elvis sang the lyrics of the retitled "Ascension Day" to his new partner. "Allen liked it. We couldn't get on the piano fast enough," Elvis says with a laugh. "I was playing the guitar, Allen was playing the piano, and then sometimes we were both on the piano at the same time, our two hands crossing over. You know you're getting to something when you're saying to each other, 'It's this chord,' 'No, it's this chord.' I could never presume to tell Allen how to phrase anything, but sometimes I would come up with a voicing or harmonic idea. We went from having nothing to different kinds of collaborations. When we wrote 'Six-Fingered Man,' we were completing each other's sentences musically."

Allen had never experienced a songwriting collaborative session like that before. "Elvis came so well-equipped," he says. "He comes with ideas. Elvis was the general leading us to the hill."

Toussaint songbook tunes, including the funked-up "On Your Way Down," the gospel-tinged "Nearer to You" and the soul cooker "Tears, Tears, and More Tears"—all newly relevant in light of Hurricane Katrina's ravages—are open to interpretation, Elvis says, then adds, "But why change something that's already perfect? Allen's arrangements have all these little nuances that are integral to the composition."

Soon after working up a batch of tunes, Elvis and Allen, who both sing on the project, headed into the studio to have, in Elvis's words, "a dialogue between people from different parts of the world."

Pegged to produce the sessions was Joe Henry, who had also produced the Toussaint tracks ("Yes We Can Can" and "Tipitina and Me") for Nonesuch's *Our New Orleans 2005* benefit album. He had been in conversation with Allen about recording an album of his material for his *I Believe to My Soul* compilation series when Elvis came up with his songbook idea.

"Elvis didn't want to get in the way of something I had planned, but I felt that Allen should have the opportunity to do whatever he should pursue," Joe says. "So, we all decided to do this together."

Joe first became friendly with Elvis when he produced Solomon Burke's comeback album, *Don't Give Up on Me*, in 2002. "When I hit problems bringing the concept together for *I Believe to My Soul*," Joe says, "I used Elvis as my sounding board and champion."

When his original pianist for the project bowed out, Elvis suggested contacting Allen, who jumped at the last-minute invite. "I was flabbergasted that he agreed," Joe says. "He pulled the project together. I keep his picture on my wall as a reminder."

Even though he knew Elvis and Allen, Joe still felt nervous about his role in *The River in Reverse*. "I'd never produced artists and their bands before," he says. "I always saw myself as a smart casting director—putting a band together and then directing the proceedings to try to make the magical and unique happen during the conversings and collisions. But here I was being asked to bring my point of view to a project where Elvis had his group and Allen had his people. As it turned out, they needed someone to take charge, to take the wheel and drive."

Joe found Elvis to be "an open-hearted collaborator who was trusting" of suggestions and Allen to be "the producer's producer and the closest person alive that has the open-mindedness and transcendence of Duke Ellington."

Day No. 1 was daunting in preparation, Joe recalls. "But the apprehension evaporated once it became clear how respectful everyone was to each other and how much we were on the same page philosophically with the material. The first day's session produced three masters and provided the template for the rest of the recording."

The group at the session consisted of Elvis's rock band the Imposters (Steve Nieve, who switched from piano to B-3, bassist Davey Faragher and drummer Pete Thomas) and Allen's electric guitarist Anthony Brown and horn section (baritone saxophonists Brian Cayolle and Carl Blouin, tenor saxophonist Amadee Castenell, trumpeter Joe Smith and trombonist Sam Williams).

PIETY STREET RECORDING

The first week of *The River in Reverse* sessions took place in late November at Sunset Sound in Los Angeles, then moved to Mark Bingham's Piety Street Recording in

New Orleans (shuttered in 2013) in early December. Nearly the entire album was performed live with minimal overdubs.

"You listen to the mix back, and you hear how much life there is in the music," Elvis says. "That's where the vitality of interpreting songs comes from. You can hear it in Allen's song 'Who's Gonna Help Brother Get Further?' I can't think of a better question to ask right now, but not in a heavy-handed way."

Elvis beams at Allen's lyrics and recites the last verse: "What happened to that Liberty Bell I heard so much about?/Did it really ding dong?/It must have dinged wrong/It didn't ding long."

Elvis loves those lines: "That's why we sing the verse twice. I like the idea of handing the words back and forth, playing it like a little group having a conversation."

Also on the CD is the urgent and angry title track that Elvis penned the afternoon before he appeared at *The New Yorker* magazine's benefit event at Town Hall in September. The lyrics in the chorus are poignant:
"Wake me up
Wake me up with a slap or a kiss
There must be something better than this
I don't see how it can get much worse
What do we have to do to send the river in reverse?"

"I wrote the song in 10 minutes," Elvis says. "I had all these images floating around in my head for a week, and they suddenly solidified into that song."

While the album has its Costello-Toussaint-composed moments of gloom, including the funerary march-beat "The Sharpest Thorn" and the disgrace-in-darkness "Broken Promise Land," *The River in Reverse* also buoys in celebration of the New Orleans sound. The uptempo "International Echo" is spiced by Allen's Longhair-like breaks and drenched in images of how the power of music cannot be denied.

"That's a song about how music comes from one city, travels around the world and then rebounds back," Elvis says. "I wanted to show the joy of that. I've never written a song about music before."

THE BRAINCHILD OF ELVIS

Allen notes that the entire project was Elvis's brainchild. "I was the yes man," he says, and adds that the band playing the album's music will be featured at festivals across the country this summer. "I enjoyed the journey, especially how the tunes would grow from one day to the next. We arrived places. It wasn't just wishbones and feathers everywhere. We took every step with integrity and faith, belief in what we were doing."

Before the hurricane and flood, there were nine recording studios in New Orleans. Only two were in business at the time *The River in Reverse* was recorded. "It was wonderful [going back]," Allen says. "Elvis was insistent about recording the album there. He wanted the authenticity because I'm from there. But we also wanted to show that there's life in the city, that this isn't a total dead zone."

Elvis experienced the city in a different way. Going to New Orleans wasn't a homecoming, but a shock of reality. "It was emotional," he says. "You arrive at an empty airport and then see blown-down signs everywhere. The first day I was there I walked around the streets and all the franchise businesses were closed. They'd just left town. Local businesses were struggling to keep going because of a lack of patrons. The first day at Piety, I asked my driver if it would be too morbid to drive me to where the flood hit the hardest. He drove me to where the breach in the levee had occurred in the Lower Ninth Ward. It was horrifying seeing the destruction at eye level after having seen it through a television lens."

Allen adds, "We'll all be coming back. Elvis wanted to bring that musical life into the album. That was the thing to do, and he followed through on it. It was the right thing to do, to breathe life into the area."

It's a first step, though Allen is a realist. He soberly says, "It's going to take a lot of money to rebuild, but it'll also take a lot of guidance. You can't just take the money [for rebuilding], throw it out there and see where it winds up."

But he remains hopeful in New Orleans' revival. "The city is the cradle of American music," Allen says. "Babies are still being born, they'll pick up a trumpet and tap into the tradition, and the music will prevail."

ELVIS HEADS NORTH IN JAZZ-FUELED ROMANCE AND PAIN

2003

This article is about his turn to jazz on his 2003 album North *after he became engaged to Diana Krall*

INTRODUCTION

In 1994, at the Concord Pavilion in the San Francisco suburbs, Elvis Costello eagerly agreed to be Blindfolded for *DownBeat*. Touring in support of his molten-hot rock album *Brutal Youth*, the musical omnivore aced the test after sound check, identifying the eclectic playlist, from Charles Mingus (nine million stars) and John Coltrane (49) to Charles Brown (75) and Johnny Cash (53: "One for every state, one for the moon, two for the outer galaxies").

Backstage at the Mother's Day concert was Lillian MacManus, Elvis's mother and biggest fan. A clerk in Beatles manager Brian Epstein's Liverpool record store and jazz club proprietress, she said that she knew during pregnancy that her child would grow up to be a musician. In fact, she listened to a range of music—from jazz and classical to the pop of the day—when Elvis was still in the womb to give him an early start as a connoisseur of fine song. So convinced of his future, Lillian even christened him with an unusual first name for remembrance sake. Ironically, in ramping up to his punk-charged 1977 pop debut *My Aim Is True*, Declan audaciously crowned himself Elvis, which proved to be a decisive, if not outrageous, nom de plume.

Mum was right in her maternal instincts. Today Elvis, 49, whose father was a jazz bandleader in London, is one of pop music's most imaginative, adventurous and honest artists. A rebel at heart and a voracious lover of all kinds of music, he has flourished as an artist primarily because of his unwillingness to be fenced in by stylistic boundaries. He has said, "I can't subscribe to limiting [myself] to one form of expression exclusively." Accordingly, he is the rare artist who has carte blanche from his record companies (today he's signed to Universal's Deutsche Grammophon) to pursue his restless musical whims and passions.

However, this has come at a cost, says Elvis in a phone conversation in August 2003 about his evocative new all-ballads, piano-based album *North*. He was talking crosstown, having briefly touched down in New York City after a whirlwind of rock dates in Calgary, Tokyo, Monte Carlo and Reykjavik, not to mention a brief stopover at one of his homes in Ireland. He's well-versed in how difficult it is to break out of the mold of expectation. Some people still equate him with punk, he says, "or whatever reduction of my career that people choose to use." But that hasn't impeded Elvis, who speaks in a rapid-fire flow of musical erudition, from moving forward. "Yet whenever I've done something new," he says, "some fans and critics act as if I've changed my religion or denied the existence of what went before."

The jazz-like sensibility of creating anew informs Elvis's projects. He's impressed by the volume of albums jazz artists have recorded—sometimes in quick succession. "Rather than repeat themselves, the great jazz musicians strike out for new ground or place the emphasis of their music differently," he says. "What's so terrifying about that? When Afro-Cuban music was embraced, that didn't mean the end to all the other jazz forms. It just made for new avenues to explore and a richer vocabulary of music to learn to speak."

A recent inductee into the Rock and Roll Hall of Fame and this year's winner of ASCAP's Founder's Award, Elvis has tread on his share of wide boulevards and learned his fill of new dialects. He cut his professional eye teeth on rock which he continues to revisit with aplomb, delved into the classical world with the Brodsky Quartet, collaborated with a range of top-drawer songsmiths including Paul McCartney and Burt Bacharach, embraced jazz alongside such noteworthies as Bill Frisell, the Count Basie Orchestra and the Jazz Passengers, and has in recent years composed tunes for mezzo soprano Anne Sofie von Otter and the orchestral score for a production of *A Midsummer's Night Dream* by the Aterballetto dance company of Reggio Emilia, Italy (the London Symphony Orchestra conducted by Michael Tilson Thomas recorded the work in June for release next year).

Last year after delivering the rousing rock CD *When I Was Cruel* and making a cameo vocal appearance on the Mingus Big Band disc *Tonight at Noon: Three or Four Shades of Love*, Elvis began to switch musical gears again in the wake of the breakup of his 16-year marriage to former Pogues bassist Cait O'Riordan and his engagement to Diana Krall. He reflected on those dispiriting then joyous experiences by writing a fresh batch of tunes.

NORTH

North, remarkably his 24th album, captures the singer-songwriter in his most intimate—heartrending and tender—performance. In addition to his longtime pianist Steve Nieve, Elvis is supported by several jazz musicians, including drummer Peter Erskine, bassists Mike Formanek and Brad Jones, vibraphonist Bill Ware, tenor trombonist Conrad Herwig, tenor saxophonist Andy Snitzer, alto saxophonist Lee Konitz and flugelhornist Lew Soloff. The latter two take end-song solos on the heartbreaking "Someone Took the Words Away" and the giddy "Let Me Tell You About Her," respectively.

Elvis wrote the bulk of the songs while he was touring with his rock band the Imposters last year. "I was completely taken over by the music I was hearing in my head," he says. "I had no choice but to respond to it. I found myself seeking out pianos, instead of guitars, for composing. The piano is not an instrument I can truthfully claim to play, but these songs required more harmonic development and expansive lyrical possibilities."

Each night after a show, Elvis hunkered down in his hotel suite and wrote songs as well as imagined orchestrations to color the mood. "For the past eight years I've been arranging for groups of musicians between 11 and 17," he says. "That's become a passion. I'm proud of the arrangements." Earlier this year he entered Avatar Studios and created *North*, a vocal album that never strays far from a balladic tempo.

North is a beauty. The melodies are strong, Elvis's voice is a revelation (his natural baritone sounds refined—quite a departure from his rock recordings where he sings higher to project above the electric instrumentation), the string orchestrations serve the emotion of the songs such as on the dark-hued "When Did I Stop Dreaming," and the story behind the album's song cycle makes for fine drama: the anguish of the dismaying opening track "You Left Me in the Dark" balanced by the hopeful end song, "I'm in the Mood."

The jazz players complemented Elvis's approach. He hooked up with Erskine working on the *Midsummer Night's Dream* project and brought him aboard for *North*. The drummer then recommended Formanek. "We all hit it right off," says Elvis. "We cut four of the most difficult songs on the first afternoon. Peter, Mike and Steve helped to establish that kind of stillness and bareness I wanted to express with these songs."

Elvis has known Soloff since 1984 when he caught him performing in Gil Evans' band. "I took my mother to New York to go to all the jazz clubs," he says. "I remember hearing Lew and being smitten by his playing." As for Konitz, he was reading the listings for club dates in New York while he was recording *North* and saw that the alto saxophonist was at Birdland. Elvis made a few calls inquiring about his availability and in a short time rang him up at his apartment on the Upper West Side.

"I asked him if he would play on one of my tracks," Elvis recalls. "And he asked me what time the session was. I told him 8 o'clock and he said his bedtime was at 9. I figured that was fine. We would only do one take."

Yet since Nieve had already flown back to London, he had to play the piano to teach Konitz the harmony on "Someone Took the Words Away." "I was terrified that I was going to fuck up," says Elvis, who plays the keys on two tunes while contributing a guitar part on only one track. "But we played two takes and that was it. Lee played two entirely different conceptions that were fantastic. Both were usable, and we went with the second take."

Elvis laughs and tells how after the session he asked Lee to sign the tune's lead sheet for his mother who used to sell the saxophonist's records in Liverpool. "Lee signed it with the same economy of his playing: 'Lillian. Thank you. Lee Konitz,'" he says. "So I framed it and sent it to her. She jumped out of her skin when she got the package."

Elvis says that her mother's reaction does not surprise him. "As soon as she started working, music was her world," he says. "That's what the beauty of music was back then. It's so global now, but back in the '30s, '40s and '50s, music was like a secret language arriving on a disc. There was a thrill then of listening to records that were hard to get. I think that's why people today are attracted to music from other cultures. It's novel. All the reference points and architecture of the music are so totally different that our imaginations get stretched."

As for his fans' reaction to *North* being such a pensive recording, Elvis is unfazed. "If it horrifies people who still have a thumbnail sketch in their minds about who I am, then I can't help them," he says with an edge of scorn in his voice. "If all they've heard is 'Pump It Up' at a hockey game, then maybe they're not ready for this. These songs, they're honest. I mean 'em. They are sung without irony. There's no theatrical quality about them. I think they work best by inviting listeners to relate the songs to their own lives, rather than having a morbid interest in what's happening to me personally."

THE ELVIS-DIANA ROMANCE

But, because the Elvis-Diana romance has become so public, that's exactly what most people will be reading into when listening to *North*. In the title song "North," which inexplicably is not included on the domestic release of the album, Elvis sings about the compass point directed at Canada and concludes: "It's something I will always carry in my heart/A place where dreams begin and life can start/Who cares what people know/Let me go…North." It sounds obvious: Costello is madly in love with a Canadian jazz singer, who, it appears, serves as his muse.

"I'm happy to say that Diana is really a remarkable artist and interpreter of song," Elvis says. He adds with a gush of enthusiasm, "My appreciation of her artistry is enormous. I've been hearing her play close up for a year now, and she's a tremendously underrated piano player. You can really hear that on her *Live in Paris* album. Diana's sense of humor and her appreciation for the history of the music is like nothing I've encountered before in a musician." Even so, Elvis feels Diana has gotten short shrift. Her talent, he says, outweighs the image. "People attribute her success to the [album] jacket. C'mon. Listen with your ears and not with your eyes."

When Elvis divorced his first wife, Mary Costello, in 1986, and married O'Riordan, whom he met while producing The Pogues second album, *Rum, Sodomy & the Lash*, fans wondered if their marital union would extend to their music. At the time, Elvis said, "We're the Sonny and Cher of the '80s," pausing for comic effect, then adding, "And I'm Cher." The two did co-write songs, including "The Judgment," penned for Solomon Burke's last CD, *Don't Give Up on Me*.

As for his relationship with Diana, Elvis says, "I know that if either of us departs from what we've been known for the other will get the blame." He laughs. "Many people who don't really think about music and don't have a lot of knowledge about it assume that we'll make records together, that we'll become a Steve [Lawrence] and Eydie [Gormé]. Nothing against them, but we don't have to naturally become a team."

Six years ago in a conversation I had with Diana, she expressed frustration with being interrogated about when she was going to unveil her own compositions. She said, "What if I'm an actor? I study Shakespeare, I perform in great plays. So that means I'm ready to write, direct and star in my own film? I'm being very careful. Writing is a private thing. I'm not going to do it until I'm ready. I asked Tony Bennett about that and he told me that he sees himself as a master storyteller. He's not wrapped up in writing his own material. He's committed to creatively interpreting other people's songs. I'm not going to write songs until I'm confident I have something to say. If I never do, no big deal. I'm already creatively fulfilled."

Will Elvis's influence prod her into penning her only songs? "Oh, Diana's been playing songs in concert that she's written," he says. "You know, I love this girl, but these songs are great. She's digging down deep. You have to go to the well of feeling about music and learn from masters and mentors as she has done and come up with something that's your own view."

Does Elvis think a new direction for Diana could upset her fans who expect her to continue playing the standards? "It's not for me to say what will come next for Diana," he says. "But I know all about this from my own experience. There's so much reward for everybody, even the record company, when you depart from what you've done in the past. It's not a brave thing. Bravery is an innocent man facing a firing squad. Rather, it's bold to step away from where you previously lived and succeeded."

ELVIS GOES MINGUS
2003

You think Elvis Costello is only a rock star? Think again. He has deep jazz veins as evidenced in his connection to jazz icon Charles Mingus.

It's a Saturday afternoon in early November 2002 and one variant of the Charles Mingus Orchestra is at Avatar Studios in New York recording four tunes for the next Mingus Big Band (MBB) album, *Tonight at Noon: Stories of Love*. It's the group's seventh CD for Dreyfus, two of which were nominated for Grammys (ironically, during his lifetime Mingus only received one Grammy—and that was for liner notes).

The MBB has not only scored numerous awards in jazz polls as best big band, but most importantly it has also inspired a surge of interest in the Mingus legacy. At the helm of the operation is Sue Mingus, in the engineer's booth with a stopwatch timing a buoyant take of "Tonight at Noon," arranged by Sy Johnson. She's pleased with the performance, which features solos by trumpeter Alex Sipiagin, drummer Jeff "Tain" Watts and alto saxophonist Alex Foster, but notes, "That's 7:18. It's supposed to be only five minutes. Oh, well, I guess we can make some cuts."

Sue, a trim, athletic-looking woman with bobbed blond hair and dressed head-to-foot in black, works to insure that everything runs smoothly. She is, after all, the guardian and champion of her late husband's music and the no-nonsense artistic director of the Charles Mingus Orchestra and MBB.

She fields the teams (she has a phone list of players several pages long with such pro/con notations as "good tone but slow sight reading" and "sublime musician but always late") and handpicks the rotating personnel for performances (on the road, including recent tours to Europe, Australia and China, and at home at the Fez where the MBB has become an East Village institution in its weekly 10-year run). She also voices her opinion on the band's set list as well as on slights by Mingus detractors, with whom she has little patience. But at the Fez, the proud den mom roots the boys on, beaming when they make a Mingus composition bloom.

Today, in addition to overseeing her guys, she's also playing host to omni-music connoisseur Elvis Costello. Wearing peach-colored tinted glasses and an untucked flannel shirt, Elvis arrives midafternoon to record "Invisible Lady," one of several Mingus instrumentals he recently penned lyrics to for a collaborative performance with the Mingus Orchestra at UCLA in September. (A little over a month later he retackled the difficult material at the Beacon Theater in New York.) While the orchestra records another speedy take of "Tonight at Noon," Elvis gives the band a thumbs up and converses with Sue about his number.

After a short break, Elvis goes into an isolation booth with the lyrics in front of him. He waits for Michael Rabinowitz's bassoon open, then joins in with the horn-swelling swing of the band, keeping time with a pencil that he uses like a baton. The tempo slows for the chorus, with Elvis emotively singing into its mysterious heart.

After an instrumental interlude highlighted by Conrad Herwig's trombone musings, Elvis returns for a soaring vocal finale that is literally spine-tingling. He works up a sweat on another take, then hangs out to meticulously fix a couple mistakes.

"My dad gave me my first Mingus album, *Oh Yeah*, when I was 13," Elvis says after the session. "My parents encouraged me to listen to all different kinds of music. I really liked that Mingus record because it had this mythic quality. I knew it came from over the seas. I liked the singing and cajoling that was going on. When you're young, you like the shouting. But I also knew that there was someone very powerful driving it along."

Elvis didn't return to Mingus until years later after he made his mark as an upstart rocker. "Around the same time as I was listening to my first Mingus album, I was also listening to the Jefferson Airplane, Marvin Gaye, Lou Rawls," he says. "And as a teenager, I was into the Beatles and the whole Motown thing and also songwriters like Burt Bacharach. I was listening to a lot of pop music and then a little bit of Latin."

When he first started playing music, Elvis had this fierce allegiance to pop. "But within three years of performing and recording, I realized I had exhausted my interest in all the pop and rock I had grown up listening to," he says. "So I bought a piano and began to teach myself music on a deeper level. I listened to Debussy for six months, and then Miles Davis for six months. I studied the ballad style by listening to Billie Holiday, and I checked out samba. Then I remembered Mingus."

After his years of pop stardom, he was ready to return to the sounds of his youth. The timing for his reintroduction to Mingus was important for Elvis. "My philosophy is that music waits for you to be ready," he says. "When I was young, Mingus's music sowed a seed in my imagination. I returned to it and could hear the gospel elements from his church upbringing and better understood the harmonic complexity of what he was doing. Each time I listen now, I hear how deep his music is."

As for performing and recording with the Mingus Big Band and Mingus Orchestra, Elvis marvels: "It's astounding. Mingus's music becomes so much more vivid to me when I'm with the band face-to-face. I become increasingly aware of the music's complexity. I'm really fortunate to be able to record with them and have a relationship to this album."

As for writing lyrics to Mingus's music, Elvis replies with a sense of awe. "Recently I started listening again to a lot of Mingus's music and ended up writing words at Sue's suggestion," he says. "The titles of his compositions are a gift to a songwriter like me. I wanted to avoid vocalese and to follow the melody line. But I also came up with new melody lines. In that way I feel like a soloist. I'm not improving Mingus compositions. It's as if I'm doing solos on them."

INTROVERT MEETS EXTROVERT: ELVIS COSTELO AND BILL FRISELL JOIN FORCES
1998

In 1998 I interviewed Elvis at home in Ireland for this DownBeat *article about The Sweetest Punch, Bill Frisell's arrangements of tunes Elvis co-wrote with Burt Bacharach for their album Painted From Memory.*

"*The Sweetest Punch goes to another place where Bill and I are both comfortable. We each make music by following the natural flow rather than trying to jump the hurdles that words like pop and jazz end up becoming. Music is like a liquid.*"—*Elvis Costello (1998)*

PAINTED FROM MEMORY GETS THE SWEETEST PUNCH

Musical omnivores gravitate toward each other. That's especially true if they also happen to be recording artists. Unencumbered by sectarian tastes, they take an expansive approach to music appreciation, listening with open ears and then comparing notes. While eclecticism in the creative process can result in postmodern fluff—art that's as contrived as it is tedious—that kind of receptive mindset can bust open new doors. Why stay in a safe neighborhood when you can venture out to other boroughs to explore alternatives to the status quo? After all, that's how both Latin jazz (thanks to the percussive Afro-Cuban connection) and rock 'n' roll (popular song gets it on with rhythm & blues) were born.

While neither artist is perched on the cusp of creating a new varietal of music, both guitar virtuoso Bill Frisell and pop song maestro Elvis Costello possess an insatiable appetite for sounds of all persuasions—the former rooting his repertoire in jazz but freely expressing himself by infusing his music with a range of styles from country to John Philip Sousa marches and the latter equally at home pounding out punk-infused rock and crooning with a classical string quartet. It's this simpatico spirit of breaking down boundaries that makes for the ideal pop-jazz crosscut they pull off on *The Sweetest Punch*, Bill's arrangements of tunes Elvis co-wrote with songsmith Burt Bacharach for their album *Painted From Memory*.

Released nearly a year after the Costello-Bacharach collaboration, Bill's companion disc, largely an instrumental recording, showcases his genius for developing lyrical arrangements. Supported by a stellar septet and guest vocalists Cassandra Wilson and Elvis himself, Bill stays faithful to the Elvis-Burt song structures while at the same time applying refreshing new brush strokes of tonal color.

"I don't really know how to define a record like this," Elvis while discussing the project released on newly revived Decca Records, a division of the Universal Music Group. "I suppose you could call it an album of ensemble playing where the melodies have been reharmonized and revoiced away from the instruments the tunes were originally written for. But, overall this is music that doesn't fit in any genre comfortably."

In signing with Universal in 1998, Elvis was given free rein to fit his often hard-to-categorize recordings into the appropriate label owned by the recording giant. "I'm hoping Decca will be a new place to put music without using that dreadful C-word," he says. "You know, that word that begins with C-R-O-S...But this record isn't crossover...Oops, there I said it."

Elvis laughs and adds, "*The Sweetest Punch* goes to another place where Bill and I are both comfortable. We each make music by following the natural flow rather than trying to jump the hurdles that words like pop and jazz end up becoming. Music is like a liquid. If you spill water, it runs in many different directions. It doesn't line up in a neat procession. To my mind, following the flow without analyzing or being afraid is the most human thing you can do as an artist. It feels a lot more natural than sitting in a box."

Bill was thrilled to be asked to come up with instrumental arrangements of the Costello-Bacharach material. "I love working with Elvis because he's so encyclopedic with his knowledge of all kinds of music and he's so spontaneous," says the 48-year-old Bill. "I've been a big fan of his music since his second or third Attractions album. A friend played me one of his albums in the early '80s, and it hit me how different he was from everyone else doing pop music then. Then I saw him on *Saturday Night Live* just by himself with an electric guitar. It struck me how rocking and strong a performer he was. I remember thinking that he wasn't a one-record fluke, but a serious musician unafraid to take chances."

While they may share the same penchant for musical adventure, Bill and Elvis couldn't be more dissimilar in personality. It's a classic case of introvert meets extrovert. In conversation, Bill is reticent, unassuming and pensive, often pausing mid-thought to make sure he stresses exactly the point he's intent on making. He's a haltingly articulate speaker. In the other court, Elvis talks a blue streak as if he were in a caffeine buzz. Slightly cocky yet sincere, he bubbles over with ideas, so much so that you get the impression that perhaps he has a difficult time shutting off the spigot once it's opened.

"I tend to fly with words and Bill's just the opposite," says Elvis in a phone conversation from his home in Dublin, Ireland. When told that both their hectic schedules necessitate the interviews being done separately, he adds, "That's fine. Actually, I'd be afraid that if we were together I'd do all the talking and Bill wouldn't be able to get a word in edgewise."

MUTUAL ADMIRATION CLUB

The Sweetest Punch was born soon after Burt and Elvis decided to work together on a full album's worth of new songs, which made pop music headlines (read: Esteemed Songwriters from Different Generations Join Forces). They had already teamed to write "God Give Me Strength" for the film *Grace of My Heart*, an over-the-telephone collaboration that proved to be so successful that they made plans to write more songs together. So the pair met a year later and began crafting, then finessing new compositions.

"Even when we were still writing, the idea got bandied about that we would also commission an instrumental project," says Elvis. "I was extremely anxious not to get the hippest rhythm section and the hottest tenor saxophonist in town to blow over the changes. I thought that could only lead to disaster. I felt strongly that a chamber group approach or something similar would be more appropriate."

Enter Bill, with whom Elvis had worked briefly on two other occasions: in 1992 on producer Hal Willner's Charles Mingus tribute album *Weird Nightmare* and again in 1995 when the pop star asked the jazz guitarist to perform with him in a duo setting at the Meltdown Festival in London (the resulting live recording became *Deep Dead Blue*).

"Bill brings to his music an instinctive feel that I thought was important for the songs Burt and I wrote," says Elvis. "It's clear in all the choices he makes in his music that he had the right combination of poignancy and history for the job. I was so madly curious to see what Bill came up with because he's not only a great soloist and composer, but also an arranger to be reckoned with."

He remembers his first encounter with the guitarist when Willner enlisted both to play on the tune "Weird Nightmare." Elvis had just come off his *Kojax Variety* project and was thrust into a situation that he initially thought was over his head.

"I didn't know Hal's approach, which was basically to put a bunch of characters into a room to see what would happen," Elvis says. "Plus, Hal used those Harry Partch instruments which are tuned to a 42-tone scale. The number had a vague D-minor tonality being sketched off these marimba-like instruments that sounded like the tolling of Buddhist bells. Hal created a scary place sonically with this wonderfully nightmarish feel, but I had no idea how I was going to sing the tune. Suddenly at the bridge Bill came in, and I thought, I'm home. He played so beautifully to complement these various unusual timbres that I just sailed right through the rest of the piece."

Likewise Bill was impressed by Elvis, especially how he came in cold to the session and nailed the challenging number in a couple of takes. While he didn't get to spend much time with Elvis during the recording of *Weird Nightmare*, Bill remembers him coming to the Village Vanguard to catch one of his shows a couple of years later. It was then that Elvis invited him to perform at the Meltdown, which he was directing that year. That's when Bill really got to check out Elvis's strength as a singer.

"Because Elvis was so busy organizing all these other shows at the festival, we barely had enough time to run through the songs we were going to play," he says. "Basically we just hit it. There was no tip-toeing around him. It was like playing with another musician. With some singers, you have to feed them what they need. But he had that spontaneous way of singing. He goes for the moment and something happens. That's what took place on *The Sweetest Punch* when he came in to do vocals on two songs. He didn't work the pieces to death. He approached the songs in a jazz way, and we had the numbers down in one or two takes."

Given Bill's well-documented love for pop music of all stripes (trying naming another jazzer who covered a Bob Dylan song and a Madonna number on the same album) and Elvis's depth of jazz knowledge, it make sense that the two found common ground. The Elvis-Burt link, on paper a promising pop music marriage, was also not very surprising.

But what about Bill's opinion of Burt, often derided as a purveyor of sappy pop tunes? In the '60s, he composed with lyricist Hal David numerous Top 40 hits, including Tom Jones's "What's New Pussycat?," B.J. Thomas's "Raindrops Keep Falling on My Head," Dusty Springfield's "The Look of Love" and a slew of Dionne Warwick chart toppers like "Do You Know the Way to San Jose?" and "I Say a Little Prayer." Even though Burt filled his songs with odd time signatures and atypical orchestrations, wasn't this a stretch even for the jazz guitarist with such idiosyncratic tastes?

"Are you kidding? Burt Bacharach's music is larger than life for me and has been interwoven into the fabric of my entire career," says Bill. "The whole time I was learning about music, his songs were always there. Sure, you tend to take his songs for granted, but try to play them and you discover how technically complex they are for popular music."

Bill recalls his high school Top 40 gigs when the bands he played in covered tunes by James Brown, the Temptations, the Beatles and Otis Redding. But when it came time to work up a Dionne Warwick hit, well, the guitarist found himself treading in deep water. "I learned songs by listening to records and figuring out the chords," he explains. "I'll never forget trying to do 'Alfie.' I got the first line, 'What's it all about....' Then it was oh-oh. I couldn't continue. There was something going on that was way more harmonically sophisticated than anything I had dealt with before." He laughs, then sheepishly concedes, "So I just gave up."

When Bill began working on *The Sweetest Punch*, he marveled at how the songs Burt and Elvis crafted were just as challenging. He notes that the songs were simple enough on one level to easily enter into a listener's subconscious. But, again, playing them was another matter entirely. "The melodies unravel so freely," Bill says. "The way a phrase will continue longer than it's supposed to before the chord changes reminds me of Ornette [Coleman] or some old blues guy. There's a logic to it, but the music is really tricky and difficult to play."

FROM PAINTED BY MEMORY TO THE SWEETEST PUNCH

The jazz catalog is full of tunes based on pop tunes of the day, but to the best of my knowledge, recording an instrumental interpretation of a collection of songs while the original project is still a work in progress is unprecedented.]

"I always hoped there would be another life for these songs beside me singing them," says Elvis. "In fact, even though the tunes Burt and I wrote are meant to be done as vocal pieces, most of them existed as music first. *Painted From Memory* was not governed or driven by lyrics, but by mood. The mood of the music led naturally to the lyrics. The music communicated in a way that the lyrics underlined later."

Elvis and Burt composed the songs over the course of several months, usually in five-day stretches. In between the sessions, the two independently worked on finessing the melodies and developing lyrics that fit the music. On the last day of writing, the pair made a few tweaks and gave each other homework assignments before the recording sessions were to start six weeks later. Elvis refined the lyrics and Burt developed the orchestration. Their final task together was to draw a roadmap for Bill.

"We photocopied all the song manuscripts and lyric sheets, and we made a tentative vocal rehearsal tape of Burt playing the piano and me singing the tunes," Elvis says. "Burt also had written out very early four-line sketches of arrangement ideas. So, literally with the ink still wet, we parceled it all up and sent it off to Bill. We didn't talk with him about what band configuration he would use and how he would arrange the songs, but obviously we were hoping that he was going to come up with something quite different than what we planned."

The package that landed on Bill's doorstep the next day was, in his words, "pretty overwhelming." He explains that coming up with his own interpretations of other people's songs requires time—sometimes several years of the melodies incubating themselves within him before he's inspired to put his own distinctive slant on them. In the case of the Elvis-Burt tunes, he had a relatively small window: two months to write the arrangements, rehearse a band and record the music. "That isn't much time, especially as I get older and my brain starts slowing down," he quips. "I wanted to take the 12 songs they gave me and internalize them as deeply as I could."

The first thing Bill did was translate the material into his own world by re-envisioning the songs on his guitar. In that way he distanced them from the keyboard on which the tunes were originally composed. From there, he approached the arrangements in the same manner as when he works on his own compositions. Instead of taking cues from the lyrics, Bill says that he "obsessed over all the notes." Then he put together his dream band, featuring clarinetist Don Byron, alto saxophonist Billy Drewes, trumpeter Ron Miles, trombonist Curtis Fowlkes, bassist Viktor Krauss and drummer Brian Blade, to give voice to his vision.

Bill pays tribute to the songwriters' melodies on *The Sweetest Punch* by viewing them through a different lens. So, in lieu of the full orchestration on the Elvis-Burt version of the melancholic beauty "In the Darkest Place," Bill offers a four-horn tonal color, a reflective guitar chime and a sorrowful trumpet cry. Instead of the strings and schmaltzy ringing bells on "The Sweetest Punch," Bill whimsically paints dark hues. Gone are the trademark Bacharach flugelhorns on "Toledo," replaced by horn-guitar harmonies and a catchy Byron clarinet solo at the close. Even though the overall flavor of Bill's interpretation is quiet and relaxed, he does accentuate the tension inherent in the song "Such Unlikely Lovers" by letting loose with a stinging solo.

After Bill completed the instrumental tracks for the album, he and producer Lee Townsend brought in guest vocalists Cassandra Wilson and Elvis to overdub their parts. "It's my only regret in the whole process that I couldn't get to record live with the ensemble," says Elvis, who at the time was still knee-deep in the *Painted From Memory* recording sessions. "But I was very pleased to sing with Cassandra, who I greatly admire but hadn't met before. When we sang 'I Still Have That Other Girl,' we did it like we were having a conversation, like she was admonishing me. Because of Bill's arrangement this song came off with a humorous touch, which is much different than the version Burt and I cut."

Elvis also sings on "Toledo," which in Bill's hands is manifest with a different rhythmic sensibility and vocal phrasings. "Sure, I was nervous at first because I had to come up with a new interpretation of a song so soon after doing the original," says Elvis. "But I solved that by reacting instantly in the spirit of jazz to the new architecture Bill had built."

In listening to *The Sweetest Punch*, Elvis discovered plenty of other surprises. He likes Bill's art-song take on "What's Her Name Today?" with its almost delirious pulse, the ominous visual quality of "Such Unlikely Lovers," the element of French fairground music in the second run through "Painted From Memory" (Cassandra gives an alluring show-stopping read of the tune earlier on the disc) and Byron's clarinet part after the sketch-like intro of "My Thief." "The subtlest things really touch me," says Elvis. "Some people may be surprised that there's not a lot of improvisation. But these songs are very new. Maybe if they're more well-known ten years hence, you could take them out on new flights."

As for Bill, he didn't get a chance to hear the finished *Painted From Memory* project until several months after he completed his version (which was originally slated to be issued simultaneously as a companion disc, but was pushed back on the release schedule for several reasons, including a fear of having the two CDs compete against each other on the marketplace).

"My initial reaction was, wow, I know these songs," says Bill who adds that he was pleasantly surprised to hear an edge in the beauty, especially since he was anticipating more lushness. "It was weird hearing a new album when you're already intimately familiar with all the tunes. It's a bizarre thing that I'm guessing will never happen again."

DOWNBEAT BLINDFOLD TEST

1994

This was Costello's first Blindfold Test. I got him to agree to do it in his backstage dressing room at the Concord Pavilion arena in Concord, California.

Booker T & the MG's

"Slip Slidin'" (from *That's The Way It Should Be*, Columbia, 1993) Booker T. Jones, keyboards; Steve Cropper, guitar; Duck Dunn, bass; Steve Jordan, drums.

Is this the new Booker T & the MG's album? Filling in for [late drummer] Al Jackson is probably the toughest chair to fill in the whole of music. It's great to hear them playing together again even if one of the crucial members of the band is gone. But it's difficult to have the same kind of affection for this new piece. It's a much more relaxed sound. It's not as tense as the earlier material that had an edgier feel to it. This sounds so much more mature. It's great nonetheless. I hate having to give a star rating, but I'll give this 5 stars for them just being Booker T and the MG's even without Al Jackson.

Latin Playboys

"Same Brown Earth" (from *Latin Playboys*, Slash, 1993) David Hidalgo, vocals, guitar; Louie Pérez, drums; Mitchell Froom, keyboards; Tchad Blake, bass.

I play this record all the time. I love it. I'll give this one 10 stars. David Hidalgo has such a great imagination. He could very well be a Duke Ellington some day. On this album, you could say a certain song doesn't sound finished, but that's the whole beauty of it. These songs are about real things like people eating too much food and getting a bellyache. I also like the messing around with distorted sounds on this album. It's like getting somebody's home demo before the producer gets a hold of it and ruins it. Compared to all the other formularized music, this is like the creating of an upside down world. This album proves there's hope for the corporate music industry, which was willing to bankroll this. Michael Bolton should be locked in a room and forced to listen to this record for ten years. No, I take that back. He should just be locked in a room and kept away from any other soul records he might cover.

John Coltrane

"Giant Steps" (from *The John Coltrane Anthology*, Atlantic Jazz/Rhino, rec'd 1959) Coltrane, tenor sax; Tommy Flanagan, piano; Paul Chambers, bass; Art Taylor, drums.

This sounds like it was made yesterday. It has an incredibly clean sound. It's not a new record, is it? If it is, then the sax player is doing something similar to what was recorded in the late '50s, early '60s.

DO: *I'll give you a clue. It's a remastered album.*

It's been incredibly remastered. That's not fair, especially after playing the Latin Playboys record that was made to deliberately sound murky. So, I'd say it's Coltrane. It was disconcerting at first because it sounded too clean. I thought maybe this was a trick question, where there was something weird going on like when a Charlie Parker solo was taken off a record and a new backup band was used. Stars? Can I give 49 for this one? Coltrane was one of the few people who could play as many notes as this without becoming boring. When guitar players do this, I just want to shoot them.

NRBQ

"I Want to Show You" (from *Kick Me Hard—The Deluxe Edition*, Rounder, rec'd 1975) Terry Adams, keyboards, vocals; Al Anderson, guitar, vocals; Joey Spampinato, bass, vocals; Tom Ardolino, drums; Donn Adams, trombone; Keith Spring, tenor saxophone.

It's NRBQ, isn't it? Oh, this is great! They play an amazing range of music. Terry Adams is a wonderful musician. Inside that track, there's so much going on. The vocal harmonies sounded like the Band. The saxophone could have been from the Neville Brothers or Ornette Coleman. Plus Al is working on a Bob Wills guitar sound. It's terrific to get all that in one piece without shoving any of it in your face. NRBQ is probably the greatest group in America. They defy all attempts to categorize them. They don't obey any of the rules. They're in that same alternative universe as the Grateful Dead. Did I give them any stars yet? They deserve 5006.

Charles Mingus

"Don't Be Afraid, the Clown's Afraid Too" (from *Let My Children Hear Music*, Columbia/Legacy, rec'd 1972) Mingus and ensemble.

Nine million stars. It's Mingus. I love the tuba, and I love the burlesque element in his music. His work is the greatest. It's a bottomless well of music. I can't think of a composer since the '40s who is as imaginative as Mingus. There's such a freedom in his music that allows for spontaneity. It's mindboggling. Jazz is such a limiting name for what he did. It's truly American classical music. It's a great shame he wasn't as recognized as he should have been.

Charles Brown

"B & O Blues" (from *The Swingtime Records Story*, Capricorn, rec'd 1948) Brown, piano, vocals; other band members unlisted.

This is Charles Brown. It's an old one. His voice has gotten deeper as he's gotten older. It's wonderful. He's a terrific piano player, and he's got great style. His music is real and it's got humor. I love his voice. He's been an inspiration to me. I've gone to a number of his live shows and I love him. For this piece, I'll give 75 stars.

Johnny Cash

"The Beast in Me" (from *American Recordings*, American Recordings, 1993) Cash, acoustic guitar, vocals.

[Two chords into the song] It's Johnny Cash. I know this song well because Nick Lowe wrote it. Nick, who was married for several years to John's stepdaughter Carlene, tells a funny story about writing it. They lived in England, and Johnny was spending some time with them. Nick stayed up all night once to write a song for him and by 3 or 4 in the morning he was convinced he could hear Johnny sing it. The next morning, somewhat chastened, he played it for him in a small, wimpy voice. And that was that. John put it away for years until it surfaced on this new album, which is terrific, wonderful. The sound is great. Johnny's got such a recognizable style. I'll give this 53 stars. One for every state, one for the moon and two for the outer galaxies.

Astor Piazzolla & The Kronos Quartet

"Fear" (from *Five Tango Sensations*, Elektra Nonesuch, 1990) Piazzolla, bandoneon; David Harrington, violin; John Sherba, violin; Hank Dutt, viola; Joan Jeanrenaud, cello.

Is that the bandoneon? Then it must be Astor Piazzolla. I love the sound of his instrument. The bandoneon works well with the strings. But I have no idea who he's playing with. I like this a lot, even though it doesn't send me leaping around the room like the Mingus piece. Who's the ensemble? Kronos? I'm not all that familiar with their work. I do think it's great they exist and are always looking for the bridge between genres. I like unusual combinations of chamber music. I'd like to hear this again. 5 stars for the daring-do of the collaboration.

Etta James

"Embraceable You" (from *Mystery Lady—Songs of Billie Holiday*, Private Music, 1993) James, vocals; Cedar Walton, piano.

Is this Jimmy Scott? If it's not him, it must be Dinah Washington. It's not? It's a bit hard telling whether this is an old or new take. It's Etta James? She usually sings in such a harsh, bluesy way that it's nice to hear her sing this softly. This is really a new path for her. This shows me she can sing in lots of different styles. It's great. Great soul. 9 and 3/4 stars. I suppose if this was Jimmy Scott, it would have had a wilder feel to it.

Charlie Haden—
Wide World of Wonders

When I lived in the Bay Area, I came into friendly contact with Charlie Haden a lot. Not only was he a grand master of the jazz bass, but he was also a top-tier conversationalist. He philosophized with a Left Coast new-age sentiment ("I love beautiful music from the heart and purity of someone's soul to give back to the universe because the universe has brought all of us together").

He quibbled over the term jazz ("I can't even call it jazz what some people are saying is the art form of jazz. As a matter of fact, I hate jazz").

He shared entertaining anecdotes, including his response to a cell phone ringing during a performance ("I stopped playing in the middle of my solo and said, 'Suicide hotline—please hold'") and his comic experience of surviving supermarket Muzak (what he calls "brain-damaging, back-beat, dysfunctional noise, or Maytag music).

We liked each other and that was special.

CHARLIE SITS AND TALKS
1995

At age 59, jazz bassist Charlie Haden is a 57-year veteran of show business. He's one of the heavyweights of the jazz world and a prolific recording artist, both as leader and top-notch session man. We're sitting in the sparsely populated lounge outside the main dining room at Claremont Spa & Hotel in Berkeley, California, where he's staying during his five-night headline engagement at Oakland's prestigious jazz club, Yoshi's Nite Spot, with jazz elder saxophonist Benny Carter and upstart pianist Eric Reed.

Looking dapper in a gray shirt and gray corduroy vest, Charlie wants to start out by expressing how he approaches music. "If you think back, the music that moves you the most is that which is the most honest, vulnerable and true," he says. "Part of my mission as a musician is being committed to bringing beauty to the world. I do what I do because I feel it with my heart and soul. I approach music with a willingness to give up my life for every note."

It's an early Saturday afternoon in June, and Charlie appears to have recovered from whatever bug that made him feel a tad under the weather earlier in the week. His walk is brisk, and he says he's excited to talk about his years in the music business.

When we're fully ready to have a long talk for a 1995 *Strings* magazine cover story, Charlie shakes his head and says we've got to find a different place. The lounge won't do as the place for him to be fielding questions this afternoon.

"I can't talk when this is playing," Charlie says, in reference to the soft, canned, elevator-like music filtering into the lounge from speakers set into the high ceiling. His disgust with flowery background music prompts us to find a conference room nearby where we finally park and, with Charlie sipping a cappuccino, begin our bass conversation.

It's no surprise that one of the main themes Charlie keeps returning to is how reverentially he approaches music.

Charlie made his professional music debut when he wasn't yet 2 years old as Little Cowboy Charlie with the Haden Family Band, a well-known country and western group helmed by his parents. He continued performing with his family throughout his high school years, even though by that time he had become a jazz fan. While he didn't start playing bass until he was 14, he was convinced he would be performing as a jazz bassist as soon as he was able to leave his Midwest home. At 19, he moved to Los Angeles to attend the Westlake College of Modern Music, which Charlie eventually quit because he found a home in the jazz clubs.

With his closely cropped hair and eager smile, he still has that Cowboy Charlie boyish look about him. But during our conversation, you can tell that he's lived the jazz life, especially when he reminisces about jazz colleagues who weren't able to handle the fast life. He recalls the joy of working with people like cool-jazz trumpeter/vocalist Chet Baker, who died an early death, and wishes he had had the opportunity to perform with piano great Bill Evans, who also died prematurely.

As if thinking of his own bout with substance abuse in the mid '60s, Charlie, at one point in our conversation, says, "The most important thing as a musician is to be healthy so you can stick around long enough to give your gift back to the world. You can't deprive the world of your gift. All of today's musicians have to be squeaky clean. They must be in great mental and spiritual shape to play this music at their full power. They have to stay away from all chemicals including alcohol. You cannot be at your full creative power if you are sedated. Bird [Charlie Parker] was a great musician in spite of his addiction, not because of it."

After his SoCal landing in the jazz world, at 21 Charlie made his way to New York, the center of the jazz universe, in the band of one of the new revolutionaries of the idiom, Ornette Coleman. It was Charlie's melodic bass patterns that undergirded the new-styled free jazz Ornette's quartet played. Charlie's improvisation independent of the chord changes of the pieces made him an instant star.

In subsequent years, Charlie performed in the bands of dozens of contemporaries before launching his own solo career. His first solo project came in 1969 with protest piece album *Liberation Music Orchestra* that featured a big band that overtly mixed jazz and political critique and garnered the bassist a composition Guggenheim Fellowship in 1970.

In recent years, Charlie's formed Quartet West in 1986 to rekindle his love for the music of the '40s and early '50s. His project featured saxophonist Ernie Watts, pianist Alan Broadbent and drummer Larance Marable. It has released several albums, including *Haunted Heart*, which was nominated for a Grammy Award in 1992, and *Always Say Goodbye*, which was named Album of the Year in *DownBeat* magazine's 1994 Critics Poll. Charlie was also named top bassist in both 1994 and 1995.

Charlie's most recent studio album is *Steal Away—Spirituals, Hymns and Folk Songs*, a bass-piano duo date with Hank Jones of such gorgeous melodies as "Wade in the Water," "Sometimes I Feel Like a Motherless Child," "Swing Low, Sweet Chariot" and "Amazing Grace" that are deeply ingrained in American gospel culture.

The album was recorded in Montreal in 1994, after Charlie and Hank premiered the project at the Montreal Jazz Festival concert. When they took the stage, the full house at Theatre Maissonneuve knew the piano-bass duo would be performing spirituals, hymns and folk songs, but audience members had no idea how elegant, moving and arresting the listening experience would be.

As a matter of fact, it wasn't until the eighth number—a sublime rendition of that hopeful anthem of the Civil Rights movement, "We Shall Overcome"—that concert goers emerged from their rapture long enough to applaud the extended improvisation Hank offered. Before that, the playing had been so heartfelt and reverential that it seemed as if you were at a meditative church recital where clapping was appropriate only after the last note of a piece was played.

In addition to working on his own projects, Charlie has been busy lending his bass lines to albums by such jazz stars as Abbey Lincoln, Bill Frisell, Ginger Baker, Kenny Barron, Joshua Redman and Toots Theilemans as well as pop singer Rickie Lee Jones. He's also contemplating collaborating on a new Haden family project, this time with his own children, his 27-year-old son Joshua, and his 23-year-old triplet daughters, Rachel, Petra and Tanya. He and his wife Ruth live in Santa Monica, California.

THE CONVERSATION

Why did you decide to play bass?

I come from a musical family. My parents performed on the Grand Ole Opry as a team. When each child was born, we were added to the family band. I was born in Shenandoah, Iowa, where my family was singing on this radio show on this big station called KMA. This was before television, and they were on a lot of radio stations that covered vast areas. So, when I was 22 months old, I sang my first song on the radio. I was billed as Cowboy Charlie. From that point on until I was 15, I sang on the radio every morning and afternoon. We moved all over the place, but most of the radio we did was in the Midwest.

One of my brothers Jim (he was called Smokey Mountain Jim) had started to play bass on the radio after one of the guys in the band left. My dad needed a replacement, so

Jim, who was five years older than me and had been playing the guitar, was the likely candidate. As soon as he started playing, I noticed how the bass made everything sound deeper and better. It added so much fullness to the music. I loved the way it sounded. So, every chance I got when Jim was leaving to go to school or going on a date, I'd grab his bass and start playing it. I was 14 at the time., especially around Springfield, Missouri

Your brother was also a jazz fan, right?
That's right. He bought records. So when I was trying to learn how to play the bass, I'd play along with his records. That's how I first became interested in jazz. Plus, when I was 14, my dad had taken me to see a Jazz at the Philharmonic touring show in Omaha, Nebraska. We were doing a weekly TV show in Omaha at the time. So we went to this concert. I heard Charlie Parker and Lester Young, and I knew right then that this is what I wanted to do.

That was it. I knew nothing could stop me from playing jazz. That was all I thought about. I formed a band in high school. We called ourselves the Cool Four. I played bass, and we'd perform at assemblies and other school events.

Around this time my dad decided to take a break from show business and touring. So we moved back to Springfield, Missouri. My dad was a fisherman who loved fly fishing, so he built a lodge out near this new lake called Lake Bull Shoals in this tiny town called Kisseemills, population about 100. I finished high school in a town called Forsyth, which is very near Branson, a town known for its country music today. I was still playing bass and was playing along with records I was buying, but there weren't any other musicians around to play jazz with at Forsyth High. My senior class had 30 students who all belonged to Future Farmers of America and wore their FFA jackets to school. I used to invite some of my friends to the lodge and play them Charlie Parker and Billie Holiday records. They thought I was crazy, but I did convert a few.

So, you knew you didn't have a future in music there in the Ozarks.
Right. I knew I had to move away after I finished school. At first, I was interested in Oberlin Conservatory of Music in Ohio. I had read about the school and contacted it for a scholarship application. I didn't know any classical music on my bass because I had never taken lessons. But the band director at Forsyth High got a hold of a little classical piece for bass. I taught myself how to play it, recorded it on a tape machine and sent it to Oberlin. They gave me a full scholarship.

I was planning on going until I read an article in *DownBeat* magazine about this school in Los Angeles. It was called the Westlake College of Modern Music, and it was like the Berklee School of Music in Boston. I decided that would be a better place to go because they had teachers and students who were centered around playing jazz.

I had also been to Los Angeles once before in 1946 or '47 when I was nine. My mother's

Aunt Margaret was an aspiring actress who was on track to become a movie starlet. But she discovered she had a heart murmur, and the movie studios wouldn't insure her. So she was dropped. My mother, my sister Mary and I drove to see her in Long Beach. I'll never forget it. It was during the heyday of the Raymond Chandler film noir period. I saw Sunset Strip, the corner of Sunset and Vine, all the major radio network buildings. It left an impression on me.

But it was the jazz connection that really drew you to Los Angeles.

Yes. Besides playing the bass, I was listening to a lot of jazz. It was difficult to get jazz records in Springfield. You had to order them. Every once in a while, a stray record would come into the Hoover Music Store. I spent all my time there after school, sitting in the listening booths to everything I could get my hands on. I listened to all the greats like Charlie Parker, Thelonious Monk, Bud Powell, the Duke Ellington band, the Stan Kenton Band with Art Pepper. One of the people I listened to a lot was Hampton Hawes. I loved his piano playing so much. Someday, I thought, I'm going to play with him.

When I was 15, I went to see Stan Kenton's group play in Springfield. I talked to a couple of the guys in the group and then went to the hotel after the dance. I had been in the booths so much that I decided to knock on the door of the room at the Colonial Hotel. The guys I met opened the door. All over the room there were bottles of gin, vodka and bourbon. I told them how they great they had sounded. And they said, you wanna play jazz, and I said yeah! They said, look around the room. You want to end up like us? And I said yeah! You want to tour and do a lot of one-nighters in smoky jazz clubs? And I said, yeah, that's what I want!

So you headed off to Westlake as soon as you could.

I had to wait awhile to make enough money to go. I started playing bass on this weekly TV show called *Ozark Jubilee* which originated from Springfield. Musicians from Nashville would come and play. I performed in a band led by Grady Martin, who was the band leader of Red Foley. I saved as much money as I could to pay my way through school. I was also selling shoes at the Walkover Shoe Store.

The manager of the store was a drummer. He wasn't very good, but he had a band that I played with a couple of times. But as soon as I had enough saved for my tuition and a Greyhound bus ticket to L.A,. I packed my bags and my bass and I were gone.

I was so happy to leave. One of the things I didn't like about the Midwest was the racism. It's beautiful country, but I found it real backwards when it came to values and education. My mom and dad weren't that way. They were interested in all kinds of things. I remember my mother taking me to an African-American church when I was a kid. We went into the back row and listened to the gospel choirs. I loved it.

I hated the racism in Missouri. I didn't understand it at all. I thought I'd be getting away from that when I got to L.A., but it was still there. It just had a more cosmopolitan spin.

Getting to L.A. was a big culture shock for a boy like me from the Midwest. I'll never forget the L.A. bus station waiting for the people at Westlake to pick me up. It was unreal. I had never seen anything like it in my life. There were all different races, people from Mexico and China, African Americans.

Didn't your education at Westlake pale in comparison to what you learned in the clubs?
Westlake had some pretty good teachers, but I did start going to jam sessions in clubs so I could find players better than me to play with.

One night I was in Tiny Naylor's Drive-In at the corner of La Brea and Sunset. It was 3 o'clock in the morning, and I was doing my homework there. I looked down at the end of the counter and I saw this guy who looked like Red Mitchell, who played bass with Hampton Hawes. So I introduced myself and told him how much I enjoyed his playing. Then I said that I really wanted to meet Hawes.

Red invited me over to his house to talk. I went there every Sunday for a month. He'd play piano and I'd play bass. We also talked a lot, about being on the road with different bands like Woody Herman's. I asked him a lot of questions about living the jazz life and playing music.

One day he called me and said that he was playing at a club in East L.A. with Art Pepper but couldn't finish the gig because he had a recording date lined up. So Red said, "Why don't you come down and sit in on a couple of tunes. I'm sure Art'll hire you after he hears how you play. So I went to the gig. Red introduced me to Art and I played Red's bass. I was scared to death, but Art turned to me and said, "You've got the gig the rest of the week."

That first night Sonny Clark was playing the piano. But the next night, guess who was there? Hampton Hawes. We ended up becoming close friends and playing a lot together.

Being a young kid from the Midwest in the big city, were you worried that jazz musicians wouldn't give you the time of day?
The big city jazz musicians are very open people. I never had any trouble. But that may have been because I was possessed. There was nothing that was going to stop me. I used to go to jam sessions, walk up to the bandstand, grab a guy's bass and say I wanna play. I met a lot of musicians that way. I think people who are involved in music are always looking to make it sound better. If you can play, people welcome you.

My experience playing with Art Pepper was good because I met a lot of other musicians. I was at another jam session when I met [pianist] Paul Bley who had just come from New York. His bassist had to return home because his wife was having a baby, so I sat in with him too. He liked my playing so much that he invited me to play with him at a gig he was starting at the Hillcrest Club on Washington Boulevard between La Brea and Crenshaw. I met a lot of other people there at the

Sunday afternoon jams when a lot of musicians sat in with us. We packed the club every night the rest of the week. We were there for months.

How did you meet Ornette Coleman?
Around this same time, I went to this club called The Hang on Wilshire Boulevard on one of my nights off. I was listening to this band when this guy came up to the stage and asked the leader if he could sit in. He took out an alto sax that was made of plastic and he started playing. That whole room lit up for me. I had never heard anything like that in my whole life.

Pretty soon, the leader stopped playing and told this guy to put his sax away. He did and then disappeared out the back door before I could catch up to him. The next night I told Lenny McBrowne, the drummer in Bley's band, about this brilliant alto player I had heard playing on a plastic sax. He told me that was Ornette Coleman. I said, could you introduce me to him. The next night Lenny brought him to the club. I told Ornette how great I thought his playing was. He told me to come over to his place to play after my gig that night.

That was the beginning of a whole new world for me. I was finally able to play music the way I had been hearing it in my head. You see, what Ornette was doing was playing in a free way in which you didn't have to improvise on chord changes. We started rehearsing every day with trumpeter Don Cherry and drummer Billy Higgins. We were all thinking the same things musically. It was a matter of everyone being at the same place at the same time. The quartet blossomed and soon after we made our first record together.

Why were you so attracted to playing free?
It's not that I didn't like playing on the chord changes. That's what inspired me to play jazz in the first place. But I was hearing other ways of playing that didn't involve the written chord structure of the composition but involved the emotion of the piece. I wanted to play on the feeling and the inspiration of the piece instead of sticking to the chord structure. During the jam sessions back then, I'd be playing along with the chord structure but then stay on the bridge of the song for a while and just play on that. A lot of the musicians I played with didn't like that. So I had to choose carefully when I would play that way. A couple of people at Westlake were thinking about playing in different ways, but it was for the most part pretty much a straight-ahead jazz scene. You've got to remember that jazz was still a young art form then. Bebop was still relatively new.

I was just hearing another way of expressing myself through the music that was deep inside me. It's hard to explain in words when you improvise on a feeling rather than a chord.

It's interesting that the music that Ornette was playing originated on the West Coast. What was it like going to New York where the music you were playing was met with a lot of criticism from jazz fans and musicians alike?

Obviously, the criticism was inside me. It's hard to explain and what you were doing didn't feel good, but we weren't thinking about that. We were just excited to be able to play for people. We had been playing the Hillcrest in L.A., but the crowds were dropping off so we got fired and figured we were ready for New York by that time anyways.

Our time in New York was very inspiring and challenging. It was a time of exploration and discovery. We weren't trying to show off there. We just wanted to present what we were doing to people.

Were you surprised by the negative reaction?

We were playing controversial music and people were putting us down, but on the other hand, we packed the Five Spot every night. It was so lucrative for the owners of the club that they opened up another place called the Jazz Gallery on St. Mark's and Second Avenue. We were only making $490 a week, but they were making a lot of money. But it wasn't just the jazz crowd coming to hear us. Everyone in the art world—painters, composers, actors—came to the Five Spot to hear this band of funny looking guys from Los Angeles who were wearing short little coats and playing free styled music with weird horns. They hadn't heard anything like us. As far as I'm concerned, we knocked everybody out.

That's the way it's gone down in the history books. In the Ornette Coleman boxed set of CDs, Beauty Is a Rare Thing, *which chronicles that period, you open the piece "Focus on Sanity" with a moving bass solo. It's a very melodic part, which isn't what most people associate with Ornette's music.*

But Ornette's music is so melodic. He approaches music with a strong folk music sensibility. His pieces sound like folk songs. When he improvises, you can hear the folk and blues influences in his magical melodies. Innovators like Ornette are rare. He brought a strong message and changed the course of jazz. He added to the genre's vocabulary the way Louis Armstrong did in the swing era and the bebop guys did after that. When our quartet played together, we did everything with intricate precision. We played freely, but it was like clockwork. We could start together and stop on a dime together. We were in top-notch shape.

You've performed with so many people from Ornette to jazz singer Abbey Lincoln to pop singer Rickie Lee Jones. How do you approach playing with artists from such different musical backgrounds?

The bassist's job is to make everything sound better and deeper. As for the variety of people I play with, I like working with musicians who share the same honest, creative, human values I hold. I value depth and beauty in music. With the bass, I try to enhance that and inspire everyone to play at that same level. My payback is to inspire the musicians I play with and get them to play the greatest they've ever done. I think the bass is an instrument that's conducive to that.

When I was a kid listening to classical music, Broadway tunes and folk music on the radio, I could always tell when the bassist stopped playing. The fullness and deep sound of the music stopped until the bass came back in. I can hear that even in a choir. I think that love of the bass sound is why I prefer a chamber orchestra to a string quartet. I'd rather hear eight basses, nine to ten cellos and several violas and violins instead of just hearing two violins, a viola and cello. I'm a romantic in that respect. I love adagios and the fullness of pastoral music. I love Rachmaninov and Ravel. And Bach. He was the greatest bass player who ever lived. He heard the greatest bass lines. You won't hear better bass lines than those that he uses in his compositions. If he had been given a bass to play, that cat would have been great at it.

Everybody hears music differently. The guy who was driving us to our gig at Yoshi's was telling me that he doesn't like Bartók because he doesn't like the dissonance in the music. I responded by saying that everyone hears differently. You hear chords in a different way than the person sitting next to you. It's like how everyone has different fingerprints. That's just the way it is with appreciating music. The role of the bass is to make everything sound as beautiful as possible.

In watching you perform, I'm always amazed how deceptively simple your bass playing is. The other night when you were playing with Benny Carter and Eric Reed, you were playing the bass lines right on the beat and bringing out the melodies of the tunes the trio was playing.

I like playing melodies because I grew up singing melodies. That's all I did when I was a kid. That's inside me. That's why when I play my bass lines or solos, they come out as strong melodies. As far as playing on the beat, I had to play that way with Benny and Eric. They're both marvelous improvisors. Since there wasn't a drummer in our trio, I had to play on the beat to keep everything flowing. When they improvised, they were playing behind the beat a lot, so I had to keep the time. When you play with a drummer, you can be more flexible.

Playing without a drummer brings up how you are plagued by tinnitus.

Yeah, it's something that I've developed in the last 20 years. I think it's genetic. Some people have ears that can take more punishment.

My ears are sensitive. My hearing is so acute that it's like the volume is turned up in my head.

You've probably gone to rock concerts where you come home and your ears are ringing. I started developing that ringing from playing next to the cymbals on stage. I had ringing at the end of evening shows. One morning I woke up, and the ringing never went away. It keeps getting louder and louder and louder.

Other musicians in history I believe had the same thing. Beethoven had extreme ringing in his ears, and I think Schuman had such bad ringing that it put him into an insane asylum. It's very heavy if you can't acclimate yourself to it because there's no cure and no way to lessen it. It's something you have to live with. I have to take a lot of precautions. I play with earplugs, and whenever I do play with a drummer, there has to be plexiglass to separate us onstage. When I record, I have the headphones turned down low, I use earplugs and I play in an isolation booth.

Has it affected your hearing overall?
That's the funny thing. My hearing keeps getting better. I take ear tests and I go over the limit. I subscribe to this magazine called *Tinnitus Today*. A lot of people have this problem. Barbra Streisand and Michael Brecker are two musicians who come to mind. But then there are people like Tony Randall. We all have to work out how best to deal with the problem.

You've said that during the Ronald Reagan-George Bush presidential years, the arts got wiped out in this country.
That is so true, but it was also a period of time when the music industry built up a kind of music that had a powerful volume. It kept getting louder and louder. Now you can't go to a house for a dinner party without trying to talk over a thunderous kind of boogaloo beat. Look at the kids driving around in their cars that have the bass so loud they're shaking from side to side. Either people have forgotten—or the younger kids may never know—what real music sounds like. Real music is supposed to sound like silence. It's like going into a forest. You have the silence. It's the same with composing. You have to stop and have the calm before you have music.

When Benny Carter plays, you can hear his song coming from his reed. If you amplify it 200 decibels, you can't hear his reed. Then you have these rock groups that come out on stage with amps that look like the World Trade Center. What is that doing to the human psyche and to the human spirit? It's destroying it.

Every morning outside my bedroom window is this mockingbird that starts singing at 4 in the morning. It does different bird warbles. It's beautiful. That's the way music is supposed to be. Music starts with the simplicity of a child and ends up expressing the humility of a wise man. It has to have that. Most people will never have the opportunity to be taught humility by the experience of beauty.

I was just reading about pianist Keith Jarrett, with whom you played for years. I was really struck by a comment he made about the loss of melody in music. He said that since melody was so tied into the health of the soul that our modern culture is going through a crisis of the soul because melody is no longer put on a pedestal in modern music. Is this why you decided to do the Steal Away *project with Hank Jones?*
In a way, yes. I've been wanting to do something with those hymns, spirituals and old folk songs as a way of reacquainting people in this country with how these beautiful songs come from such a depth of human spirit. We're living in a culture

where a shallowness is bred by hate, greed and racism. That has a tendency to stifle creativity and depth of spirit. These particular songs counteract all the madness in this country. The spirituals were born out of a liberation movement when African slaves struggled to be free, and the hymns came from England, Ireland and Scotland and were songs of the poor in the Appalachians and the Ozarks struggling to be something better. All these songs should be treated with respect. It seemed important to me to record these songs as a healing process, to remind people about the beautiful songs from this country.

Again, there's a simplicity at work in these pieces. In Montreal in the summer of 1994 when you premiered these pieces, it was as if the audience was in church. Why did you keep the songs so simple?

All the tunes we played are sacred songs. Hank and I had a long talk before we performed and recorded these pieces about how we should play them. Some of the tunes lent themselves to being improvised upon, but we felt that others like "Swing Low, Sweet Chariot" and "Steal Away" should be played without improvisation as a way of reverence for the meaning of the tune. I had been performing "We Shall Overcome" with my Liberation Music Orchestra. We played it straight, then went into the blues. I suggested to Hank that we do the same thing and he agreed. Later when we went into the studio to record the songs for the album, it really was like we were in church. A couple of times. we even looked up and said, "Forgive us, O Lord, for that flatted 13th."

This reminds me of your series of quartet albums, including Always Say Goodbye, *which won* DownBeat's *Critic's Poll Album of the Year in 1994. Those albums play up the theme of nostalgia for old times when life was simpler.*

Well, I do believe in nostalgia. I'm attracted to the notion because it helps take people away from all the madness and violence of our culture today. I see my albums as a way of returning to roots and recognizing that popular music has a deeper value. Young people today have been taken over by the media and the recording industry, but I think it's important to broaden musical horizons. As for the nostalgia part, it's a reminder that you have the ability to dream about how you want your life to be. I think music can draw people closer to that reality. The songs on *Steal Away* are about how everyone is a creative human being. Everybody means something to this universe. I think it's good for music like this to be heard.

This is a bit of a digression, but I'm curious about your bowing. You don't bow very often,

Once in a while when I want to evoke sounds of life. For example, I did an album with Keith Jarrett several years ago on ECM called *Old and New Dreams*. There was one song called "Songs of the Whales." I bowed the whole thing, using the bow to sound like whales. But I don't bow very often. It's difficult to master. The great string players in jazz all started out with classical training, which is almost all arco playing. But I knew when I was younger that I wasn't going to be a classical musician. I think there's something inside of you that has to be attracted to either being an interpretive musician, which is the classical world, or an improvising musician, which is what I do.

One of the things I did when I went to Westlake was to hook up with this teacher, Herman Reinshagen, who had been the principal bassist under Toscanini in the New York Philharmonic. He moved to Los Angeles with his wife when he retired, so I looked him up and took seven or eight lessons with him. He was in his late seventies or early eighties. Top-name jazz bassists like Ray Brown and Charles Mingus had studied with him.

The melodies I hear when I improvise are in a pizzicato context. If I were a musician like Keith Jarrett or Wynton Marsalis who can play both jazz and classical well, I'd have to practice a lot. But I'm not inspired to do that.

So I called Herman up and went over to his house and met with him in his music room, which had beautiful basses in every corner. I brought my bass over and he asked me to play. He immediately said, "I know you're not interested in playing classical music." I told him that was true, but that I wanted to learn more about the instrument. So he said, "OK, I'll play for you, and you play for me." So I improvised and played jazz, and he'd play classical pieces for me. He wrote out different fingering techniques for me to practice. We had a ball together. He was a great teacher.

You've played with so many musicians and been involved with so many different musical projects throughout your life. What would you like to do in the future?
I'd love to do something with a chamber orchestra. I've wanted to do that ever since Keith Jarrett released *Arbour Zena* (1975). He wrote this piece with strings that I really loved. So I've thought of doing an album of adagios for chamber orchestra and solo bass violin. I'd like to work with different composers who know my music and my improvising. That'd be great.

I'd also like to do a country album with someone like Vince Gill or Chet Atkins. When I was a kid, most of the musicians I met were country singers. I was lucky to be brought up around people like the Carter Family, Chet Atkins and Roy Acuff. My dad knew them all.

Country is the other musical art form besides jazz that was born in the United States. I'd love to do a country family album with my daughters and son someday. My two daughters in the band That Dog opened a show for Johnny Cash awhile back. So I taught them the Carter Family song "Single Girl, Married Girl." After they sang it, June Carter, Johnny's wife, came backstage and asked Rachel and Petra, "Are you the Haden girls? Are you the daughters of Little Cowboy Charlie?"

Your children are all successful artists and they're all stringed instrument players. Did you force them to play?
I didn't force them into any kind of music on their way to becoming. They were surrounded by great music at home, and they sought out their own the music they

felt close to. They all love jazz. My son Josh was the first person to hip me to some great rock bands like the Minutemen, Firehose, Black Flag and the Meat Puppets. He had a band called the Treacherous Jaywalkers that recorded a couple albums for the SST label. He's got a new band called Spain that just released an album on Restless Records. He's a gifted performer and singer. I'm real proud of him.

Josh started out on guitar and switched to bass. One day he asked me for a bass and I got him one. He asked for an electric bass. I didn't tell him he should learn how to play an acoustic bass. I just got him an electric. You can't try to change your kids' ways because they'll just rebel. They'll tell you what inspires them, and then you have to encourage their inspiration.

My daughters also have great concepts as musicians. Rachel started playing piano, then took up the guitar, and now she too plays the electric bass. Petra is a violinist. She has perfect pitch. She left some music on my answering machine the other day. She had recorded all the parts of a Bach piece on her four-track. She played all the voices by ear. My other daughter Tanya lives in San Francisco and goes to San Francisco State where she's studying to be an animator and painter. She also plays cello and has appeared on both the That Dog albums. I'm real proud of all my kids.

CHARLIE'S GEAR BOX 1995

Charlie's upright bass is his pride and joy. It was made circa 1840 by the famous French instrument maker Jean-Baptiste Vuilliume. "He mostly made violins, violas and cellos," Haden says. "He made only a few basses and I got one. It's one of the greatest instruments I've ever played."

He uses Golden Spiral gut strings for his G and D strings and Thomastik Spiro Core gut strings for his A and E strings. The Golden Spiral strings were made by Kaplan, which was sold to D'Addario, which plans to phase out the line, according to Charlie, because the company can no longer secure high-quality gut. "But they're supposed to make special strings for me," he adds, "because that's all I ever use."

Charlie also uses a Gallien-Krueger 112 MBE amplifier and a pickup made by a young Swiss bass player named Stephan Schertier. "The pickup is the first one I've found that amplifies the instrument without taking on a personality of its own," Charlie says. "Instead, it takes on the personality of the instrument. That's what you need. You want to be playing your bass and not your amplifier. Some guys spend $10,000-20,000 for a great instrument, then put on metal strings and an inferior pickup, and the bass ends up sounding like a Fender electric."

For composing, Charlie uses his bass as well as a Baldwin piano, though, sometimes, he says, tunes come to him in unpredictable ways. "The other day I had a dream that I was in a recording studio listening to a tape of a composition I had written," he says. "It was being played by strings, but the sound was very loud. I asked the engineer to turn up the sound and I heard the melody. At that point, I woke up and immediately wrote the melody down."

CHARLIE'S QUARTET WEST WITH STRINGS OPENS THE 1999 SAN FRANCISCO JAZZ FESTIVAL

1999

Playing music with passion is Charlie's professional credo. Even when the jazz bassist informally talks about his career, he keeps returning to one theme: the importance of approaching music reverentially.

A month before his show at the San Francisco Jazz Festival's press luncheon where the lineup for this fall's classic was announced, Charlie briefly spoke to the assembled scribes and explained why he chose to premiere his latest project here.

"San Francisco's festival is one of my favorites because it has remained true to presenting beautiful and deep-valued music," Charlie said. He's openly pleased that his lush and lyrical *The Art of the Song*, complete with a string section and guest vocalists Shirley Horn and Bill Henderson, opens this year's 17th annual jazz celebration on Wednesday. "Randall Kline is one of the few jazz festival directors today who has not watered down his festival with pop music."

As for the concert itself, Charlie says in a telephone conversation from his Malibu home a few weeks later that he hopes festivals in such jazz centers as New York, Boston, Philadelphia and Chicago get the message. "I want others to see how elegantly this art form can be presented," he says, "Jazz really needs this. It's in a sameness mode right now. There aren't many innovators who are offering changes for presenting music."

Charlie's *The Art of the Song* performance features music from his sixth album recorded with Quartet West, a Los Angeles-based group he founded in 1986. He formed the band—featuring pianist and arranger Alan Broadbent, saxophonist Ernie Watts and drummer Larance Marable who replaced charter member Billy Higgins after the first recording—to rekindle his love for music of the '40s and early '50s.

Called a "highly unusual and incredibly charming" album by liner note writer Orrin Keepnews and deemed one of his personal favorites by the leader himself, *The Art of the Song* comprises tunes Charlie has been collecting over the years. He says he wanted to not only showcase numbers that had rarely been recorded but also highlight complete melodies that tell a story.

There are several classic numbers including Cy Coleman's "I'm Gonna Laugh You Right Out of My Life" and Leonard Bernstein's "Lonely Town" as well as two classical pieces by Rachmaninoff and Ravel given chamber jazz treatments and a couple of Haden originals with lyrics penned by Arthur Hamilton.

If the swells of orchestral beauty and the timeless quality of the songs serve to play up the theme of nostalgia, that's fine with Charlie, whose Quartet West projects in the past have conjured up that same spirit. As he had told me a few years ago, he reiterates that he champions the notion of nostalgia.

"I do believe in nostalgia because it helps take people away from all the madness and violence of our culture today," he says. "I see my albums as a way of returning to our roots and recognizing that popular music has a deeper value. It's a reminder that you have the ability to dream about how you want your life to be. I think music can draw people closer to that reality."

For *The Art of the Song* project, he decided to enlist the services of two vocalists he admires, Bill Henderson and Shirley Horn. Of the former Haden says that the L.A.-based singer is one of the best male vocalists in jazz, although he's not as well-known because he also has a career as a television and movie actor.

Charlie was equally delighted to work with Shirley, who rarely performs on projects outside of her own gigs (the pianist-vocalist opens the show with her trio). "Shirley is a legend," Charlie says. "She's been singing and making records for years. She's the only female vocalist I can think of who sings on the level of Billie Holiday. This summer Shirley and I played at the same festival, the Jazz on the Water Festival in Portland, Oregon. She sang a couple songs with Quartet West. After the show she asked me, 'How many songs can I do in San Francisco?' And I told her as many as you want."

The San Francisco Jazz Festival show marks the first time the chamber orchestra and Henderson and Horn will perform this material in concert. Charlie is excited by the prospects. "I've never heard Shirley and Bill sing better than when we recorded the album," he says. "So for this show, I want us musicians to inspire them to sing better than they ever have in their lives."

Even though Charlie had gone from Los Angeles to New York with Ornette Coleman to spread the gospel about the new-styled free jazz, he remembers well his times gigging on the West Coast, especially in San Francisco. "Oh, yeah, my first trip to San Francisco was in in 1957 at the Jazz Workshop playing with [pianist] Paul Bley," he says. "Around the same time I was playing with Ornette and Don Cherry at a club called Mr. Smith and jamming a lot at Jimbo's Bop City, where the tenors were all standing in line waiting to play and the bassists all had bleeding fingers."

"If you think back," Charlie says, "the music that moves you the most is that which is the most honest, vulnerable and true. Part of my mission is being committed to bringing beauty to the world. I approach music with a willingness to give up my life for every note."

THE ARTISTRY OF THE DUO PERFECTED

2018

This article was published in 2018 in the now shuttered QWEST.tv magazine.

When Charlie died on July 11, 2014, the youthful-looking, acutely reasoned and fervently committed peace-seeking devotee to political activism left us with a variety of advanced music that documented his legacy as a pioneering solo artist beyond his groundbreaking collaboration with the iconic shapeshifting contrarian Ornette. With Carla Bley, he formed his leftist-leaning Liberation Music Orchestra in 1969 and later after moving from New York back to Los Angeles launched his more bop-oriented Quartet West project in 1987. But where Charlie was at his most soulful and insightful best was in his duo adventurers with such a diverse cast as Pat Metheny, Keith Jarrett, Hank Jones, Jim Hall and even his former avant partner Ornette. Haden was quoted in his website blog: "Before music there was silence, and the duet format allows you to build from the silence in a very special way."

In an NPR interview about his 2010 duo album *Jasmine* with Keith Jarrett, Charlie said, "The priority is to create something new that's never been before. And you put your life on the line every time that you play."

Keith added: "We're trying to find the dynamic—not exactly blend, but add the right color at the right moment based on what the other player is playing."

Charlie recorded well over 20 albums of his intrepid duo explorations with some previously unreleased sessions only eventually seeping into the album world, especially on Impulse! In 2014 the label released Charlie's duets with guitarist Jim Hall—a sublime show that had been recorded in 1990 at the Montreal International Jazz Festival.

It was about time, as the release was a posthumous affair, given that Jim had passed away the year before. In 2015, label also offered the rare duo date with pianist Gonzalo Rubalcaba (who Charlie mentored after discovering him in Cuba). It's another moving live documentation, *Tokyo Adagio*, from a 2005 date at the Blue Note Jazz Club in Tokyo.

At the Haden memorial produced by his wife Ruth Cameron Haden at New York's 1,500-seat concert venue Town Hall on January 13, 2015, numerous collaborators gathered together to pay their respects. Cameron reflected on her husband, noting that "he felt a responsibility to impart beauty to the world and see creative music as an alternative way of looking at the world. He felt at home and safe when he played music. He faced challenges in his life—polio and addiction—and he felt like he had to keep a constant vigil. He would say, I'm in trouble when I put my bass down."

One of the performances at the show featured pianist Brad Mehldau dueting with saxophonist Lee Konitz. It was fitting given that the two had recorded with Charlie on 1997's *Alone Together* album on Blue Note and again with Paul Motian on drums in 2011 for the *Live at Birdland* ECM album. At the memorial Brad acknowledged how Charlie, a one-time heroin addict in his twenties, had helped him through dark times of his own. "Charlie was a musical and spiritual mentor to me," he said.

Charlie had recognized Brad's ability to advance the language of jazz with his distinctive voice on the piano and his harmonic sophistication. He eagerly sought future encounters with his soulmate, which led to an invite from the Enjoy Jazz Festival in Heidelberg, Germany to play together in November 2007 in the art nouveau cathedral, the Christuskirche, in Mannheim. It was their first duo appearance and was recorded. Haden possessed the tape that he listened to often and desired to have it be documented as a live album. That dream came true in October when Impulse! Records/Universal Music Canada released *Long Ago and Far Away*—yet another brilliant addition to the Charlie Haden duo oeuvre. Brad reflected on the concert: "It's thrilling to play with someone who improvises like this…Ornette's quartet often was free of a fixed harmonic schema…and Charlie was improvising the harmony from the ground up."

Long Ago and Far Away opens with Brad and Charlie in a playful anarchic space on "Au Priv" with the pianist at times dancing the melody with the bassist surrounding him with a soft lyrical tenderness, setting the improvisational fluidity to come. Like most of Charlie's duo shows, this has the emotional undercurrent of quiet—a contemplative spiritual realm.

There are also no repertoire surprises, but a deep element of listening and conversing at work throughout. The title track, an Ira Gershwin and Jerome Kern tune from the 1944 film musical *Cover Girl* (starring Rita Hayworth and Gene Kelly), has Brad stepping up with a tinge of swing and a staccato single-finger fling in the midst while Charlie, intent on his partner's searches, brings his bass to a space of new ways of hearing the tune. The pair also relaxes into solo transcendence on one of Charlie's all-time favorite tunes, "My Love and I," composed by David Rasmin for the 1954 film *The Apache*. The bassist, who recorded the number with Quartet West, is on the record as describing the song as having "a deep melody and very deep chords."

The entire live recording has that pleasing mystical sense of tension and release, with each improviser developing the other's ideas, bouncing off each other's inventiveness, in a relaxed trust. They are two storytellers having a loving conversation.

This new chapter of Charlie duos brings to mind more from his heralded history as an artist eager to engage in free musical discourse. Below is a very selected list of Charlie Haden duo heroism on record:

- *Closeness* (with various artists, A&M/Horizon, 1976) Charlie loves duets, so why not link up with four of his friends to have some fun and lay down eight tracks. It's lovely Charlie with Ornette Coleman, Keith Jarrett, Alice Coltrane and Paul Motion. Quite a feast.
- *Soapsuds, Soapsuds* (with Ornette Coleman, Artist House, 1979) Some listeners call this one of the greatest Haden duos ever. There's a good reason as he and his former band leader Ornette Coleman push boundaries in this raw and

edgy setting, inspiring each other in an active way. It's all about telepathy here with Ornette on tenor sax and trumpet playing peek-a-boo in counterpoint to Charlie's sonic lyricism and pizzicato dissonance. Great track: "Mary Hartman, Mary Hartman"—the theme from the bizarre late-night soap opera on TV at the time where Ornette blows and Charlie scampers his bass line in support. It's one of Charlie's hardest albums to track down. Rare.

- *Steal Away: Spirituals, Hymns and Folk Songs* (with Hank Jones, Verve, 1995) A true gem, this meeting of two icons praising with spirituals, hymns and folk songs is a rewarding spin through music that had largely been forgotten by the fast pace of our culture. Charlie and Jones lovingly play the melodies straight from their hearts on piano and bass. In the liner notes, Abbey Lincoln wrote: "Hank and Charlie together are a magical, musical entity....[they] use a brilliant, simple, masterful approach to these forever songs."
- *Beyond the Missouri Sky (Short Stories)* (with Pat Metheny, Verve, 1997) Both the guitarist and bassist shared Missouri lineage which prompted them to contribute their originals as well as old-time music from the Midwest and popular tunes. While Metheny's guitars dominate the proceedings, Charlie plays the intimate card with gorgeous lyrical basslines that rudder and drive the songs. A big hit in the jazz world as well as a Grammy winner for best jazz instrumental performance. At the memorial where Metheny fingerpicked three of Charlie's tunes on acoustic guitar, he said, "Even though he was 17 years older than me, Charlie was like a brother in that we understood each other without talking."
- *Jasmine* (with Keith Jarrett, ECM, 2010) In the liner notes to this charged album, Keith writes: ..."Art is dying in this world, and so is listening...Charlie and I are obsessed with beauty. An ecstatic moment in music is with the lifetime of mastery..." With pockets of high energy mixed with contemplation, this is one of the best duos Charlie created with pure and robust spontaneity.
- *Charlie Haden Jim Hall* (Verve, 2014) From the onset, Charlie syncs up with the guitarist on an almost rowdy take on Monk's "Bemsha Swing." It's a travesty this tasty live recording mostly of standards but with originals had to wait nearly 25 years after it was recorded in Montreal. The two circle each other, listen to each other and open up wide spaces for lengthy improvisation on ballads and swingers. Pat Metheny commented in the liners: "This is a recording for the ages."
- *Tokyo Adagio* (with Gonzalo Rubalcaba, Impulse!, 2015) After meeting and hearing the young Cuban pianist in Havana, Charlie went to bat to get him a recording deal in the U.S. in the midst of the embargo, proving what a talent he was to Bruce Lundvall who pulled some sleight of hand with the Cuban government and signed him to Blue Note Canada. Gonzalo always touched base with Charlie, but this 2005 meeting in Tokyo at the Blue Note Jazz club has the markings of journey music with great respect. Some of the tunes are uptempo, some soft spoken, but all with a generosity and romanticism of improvisation.

CHARLIE GETS DOWNBEAT BLINDFOLDED
1997

Why is the Blindfold Test is so revealing? It is not a big publicity push for a new album or a battle of wits with an obnoxious journalist quizzing an artist with inane questions that could easily be answered by an internet search. Blindfolding means just that. Playing a track of music to elicit reflections on the nature of the tune and the musicians who set it free to the universe of sound. The Blindfoldee gets to talk about what he or she loves to talk about: music and more music!

Here's my first encounter with Charlie for a live DownBeat *Blindfold Test in 1997. Always a favorite at the Monterey Jazz Festival, he's an eager participant for what is his first BFT. Entertaining, opinionated, wise to the bone. The crowd loves his every word.*

Charles Mingus

"II B.S." (from *Mingus Mingus Mingus Mingus Mingus*, Impulse, rec. 1963/1995) Mingus, bass; Jaki Byard, piano; Eddie Preston, Richard Williams, trumpets; Britt Woodman, trombone; Don Butterfield, tuba; Eric Dolphy, alto sax, flute; Jerome Richardson, Dick Hafer, Booker Ervin, saxophones; Walter Perkins, drums.

I love listening to musicians I love and respect. Mingus was a great composer and musician and a very strong human being. I think this piece is beautiful. It's worth more than 5 stars. More like a 100. I played in the first Mingus Dynasty Band. Sue Mingus asked me to play, and it was an honor. The first rehearsal was at the Mingus apartment at the Manhattan Plaza. As I took my bass out of its case, I felt this presence. I turned around, and there was this portrait of Charlie on the wall.

Mingus used to call me Bass. We were both playing in Miami once, and he called me in my hotel room. He said, "Bass, they've got a terrible bass here for me to play. Can i borrow yours?" I said, "Man, you can have my instrument." Five stars for this.

Rob Wasserman

"Dustin' Off the Bass" (from *Trios*, MCA/GRP, 1994) Wasserman, Willie Dixon, Clevinger basses; Al Duncan, drums.

Oh my goodness. I'm not going to attempt to say who this is. I really don't listen to that many bass players. But this person is a great musician with great intonation, great sound, great ideas, imagination and creativity. I really loved it. Stars? 5. And a half. I know the tune, but I can't think of the name of it. I've played it before, but it's been a long time. The way this is rendered shows the dedication and devotion to playing beautiful music. Nothing like a good sense of humor. That's beautiful. I love hearing humor in music. And I like the title, "Dustin' Off the Bass." I have no idea who this is, but I really like it. They're having a lot of fun, and their time is really strong. They're playing this song like it's meaningful to them. That's important. 5 stars. It's Willie Dixon? Yeah, that's him singing all right. He was a great bass player.

Milt Hinton

"Indiana (Back Home Again in Indiana)" (from *Laughing at Life*, Columbia, 1995) Hinton, bass; Richard Wyands, piano; Dave Ratajczak, drums.

There are probably only two bass players that this could be. One is Milt Hinton. I think that's who it is. His intonation on the bass is very deep and recognizable to me. Plus, no one slaps the bass the way he does. Milt is the only person i could tolerate hearing this tune, "Back Home Again in Indiana." This melody has been played straight so many times. I like to play a standard without playing the melody. Sometimes I'll just improvise on a piece and maybe play the melody at the end, if at all. But Milt can do whatever he wants to.

We were judging the bass competition at the Thelonious Monk Institute in Washington, D.C. a few years ago. We were in a limo on the way to the competition, and I guess I was staring at him. It was embarrassing. Milt said, "Charlie, what are you staring at?" and I said, "Man, I want to do everything you do. I want to take the vitamins you take, the food you eat. Whatever you do, I want to do." Milt cracked up. Oh, yeah, stars: easily 105.

Ron Carter

"Mr. Bow Tie" (from *Mr. Bow Tie*, Blue Note, 1995) Carter, bass; Gonzalo Rubalcaba, piano; Lewis Nash, drums; Steve Kroon, percussion.

Well, first of all, the bass was mixed too loud. It's probably Ron Carter. On piano, that's Gonzalo Rubalcaba. The piece was nice. It sounds like it could have been written by Gonzalo. Maybe it's a Cuban song. I love Gonzalo. He takes a lot of care and listens while he's playing. On this track, he's playing very thoughtfully and with a gentleness and stillness. He has the ability to play with tenderness, then strength, then emotion. That's rare in the '90s when rock and pop keep pushing the volume up and up and up and even jazz is getting louder and louder. Pretty soon we won't be able to hear the humanness in the instruments.

The first time I heard Gonzalo play I was in Cuba with my Liberation Music Orchestra. After we went on, this group played with a 23-year-old kid on electric piano. When he started to solo, i thought, what is that? I went backstage and told him through a translator that I'd love to play music with him. The next day just the two of us went into a studio in Havana and played all day.

I'll give this piece 5 stars for Gonzalo. The tune on the whole was nice, but what impressed me was Gonzalo's inspiration and improvisation.

Ray Brown

"Mack the Knife" (from *Super Bass*, Telarc Jazz, 1997) Brown, John Clayton, Christian McBride, basses

That's Ray Brown. And there's Christian McBride. And the third bassist is John Clayton. Well, I love them all. They're all great musicians, and they play with a lot of love, tenderness and joy. Ray was one of my heroes ever since I heard him play with Charlie Parker. Listening to Ray and Kenny Clarke together was like hearing the waves on the ocean. Christian is one of the young musicians i really admire. I hear a lot of young musicians today, but few like Christian are playing with much innovation. I first heard John Clayton when I was a judge at a Notre Dame Collegiate Festival. John was with a university band, and I judged him the best musician of the entire festival.

It's tough trying to hear who's who when three bassists are playing together. The sound is kind of dark. On this tune, they're all playing in the same register. But when Ray went up into a higher register, I could immediately hear his melodic identity. As for Christian and John, I guessed them because i knew Ray had made a record with them. Stars? For those three bass players, all of whom really strive to get a beautiful sound on their instruments, it has to be 100.

CHARLIE GETS DOWNBEAT BLINDFOLDED—AGAIN

2005

In DownBeat's *fifth annual live Blindfold Test at the 2005 International Association for Jazz Educators annual convention in Long Beach, Calif., Charlie listened, reflected and weighed in on music by bass players recorded within the last decade. This was Charlie's second live Blindfold Test with me in front of an audience.*

Ron Carter

"N.Y. Slick" (from *The Golden Striker*, Blue Note, 2003) Carter, bass; Mulgrew Miller, piano; Russell Malone, guitar.

I love the sound that all three musicians get out of their instruments, and I love the way they play together. It reminds me Oscar Peterson and Ray Brown with either Herb Ellis or Jim Hall. But I have some styling doubts about this being Ray Brown. The way the pianist plays those beautiful voicings with his left hand while he was soloing with his right makes me feel real close to Oscar. Another person who did that was Ray Bryant and of course Horace Silver. But the person who really did it was John Lewis, but this isn't Percy Heath.

I have never heard this song before, and it's not something I would play. I'm an adagio guy, and that's a little too cutesy pie for me. Not that I have anything against that. It reminds me of "The Surrey With The Fringe On Top." Every time I hear that song I cringe, especially with the eighth notes played at the end of the phrase. It reminded me of when my parents had a farm. Every morning the chickens woke us up playing "Surrey." But it's difficult for me to tell who this is exactly because I don't listen to things like this.

(After audience member guesses) Yes, that's Mulgrew. I love his left hand. He uses sevenths and thirds in the bass line, which I love. Russell is a great guy with a great sense of humor, and I love Mr. Carter's playing.

Dave Holland Big Band

"Happy Jammy" (from *Overtime*, Dare2/Sunnyside, 2005) Holland, bass; Antonio Hart, alto and soprano saxophone, flute; Mark Gross, alto saxophone; Chris Potter, tenor saxophone; Gary Smulyan, baritone saxophone; Robin Eubanks, Jonathan Arons, Josh Roseman, trombones; Taylor Haskins, Alex Sipiagin, Duane Eubanks, trumpets, flugelhorns; Steve Nelson, vibes; Billy Kilson, drums

This was very linear, a kind of abstract linear. The sound and the concept of the bass player was either Dave Holland or someone very influenced by him. When I first met Dave he was playing electric bass with Miles and played opposite Ornette's band. It seemed to me that he took to the electric and was more comfortable playing that than when he picked up the acoustic bass. The way he plays acoustic is very linear, like how you hear electric bassists playing melodies. Remember, I'm not saying this is bad. I'm not being judgmental because who am I? I don't believe in judging anybody else's creative output. That's not my job. I have enough just to play the bass, let alone talk about it.

I believe this is Dave's big band. He's a great musician. I admire him for trying to find something new in the music. That's so important. I heard different approaches to harmonies, melodies and voicings that Dave does very well. It's part of the way he hears music. It's in his bass playing too. I'm glad there are people like Dave Holland in the world who are thinking and discovering new ways of playing music to make it more meaningful, pure and from the heart.

John Patitucci

"Chovendo No Roseira" (from *Songs, Stories & Spirituals*, Concord, 2003) Patitucci, bass; Luciana Souza, vocals; Ed Simon, piano; Brian Blade, drums

I have to admit I don't have as much time as I used to for listening to music. I used to listen to music every day. Now I'm either playing or writing. After a strenuous day, Ruth and I sit down and listen to something beautiful like this to put our minds at rest before we go to bed. I have never heard this. It sounds Brazilian. The piano sounds influenced by Brad Mehldau, but I'm almost positive it isn't. The bass sounds like he could be influenced by Larry Grenadier. But all that doesn't really matter to this piece of music. What matters is the communication among the musicians and what gets communicated to the listener. It's very pleasurable. I know this singer. I just can't remember her name. I liked it. It's very pleasant.

Avishai Cohen

"Come Together" (from *Lyla*, Stretch, 2003) Cohen, bass; Mark Guiliana, drums

This piece was completely unnecessary to me. There were repetitive chords, repeating over and over, without really going anywhere. And I don't feel close to the bass being bowed except in classical music where a composer like Rachmaninoff wrote specifically for the bass. I've used a bow now and then, but this piece, I have no real association with it. I have nothing positive or negative to say. It's just something you put on a record player.

(After being told it's a Beatles' song): I was in the studio with Ringo Starr for his last record *Ringorama*. He called me in to play jazz on my acoustic bass. After the session, Ringo said, "Charlie Haden doesn't play jazz; he plays music."

William Parker

"Goggles" (from *In Order To Survive: Compassion Seizes Bed-Stuy*, Homestead, 1996) Parker, bass; Rob Brown, alto saxophone; Cooper Moore, piano; Susie Ibarra, drums

(A few minutes into the piece) OK, OK, that's enough. It's very difficult for me to listen to music that's played out of tune. And it was such a repetitive motif behind the out-of-tune playing. That's it. That's all I have to say. I don't know who William Parker is, or any of the other players. It's not that I didn't like it or I feel it's bad. I either say I feel close to something or not. And I didn't feel close to this at all.

Keith Jarrett Trio

"The Out-Of-Towners" (from *The Out-Of-Towners*, ECM, 2004) Jarrett, piano; Gary Peacock, bass; Jack DeJohnette, drums.

Someone showed me a video in the early '70s of me and Paul Motian playing with Keith Jarrett. I always play with my eyes closed so I never know what's going on. But while Keith was singing or warbling or whatever it was, he was always looking at me. I thought maybe it was just one night, but he kept doing it. Paul told me, "For some reason what you were doing inspired him." I used to call it, as if to a team of horses, whoooah.

I know this wasn't me playing, so it could have been either Palle Danielson or Gary Peacock and Jack DeJohnette. Keith doesn't play with very many rhythm sections. I love Gary and Jack. Not too long ago, I played with Jack on Alice Coltrane's record. It was nice to talk with him about the old times. And Gary is such a great musician and wonderful guy. But it's really hard for me to listen to him in this trio because I keep hearing the bass notes I would have played instead.

The Lost Chords

"Red" (from *The Lost Chords*, ECM/WATT/32, 2004) Carla Bley, piano; Andy Sheppard, saxophone; Steve Swallow, electric bass; Billy Drummond. drums

I know who this is. It's Carla Bley. I can tell by the way she's playing. She's very shy. She doesn't think that she can play. She holds back a lot, but the truth of the matter is that she can really play and she shouldn't hold back. She's a great musician and pianist. Last summer we toured together and recorded a New Liberation Music

Orchestra album. One of her songs, "Blue Anthem," is incredible. Last summer, I had to talk her into taking a solo, and then she was glad she did.

I know that's Steve Swallow on bass. When he switched to electric bass, it broke my heart and I called him and told him that. Steve said he wanted to play the electric. So, I said, "Will you still make a record with me someday that's only acoustic?" He said, "Charlie, only with you." So I still have to hold him to that. There's something about Steve's playing where I don't identify the sound as an electric bass but as a completely other instrument that happens to be hooked up to an amp. It doesn't sound like a regular electric bass. It sounds more like an acoustic-electric analog bass.

Discovering your own sound like that is what I tell my students at Cal Arts. You hear music different from anyone else and you create a different sound from anyone else. It's really a miracle when you're able to bring out the sound you hear in your soul through your instrument.

John Lee Hooker— King of the Boogie

John Lee Hooker may have been a small man, but he was a giant musician who influenced generations of guitar players seeking to fully discover the blues. One of modern music's most important contributors was the son of a sharecropper in the Mississippi Delta. He was the youngest of eleven children who picked up the guitar and never looked back.

Today, John Lee sticks to his standard menu of rollicking boogies (he is, after all, the King of the Boogie) and smoldering ballads rooted deep in the Delta tradition.

While writing hits and just scraping by throughout his career, John Lee made a blues comeback in the 1990s that made him a star among stars. Getting the opportunity to meet and converse with John Lee is one of the thrills of my music writing life. Even though my story appeared in the front cover of DownBeat, *it is at this point impossible to find.*

Four years after our hang out, John Lee passed away at 83 after touring in Europe.

YOUNG AND FIESTY AT 80
1997

In mid-March 1997, I go to San Francisco's Peninsula to converse with John Lee Hooker in his home for a DownBeat (true to its motto of Jazz, Blues & Beyond) feature article. Photographer Stu Brinin joins me. As Stu always told me, writing is one thing, but when you add a photo, it's a winner. We score the cover.

John Lee's couch dwarfs him. He looks small, sunken into the pillows when we walk in. He's wearing a conservative blue suit with a bright red shirt, suspenders, a loud tie with brightly colored designs and black socks with white stars. His mouth is turned downward making him look tired, solemn, almost morose. But the first thing he says breaks the ice. He introduces himself with a jocular, almost boyish charm, mumbling in a bass tone, "Hi, I'm the Boogie Man." He smiles, his eyes sparkle and all traces of gruffness vanish

We converse for a long time—a rarity for the man who grants few lengthy interviews these days. John Lee, who turns a young and feisty eighty this summer, is a man of few words. When he talks at length, he tends to repeat words and even stutters in a rhythmic pattern, which echoes his extemporaneous vocalization. John

Lee has endured so many interviews over the years he's lost count of how many times he's had to explain why he sings the blues. However, he still likes to recount how he gravitated to the music.

John Lee has come a long way from his humble beginnings as a kid in Mississippi and then as a burgeoning star on Detroit's blues scene. Today, an undisputed master of the blues, he's finally reaping the fruits of his devotion to the blues. That's reflected at his suburban home. He owns several cars—most of which are parked outside on his street's cul-de-sac—including a Lincoln Continental stretch limo and a brand new jet black Jaguar that still sports dealer plates. Inside, he's got a mantle full of photos of him posing with VIPs, including President Bill Clinton.

Over the fireplace is a rack that holds a baseball bat autographed by all the members of the San Francisco Giants, and on the wall behind the couch is a framed Duke Snider Los Angeles Dodgers' uniform signed by the former slugger. John Lee loves the game and is already counting the months off on his hands until his beloved Dodgers settle into nearby Candlestick Park for a four-game series against the home team.

On the floor are two Epiphone guitars, including a John Lee Hooker special edition model. He's breaking them in, testing the bend of the strings. He gets the guitars gratis, he notes proudly. "Same as these hats," he adds, taking off a black fedora with a silver two-quarter-note pin on the side of the crown and the words The Hook on the label inside. "This young guy from Chicago makes 'em and sends 'em to me," he says.

Even though John Lee officially retired from the full-time road a couple of years ago, there's no silencing the man or his deep-souled music. In his twilight years, the blues has been good to John Lee. He's got financial security (thanks to a string of top-notch albums, including his 1989 million-selling comeback disc, *The Healer*) in addition to well-deserved recognition by fellow musicians and a new generation of listeners smitten by the numbing beauty of his guitar's shivery minor chords.

The blues has not only been a wellspring for John Lee, but also a fountain of youth. Prime example: a rare performance at the Fillmore in San Francisco in early March shortly before our conversation. At the sold-out concert, the fragile-looking headliner rose from the chair he'd been sitting on throughout the lengthy set and vigorously paced the stage during his trademark end-of-the-show boogie. John Lee was pumped up, pushing his Coast-to-Coast Blues Band deeper into the chugging rhythm and shaking hands with the enthralled crowd crammed in front of the stage.

Even longtime fans of the Hook found the spirited concert to be one of his most exhilarating performances in recent years. Part of the success could be attributed to close friends Carlos Santana and Charlie Musselwhite making unannounced guest appearances. Plus, the show was a CD-release party of sorts, celebrating the fresh-off-the-presses *Don't Look Back*, another primo album that was produced by blues buddy Van Morrison. But John Lee also credits the audience members, most of whom were in their twenties and thirties.

"Yeah, yeah, lot of 'em were young, just school kids really gettin' into the blues," says the blues elder. "They want to know about the real down blues. They're beginning to learn that the blues is the root of all music. I looked down at those kids rockin' and smilin' and, that's right, they put energy into me. There aren't that many older people at my shows. I'm still tryin' to figure that one out. But those young kids, they're into it. Heavy too. One thing I can say is whoever comes gets the real thing."

Hook's not bragging. He's speaking the truth—and in the business of singing the blues, integrity is the bottom line. Try to fake the emotion? He'll have nothing of that. He's been a blues man since his early Delta days growing up in Clarksdale, Mississippi, where he learned, grassroots style, that there's no substitute for a little bit of self-confidence and a hefty dose of perseverance.

"The biggest thing to learn is just hang in there if you want to play the blues," John Lee says when asked what advice he has for aspiring blues players. "You can't get dis-encouraged. If you're not serious, don't even try. If you are serious, you can make mistakes, but keep going. It's not easy, but if you love it, don't let no one talk you down. If you're a singer, hang in there. Guitar player, hang in there. You may start out rough, but keep on plucking. When I started, I didn't have no guitar. Just a piece of rubber on a wall." He strokes an imaginary string. "I just plucked it and sang along."

THE BEGINNINGS

John Lee credits his stepfather, Will Moore, as his earliest musical influence. A Louisiana-born guitarist, Will married his mother and filled the house with the sound of his gritty rhythmic blues. "I saw him play and decided that was what I wanted to do," recalls John Lee. "He helped me along the way to the style I'm playing today. I took it from him. It's too bad he couldn't have taken it himself. If he's somewhere listening—in heaven or wherever—he's saying this is what I taught the kid."

As a youngster, John Lee played country dances with Moore in Clarksdale for several years until he decided to move up river in the early twenties to Memphis with guitar in hand. He was only 14. "I was just a blues kid running around away from home," he says with a big smile. "I stayed there awhile, living at a boarding house and playing my guitar for house parties."

Soon after when he was in his twenties, John Lee was on the move again, first to Cincinnati where he worked as a janitor and a movie theater usher during the day so that he could play the blues at nighttime house parties. A couple of years later, lured by better job prospects, the 26-year-old John Lee landed in Detroit in 1943. "I worked in factories and steel mills—any work I could get," he says. "By that time I was old enough to play in bars and nightclubs where people were saying, 'Whoa, that kid can sing, that kid can play.'"

In the ensuing years, John Lee became part of the city's burgeoning blues scene that was centered on Hastings Street, Detroit's equivalent to Maxwell Street in

Chicago. "Those were the days," he says, laughing as he reminisces about the street he immortalized in the lyrics of "Boogie Chillen."

"Anything went," he says. "Wild, wild, old street. Anything you want, they had it there. The club scene was good. All the blues bands would come to town and play there." John Lee didn't play on Hastings at first. He was over at the Apex Bar on Russell Street. But he did his fair share of hanging on Hastings. "Whatever you wanted," he says. "I didn't use drugs, but they were there. Drink, women, everything. Ain't no mo' Hastings Street. A freeway's there now."

I point out that it's interesting the street where he currently resides is named Hastings Avenue. He laughs. "It sure is. I think about that all the time. I'm on Hastings again. But this Hastings ain't nothin' like the old Hastings. This is quiet, real quiet. Back then everything was open all night. The clubs never closed."

In 1948, John Lee was discovered by Elmer Barber, a Detroit record store owner. "Elmer would take me back to his shop each night and record me on blanks," he says. "He'd give me wine, I'd play and he'd cut the records. He'd say, 'Oh, kid, you got somethin' there.' That's when I worked up 'Boogie Chillen.'"

THE LIFE OF BOOGIE CHILLEN

Barber took John Lee to meet Buddy Besman, the owner of a tiny label called Sensation Records. He decided to release "Boogie Chillen," which overnight became a huge hit. "It got so big he couldn't handle it," John Lee recalls. "Buddy had to take it to another label, Modern Records. Now that was a big label, a big crooked label. That record just shot up the charts. All over, wherever you went, you'd hear 'Boogie Chillen,' and then 'I'm in the Mood.'"

Released in 1948, "Boogie Chillen" sold a million copies. As was the case with most blues—and later R&B—musicians, John Lee didn't earn a penny.

"Modern made money, but they didn't give it to me," he says. "They made tons. I got peanuts. When I was with Modern, they said they never made a profit off my songs. I knew they were crooks, but there was nothing I could do."

John Lee didn't know how to fight even as he knew he wasn't being treated fair. "Those were rough days back then," he says. "If you were a blues singer, all the companies were crooks. I think most of those labels are gone now—Vee-Jay, Chess, ABC. It's a good thing. I'm with a good label now. Pointblank/Virgin treats me real good."

John Lee pauses, and then adds with a wink behind his sun-glassed eyes, "I've got a good lawyer now who makes sure they treat me good."

Back then even though his songs were becoming jukebox hits, the only way John Lee could make money was by taking his act on the road. His Detroit-born, Oakland-based daughter Zakiya Hooker remembers when her dad graduated from the Detroit club scene. "He'd be on the road for two to three months at a time," she says. "He'd always come back home bearing gifts. It was like Christmas."

John Lee laughs. "Oh, yeah, I was Santa Claus," he says. "I'd always bring the kids somethin' to let 'em know their dad loved 'em." But I remind him about the time that he presented Zakiya with a sewing machine and his son Robert with an organ. The only problem, according to Zakiya, was that she wanted to learn how to play the keyboards too.

John Lee laughs again and explains, "Well, Robert was going to music school to learn how to play. They taught him scales and theory, but they couldn't teach him the feelings. You can't learn that in school. He went with his feelings on his own. Boy, he could smoke on those keyboards. He's in the church back in Detroit now. But when I used to take him on the road with me, he'd have people on their feet every night. He's fantastic."

Meanwhile, in 1993, Zakiya recorded her domestic debut with the remarkable soul-R&B collection *Flavors of the Blues* on Pointblank/Virgin. She proved to be a good student of her dad. John Lee schooled her well.

He philosophizes about the best blues education. "After you learn what you learn, throw the book away," he says. "Put your heart and soul into it. I don't ever look at no book twice. The book is here in me."

John Lee taps his chest and then his head. "Here and here. I can write a song in ten minutes, just like that." He snaps his fingers. "You say a word and it can mean a song to me."

JOHN LEE'S BLUES WORLD

1997

When I was writing the long-form piece on John Lee Hooker for DownBeat, *I decided to seek other voices who could speak about the Hook's personality and importance. I linked up with his 49-year-old daughter Zakiya Hooker and his 47-year-old producer/ bandmate Roy Rogers of slide guitar fame.*

Arriving at Zakiya's home across in Oakland, she giggles and rolls her eyes when recalling the recording session with her dad for her latest album *Flavors of the Blues* released in 1996. She's in the Boom Boom house studio she shares with R&B producer-husband Ollan Christopher Bell (aka Chris James).

It took John Lee a long time to recognize Zakiya's vocal talent. She laughingly tells a story of a disastrous studio session with her dad's band in the mid-'80s. That closed the book on working together at the time. He didn't like what he heard. Not enough of the deep-dispirited blues is my guess. However, today he is proud of her accomplishments. "Oooooh, she's good," he says. "My main favorite on her new album is that song 'Stones in My Pathway.' They're all good, but that one is ooooh mmmm."

John Lee appears on Zakiya's album, dueting with her on the song "Bit by Love (Hard Times)," which turned out to be a true family collaboration. "Daddy said he'd be happy to sing this song 'Hard Times' that I wrote," she says. "I explained to him that it was a tune about going through the rough times of life. I didn't give him any lyrics because I knew he'd just make up words on the spot anyway."

Shortly before the session, Zakiya talked with her dad on the phone and he told her that that he was working on a new song. "Daddy sang it over the phone to me," she says. "It went 'We all been bit by love.' I told him I liked it. Well, on the day he came to the house to record, I cooked him dinner first, then we went into the studio. We started playing 'Hard Times,' but then he picked up his guitar and started singing 'Bit by Love.' And that was it. But it worked, better than what we originally planned."

When recounting the story to John Lee, he laughs again. "Well, I always change things. It wouldn't be me if I didn't. I love making U-turns and doing things my own way."

Talking to him in his Marin Country home, Roy Rogers concurs. While these days he's cruising along with his own successful recording career (his most recent CD, *Rhythm & Groove*, was released on Pointblank), Roy served as the slide guitarist in Hook's touring band from 1982-86 and produced all of John Lee's mega sellers in the late '80s and '90s, beginning with *The Healer*.

"Lucky for me, I got the call to produce the comeback," says the seasoned producer who enlisted the support of several John Lee fans, including Bonnie Raitt, Robert Cray and Canned Heat. "I loved working with John in the studio. He defines things. That's the way it should be. He's so strong you just want to weave what you're playing around what he's doing."

Roy recalls Rolling Stones guitarist Keith Richards' reaction to working with John Lee on a new version of his classic "Crawlin' King Snake" for the *Mr. Lucky* CD. "Keith said all he wanted to do was just stay out of John's way," Roy says. "He just wanted to support him and let him do his own thing."

Roy emphasizes that allowing for spontaneity was crucial. "We took great care in picking the right songs, and we talked about tempo and groove before the sessions," he says. "But nothing was completely defined. I knew better from playing with him for several years. I knew everything would twist and turn. You can set the outline and John Lee will interpret the tune from there. And it will be better than you ever thought possible."

While John Lee takes great pride in being unpredictable in the studio, he also values efficient use of time. "Oh, yeah, I don't mess around," he says. "I do what I do, and I hardly ever make two takes. Carlos [Santana] and I work together a lot." Emulating the slight accent and hushed sweetness of Santana's voice, John Lee continues, "Carlos says, 'I don't know how you do it, but you get it. And it always comes out on the first take.'"

When I ask John Lee how he "gets it" so quickly, he cuts right to the core "It's the feeling," he responds. "It just comes to me. It feeds something into me. It comes just like that."

He snaps his fingers. "And I respond just like that."

He snaps again. "Comes out perfect," he says. "If you do a song over and over and over and over again, you wear yourself down. The first or second take always sounds better because your voice is fresh, and the song is fresh in your heart. The more takes, the weaker you get. You wind up using the first take anyway."

DON'T LOOK BACK

Right about the time when I sat down with John Lee in 1997 for our wide-ranging conversation, he was basking in the release of his newest CD, *Don't Look Back*. On it the bluesman continues to advance his raw and hypnotic attack with swaying and surging power.

For this sumptuous hot plate of steaming blues, he's in the good company with old friend Charles Brown, who contributes sparkling piano and organ support. Plus, Van Morrison not only produces most of the album but also sits in. There aren't any big surprises on the disc. John Lee sticks to his standard menu of rollicking boogies (he is, after all, the King of the Boogie) and smoldering ballads rooted deep in the Mississippi Delta tradition.

John Lee opens with a flaming take on one of his old hits, "Dimples," featuring the band Los Lobos leading the boogie charge. "It's a hot thing," John Lee says. "It kicks. Those guys know how to play it too. They kick it. I like doin' the old tunes because some generations, especially the young kids, have never heard 'em."

John Lee breaks into a run through "Spellbound" and a shuffle through "I Love You Honey," but the best tracks are the slow-dripping tunes. He taps into a deep reservoir of the blues with his trademark talkin'-moanin'-stutterin'-mumblin'-chucklin' vocal delivery. The beauty of the pack is "Blues Before Sunrise," which features Dirty Dozen Brass Band members Gregory Davis and Roger Lewis on horns.

Another highlight is John Lee's mesmerizing take on Jimi Hendrix's "Red House." "Jimi's dad asked me to sing that song on this album," John Lee says. "He called me and asked me to do it. And I did it. Oh, yeah, red house o' yonder."

Did John Lee know Jimi? "I didn't, but I wanted to." He shakes his head. "He was such a young guy when he died."

Van, who finally found space in his schedule to produce his hero, joins John Lee for emotive duets on four numbers, including the title tune of the former's latest CD, "The Healing Game," where the pair puts on a moving display of impromptu blues testifying.

"I've worked with Van for years," says John Lee. "We respect each other's feelings. We got love for each other. I love ol' Van. When he and I get together, we lock in."

While some musicians spend weeks and months finessing an album in the studio, John Lee figures it took him a week to complete *Don't Look Back*. He and Van reviewed the songs, discussed them briefly, then rolled the tapes. "I told 'em all, just follow me," John Lee says. "Van knows how I play and so do the other guys from my band. They know me like a book. We'd go over a song a few times, break through it and then I'd say, 'Let's go, let's take it, let's not mess around, I've got other things to do.' Ummm fhmmm."

Even though John Lee's music fell out of style during the rock-encrusted '70s, these days he's feeling the blues is on a roll. He says its popularity is reminiscent of the '60s when blues was part of the folk music revival. "I call 'em the good ol' days," he says. "I'll never forget 'em. I used to hang out in Central Park with Bob Dylan and Joan Baez and play in coffeehouses with Sonny McGhee, Brownie Terry and Odetta."

As for the future of the blues? John Lee returns to the subject of those youthful audiences coming out to catch him. "I tell you what, further down the line, as years go by, the blues is gonna be even more popular," he says. "It looks real good to me right now. It's right on top, and the young people will be coming back for more. A lot of people are playing the blues today. I see 'em. I hear 'em. They're playing the blues, but not the deep blues. Not like me. People cry when I sing."

As for John Lee's songwriting creative process, how does it work? Does he start with a word or a phrase, then pull out the guitar? Or is it the opposite? "What I do you'll never knows," he says with a smile. "And no one else will ever know. I get my guitar, and I just get it together."

There's nothing worse than living legends resting on their laurels—ambling onto the stage, drifting through the motions, snatching paychecks, and scramming. The audience expects cherry bombs; it settles for duds. The songs vaguely please, but their blood has been sucked dry. Fans still pour on the adulation, but the emperors ain't been wearing clothes for years.

Not so for the enlivened John Lee. He defies the norm.

Freddie Hubbard—
An Infamous Blindfold Test

By 2002, I had produced several live DownBeat *Blindfold Tests for the International Association of Jazz Educators (IAJE) conferences, including Ron Carter, Jason Moran, Charlie Haden, Joe Lovano with Greg Osby. But the most famous/infamous BFT came in January 2002 when the IAJE wanted me to meet up with Freddie Hubbard. He was ill at the time—congestive heart issues—so it wasn't certain that he would be able to get out of bed and attend the blindfolding at the conference center in Long Beach, California. It wasn't until two hours before the scheduled event that I found out Freddie was on his way.*

I had my set list ready to go, and Freddie was greeted by a full house of ecstatic fans ready to hear his wisdom. My list of tunes consisted of music that he would probably be familiar with as well as music that he likely had never heard. The purpose of a Blindfold Test isn't to stump the musician, or for them to try to quickly guess every player, but more importantly to reflect on what is being played.

As you read below in the writer's cut of this session, Freddie had his vehement opinions. The crowd loved it! After the event, Michelle Kuypers, program manager and booker at the North Sea Jazz Fest in the Netherlands, approached my editor Jason Koransky, and requested that I start doing live BFTs at that festival. The gig lasted 17 years!

BLINDFOLD TEST – FREDDIE HUBBARD
2002

This Blindfold Test, Hubbard's first, took place in front of a rapturous audience at the International Association of Jazz Educators conference in in January, 2002. Before he settled in, he said, "I'm so happy to be here. I've been wanting to get on this DownBeat *thing so I can cut up these young boys. But, then again, I haven't heard most of the young kids…I wanted to come here today to say that we're all in this music together—and that it's up to educators to keep it going."*

Sonny Rollins

"Bluesnote" (from *Sonny Rollins: The Blue Note Recordings*, Vol. 1, Blue Note, rec'd 1956, 1997) Rollins, tenor saxophone; Donald Byrd, trumpet; Wynton Kelly, piano; Gene Ramey, bass; Max Roach, drums.

(almost immediately) Well, you can stop that right now. (wild applause) No, turn it up. You know what? I heard from that trumpet player just two hours ago. That was Donald Byrd, right? I had a little altercation, a congestive heart failure that put me in the hospital till last Thursday. So Donald Byrd called me to see how I was doing. And, you know what else was so strange? When I was in the hospital, Sonny Rollins and Max Roach both called me. I worked with all those guys. As a young person (whistles) man, it was rough, but they passed a lot of information on to me. All those guys on this record were instrumental to me in even wanting to play this music. They were all great, all big time, all making it.

Donald Byrd was like a big brother to me because when I went to New York and started making records for Blue Note, he was one of the guys who taught me how to go about the business. He taught me how to phrase with people like Sonny Rollins because he had done a lot of recording and playing with those guys. So it was a thrill to play with him before I had to go into the studio. Donald Byrd taught me everything. Along with Kenny Dorham, Donald was playing long phrases back then, more so than other trumpet players. He'd play 12-bar phrases without taking a breath. And I thought that was pretty good.

This is one of my favorite records. I listen to it every day. It's funny that you played it. I have nothing but love for this. This would be good for all the kids in their studies at school to listen to. They could hear the camaraderie amongst the players to create the music. There's no rush or hard bashing. That's so good to hear. So many players are trying so hard to get their point across, to express themselves when they need to relax and just play.

That was Gene Ramey on bass, right? It's not Tommy Flanagan on piano, is it? I couldn't tell because we faded before the solo. Who is it?

(audience is offered the opportunity to guess) Wynton Kelly? No shit. (audience laughs) I watched Wynton go through all the cats because he could play any kind of style.

Roy Haynes

"Diverse" (from *Birds of a Feather: A Tribute To Charlie Parker*, Dreyfus, 2001) Haynes, drums; Roy Hargrove, trumpet; Kenny Garrett, alto saxophone; Dave Kikoski, piano; Dave Holland, bass.

I love that. These are really guys who appreciate the bebop period and there's one guy I recognize right off. I know that's Kenny Garrett on alto sax. I had a lot of experiences with him on tour. We worked together for a couple of years. In his early days, sometimes he'd go off and I'd ask him if he really knew where he was going. I told him you have to be careful. Sometimes you can make a run and go outside the chords, but you may have a piano player who can't follow you to join in. But Kenny, he's figured that out now. I love that.

The trumpet player? I'm a little perplexed. Could it be that kid Stafford? James. Is that his name? Oh, Terrell, yeah. I heard him recently in Europe at a festival and he sounded good. You know, it could be that kid who did a record on me. What's that guy's name who plays the trumpet and did a tribute? Marcus Printup. Could that be him? It wasn't? How many chances do I get?

What am I hearing here? I like the trumpet player, but he's making the same mistakes I used to make. He's too close to the microphone and it changes the whole sound and feeling of the record.

A lot of times, if you're too close to the microphone, you don't let it breathe. I'd see Miles close to the mike, but he was playing soft. I was playing hard. I think the kid here was too close to the mike, but I like his conception. From my era, you listen to the kids of a new era and right away I can tell if they sound like someone I've heard before or if they're trying something new. It's difficult to find young kids doing something new. But there are a few reaching to come up with their own sound. This guy sounds like he's reaching.

It's not Tom Harrell, is it? It's Roy Hargrove? Wow, I thought he sounded like me. That was Roy? You know what I like about this? He's playing more of his own stuff. He's a younger guy who's reaching. I like him very much, but here he's changed up a little bit with his style.

Booker Little

"Man Of Words" (from *Out Front,* Candid, rec'd 1961, 2000) Little, trumpet; Julian Priester, trombone; Eric Dolphy, alto saxophone; Don Friedman, piano; Ron Carter, bass; Max Roach, drums.

I know who this is. It's Booker Little. My experience with him was working in Slide Hampton's band. We both played trumpet in his octet. Every day I'd go to work and Booker was like a machine. He played clean and with great articulation. As you can hear, he had such control of his breathing. That's what I most admired about him. He was relaxed most of the time, but I still feel like he played tight, not as open as I like. His conception wasn't like mine. Just before he died I felt like he was loosening up a little more. It's one thing to play correct and play straight. But you've also got to come up with something new once in a while from what you normally do.

Booker was 22 years old. Sitting next to him, I watched his lips swell up and I watched his fingers. He played fast and high. I had never seen anything like it in my life. Can you imagine playing that well at 22, and there I was sitting next to that brilliant young man. He had leukemia and didn't know it. There we were on the bandstand together and within two weeks he was dead. Had he lived, there's no telling what he would have done. Can you imagine?

This tune? This is a dirge-type song. (crowd laughs at the word choice faux pas) Did I say the wrong word? Booker was thinking about some sad stuff when he was playing. He wanted to express himself that way. I like this piece and Booker Little was great.

Russell Gunn

"Epistrophy" (from *Ethnomusicology, Vol. 2,* Justin Time, 2001) Gunn, trumpet; Andre Heyward, trombone; Kebbi Williams, tenor saxophone; Marc Cary, piano; Carl Burnett, guitar; Lonnie Plaxico, bass; Woody Williams, drums; D.J. Apollo, turntables.

(makes faces at clanging electric guitar rhythm, laughs at the funky bass lines, exaggeratedly opens his eyes wide at the sound of the turntablist, then opens his eyes even wider when theme gets played) I don't wanna hear this. Turn it off. Really, I don't wanna hear anymore. And I don't want them (he points to the audience) to hear this. If I don't like it, I don't have to hear it, at least not today.

See how these record company people come up with some bullshit like this. This sounds like the theme from *Peter Gunn*. It's coming up with this hipness that has nothing to do with Monk's melody. When this kind of shit gets put out there, it makes me mad. It's like not appreciating what Monk did when he wrote this. Putting some funky beat and funny stuff on it, well, this destroys the music. We gotta stop doing that. (applause)

Monk played at the old Five Spot in the Village, and he'd play this tune every night with cats like Trane and Sonny Rollins. And to hear this bullshit, well, you gotta get over that, people. You know there are kids listening to this bullshit who never heard nobody. And they like it 'cause it's got a beat, but it don't mean nothing for the real thing. You know you have to stay real some time and not do some bullshit. (applause)

Kids go to school to learn music, then they hear some stuff like this. Where does it go? Where does it take you? Nowhere. The music [that Monk wrote] by itself is too great.

I tried a couple of times in the '70s to mess with the beats, playing the hot licks to go with the groove. But all that stuff that I practiced, busting my chops early in jazz and classical music…then to play some simple stuff over a broken rhythm, well, that doesn't make sense to me. (applause)

Art Blakey & the Jazz Messengers

"Afrique" (from *The Witch Doctor*, Blue Note, rec'd 1961, 1999) Blakey, drums; Lee Morgan, trumpet; Wayne Shorter, tenor saxophone; Bobby Timmons, piano; Jymie Merritt, bass.

(during trumpet solo) Wow! (while listening, he laughs, dances a little in his seat, makes oooh and ahhh faces) I know this. This is Art Blakey, Lee Morgan, Wayne Shorter, Bobby Timmons.

When I first got to New York in 1958, I went to Birdland to hear Art Blakey and the Jazz Messengers. He had with him Lee Morgan, Hank Mobley and Bobby Timmons. When I heard this young kid on the trumpet, Lee Morgan, whew, I thought about going back to Indianapolis. I was 20, 21 and to hear someone else playing the trumpet like that and expressing himself, well, it was frightening. I thought, you know, I gotta get into this myself. But I admit I had many a sleepless night trying to figure out if I should even bother going on.

Art Blakey. The way that guy played drums. When he played on the bandstand behind you, it felt like he was kicking you, but he also made you feel grounded. He'd play his drums and I could feel the vibrations go out the drums, through the floor, into my feet and then up my legs. I was shaking. People used to think that he was mumbling and jumbling around too much, but I could see him building all these rhythms at the same time.

Working with Art Blakey for three years was the best experience I ever had in a small group. I learned so much about rhythm. Those were the good days. He took me on the road with him to Europe, Japan, South Africa. We played bars like you wouldn't believe. I remember this one place in St. Louis called the Mardi Gras that had balloons hanging from the ceiling.

Art had me playing so long and so hard that some nights I had to soak my chops in ice after. You know you're playing your heart out, and you're in the heat of the moment and everybody's hollering and you're feeling good. But if you're tired, you start playing the trumpet with your flesh instead of the wind. That's how you get all that scar tissue. It's like Louis Armstrong. He played with brute strength. And I ended up with a bubble on my lip just like him.

That's what I like about a lot of the young kids today. They're doing it right. You get tired, you need to put that trumpet down. Otherwise you can do long-time damage.

Hugh Ragin Trumpet Ensemble

"Finger Filibuster" (from *Fanfare & Fiesta*, Justin Time, 2001) Ragin, Clark Terry, Omar Kabir, James Zollar, Dontae Winslow, trumpets; Craig Taborn, piano; Jaribu Shahid, bass; Bruce Cox, drums.

First of all, that's Clark Terry. Like I said before, when you have your own sound, you can tell right away who it is. We got together a couple of months ago, and he was helping me with my embouchure. He had a way of playing the trumpet that I could never get. He has one of the best embouchures and he was great—he could play the horn upside down, even play two horns at the same time.

The other trumpet player confuses me. It's an older guy, and he's not well known. It's almost as if the second guy was playing like Clark, but the articulation isn't as good. Overall, this sounds like a jam session record that's predicated on Clark Terry's playing. I didn't hear that much composition-wise or with soloing. It was a jam session, which is cool, but there's not too much happening. But Clark Terry, I can hear him in there. My God, he can play that trumpet. I'd listen to Clark Terry anywhere.

Lester Bowie Brass Fantasy

"In the Still of the Night" (from *The Odyssey Of Funk & Popular Music*, Birdology/ Atlantic, 1998) Bowie, trumpet; Bob Stewart, tuba; Joshua Roseman, trombone; various others.

(after about a minute and a half into the piece) Do I have to listen to this? That's it. Take it off. This music sounds like church music to me, like the Salvation Army thing. The Salvation Army band would play something like this, pray, then go out of the church and go back to their KKK meetings.

It didn't feel right, like the motive wasn't right in doing this tune. It's like listening to Barry Manilow or to Billy Eckstine. See the difference? (crowd laughs) I wouldn't want to be playing music like Barry Manilow.

It's Lester Bowie? Oh, yeah, I knew Lester. He liked poking fun. But you've got to be careful with that shit. I love Bowie, but I don't like hearing him play that.

My mother used to make me play trumpet in church. (laughs from the audience) No, don't laugh at me. She said unless you're playing your trumpet in church, you're not glorifying God, which makes a lot of sense to me now. But she had me playing "Nearer My God to Thee" when I wanted to be playing bebop Charlie Parker. This was in the early '50s when I wanted to play "Donna Lee." But she didn't want me playing the devil's music. So I said, what makes this the devil's music and what makes him the devil? But she just replied, you're not going to play that. She never did go to clubs to hear me.

Do you know how hard it was for guys like Bird and Art Blakey to play jazz? It wasn't easy. People wanted them to get off the stage. I saw how hard it was for those guys to get gigs. But they kept on playing. That's what made me want to play it. It takes time and study. You can't just pick up an instrument and do it.

In Japan and Europe, people love me. I was in Europe a couple of months ago and my chops was in and out. But the audiences didn't care. They heard the albums I'd done over the years, and they were just hoping that I could do some of that. Everybody here is so concerned with what I sound like today."

I know there are lots of cats in America—young white boys and black boys—who can play rings around Wynton Marsalis, who can kick his ass. But what makes Wynton great is that he can play both jazz and classical, which is good. I've heard him cut up cats like Lee Morgan and myself, cats who didn't have as much training as he did. But he'll never get that side [of who we are] 'cause he wasn't there during that period [when we were coming up]. We didn't know how to hold the mouthpiece to save our embouchure, to save our chops, to play clear without hurting ourselves. And he'll never know how we played our butts off trying to create something new. But since I got sick, I don't worry about what people think. You just get your own thing together and do the best that you can."

It took people like me, Lee Morgan and Booker Little several years to build up a name. Now record companies sign you, and if you don't have a successful first record, they get another guy.

Bobby Hutcherson— California Dreaming

I had interacted with Bobby often, from his gigs with the Timeless All Stars (with Cedar Walton, Harold Land and Billy Higgins, etc,) at the old Yoshi's jazz club on Claremont Avenue in Oakland to his shows at such festivals as the North Sea Jazz Festival, in The Hague. It was here when he entertained fellow performers at breakfast with his wild, hilarious stories. I listened in. Amazed.

I did a phone interview with him for a local Bay Area paper. He was polite and answered my questions, but he was pretty much cardboard—just fielding another youngster probing his artistry.

A few years later at my annual live DownBeat *Blindfold Test at the Monterey Jazz Festival, the best option was Bobby who was playing there with his band. I worried that his reflections on the music I would be playing him would be just a response going through the motions. But as soon as I played him the first tune in a set of vibes music, he came alive with waves of humor—taking center stage even if he wasn't at play with his mallets. It was a hilarious set—one of the most memorable live Blindfold Test sessions in my 24-year run at the festival.*

In 2013, I got the opportunity to converse with Bobby again about his rollercoaster ride through the jazz scene. Of note, Bobby passed away three years later.

BOBBY HUTCHERSON: CALIFORNIA DREAMING
2013

The picturesque stretch of Highway 1 along the Pacific Ocean coastline between San Francisco and Santa Cruz may not be as dramatic and isolated as the spectacular Big Sur drive farther south below Monterey. But, except for a few close-to-the-cliff curves where a car could accidentally soar off the pavement and plunge 100 feet to the jagged, saltwater-drenched rocks below, this relatively unknown span of two-lane blacktop makes for a cruiser's paradise.

Twenty miles south of San Francisco on Highway 1 sits the sleepy, idyllic town of Montara, population just shy of 3,000. Its lighthouse, built on the point in 1875, has been converted into a popular hostel, and the mile-long state beach is one of the finest on the coast.

Just off the main drive, hunkering down for yet another damp winter by feeding his brick fireplace with split Monterey pine, sits Bobby Hutcherson, the innovative National Endowment for the Arts Jazz Master who forever changed the progressive potential for the vibraphone with his improvisational mallet prowess.

While he didn't pioneer the full blooming of the vibraphone from being a novelty instrument—Lionel Hampton deserves the props, followed by Red Norvo, followed radically by Milt Jackson—Bobby took the vibes to a new level of jazz sophistication with his harmonic inventions and his blurring-fast, four-mallet runs across the metal bars amplified with motor-driven resonators. Today, he's the standard bearer of the instrument and has a plenitude of emulators to prove it.

Even though Bobby's stick action may have slowed a tad, his passion for music surely hasn't, evidenced by 2012's album *Somewhere in the Night* (Kind of Blue). Recorded live in 2009 at Dizzy's Club Coca-Cola at Jazz at Lincoln Center, and produced by Todd Barkan, the programming director at Dizzy's who knows Bobby well from his days running the famous Keystone Korner jazz club in San Francisco. [*In 2018, Todd became an NEA Jazz Master, and the next year he and Michelin-starred chef Robert Wiedmaier re-launched the Keystone Korner in Baltimore's Harbor East.*]

The disc captures the vibraphonist collaborating with B-3 organ maestro Joey DeFrancesco, guitarist Peter Bernstein and drummer Byron Landham. It's a rousing bebop-to-blues-to-ballads outing where Joey delivers fire with his brio and brusque voicings while Bobby gracefully dances with a cool finesse that thrills and even tosses in vibes fillips to complement his partner's sprightly velocity on Duke Ellington's "Take the Coltrane."

But since that gig, Bobby has been laying low for several reasons, one of which is a well-deserved respite from the career-long full-tilt action that made him one of jazz's most prolific recording artists, as a leader and as an in-demand session man.

"It's nice and green here, and it's raining like mad," Bobby hoarsely says in a bicoastal telephone conversation. "Montara is wonderful." The 72-year-old Los Angeles native made his way to New York in the early '60s and then, unlike most of his peers, returned to the Golden State in 1967. He continued his bandleading duties for Blue Note Records from his West Coast base, first in L.A. and then later in San Francisco. It was his experimental soul-blues 1971 Blue Note recording *San Francisco*, featuring the funky hit tune "Ummh," that solidified his stay.

"That song and album got a lot of airplay, so I made some money," Bobby says with a laugh. "My wife and I agreed that we should do something special. So in 1972, I bought an acre of land in Montara and built a small house on it. The acreage and house cost me $39,000. That was one of the smartest investments I've ever made."

Born in Pasadena in Los Angeles County in 1941, Bobby's jazz education came from his older brother Teddy. He listened to records by Art Blakey in his room with his friend, Dexter Gordon—the future tenor star whom Bobby was destined to play with years later (on records as well as in the CBS All-Stars band at Havana Jam in 1979 and in Bernard Tavernier's 1986 film *Round Midnight*).

Even though the young Hutcherson was surrounded by jazz, he didn't fully dive in until he was in his late teens. He was walking down a Pasadena street and heard Milt Jackson's swinging vibes blaring from the speakers of a record store. The tune was 'Bemsha Swing," a track on the album *Miles Davis and the Modern Jazz Giants* that was recorded in the mid-'50s and released by Prestige Records in 1959.

Bobby immediately bought the album, wore it out listening to it, and then began saving money while working as a bricklayer with his mason father to buy a vibraphone like his new hero.

Bobby's older sister, Peggy, was a singer who performed in Gerald Wilson's 17-piece jazz orchestra (she was later a Ray Charles Raelette). She dated locally based reedman Eric Dolphy and later tenor saxophonist Billy Mitchell. She helped to introduce the young vibes player to the active L.A. jazz scene.

After he got his instrument, Bobby began gigging in town with friends, including bassist Herbie Lewis. He played with Eric as well as saxophonist Charles Lloyd at such venues as Pandora's Box on the Sunset Strip.

Through his sister, Bobby got to know Billy, who had recently left the Count Basie Band in 1961 and co-founded a new group with ex-Basie trombonist Al Grey. "Billy needed someone to play piano parts on the vibes," Bobby recalls. "My first gig with them was at The Jazz Workshop in San Francisco opposite Charles Mingus. Billy then asked me if I wanted to go with them to New York where they were going to play Birdland, opposite Art Blakey."

That's where Bobby got his first taste of the city's strange grit. The date with Billy and Al was a two-week stint. As Hutch was assembling his vibraphone for the first night, the cigar-smoking emcee of the club, Pee Wee Marquette, blew smoke in his face and told him to get off the stage. "We don't need you," he said. "We've already got Lionel Hampton and Milt Jackson."

Marquette was known for making it hard for emerging youngsters to get recognition by deliberately mispronouncing their names.

"He'd mess your name up unless you gave him a nice tip for the announcement," says Bobby. "At first he called me Bubba Hutchins and other names. People would laugh. It was a two-week engagement, so finally after the first week, I gave him five bucks. The next week he introduced me as Bobby Hutcherson."

The Mitchell-Grey band went on the road, mostly on the chitlins circuit, and then broke up, leaving Bobby to fend for himself in New York. He settled in, living in the Bronx on 165th Street. "I grew up with grass and trees," he says with a laugh. "New York City was quite a different spot. But I knew I had what was best to get things going musically."

Even though the Mitchell-Grey band disintegrated, Bobby contributed to recording dates by both musicians as well as took on moonlighting gigs as a taxi driver to make his rent. As he began branching out more on his own, he soon faced the New York scene full on. He linked up again with Herbie Lewis, who was playing with trumpeter Art Farmer and saxophonist Benny Golson in the Jazztet, alongside Grachan Moncur III on trombone.

Herbie was hosting jam sessions at his pad, and Moncur, after hearing Hutch play, said that it would be good for him to meet saxophonist Jackie McLean, whose band he was also playing in.

"Jackie liked what I was doing with four mallets, so he asked me to play with him at the Club Coronet, where he was introducing a young drummer from Boston," says Bobby, who doesn't feel that he needs to identify Tony Williams (who was 17 at the time). "Jackie called Alfred Lion at Blue Note to see the band. Lion wanted to record the group, so we all went off to Rudy Van Gelder's studio."

The 1963 album was McLean's classic *One Step Beyond*.

Bobby continued playing with an assortment of Blue Note artists, including Moncur, Andrew Hill, Grant Green and L.A. pal Eric Dolphy. "Eric had heard about this new young band Jackie had put together for the Coronet date," Bobby says. "He came in and was surprised to see me. He told me that he wanted me to do some gigs. Eric had a thing. He played two octaves, playing the chords from the first octave followed by chords from the second. He opened up these amazing possibilities."

Case in point: Eric's sole Blue Note album, the 1964 classic gem *Out to Lunch*, where Bobby displayed the avant-garde modus operandi to expect the unexpected, collaborating with Williams, trumpeter Freddie Hubbard and bassist Richard Davis. Offering unpredictable floating accents and sly drop-ins, Bobby shined throughout, including the Dolphy-penned track "Hat and Beard" (inspired by Thelonious Monk) where the vibraphonist contributed plunks, splashes and shimmers that have a prankster vibe.

"I began hearing all these other ways of playing," Bobby says. "That was wonderful for me to be living in New York and be a part of the jazz renaissance of that time."

Early in his Blue Note stint (which continued until 1977), Lion gave him carte blanche to record his own albums as a leader. "He told me, 'Listen, you make all the albums you want. Just call me and you can record.' So that's what I was doing every couple of months."

This estimation confirmed what others in the jazz world had already realized: Bobby was an adventurous improviser who wasn't afraid to barrel through the barriers of the dominant hard-bop jazz world.

Bobby's Blue Note debut, *The Kicker*, was recorded at the end of 1963 but was mysteriously shelved until 1999.

Other sessions met with the same stockpile treatment, including *Spiral*, recorded in 1968, and *Medina*, recorded in 1969, which were released on CD in 1998 as a double album.

But several of Bobby's outings managed to see the light of day in the '60s, including his first album to be released, 1965's *Dialogue* (made during the time that he was playing with Archie Shepp).

His 1966 masterpiece *Stick Up!* was his first date with McCoy Tyner and featured his collaboration with Joe Henderson.

Bobby's New York experience came to an abrupt close in 1967 while he was recording a date with Andrew Hill. At the rehearsal he and drummer Joe Chambers took a break, scored a couple of joints and kicked back in Central Park. They were busted by the police and thrown into jail.

Musician friends at the club Slugs' passed the hat to post bail for him. But Bobby lost not only his cabaret card (the guarantee to perform anywhere in New York that was abolished not long after) but also his taxi driver's license. So, he moved back to Southern California, where he joined up with hard-bop tenor saxophonist Harold Land and began their long-running creative union, starting with Land's 1968 quintet record *The Peace-Maker* (Cadet).

With the cabaret card no longer needed in New York, Lion called Bobby to continue his recordings—this time as a collaboration with Land. The underappreciated band recorded seven albums for Blue Note, beginning with 1968's *Total Eclipse* (with Chick Corea on piano) and continuing through 1975's *Inner Glow*. The former proved to be a marquee outing for the group where hard-bop entered into the exploratory zone. The album dips in and out of Bobby's daredevil sensibility, with inventive vibe romps and pure elation. The trippy finale, "Pompeian," is a questing voyage with a whimsical open and close and a complex middle section that is avant-leaning and charged as Bobby paints dark colors on the marimbas.

"I had been doing a lot of writing then," he says. "I was experimenting with moving intervals in my playing, doing seconds and thirds to fourths and fifths. It was creating a different sound instead of typical jazz lines. The intervals were opened up. The idea was to try to make it sound simple even though it was music that was hard to figure out. Harold started playing the intervals, too, so that we could bounce off each other. Actually, I got a lot of my ideas from Joe Chambers, who was always trying to change the recipe. 'Pompeian' is full of the intervals playing — which actually reflected the scene that was going on in San Francisco at the time."

In addition to Corea, other pianists joined the Hutcherson-Land band, including Joe Sample and Stanley Cowell. "Joe hipped me to Stanley," Bobby says. "He was a guy with a direction. He had great ideas, and he showed me a lot about beats—playing on top of the beat or in the beat or behind the beat. He would create a whiplash situation, like a weather system that comes in and creates a *pow*. And then it circles around and *boom!* It's almost like a punch line. It's the kick like the tail end of a cup of coffee."

Currently chairman of the jazz program and professor of jazz piano at Rutgers University, Cowell began his New York experience in the '60s with Max Roach. Then he was called by Miles Davis, but quit after playing two gigs with him in Montreal and Boston. The situation was too controlled for him, so he worked with Charles Tolliver and then Stan Getz, connecting often with Joe Chambers, who brought him into the Hutcherson-Land fold.

"Bobby was one of the most relaxed people," Stanley says. "He was a wonderful player, but he did it in a relaxed way. When we were touring, he never rushed to the airport. We'd all be panicked that we were going to be too late, but he just relaxed and took his time — and we never missed a flight. Behind his back, we called him California Dreamer."

Stanley says that the band was definitely in the zeitgeist of the turbulent anti-establishment era. "We were all embracing the political content of the music, versus issuing the traditional and conventional," he says. "Our approaches varied. We used sounds prevalent at the time and played in a free form. Our resources were expanded as we set out to re-examine the music. The apex for me came at a concert we had in Antibes [France]. There were great moments at that show where we combined pulses with a great deal of freedom within a fixed form. Bobby was doing these incredible cadenzas. The last time I saw him, he still was. He's a happy person."

Bobby's move from SoCal to San Francisco was hastened by a Pasadena friend, Delano Dean, who opened up the Both/And club (which is where he met his second wife, Rosemary Zuniga, who was a ticket-taker). There was a lot of activity in SF, not only at Keystone Korner, The Jazz Workshop and the Blackhawk, but also in Golden Gate Park. He set up roots in the city and later, Montara.

Joe Henderson also made the move to San Francisco. The tenor saxophonist and vibist formed a trio with drummer Elvin Jones and toured the country. "Joe and I became very close," Bobby says. "He always had a hair-cutter there. When we were on the road, I brought along a pair of shears and gave him haircuts."

One time after a tour, Joe called Bobby in the middle of the night.

He said, "Hey, Bobby, what are you doing?"

Bobby replied, "What's going on? Is there some record date or a concert?"

"No, will you come over and give me a haircut?"

"It's 4 a.m."

"Come on over and we'll have a good time."

Bobby went, snipped and ended up staying there until the next afternoon, hanging out and talking. He heartily laughs when he tells the story, adding that he's got so many more great stories that his wife and three sons have encouraged him to write a memoir.

He laughs again, then notes that he's slowing down. "I'm not the dynamo I used to be," he says, laughing again. "I have emphysema, and I'm breathing oxygen while I'm talking to you. I can't play long solos like I used to be able to, and I don't play quite as fast because that takes a lot of oxygen."

During the winter months with Montara's cold, wet weather, it's been rough for Bobby, who has been hospitalized several times in recent years. Still, he says, "My doctor keeps telling me I'm doing well. That way I can continue to share my life and my music. What a reward that is."

Joey DeFrancesco seconds that notion. "Bobby is the greatest vibes player of all time," he says. "Milt Jackson was *the* guy, but Bobby took it to the next level. It's like Milt was Charlie Parker, and Bobby was John Coltrane."

Joey first played with Bobby in a duo setting in 2002 at Pittsburgh's Manchester Craftsmen's Guild, on the suggestion of the executive producer, Marty Ashby. The pair continued playing in a trio setting with a drummer.

As for *Somewhere in the Night*, Joey says, "It was incredible. The music was harmonically deep and so soulful. Bobby picked everything to play. When you play with a legendary guy, you let them play in their element."

One time in recent memory, Bobby says he was totally out of his element when he was asked in 2003 to be a founding member of the SFJAZZ Collective. He was the elder statesman working with an array of young jazz stars, including saxophonists Joshua Redman and Miguel Zenón, trumpeter Dave Douglas and pianist Renee Rosnes. On Jan. 23, 2004, Bobby played at the SFJAZZ Center's grand-opening concert and stayed with the collective until 2007.

"That was four wonderful years, and I was the old guy in the group," Bobby says. "It was something completely new to me. I was thrilled to play, but I was also very humbled. What a learning experience that was — being with the younger players. I learned forgiveness, to forgive myself. I wasn't able to play as fast, and sometimes I'd miss notes and feel bad. But all the players made me realize that I had to forgive myself and keep going. That was the biggest lesson. And I continue to work on this every day. It's a good practice."

Looking back at his career now, Bobby waxes philosophic. All the trophies he's received and the plaques pegged on his walls aren't the point, he says. "Slowing down, I see a lot more," he says. "The real plaque for me is to be able to share my music with others." He pauses and then adds, "There's still a lot to be revealed."

Abdullah Ibrahim—Musical Depth

*"The black eagle has only one wing and is blind in one eye. It can't fly.
We're working today to get our eagles flying again."–Abdullah Ibrahim*

*I first met the piano maestro Abdullah Ibrahim in his hometown of Cape Town, South
Africa in 2004. Below is the writer's cut of my article on our conversation for* DownBeat.
*Fifteen years later I was on the beat for the magazine again, this time meeting up with
Abdullah at the INNtöne Jazz Festival in Upper Austria.*

*The two conversations have largely been in the landfill since then. So, here, I
unearth them to showcase his wisdom.*

CAPE TOWN & BEYOND WITH DUKE
2004

It's a week of profound anticipation. It's early April in 2004 in Cape Town, South
Africa, and the town is preparing for the fifth anniversary of the North Sea Jazz
Festival Cape Town while the entire country is gearing up for the upcoming elections
that mark the 10th anniversary of democracy. At the pre-festival press conferences
featuring the marquee artists, questions center not so much on the music but on
the significance of the twin commemorations.

Perhaps the most renowned expatriate, 72-year-old singer Miriam Makeba,
affectionately known as Mama Africa, expresses her enthusiasm for being able
to live again in her homeland following the dismantling of the apartheid regime.
"Ten years later, I'm even more pleased," says Miriam, a staunch supporter and
cheerleader of Nelson Mandela's African National Congress party that a few days
later again dominated the vote. "South Africans have fought hard to hold onto our
new freedoms. We've accomplished more in a decade than many democracies."

Pianist Abdullah Ibrahim, inarguably South Africa's most renowned jazz instrumentalist and a sage at heart, is far less forthcoming. In fact, he refuses to be a poster
figure for either the festival or the ANC. He's prickly and circumspect during his
session with journalists who press him on his opinions of the dual anniversaries. A
Cape Town native who today lives in the Kensington district of the city as well as
still shuttles on occasion to his Chelsea Hotel digs in New York, Abdullah downplays

his first appearance as a leader in his hometown festival. He calls it "just another gig," then complains about the underbelly of South Africa's miracle of freedom. He says, "What about AIDS, poverty and the crime rate? And Cape Town is losing the vestiges of the real Africa. After 10 years, are we really in charge of our own fate? The circle is broken here. We have lost the natural rhythm of the universe."

Abdullah's fellow countrymen bristle as much at his seemingly politically incorrect opinions as his cantankerous attitude. They ask him why he has become so disillusioned. He smiles, replies that he's quite clear about what he sees and feels in his heart, then ends the interview with a parable: "The black eagle has only one wing and is blind in one eye. It can't fly. We're working today to get our eagles flying again."

The next morning in his hotel suite, Abdullah, who will turn 70 on October 9, grins at the mention of the previous day's upset when he turned the press conference on its head by posing more questions than he answered. "The problem is people don't understand the creative process," he says. "They have a preconceived idea of where I fit in and what I have to say. If you assume something about me, I'm not going to go there. If you want to know what's happening politically in the country, why not speak to the ANC. I didn't hear anyone asking me about my music."

Abdullah sighs. "People can stand on a soapbox at a press conference," he says. "But the proof is on the stage, in the headphones. Everything else is peripheral."

At first glance, Abdullah looks to be perpetually locked into a solemn visage, his eyes intense, no-nonsense, and his gaze weighty, thoughtful. He tells me he drives nearly every day to Table Mountain, the massive 3,500-foot sandstone plateau that overshadows Cape Town. Not only are the views spectacular—the fog lazily dissipating to reveal the hills and city's downtown below and the chilly blue seas beyond—but the mountaintop is the perfect place for rumination, an exercise the pianist embraces. "When you go there, the mountain gets a hold of you," he says with an earnest voice of mythical authority.

However, a moment later, Abdullah's eyes brighten as he talks about his mentor Duke Ellington and how the maestro would pick the lint off the shoulder of your jacket when he had something important to say to you. He laughingly recalls going to New York for the first time and anxiously asking Ellington for advice. "Duke looked at me and while picking the lint off my shoulder said, 'Survive.'"

Abdullah is eager to expound upon the spiritual precepts of his jazz survival. The journey includes leaving the oppression in South Africa in 1963, living as an expatriate in Switzerland and later the U.S., being discovered and recorded by Ellington, experiencing the doldrums of the jazz life, overcoming professional obstacles and finally returning home to Cape Town in 1990—in the aftermath of the bloodless revolution yet prior to the first free national elections that swept Mandela into power.

Abdullah has recorded numerous albums in a variety of different settings, but he beams when talking about his trio. "I didn't come here to play a concert for reviews," he says, in reference to his upcoming festival show with his longtime stateside rhythm team of bassist Belden Bullock and drummer George Gray. "For us, it works on a whole different level. That's how we live. It's as if we're in a state of stunned discovery on the beauty and power of God through the music."

As a child, Abdullah was surrounded by music, from traditional African songs to African-American religious hymns and spirituals in the African Methodist Episcopal church in his Kensington neighborhood. He also tuned in to jazz on Voice of America radio broadcasts. Hearing Albert Ammons' piano boogie-woogie inspired him to learn the instrument his grandmother played in the AME services.

Born Adolphe Brand, he earned the nickname Dollar because he always carried the currency to the docks to buy jazz records from visiting American sailors. In 1951 at age 17, he broke into the professional ranks with the big band Tuxedo Slickers. "That was my training because apartheid policies didn't allow us into music conservatories—or into medical school," he says. "We played Glenn Miller and Tommy Dorsey tunes as well as the traditional music from here. During that time, it was hard to distinguish between Count Basie and South African music. It was that close melodically, harmonically, rhythmically."

Abdullah loved Basie but was floored by Ellington. "I was more drawn to Duke as a pianist, composer and arranger," he says. "There's no way to escape his influence. But in those days, I couldn't get his arrangements because they were closely guarded and not published."

In 1959, Dollar Brand met alto saxophonist Kippie Moeketsi, now a legendary jazz figure in South Africa, and with him and trumpeter Hugh Masekela formed the Jazz Epistles, the country's groundbreaking modern jazz ensemble. A couple of years later, he was asked to accompany vocalist Sathima Bea Benjamin, a young star on the Cape Town scene.

"At first I said no because I had no interest in playing with singers any longer," Abdullah says. "But I went to a rehearsal and I saw this beautiful lady and I thought, 'Well, I'd better do this gig.' I asked her what she wanted to sing and she said 'I Got It Bad and That Ain't Good.' What's amazing is that I had just been working on that song. So it was meant to be." They were married soon after.

South Africa's apartheid policies became so stifling in 1963 that Brand and Sathima left the country on the invite of a Swiss friend who secured them a regular gig in a Zurich club called Africana. The pianist enlisted his Cape Town trio, bassist Johnny Gertze and drummer Makaya Ntshoko. Soon, they began to meet all the American jazz artists traveling through the city, including Errol Garner, Art Blakey, Cedar Walton, Freddie Hubbard, John Coltrane and eventually Duke. "Sathima and I really wanted to meet Duke, but the night he was in town the club wouldn't let me go," Abdullah says. "Sathima went and I don't know how she did it, but she convinced Duke and the whole group to come see our last set." He pauses, then laughs, "It was scary."

Duke liked what he heard. The next week he took the Dollar Brand Trio to Barclay Studios in Paris and recorded the band for Reprise Records, Frank Sinatra's label for which he was doing A&R work. The LP, *Duke Ellington Presents the Dollar Brand Trio*, released in 1963, introduced the pianist to the world.

(Remarkably, a session with Sathima was also recorded, with her piano accompanists including her husband, Ellington and Billy Strayhorn. The master tape was lost but eventually a dupe was discovered in the possession of Barclay chief engineer Gerhard Lehner and released a few years ago on Enja as *A Morning in Paris*.)

Other early Dollar Brand highlights were Abdullah's appearance at the Newport Jazz Festival in 1965 with bassist Gene Taylor and drummer Joe Chambers and filling in for Ellington on five East Coast Orchestra dates when the bandleader was in Los Angeles working on a film score. Abdullah briefly toured with Elvin Jones in the mid-'60s, but has rarely stepped into a supporting role since, other than backing up his wife. In the late '60s, he converted to Islam and adopted a new name. In the mid-'70s, he briefly tried to return to live in South Africa but found the politics there even more onerous. In 1976 took up residence with his family in New York.

Abdullah went on to record numerous albums, the majority of which have been released by Enja. (Many of his CDs are currently being reissued in North America by Justin Time Records, including two superb trio recordings, 1998's *African Suite* with orchestral support and 2000's *Cape Town Revisited*.) His style is an amalgam of Ellington's elegant touch and the buoyant and complex subtleties of South African music. And it also bears an affinity to Thelonious Monk's quirky, unpredictable genius.

Abdullah's first encounter with Monk came during his tenure in Zurich. "I went into his dressing room and told him I was a pianist from South Africa," he says. "I thanked him for his wonderful inspiration. He looked at me quizzically and walked away, then looked at me again from across the room. After a minute he came back and said, 'You're the first piano player to tell me that.' And I thought, 'Whoa, that's heavy.'"

When he first heard Monk's music, Abdullah was immediately drawn to it even though colleagues thought he couldn't play and was faking it. But he knew better. "I remember my first compositions where people complained that what I was playing sounded false," he says. "But it all sounded fine to me. That's the same with Monk. We shared a kinship. When I was a young man in Kensington, I listened to 78s that were so old the print on the labels was worn off. I was fascinated by this one piece that I played over and over again. Later I discovered it was Debussy's *Prelude to the Afternoon of a Faun*. It was fascinating. When I finally heard Monk, it reminded me of Debussy in a way and was a confirmation of his brilliance."

Abdullah was also attracted to the architecture inherent in Monk's work. "A lot of people complained that Monk's meter changed and that his bars were irregular," he says. "But I never had a problem with that. When I started composing I spent a lot of time in shantytowns where my musician friends lived. I'd sit in the ramshackle homes that people had built from pieces of wood and iron. There were strange angles and doors were ajar. That was reflected in my music."

When Abdullah finally returned to South Africa in 1990, the transition was traumatic. "It took me a week to walk from my door to the front gate," he says. "Then it took another week to go to the corner and back. In the third week, I managed to walk around the block. I slowly began to venture out. I checked in with other people who had been living in exile and they shared the same experience."

Did returning home have an effect on his music? Abdullah replies that it was as if he had never left. "We live in dream time like the aboriginal people. What we see physically is a dream, so in some sense I never left. That is the strength that we find within—the discovery of the self."

To further explain, Abdullah talks about his 50-year training in the martial arts. "I studied with the masters," he says. "They'd always say, 'No mind. No mind. You think too much.' They were saying if you think about doing things your creativity will be curtailed. The samurai loses his fear and becomes totally fearless. The same holds true for jazz. You can't be afraid to make mistakes. My martial arts teachers always told me, 'When you make a mistake, make a good mistake.' Just like you have to remove the fear of making a mistake while improvising, you also have to lose that fear in your personal life. You have to operate on faith."

SOUTH AFRICA TODAY

Abdullah relates that to what is happening in South Africa today. "We are the microcosm of the world to come," he says. "We have overcome apartheid with a minimum of conflict. We reached resolution through negotiation, without resorting to war. We begin to understand all this through the music, to repair the fragmentation in our immediate community and on a global perspective, to reconnect the circle that has been broken."

While he's approaching 70, Abdullah is not slowing down. He continues to tour regularly, with upcoming dates in such classical music venues as the Cologne Philharmonic Hall and the Frankfurt Opera House. He also has new projects in the works for Enja, including a project with Hamburg Radio's NDR Big Band, further cementing his long-term association with the label. In addition, he hooked up with kwaito TKZ band member Tokollo to do a hip hop remix of "Soweto," a tune he penned in 1970. Then there's the M7 Project Ibrahim started in Cape Town that addresses other issues beyond music, including medicine, meditation, martial arts and movement.

A German film crew is working on an Ibrahim documentary during the festival. They filmed him on Table Mountain and in Kensington, and this evening they'll be taping his trio date at Rosie's, a 1,500-seat theater in Cape Town's new Convention Center. Abdullah excuses himself to go to sound check but promises "some goodies" at the show. "I can't wait until the night, after the sun goes down," he says. "Then I can do the trance dance and be my real self."

He doesn't disappoint. His transcendent appearance with bassist Belden Bullock and drummer George Gray is the highlight of the festival. Together they embark on journey music that changes shape, color, tempo and ambiance from the airy to the exclamatory. A poet on the piano, Abdullah chimes chords, sprinkles single-finger notes and drifts into a state of lyrical grace. He splashes like Monk, throws in a dash of boogie-woogie, walks the blues with his left hand and sketches a melody line with his right.

The audience is hushed in rapt appreciation. The trio breathes together as they ebb and flow in segue mode from one Ibrahim tune to another, including such pieces as "Blue Bolero," "Duke 88," "African Marketplace," "Chisa" and "The Call." At the end of the set, the crowd explodes with a standing ovation—an acknowledgment of his iconic status as a musical hero of post-apartheid South Africa.

Backstage after the show Abdullah's rhythm mates are still in a state of glow. "He guides us," George says.

Belden adds, "It appears seamless, but we follow where he's going."

George nods and says, "We know what he's thinking."

"It's like magic the way he'll be in the middle of one tune and find his way to another," says Belden.

Sitting in his dressing room, Abdullah is all smiles. "It's beautiful and scary, not knowing what will happen next," he says. "We go into different places, then ask ourselves later, 'Where were you, what was that?' I never understood that when I was younger. Most of us didn't, which is why so many of us fell into drinking alcohol, smoking joints, womanizing. We thought that was what the music was about. We couldn't explain what it was that we were feeling, but I finally realized that music is a deeply moving spiritual experience."

Abdullah pauses and adds softly, "It's guidance from God."

ABDULLAH IBRAHIM: A FOCUS ON SPIRITUALITY
2019

Fifteen years after our first conversation in South Africa, we link up again in Austria to continue our conversation about the creative power of music.

In May 2019 at the INNtöne Jazz Festival in Upper Austria, Abdullah Ibrahim, the headliner of the three-day event, gives cosmic witness to the intimacy and magical beauty of solo piano to a hushed and in-awe crowd of 800 on the Jazz on the Farm's main stage in the property's repurposed barn.

The South African-born, Germany-based Abdullah (who also owns a large spread in South Africa's Kalahari Desert) plays as if he were communing with the natural surroundings, creating verdant rolling soundscapes throughout his 90-minute set. In front of him is a tattered spiral notebook which at first glance looks like a setlist. But it's a crossword puzzle of song titles that reminds him of where to go on the keys as a maestro of improvisation when the time is right.

As Abdullah told me earlier, "It's the idea of being free. It's almost like abandonment, just playing with your feel and forgetting about the notes."

Without uttering a word throughout the set, the 84-year-old Abdullah weaves a series of tunes interspersed with recurring fragments of such well-known songs as "The Wedding" and "Blue Bolero."

Known as Dollar Brand until his conversion to Islam in 1968, Abdullah was awarded a NEA Jazz Masters award this year and has just released his first new album in five years, *The Balance*, with his longtime septet Ekaya (translation: "home"). The recording has been released on vinyl and traditional CD via the upstart London-based Gearbox Records, home to such cutting-edge artists as Theon Cross and Butcher Brown.

The album enchants and stimulates with lyrical upbeat beauties that the band dives into (including a riot through Thelonious Monk's "Skippy") and also ruminates with Abdullah's solo meditations. A perfect balance of the master's repertoire, hence the title.

In a two-hour conversation with the relaxed, youthful-looking Abdullah before his INNtöne performance, I scratch the surface on delving into his storied history, including life under the South African regime of apartheid, his exile, his U.S. citizenship after his home government revoked his status, and his return to perform at the inauguration of Nelson Mandala, who called him "our Mozart."

The talk meanders in circles just like his animated serenity at the piano. The topics range from his nearly half-century practice of the Japanese nonviolent Budo martial arts discipline to his little-known creative process of writing lyrics for all his instrumental compositions.

Congratulations on receiving the National Endowment for the Arts Jazz Masters Award this year. What was it like going to Washington, D.C., to perform at the Kennedy Center for the awards show?

At first, I didn't quite catch the scope of it. It was nice to be honored in the same breath with all the great musicians I've always aspired and still aspire to. They continue to be my teachers and mentors without them knowing it. It was also getting the recognition of my music. It was not just an accolade for myself but also my band Ekaya. They were ecstatic about it. [Saxophonist/flutist] Cleave Guyton and [bassist] Noah Jackson were there playing with me.

And the award itself?

It was like being honored by my Japanese Budo teacher Sansei Tonegawa who I've been practicing nonviolent martial arts since 1960. He's taught me to enter places where I hadn't been before but with an understanding that you are well-equipped to handle the situation. He gave me a diploma that was a license to teach Budo. So I said to him, Master, you're giving me this diploma, but I don't know anything. Then he said to me, that's why I gave it to you. I don't know either. He was saying it was the beginning of a new phase. And then you have to strive harder.

We talked in 2004 and you were playing the Cape Town Jazz Festival with your trio, performing an amazing concert that you called being "in a state of stunned discovery on the beauty and power of God through music." You noted to me before the show: "You ask yourself, where were you? What was that? I never understood that when I was younger—most of us didn't—which is why so many of us fell into drinking alcohol, smoking joints, womanizing. We thought that was what the music was all about. We couldn't explain what it was that we were feeling, but I finally realized that music is a deeply moving spiritual experience. It's guidance from God." Do you still believe in that guidance?

Absolutely. We were living in this horrendous regime, but at the bedrock of our understanding of who we were and what we were was our parents and other mentors along with the unsung people in the community. We were living where everything was negated. Our traditional medicine was banned because it was considered witchcraft. So much was called witchcraft, but this is what our mentors helped us understand. It has nothing to do with religion. From early on in the community and with my parents and family, the focus was on spirituality. We mixed with everybody—Christians, unbelievers. We all understood that this was the cosmology of living together. I've carried this understanding to what we are doing with the music. It encompasses everything.

And that relates to your life as a jazz musician?

For me, jazz is the highest form of music. Early on I'd listen to Louis Armstrong and Count Basie and the boogie-woogie playing of Albert Ammons. We used to play in house parties, carnivals, in church on Sunday, at picnics and I'd play with this stride piano sound. What I liked was the incessant drum sound. I found that the basslines were actually the same rhythm of traditional Swazi drumming. Boogie-woogie gave me a way of developing my left hand. It was a grounding point for training independence between the left and the right hands. So I was playing this along with music from Africa.

How did the Jazz Epistles begin?

I had been composing and being opposed to playing alone, but wanted to play with a band so we could start to break the boundaries. The boundaries we had to overcome was this governmental thought process that blacks were inferior. We were forced to live in a system that said we do not have the mental capacity to deal with intricate things such as mathematics. But for me, I knew that was wrong from listening to the various styles of traditional African music and realizing their complexity.

So we were forever relegated to the role of being subservient. I started composing music that wasn't logical. We had already gone through the whole process of playing the traditional music, the church music and the carnival dance music. But then swing came along. There's massive complexity that people miss. When I started getting on to jazz, I loved Monk and Herbie Nichols and Duke Ellington.

Your playing is also steeped in classical music like Bach. What did that bring to your playing?

It still informs it. But you first have to talk about the government in South Africa and not wanting the music to include intricate things. But with the African music, a lot of that trickles down into the communities. When I started playing things on that level, I was booed off the stage. You know, what the hell are you doing?

In Cape Town, across from a cinema, there was a cafe that had an old broken grand piano. The gangsters in town were always having holiday there. I used to compose in that room, and you'd get completely stoned even if you didn't smoke because they were. They liked the music because they could see pictures. I didn't know if it was because they were enjoying the music or their joints.

I listened to everything. We had a gramophone that broke, but we didn't have money to fix it. So we spun the disc with one finger. I was 14. I played one 78 over and over, but the label was so old I didn't know what the music was. Years afterwards I discovered it was Debussy's "Prelude to the Afternoon of a Faun." My ears were open to this, and I transcended the instruction they were trying to place on us. Then it was "The Rite of Spring" and the Brandenburg Concertos.

I realized that it was serial music and there's this formula. So why not crack the formula. All of this music was composed by other people, so you bow to it of course. I studied with Hal Overton in New York later, and he gave me Bach preludes and fugues to study. Then he said, OK, play it to me. Because Bach was not recorded, it had to be my interpretation. So then I realized, Bach's phrasing is how he breathes, but that's not my breathing. I had to find my own voice.

What was it like meeting up with saxophonist Kippie Moeketsi in Cape Town?

When I started composing, I met Kippie. He taught me that musicians should know what our tradition is. There was this perception that people in the rural areas are dummies. So it was a social issue. For me, listening to the traditional music, I realized the complexity even just in the call-and-response.

You recorded one album with the Epistles. Is that what led you to be viewed as incendiary by the government that didn't understand or trust jazz?

The music can be very political in a bigger sense than you can even think. Here's someone who is breaking the rules. Did they really understand what we were doing? We knew it was subversive beauty. But a big thing for me was being asked to play on a significant broadcasting corporation radio show by this woman who had a weekly show. I think she was one of those musicologists. I'm sure she thought that she would keep what I played for posterity without us getting paid of course. So I played Monk's "Crepuscule With Nellie," and the government banned it.

Why?

They thought it was insurgent, and they didn't know what crepuscule meant. This was right after the Sharpeville Massacre that was a violent protest against the pass laws. Soon after, they clamped down. It became awful for all of us, painful even. At four o'clock in the morning the police knocked on my door at my house and brought me to the police station. They claimed that I hadn't paid a speeding ticket in Free State, which was the equivalent of the deep South in the U.S. then. I remembered that some years earlier, I got a ticket, but the officer tore it up when we gave him cigarettes. The police in Cape Town said I had a violation there and wanted to take me there to fix it. I said I'd pay for the violation, but they wanted to take me there. But I didn't want to because I could be disappeared. I left the country right after that.

How did you get out with a clampdown going on?
There was a commercial artist living in Cape Town who was into the music. He said, you've got to get out of here. I said, but we don't have any money. So he withdrew money from his bank and had us buy tickets on a propeller plane. After a few attempts to land first in the Congo, then Algeria, then Paris which were all going through political issues, we ended up in Zurich. Somebody introduced us to the owner at Club Africana where we played every month. When we weren't playing we went to see American artists touring, like Art Blakey's Jazz Messengers, Freddie Hubbard, Wayne Shorter, John Coltrane.

Was your music accepted in Zurich?
Not really, but later I heard that small groups of students used to come and listen for hours and sip on one Coca-Cola. We did have a lot of support from the musicians there. We were playing as a trio of fellow exiles with Johnny Gertze on bass and Makhaya Ntshoko on drums. The funny thing is we lived in Zurich on the second floor of a student's house. I didn't have a piano. One day there was a knock on the door and a piano was delivered. To this day I don't know who did this for me. It was like dream time, an African concept where whatever we achieve comes from dream time.

Then of course Duke Ellington is the person who gave you a lift up.
The club owner wouldn't let us go to see Duke and his orchestra who were in town. So my girlfriend singer Sathima [Bea Benjamin] went and met Duke. She told him he must come to hear us. I don't know what she said to him, but we were just about to close when Ellington and some of his band came. The next day he met with us and three days later had us come to Paris to record an album for Reprise Records, where he was an A&R representative. That was *Duke Ellington Presents The Dollar Brand Trio*. He also recorded Sathima with the trio and he and Billy Strayhorn playing on some tracks, but the tapes were lost until 1996.

Then you moved to New York because of the album.
The reaction to the Dollar Brand record was good. I felt like I won the election, even though I was still a fledgling. Coming to New York [in 1963] was like living

in the golden ages. I met every one. I hung out with Coleman Hawkins an entire day, just listening to him play "Picasso." And then I met Monk. I liked his music, but I thought this guy is crazy. I introduced myself, and I said, "I'm from South Africa, I think you're great and thank you very much for inspiring me." He looked at me quizzically and walked around the room a couple of times and came back again and said that I was the first piano player to tell him that. At the time many people were talking negatively about him, how he couldn't play, he didn't know the scales. I wanted to study with Monk, but I knew that was impossible. But I met Hal Overton, who arranged the music for Monk's big band, and he said he would teach me. But I had no money.

How did you take the next step?
I went through the yellow pages to look for philanthropic societies. There were 120 of them, so I hand-wrote letters to each of them. They all came back negative. But then one came back from the Rockefeller Foundation. I had said that I wanted to study, and they gave me a grant to study with Hal Overton. That's how I got to understand Monk better. Of course, I got a lot of flak from the local musicians. You come from Africa, and you get this money. Why did they give you this, and I replied because I asked for it.

So you and Sathima stayed in New York.
We went back and forth from New York to Zurich and then at one time back to South Africa. In New York, we lived in the Chelsea Hotel for some 20, 25, 30 years. We needed a place to stay when we first arrived, so Don Cherry introduced me to Stanley Bard, who was manager and part-owner. It was quite a place known an artists' hotel. It was really incredible. Really fantastic. You didn't care about neighbors playing music at 2 o'clock in the morning, and it was just a walk away from all the clubs in the Village.

Let's jump to the future and talk about your new album, The Balance. Originally it was going to be titled Jabula, which means rejoice. Why the change?
"The Balance" is an older song that we retitled. It's upbeat. It's about the concept of joy after this arduous trip that we all embark on individually. You get to a point after you think that you've accomplished all this, and you get this brief respite of joy. But you know that the road is ongoing, and that there will be more of these moments. It's a balance between all of these different moods or modes. It's like the album. There's Ekaya on many of the tracks and three solo pieces that are totally improvised. They start from scratch and can never be played the same way again.

What's your future look like?
I've formed two philharmonic orchestras of young musicians in South Africa and Milan, and we'll be doing my songs with their words. Every song I've written has lyrics, but they never come out in an instrumental setting. A long time ago I wanted

to record an album with Johnny Hartman singing, but that never happened. So the words will finally come out. These young players are unbelievable. This is a new generation. We're call it the AI Pops Philharmonic., and Gearbox is totally into recording this.

Sounds like a major challenge.

It's like anything else. It's a mental exercise where sometimes we paint ourselves into a corner. But it is very simple and profound at the same time. It is the profundity of simplicity. That's been my career.

Keith Jarrett—Reinvented

I wrote this August 2005 DownBeat *cover story on Keith Jarrett when the magazine's annual Critics Poll named him as Best Acoustic Pianist and leader of the Best Acoustic Group. My self-edited profile is below.*

The rest of the chapter dives into earlier Keith encounters regarding his New Standards Trio in 1999 and later in 2001 (on the occasion of the trio's 20ᵗʰ anniversary) and in 2008 (on its 25ᵗʰ year anniversary). All testimonies to Keith's brilliance which has again been shuttered (see end note).

KEITH JARRETT REINVENTS HIS APPROACH TO THE PIANO AND LOOKS TO DO THE SAME FOR HIS REPUTATION

2005

RADIANCE SHINES IN A SOLO SKY

The word radiance speaks volumes to Keith Jarrett.

Radiance is not only the name of his new solo CD, but it also describes the state of mind he's in on this sunny mid-April day in 2005 at his house in the western New Jersey countryside. He may not be physically beaming, but he's certainly high-spirited, feisty, talkative and quick to laugh—hardly the demeanor most people associate him with. To many concert goers and diehard fans, Keith is seen as brilliant yet growly, astonishing yet dour, someone to admire but not anyone you'd want to hang out with.

Today, a few short weeks before both his 60th birthday and the release of *Radiance* that he calls the most important of his career, Keith is in a buoyant mood, good-natured and eager to converse.

"My reputation is truly not deserved," he says, without a trace of ill temper in his voice.

What reputation?

"Oh, that I tell people at shows to stop making noise in the hall," he says, well aware that he's probably the rare jazz instrumentalist who vehemently demands an attentive audience. "It's like it's all personal to them. Oh, they say, he's always in a bad mood or he's complaining to us. Or some people come backstage to see me and don't like me to be honest about some subject."

Keith's bucolic New Jersey home that he shares with his wife, Rose Anne, is closer to his Allentown, Penn., birthplace than to New York City, a 90-minute drive away. He's lived here since 1971, has bought up surrounding land and takes refuge in his house, office and studio in a separate building where we have our conversation. There's a small gurgling brook that runs close to the house. Keith seems rested here and says his only trips to the big city are to go to the airport.

Upon my arrival at his residence, Keith is sitting in his low-ceilinged kitchen eating a rice cracker spread with peanut butter and drinking sparkling water to wash down several vitamins he takes to keep his illness, Chronic Fatigue Syndrome, at bay. Later, during our conversation, he swallows several toxin-cleansing charcoal pills, also a part of his daily regimen against the bacterial parasite that nearly permanently sidelined him.

With short-clipped, gray-tinged hair, Keith is trim and looks in good shape. He says, "People ask me why I don't look like I'm about to be 60. Well, it's because I'm always moving. I'm a walker. You don't catch me standing still.."

Even so, a few minutes later, a chiropractor who lives nearby bicycles to the house, and Keith excuses himself for 15 minutes for some adjusting that helps with his shoulder pain. (Two hours later, at the conclusion of our conversation, the chiropractor returns.)

We move from his kitchen to his studio. His upstairs office is sound-system central, with hi-fi equipment strung together with thick black cables resting on Styrofoam cushions the size of wine-bottle corks. The ceiling is red-orange and has track lighting. The walls are adorned with Swing Journal awards and a Japan gold record for his 1987 trio album, *Standards, Live*. His dark-wood desk is scattered with paper, as well as several model cars, including a red Ferrari and a gray 911 Carrera S. Underneath the desk is a box set of CDs, *Sinatra—The Capitol Years*.

Keith settles into his desk chair, relaxed. After being congratulated on his upcoming birthday, he smiles and says that this year promises to be full of significant events. "It wasn't a master plan that I know of," he says. "It just happened."

He's excited about the creation of *Radiance*, a double live solo album, recorded in Japan in 2002, in Osaka and Tokyo. The two dates not only commemorated Keith's 149th and 150th concerts in Japan, but also introduced a new awareness in the pianist's creative process.

The aging pianist, still young at heart, can still learn new tricks—only in this case there was no sleight of hand involved, just pure improvisational freedom that can only be expressed in 10 fingers forging a new relationship with the 88 keys.

"A couple of months before I went to Japan, I deliberately decided to take away all the hooks and all the things that I preferred in my playing," Keith explains. "I didn't want to be a victim of my own preferences. That's as close as I can put it. But that's what happens to players all the time. They have certain sounds and things their hands like to do better than others, and then you hear them do that all the time."

He feigns boredom.

To close the door on predictability and swing wide the portals to surprise, Keith says he had to undo everything that he ever did solo. It was like suffering a brain aneurysm that erased the ornamentation and intent but retained the touch and nuance that Keith is known for. It also helped being sidelined from solo performance for several years because of his debilitating bout with Chronic Fatigue Syndrome.

"It took that gap in my solo playing from 1996 to get to this point," he says. "I couldn't have come to understand this being on tour. I had to be at home and in the mood. In essence, I was looking at the piano, and then telling my left hand, 'Look, you haven't been let out of the cage. Is there anything you want to say?'"

THE RENEWED KEITH

The break in *Radiance* from Keith's earlier solo work is manifold. The CD is his first live solo improvised concert since *La Scala*, recorded in 1995 and released in 1997, and his CFS-recovery ballads album, *The Melody At Night, With You*, recorded in 1998 and released in 1990. Jarrett's most renowned solo performance is 1975's *The Köln Concert*, the top-selling solo piano album of all time and a groundbreaking recording in that it pioneered the art of concert improvisation with no preconceived set list.

On *Radiance*, instead of mellifluent music with expansive lyricism, a variety of spontaneous melodies rise up and disappear quickly, not be repeated again. The tunes also resisted the improviser's temptation to be named; hence, each piece is designated as Part 1, Part 2, and on, concluding with Part 17. But, perhaps most radically, none of the pieces is longer than 14:04 minutes, most clock in the 5-8 minute range and two are remarkably short (Part 4 is 1:27; Part 11 is 1:13).

Radiance news flash: In a solo setting Keith actually stops instead of a full-set segue, where in the past he'd weave melodies into a tapestry that could cover an entire wall of a high-ceilinged museum. On *Radiance*, he used smaller canvases, with the color, depth and unusual design that more resembles the flat-weaved kilims that adorn the inside of his house. This too was a revelation that he discovered in his home practice studio.

"I started to play and then would stop if I felt there was an end," he says, then asks rhetorically, "Why wasn't I doing this before? I'd be fully into the music, but maybe I was missing the whole point. I always keep a watch onstage to look at. In the past, there'd be times when I felt like stopping 25 minutes into a 40-minute set, but I'd look at the watch and say I can't stop now. I'll lose the whole flow, so I'll keep playing. But then I started to think about it the other way around. If I lose the flow, that's good because I may not want to hear what's coming next. So, I'll stop. Why keep playing? Just because you know how to do that?"

Keith laughs and continues, "And that got me fascinated in the creative process. Where's the resolution? How do pieces end? If I start to play and a minute and a half later I feel a piece is over, then I'll stop. It's the freedom to stop when stopping seems correct."

While exploring this newfound freedom, Keith was also reading mathematician Stephan Wolfram's 1,280-page tome, *A New Kind Of Science*, a book about computers and mathematical science that espouses a new paradigm for understanding how the universe works. At heart, Wolfram's book puts forth, as one critic calls it, "that simplicity begets complexity."

Why read that book in particular?

"I read a review of it and got interested in his concept."

Are you interested in computers?

"Not at all. I don't have a close relationship to them and never will."

And you read the entire book?

"Yeah." (Laughs) "I've been known to do this. I force myself. It's one of those things from Guru Dev. He said something like you must move your brains every day. So this was a challenge that I set up parallel to the music."

And the music was also a challenge?

"Yeah. I was in a no man's land. And here right in the middle of this search this book gets released. And I thought, I'm not going to overlook anything. That's a part of the serendipitous nature of improvised music."

And what did the book bring to the music?

"It got me thinking about how I had got myself locked into a slightly too complicated situation where the rules I had made for myself had been governing me—instead of making simple rules that could take me somewhere new. Making simple rules leads to more complex behavior."

Keith says he only recognized how truly profound *Radiance* was musically when he immersed himself in the material to "get everything right" in the live mixes in preparation for release. "I started to realize how important this album is," he says. "Recently I talked with an interviewer who commented, 'This is so tightly constructed,' and I thought, wow, that could be true."

In the liners to *Radiance*, Keith notes, "The event lays itself out as it happened. I was slightly shocked to notice that the concert had arranged itself into a musical structure despite my every effort to be oblivious to the overall outcome. I should not have felt this way, however, for the subconscious musical choices of sequence were made out of the personal *need* for the next thing."

Keith says he didn't realize there was such an arc to the performance until he came home and listened to the tapes. He said to himself, as if objectifying the listening experience, how did this guy know how to play that next?" He laughs. "Oh, yeah, that was me, I was there and I played. And I don't know except that there are miracles in the music to me."

COUGHING AND NO APPLAUSE

From the sacred to the profane. Then there's the matter of the coughs. Anyone who attends a Keith show, solo or with his Standards Trio, knows full well to stifle or muffle any coughing to ward off a potential wrath-of-Keith moment. But on *Radiance*, a few coughs in all their humanness survived the mix. Initially ECM chief Manfred Eicher requested the coughs be excised; upon hearing the mix, Keith disagreed.

"I'm the one who demanded the coughs back," he says with a laugh, as if to say, can you believe it? "To get his mix Manfred had to close down some of the mikes in the house. I listened to what he did and it didn't sound right. During those shows the coughs had been cues to what I did next. For example, there's one cough that determined where the end of a piece should be. I was playing very softly and I could have gone on, but that cough told me it's about ready to resolve. So, it was like getting messages from the audience."

Keith says that he told his trio band mate Gary Peacock about this part of his "epic saga of working on the live mix." And Gary said, "I thought you didn't like coughs in the mix."

Keith told him: "You're right, but it was weird. When they were gone, I wanted them back."

Gary's response: "Keith, you're even more Zen than I am."

Keith laughs.

So, on the record, is Keith now encouraging his audience to give auditory cues?

"No, good point. I don't need voluntary coughing. Besides, I can tell the difference."

Was he also surprised by the lack of applause between pieces?

"No, when that happened, I gave a little silent thank you. I was glad that the audience was uneasy. They expressed it by not applauding. They didn't know when to clap and that was so great. That was special. I knew the Japanese audience would give me a chance to try something different. Even though they weren't sure if they should clap, they were content to just sit there. That was wonderful to me because that's what I was experiencing at home in my studio. When I stopped, there was a pause to let the next [musical] thing occur to me."

In an interview a few years ago, Keith said he used to believe that his solo recordings shouldn't last, but self-destruct by a certain date. The old Keith would disappear, not to be confused with the new. Does he feel the same way with *Radiance*?

"No," he says flatly. "This is my position paper on what I feel I can and cannot do at the keyboard. The whole language is intact. There's an electricity because it was live. This album has something to do with composition in a way that the others did not. When you finish listening to it, it's not like you've experienced a transient event. What's happening here is closer to the coalescing of personal philosophy and music than a shot-in-the-dark concert. I can support this release more than any other that I can remember."

Plus, Keith adds, each listen reveals even more about the music he created out of thin air on those two evenings in Japan. "Usually after going through the process of getting an album ready for release—certifying the sound, dealing with micro-volume differences—I might be tired of it already. With *Radiance*, my interest in what I was hearing went up every time I listened to it. This kept happening after I wrote the liner notes, otherwise I would have lightheartedly suggested that the music be listened to at least 26 times before making any judgments."

While *Radiance* is his crowning moment, the CD is only the first project that will roll out between now and this fall. The double disc includes the Tokyo concert tracks, 30 minutes' worth, because "that was part the same concert in Osaka. After the first show I took a train to Tokyo, had a day off and the next thing I played were the four parts in Tokyo." The full Tokyo concert (including an encore of standards) will be released by ECM as a DVD.

Also slated for the fourth quarter is Columbia/Legacy's long-awaited funky six-CD box set, *Miles Davis—Live At The Cellar Door*, which featured Keith on electric keyboards. In the tape archives since the 1970 performance at the Washington, D.C., club, the box captures the trumpeter stretching further into the fusion zone in the company of Keith, saxophonist Gary Bartz, electric bassist Michael Henderson, drummer Jack DeJohnette and percussionist Airto Moreira (it's the same band as captured on *Live/Evil*, sans guitarist John McLaughlin, who does show up here also).

If Keith's *Radiance* is best sipped in the quiet of a listening room, then *The Cellar Door* is made for frenetic driving over the George Washington Bridge back into Manhattan, then down the Henry Hudson Parkway. It's hot, fast, exhilarating and dangerous. Keith contributes to the set's liners, writing, "You don't usually see this kind of comet go by more than once or twice in a lifetime."

Keith is pleased with the release, especially since it's the only recorded documentation of the group without McLaughlin. "I wouldn't have written any liner notes if I didn't like it," he says and laughs, "even though the Fender Rhodes was off its game during that gig. I would not have played that gig without Miles who knew I was only there temporarily because I had my own thing."

Keith disagrees with Marcus Miller's assessment of that period as Miles just wanting a funk band. "Then why was he still playing such wonderful scales that have nothing to do with funk?" Keith questions. "I believe Miles wanted us all because he knew we could get funky, but not go over the edge and become a funk band. He wanted the band to play exciting things, to surprise him. Sometimes he'd look at you and you'd think he was mad at you, but what he was really doing was looking like 'Wow!'"

Was that your last time playing electric keys?

"Yeah."

Do you own electric keyboards today?

"No. Totally not. Not interested."

Why?

"I still don't think they're anything but toys. I can get toys in a toyshop. It's hard enough getting the right audio system to represent a certain moment in music. Why bother getting an instrument to squeeze itself through wires and then pretend a volume control means something. I like the electric guitar, but applying the concept to keyboards sucks."

So, with a milestone album on his hands, what's the future look like for Keith? He has no plans to expand the trio ("That band is about consciousness; if one member changes, it dissolves"), nor to work with any other artists outside his comfort zone ("I haven't heard consciousness coming through players in so long that I'm addicted to my own band").

While he says he wishes he heard something new among the players he's listened to, Keith is disappointed. "I can only listen to a couple of minutes of performances and I have to turn them off. Unfortunately it sounds like people don't know what they're doing."

Would he sit for a Blindfold Test? "No. I'd probably sound like an opinionated asshole. Besides that would be enough to give me a chronic fatigue relapse."

So, what's on the horizon personally?

"I don't look ahead."

So, you're in the here and now?

"Yep."

No plans?

"No, never have, and if I did I would have probably missed out on things that did happen. If I had plans, even the sketchiest of blueprints, I could be stuck with the remnants of a bad idea, rather than waiting for these new things that come through the flux all by themselves. Those little nanoseconds. That's what's radiant. It's like seeing people fishing in the stream and you can see the water glimmering."

Keith pauses and he smiles. He says, "Maybe if I have a secret, that's it: Don't have plans.

RETROGRADE: STANDARDS TRIO—KEITH JARRETT COUNTS HIS BLESSINGS

1999

In an ego-driven culture, the grace of thanksgiving is rare. Too much gets taken for granted. Joni Mitchell states it well in her poignant pop hit "Big Yellow Taxi" where she laments, "Don't it always seem to go [that] you don't know what you've got till it's gone."

Keith Jarrett can relate. Struck down by Chronic Fatigue Syndrome in the fall of 1996 and confined to the sidelines by the debilitating bacterial disease, the pianist not only canceled all of his engagements but also seriously wondered whether he would ever be able to perform again. "Nobody learns to appreciate that time more than someone who was denied it," he says about the short intervals of practice he's only recently been able to handle. "Playing the piano has been my entire life."

It's difficult to imagine the dynamo at the keys stilled. One of jazz's most athletic pianists, Keith's concerts are unforgettable visual experiences. Case in point: the latest Standards Trio video, *Keith Jarrett/Gary Peacock/Jack DeJohnette Tokyo 1996*, on RCA/BMG Video (a companion to last year's scintillating ECM recording). Recorded a few months before Keith fell ill, the video captures him soaring in ecstasy, restlessly throwing his entire body into improvisational torrents. In sync with the music, he stands, crouches, bends his knees, tucks his head close to the keys, swivels his hips and sprawls elastically across the keyboard.

"It's hard for me to remember playing that way since I got sick," Keith says with a laugh shortly before traveling to the West Coast to perform trio dates in Los Angeles and San Francisco. "I don't have as much to throw into it. I have to limit myself to the keyboard a little more these days." He pauses, then adds, "Well, if I'm not really active on one number, that means I'm saving the jumping for the next."

Nearly four years since his last appearance in San Francisco, Keith took the stage at the sold-out Masonic Auditorium—only the third time he appeared in concert since contracting CFS—and it was quickly evident he was keeping the physicality of his performance in check. Instead of vigorously surrendering to the music as he did on his last visit, Keith, dressed head-to-toe in black, except for a white and black print vest, proceeded at a subdued pace, hunching over the keyboard, leaning back as if steering the notes into shape and a little later crouching as if ready to pounce.

It was the first concert of the San Francisco Jazz Festival's Swing Into Spring series, and while Keith's flamboyance was noticeably lacking, his engagement with the music was incandescent.

The ensemble interplay was especially entrancing as the trio members listened attentively, making eye contact and grinning with delight throughout the show (with bassist Gary Peacock and drummer Jack DeJohnette at one point even slapping hands after a delicious, lightly swinging number that made the house erupt with applause). It was a textbook display of intuitive musicmaking, the kind of seamless improvisation only possible when bandmates are tuned into the same wavelength (the three have been playing together since 1983, making it one of the most stable—and popular—combos in jazz).

Contorting his face and squinting his eyes at junctures of intensity, Keith uttered his trademark aaahhs of satisfaction. He embarked on mesmerizing journeys while the rhythm team offered currents of support. The trio played into the heart of such ballads as "Night And Day" and "My Funny Valentine" (the latter the first of two encores) and roused the house with several upbeat bop tunes, including Tadd Dameron's "Hot House" and two Charlie Parker classics "Billie's Bounce" and "Scrapple From The Apple." It was a triumphant show, the strongest of Keith's three shows thus far, according to his manager Stephen Cloud, and far more spirited than one might have expected given his near brush with retirement.

"It felt like forced cessation," says the 53-year-old Keith in reflecting on his sickness that kept him largely bound to his rural New Jersey house for over two years.

"I wasn't on hiatus," he says. "That wasn't the case because I had to come to terms with the prospect of never playing again. I was too sick to come to terms with anything else. A year and a half ago I'd go look at my pianos and think, yes, they're still here. Then I'd leave the room. I thought if you can't play, you can't play. I was not going to try to compete with myself after my lobotomy."

Hyperbole? Keith's not joking. "No one knows how debilitating this sickness is unless they have it," he says. "It's like if you get migraines, someone may say, oh, I get headaches so I know what's it like. But you can't imagine how bad they are unless you've had a migraine yourself. But this is a much more horrible disease." So, it's more than just being tired or burned out, a common perception? Are you kidding? I've met people who have had it for 10 years, 25 years. Some are bedridden, some can't walk across the street. It's stupid to call it Chronic Fatigue Syndrome. It should be called the Forever Dead Syndrome."

Keith contracted his illness in the fall of 1996 while touring in Europe. He was suddenly overcome by such a profound sense of fatigue that he told his wife he felt like aliens had invaded his body. He realized several months later that's precisely what happened because CFS is caused by an airborne parasite. Back home, Keith heard about a doctor who was conducting a study, treating the disease aggressively as a bacterial infection and claiming to reverse the symptoms in a relatively short time—meaning a couple of years.

"I've undergone an overwhelming amount of aggressive medication, vitamins and nutritional supplements, and I have been getting better slowly," says Keith, who actually sounds energized talking about his ordeal. "But slow is slow. The problem with this disease is that theoretically the parasite attacks cells when they're producing energy. In essence they rob the fuel of healthy cells, then infect them. As a result, any expenditure of energy makes you feel horrible. It's a total breakdown of all your bodily systems. It was hard for me to come downstairs once a day for breakfast. As for music, it got to a point where I didn't even like it. My body was telling me that I couldn't even listen to music if I wanted to maintain at least some level of health."

Easier said than done for someone whose whole life has been at the keys. A child prodigy on the piano at age three, Keith gave his first full-length recital when he was seven and toured as a classical pianist throughout his youth. In his late teens he was offered a scholarship to study with Nadia Boulanger, but instead opted to briefly attend Berklee College of Music before moving to New York in 1964. Keith began his jazz tour of duty with Art Blakey's Jazz Messengers in 1965, then a few months later joined Charles Lloyd's quartet for several years. He also joined Miles Davis in his early electric jazz projects.

Keith launched his solo career in the early '70s and immediately became a hit thanks to his lyrical pianistic approach. Since that time he has focused his attention on performing solo (both jazz and classical), with classical orchestras and in the Standards Trio with Gary and Jack. They've recorded over a dozen projects together, including a six-CD set *Keith Jarrett at the Blue Note: The Complete Recordings,* which won the 1996 *DownBeat* Critic's Poll as album of the year.

It's significant that Gary and Jack were on stage with him when Keith made his first concert appearance in two years at the New Jersey Performing Arts Center in

Newark in November 1998. "I couldn't have done it without Gary and Jack," he says. "There are no better people to be on stage with. But knowing about my condition, they were both concerned I might push too hard. There's a low ceiling as to what you can do. If you hit the ceiling, you can have a relapse. The problem is you don't know where that ceiling is until it's too late. That's when you get hammered again."

That's what happened late last summer when Keith and his trio mates met together for the first time in a couple years to rehearse for an October date in Chicago. It proved to be too taxing for him, so he was forced to cancel the engagement.

As for the Newark concert, Keith expresses ambivalence. "The show came off really well considering I wasn't fully ready to play. I wish more of me could have been at that concert, but the music itself was great."

Even though Keith knew he wasn't in his prime, he was champing at the bit to get back in action. "I heard this story about a race car driver who had a bad accident," he says. "As he was recovering, people kept asking him when he was going to race again. He said, not until he was 110 per cent. For the last two years I've been mulling that over. I knew he was right, that I'd want to be in better shape, but I also realized I was getting older every year. That's why I decided to jump back in prematurely. All the shows I have set up for the near future are based on the hope that I can do more each time."

After the San Francisco date, Keith was taking a break and then heading to Italy to test his endurance further by performing two solo dates, including one at La Scala in Milan. In June the trio is scheduled to perform at the Verona Jazz Festival (with perhaps a couple other European dates rounding out the micro-tour), and more solo shows in Japan are on tap for September. All are subject to cancellation should Keith's health suddenly deteriorate again. "Nine months ago, there was no way I was even thinking about setting up concerts. Let's just say that right now I'm cautiously optimistic."

During our conversation, Keith pops a pill and tells how he's met several people who also have chronic fatigue syndrome. After an article in the New York Times last fall, he was flooded with inquiries about his condition. (A similar phenomenon happened after I wrote a profile on him for the San Francisco Chronicle.) "People thank me for being so willing to talk about what I've gone through. They don't feel so alone."

So, is Keith ready to be the poster boy for CFS? Hardly. At one point, he interrupts and asks if we can talk about music instead of what's been eating away at his energy reserves the past two years. But he quickly backs off, "Well, that is the biggest part of my story now." But he sounds like he'd be happy to have this plague behind him and get back to the simple pleasure of playing the piano again.

In the first few months under the spell of CFS, Keith discovered that any activity drained him, even listening to music. "I got to a point where I was asking myself what the hell is music? I stopped listening completely. If you can imagine that what makes you feel the happiest can make you sick, that's what my life was about."

As he began the long, drawn-out process of recovery, Keith dipped his toes into music by listening to his most recent recordings. He wasn't pleased. "When you think you may never play again, the flaws are magnified tremendously," he says. "One of the things that jumped out at me was my long solo introductions. Critics used to write about how self-indulgent they were. Self-indulgent? Yep, you're right. And my solo albums. What the hell was I doing for 45 minutes playing solo? So, I had to start from zero. I felt the need to reinvent myself again. I didn't like what I had already recorded."

Was that true across the board? He pauses, then laughs, "Well, not everything. One of my favorites is *Book of Ways*, which I feel was underexposed. That one is special to me. But, hey, it's all in the past as far as I'm concerned. All those albums were recordings I made when I was younger."

So, in some ways, this forced sabbatical is similar to his self-imposed withdrawal from the music world in 1985. Back then, it was a crisis time that forced him to reflect more deeply on his musical vision. Keith returned to action with the cathartic recording *Spirits*.

Is there anything in his CFS experience that sheds such a positive light? "A lot of good things have come out of having this disease, but none that are expressible in art," he says. "Basically, it strips you to the bare bone, to a place where you have nothing to express. You find out what life is about and that is survival. That's a good thing to learn because it's true. Plus, if I had been gigging all the time, I'd have never had the time to notice what I didn't like about my playing and make changes."

The new Keith is basically the old Keith with slightly different inflections. For example, he says his voice is much more tuned in to bebop now than it was before. He began to move in this direction around the time of the Tokyo 1996 concert. "I've been trying to free up my left hand to play like the middle bop period where much of the real stuff of modern jazz was born," he says. "I'm adding in these little jagged things with my left hand that might get in Gary's way more. I'm trying to pay tribute to the bop-era pianists in every tune I play."

Keith chafes when asked who specifically he's paying tribute to. Still, upon a little prodding he responds. Bud Powell? "Well, if I had to name someone, sure," he says. "But I also think of Lennie Tristano even though I hate the way he played right on the beat all the time. But basically, I'm trying to hear the history of jazz as well as play into the future while playing the stupidest standard tunes. If that helps some people understand why Gary, Jack and I have a zillion recordings of standards, then good. All three of us love melody and don't like playing clever."

Obviously taking pleasure in being agitated into a feisty state, Keith asserts his opinions on the new generation of jazzers. In a nut shell, he doesn't like the posturing. Not enough of the youngsters, he contends, really know how to listen. "I'm talking about listening in a humble way, hearing where the music is coming from," he says. "This is a paraphrase, but there's a saying that goes something like, if you want to emulate a wise man, don't do what he does, figure out where he's come from."

Not only is a knowledge of history important, but Keith insists that a love of the music should be the foundation upon which an artist builds. It sounds simple. But, he sniffs disapprovingly, "Too many guys, whether they have something to say or not, are doing it because it's hip. In the past, musicians had to struggle to make it. It was hard. That's what caused drug and alcohol problems. Today, youngsters have the history behind them and the media helping them out. Success means making money, not having something important to express. All you have to do is look at album covers and see the faces of these young guys to see that they're posing."

Keith shakes his head and brings up his friend saxophonist Dewey Redman. "Not too long ago I saw Dewey and he was wondering out loud if he really had a voice," he says. "Can you believe that? He said, 'What's happening, man? I'm Joshua Redman's father now.' That's how it's perceived. I told him that of course he had a voice. He said, 'You really think so?' Dewey's trying to see straight, but it's so easy to be convinced by the rest of the world that you're not seeing anything at all."

Having been so sick and having to consider the very real possibility of a relapse, Keith counts his blessings. He's content working with the trio and prepared to resign himself to never writing any new material again. "It's too much to think about right now," he says. "If I write something that requires rehearsals, well, that's way in the future because of the energy it requires. It really doesn't matter if I ever do anything new again because the act of making music is so important. If I'm able to only do that a few times, I won't ask for more."

Even having this conversation six months ago would have been impossible, he says. It wouldn't have lasted longer than five minutes. So, Keith's slowly on the mend. But he's cautious. "The parasite isn't gone.," he says. "These days I'm thankful if I can practice a half hour in the morning and then another half hour later in the day. I'm testing my limits and hoping I won't overdo it. It's pretty scary because I could wake up tomorrow and say, oops. But so far so good."

KEITH FULLY RECOVERS (WITH STANDARDS TRIO)
2001

Sad reality: cars equipped with manual transmissions are headed for extinction. They're already becoming increasingly rare. According to auto sales records, 12.3 percent of vehicles sold in 1996 had stick shifts. That figure dropped to 8 percent in 2000. Writing about this phenomenon in a recent editorial on sfgate.com's The Morning Fix, Mark Morford opines that we have a "cultural aversion to...engaging in anything that requires practice or patience." He adds, "The demise of the clutch is where the convenience impulse meets the laziness impulse meets technology's nasty habit of doing everything for you...Make no mistake, we are losing something profound with the clutch's passing...What we're losing is 'feel,' that almost intangible thing that lets us know we're in control, that we still have some tiny degree of autonomy..."

What does this have to do with jazz and, in particular, with pianist Keith Jarrett's new CD, *Inside Out*, a brilliant live outing with his longtime Standards Trio cohorts, Gary Peacock and Jack? Well, there's not a drop of automatic jazz transmission fluid in the new album recorded at the Royal Festival Hall in London in July 2000. *Inside Out* is a small miracle in today's jazz land where market "wisdom" too often trumps creative impulse and expression, where "catching a groove" sometimes means "cruising on auto pilot."

Technique is a must in jazz; mechanical performance is deadly. Even a lot of today's improvisation sounds canned (read: pre-constructed solos practiced ad nauseum before studio time), not extemporaneous (created on the spot sans preconception).

Catching Keith, Gary and Jack live is a treat because they are so creatively present tense. They call themselves the Standards Trio because they primarily exercise their imaginations on tried-and-true songs. However, they also work like a standard car transmission—driving with the full awareness of the unexpected twists and turns on the road ahead (on steer alert every moment) and with the engaged physicality that optimum performance requires (downshifting, upshifting tempos).

That's the way Keith and co. navigated the music at this year's JVC Jazz Festival in New York in a sublime performance at Carnegie Hall. With Keith's sparkle on the keys, Gary's subtle acoustic bass lines and Jack's understated yet muscular drumming, the trio offered a jazz poetry of clarity and joy—so captivating that the house stood and brought the band out for three encores. But my memory of the two-set show is how the three played with such a radiant communal appreciation of each other's contributions. The show was one of the best instances of trio togetherness that I've witnessed.

On *Inside Out*, that co-operative spirit is delightfully captured, especially the leader's orgasmic ahhhh's and ooooh's expressed while creating spontaneous art with the rhythm team. It's as if Keith himself is simultaneously in awe and charmed by the notes he plays. Like all of his trio CDs, there are moments of lyricism, passion, fun, transcendence. But unlike any of his previous Standards Trio outings, there is only one chestnut in the five-piece collection: the end song "When I Fall in Love," composed by Edward Heyman and Victor Young. All the other tunes are experiments in free improvisation where the only material is that which Keith, Gary and Jack collectively dreamed up onstage. It's this daring excursion into the unknown that makes *Inside Out* arguably the pianist's most adventurous sojourn. As he states in the CD's liner notes, "*Inside Out* means...bringing something pure *out from the inside*, at the spur of the moment."

Free improv is a dangerous jazz sport where hang-gliding musicians can come crashing to earth in a moment's notice. But with the trio's history of performing together as simpatico musical partners, the results here are magical: 78 minutes and no dull moments. The first three cuts clock in on the average at 20 minutes. Each number has movements—not in the classical music sense, but in the literal sense as Keith, Gary and Jack open up new passageways as they perform. This is journey music.

"From the Body" opens with Keith doodling on a playful melodic phrase, moves into a flurry of keyboard statements and searching notes bolstered by Gary's heartbeat pulse and Jack's rolls and tumbles. It ends beautifully with a lingering meditation. The title track starts with an active sensibility, quiets with a hymn-like calm, then develops into a blues and excites with Keith's ecstasies on the keys.

The genesis of "341 Free Fade" is Gary's song-like solo that Keith and Jack join with plinks and rim shots. Later the drums click and clack while piano and bass play out with hide-and-seek frolic. The hard-driving "Riot" fades in for six intense minutes, part romp, part intrigue. The full 30-minute piece wouldn't have fit on the CD, so the climatic section is the take. (One wonders if someday we'll get to hear the full version?) The CD closes on a graceful note as the trio muses on "When I Fall in Love."

As noted above, *Inside Out* flies in the face of automatics. It's a three-on-the-floor masterpiece. So, what next for Keith and trio? Again from the liners, the pianist gives a clue: "We will be releasing more of this kind of thing in the near future, and it will be even more 'radical.'"

STANDARDS TRIO—HAPPY 25

2008

Two years earlier in a conversation at his New Jersey home, Keith waved off any suggestions that he might ever expand his Standards trio of Gary and Jack. "This band is about consciousness," he said. "If one member changes, it dissolves." He paused, then added, "I haven't heard consciousness coming through [other] players in so long that I'm addicted to my own band."

Keith echoed the same sentiment this past summer at his annual Carnegie Hall show as part of the JVC Jazz Festival. At the beginning of the second half of the show, in a rare gesture, he addressed the audience. "I want to publicly thank John and Gary for the music," he said. "A lot of people ask if I'd want to play with other musicians. But I feel that this group is still forming."

Indeed, on the eve of the group's 25th anniversary as arguably the greatest working band of all time, ECM is releasing two different documents in celebration. Arriving this fall is a new double album, *My Foolish Heart*, recorded live at the Montreux Jazz Festival in 2001. It's the trio's 18th album, all of which have been released by the label. In January ECM delivers a remastered box set, *Setting Standards*, bundling for the first time the trio's debut recordings—*Standards, Vol. 1*; *Standards, Vol. 2*; and *Changes*—all recorded in the same session at New York's Power Station in 1983.

Keith is pleased. "As long as we have integrity and respect amongst ourselves, we'll keep on playing," he says, in a recent telephone conversation. "That's the way it was from the very first note, in the very first session. As time has gone on, it's easier for us to understand what a privilege it's been and continues to be to play together. It's mind-boggling how the music is so complicated and yet so simple. We don't bring any baggage. We wake up, get into the appropriate state of consciousness and play."

While the band members have other gigs, they all keep their calendars open for the annual tour, which averages about 12 dates per year, says Keith says. "Normally you feel exhausted after touring, but when we play there's a level of ecstasy and concentrated focus that gives us energy," he says. "All I can say is that it's the best the trio has ever sounded on the last two tours we did, in Japan and Europe."

Gary attributes the band's longevity to trust. "We all surrender to the music and we're all 200 percent committed to the melodies in the American songbook," he says. "But, if someone had told me at the time we started that I'd be playing in the same band, even for 10 years, I would have thought they were a couple of sandwiches short of a picnic. But we have stayed together, by immersing ourselves into these great songs, by engaging in a spirited symbiosis and reaching a depth that's rare to achieve. After 25 years, it's like family."

"We've all gone through lots of changes since we first started," says Jack. "But it still feels good. We're older now, and the music has its wisdom, but we play like we have nothing to prove. Our faculties are still there, and we challenge each other and have fun."

In reflecting back on the trio's beginnings, Keith recalls the early '80s as a time where "there was lack of joy in the music. Something was missing. It was all about that you had to own the music, you had to write it, you had to arrange it. So, then I thought about being a sideman, where you're not in charge and you can just show up and be yourself. What if you could form a band to personify that? Instead of one person in charge, three could be."

Keith chose the trio format, thus avoiding horns or a chordal instrument like guitar from muddying the mix. "It's like Japanese flower arrangements, " he says. "You put a fourth flower in and it looks weird. I wanted three of us to play together, to stop at any time, to keep going as long as the music has enough integrity."

Jack notes that he and Keith had played together in Charles Lloyd's quartet in the '60s and shortly with Miles Davis, then recorded the duo album *Ruta and Daitya* (1971, ECM). All three joined for the first time on Gary's album *Tales of Another* (1977, ECM). But it wasn't until six years later that they reconvened. "Keith had the idea to form a band where we would use standards to jump off for improvisation," Jack says. "He talked to Manfred [Eicher], and I agreed to try it, to play as long as long as it feels good."

Since Gary had used the American songbook as the text for a class on theory and ear training that he taught at Cornish College in Seattle, he initially thought the idea of playing this exclusively wasn't to his liking. "At first, I said I wouldn't do that," he says. "But then I thought about it. If Keith is proposing this, he must be setting out to do something different."

So, Keith assembled Gary and Jack to a dinner before the sessions to talk about his ideas before committing them to a recording. "I was fired up after we talked," says Gary. "I was thinking we were going to just do one album, but we just kept going so that we had three albums done in a day and a half. It was very special. It was very unique."

As for the new album, *My Foolish Heart*, that too was a distinctive event and a departure from the norm. "I've been waiting for the right moment to release this album," says Keith. "This is special. In a nutshell, this is a unique representation of the bandwidth of material we feel comfortable playing."

He recalls the evening in Montreux well. The room was hot and uncomfortable, the sound was bad and the piano was lousy. Plus, he felt the Swiss audience was responding to the trio's music with a detached sense of apathy. "There was nothing about playing there that night that suggested something special would happen," he says. "But I was absolutely committed to finding out what would move the audience. I was compelled to do something different. So we played music that we had never played before and have never played since."

The icebreaker turned out to be ragtime music. Gary recalls that during sound check, Keith was noodling around playing stride piano. "That's part of my roots," Gary says. "It's some of the earliest jazz I heard. So I told Keith, why don't we do that? So, the three of us just started playing around."

"I felt fine fooling around in sound check, but I had no plans to go out on a limb and play that in concert," says Keith. "But I did it on the spur of the moment and that's when the audience came around. We played two ragtime numbers and then a third with a modern jazz middle. As a result, as a trio we found a new place we hadn't explored before."

Keith felt the time to issue *My Foolish Heart* is now, especially in light of ECM's boxed set plans. It's his way of testifying that the Standards Trio is still vital, energized and alive to new possibilities.

So, another 25 years? Jack laughs and says. "That's a long time and a lot of music. I don't know how much longer we can play, but we still feel the music and we still have a long way to go."

"We haven't rehearsed in years," Gary says. "If we decide to play a new tune, we work on I, in sound check. We go out and never discuss what we're going to play. Keith usually starts things off, but there are always surprises. That's keeps us aware of being on the edge. Sure, there's uncertainty about how long this can go. But there are no guarantees in anything, which is why I see the trio as a life-and-death situation. Every night is the first note and the last note."

END NOTE

In 2018 Keith suffered two strokes (in February and May) that partly paralyzed his left side. He is still able to play his piano with his right hand, but it's unlikely he will ever perform again.

His last concert took place at Carnegie Hall in 2017. In the past he had often exhibited an aggressive stance with his audiences. Prime example: in 2007 at the Umbria Jazz Festival in Italy, he abruptly had his trio leave the stage after he had curtly warned the crowd to not take pictures.

At the Carnegie Hall show a decade later, Keith was quite the opposite. Performed shortly after Donald Trump won the presidency, Keith set up a microphone away from the piano to periodically rail against the political turmoil and made other humorous asides throughout the concert. He was having fun and even applauded the audience after his performance for bringing him to tears.

Elvin Jones—Ferocious Beatmaster

The jazz Jones family, big band leader Thad, piano maestro Hank, and drummer Elvin, all made their individual marks in the jazz world. All spiritually attuned icons. My strongest connection was with Elvin who made bis name in Detroit's late '40s bebop scene before heading to New York to join the bands led by Miles Davis, Charles Mingus, Sonny Rollins. But it was his association with John Coltrane and his earthmoving quartet that graced Elvin with a future of pioneering drum work.

After seeing Elvin so many times on stage, it's a surprise meeting him in person. In concert, he looms over his kit—a brawny, towering beatmaster who unleashes torrents of potent polyrhythms. Even from a distance he appears to be larger than life—an illusion created by the authority of his drumming.

But he looks different in the living room of his Central Park West apartment on the Upper West Side of Manhattan—in the same building that houses fellow drumming ace Max Roach and where the drumming master Art Blakey once lived. Here Elvin is a mere human—trim, not quite six feet tall and more prone to laugh than to bowl you over with a barrage of ferocious drum blasts.

FASCINATING RHYTHM
2000

When jazz drumming legend Elvin Jones sets up shop this next weekend at SFJAZZ 2000's fourth in a series of Spring Season concerts, he'll be demonstrating why he's the most dynamic and influential drummer of the last forty years. While he's best known for his "circle of sound" timekeeping in saxophonist John Coltrane's classic quartet of the early '60s, Elvin has also been at the helm of a successful solo career, crisscrossing the globe with his group the Jazz Machine and recording albums on a regular basis.

At age 72, to what does Elvin, whose black hair only has a dusting of gray, attribute his career longevity? "Grapefruit juice," he says, beaming his distinctive wide-mouthed smile, holding his glass up with his thick muscular fingers and taking a gulp on this sweltering day in early May.

He pauses for effect and adds, "And, of course, other assorted juices."

He laughs and relates how pianist Thelonious Monk once told him that it wasn't worth the hassle quitting the little vices. "Monk said, do what you want as long as you don't lose your soul."

Given Elvin's soulful command of the beat, he should keep those fluids flowing.

"You think my playing is ferocious?" he asks, then takes a drag on his cigarette and laughs again. "Maybe it sounds that way, but what I do is about as far as it gets from ferocious. The drum kit is a sophisticated instrument that you have to learn to stroke just right to create the dynamics. The sound gets you right inside and makes you feel. I may hit the drums hard but I also sketch out all the little nuances that occur within a composition."

Elvin never had any desire to play another instrument. Born in Pontiac, Michigan in 1927, he was the youngest of three boys who all went to the head of the jazz class. His oldest brother Hank plays piano and is still active today at 81, and his other brother Thad who died in 1986 at the age of 53 played trumpet and co-piloted the Thad Jones-Mel Lewis Orchestra.

"When I was a kid, we had a piano in the house and later my uncle brought a trumpet by," says Elvin, his blue shirt unbuttoned in the heat and small beads of sweat accumulating on his forehead, not like the rivulets when he performs. "Even if I wanted to learn piano, I'd probably get two minutes each day because my sister played too. But the other instruments didn't interest me. Since I was two and saw the Ringling Brothers circus parade march down the street in front of our house, I wanted to bang the drum."

In junior high at the age of 13 Elvin started to learn to control the drumsticks and read music under the tutelage of Fred N. Weist, who later moved to Oakland where he taught band at McClymonds High School. (Elvin says Weist's widow Dorothy still lives in Oakland and attends his shows when he performs in the Bay Area.) But it wasn't until he enlisted in the Army Air Corps in 1946, playing the timpani in the orchestra and the hefty 30-inch bass drum in the marching band, that he heard jazz for the first time.

"I heard an old scratchy 78 of Dizzy Gillespie doing 'Salt Peanuts' with Big Sid Catlett taking an intro on brushes," Elvin recalls. "What in the world is this? I thought. Then I heard a Max Roach record and Chick Webb playing the tune 'Lisa.' That turned my motivation around 180 degrees. I wasn't interested in doing the Corps 'Operation Happiness' stage show anymore. I set out to pursue jazz.'"

When he returned home to Pontiac after his stint in the service, Elvin headed for Detroit where drummer Art Madigan of Woody Herman's Third Herd took him under his wing. Ten years and many on-the-stage lessons in keeping time later, Elvin joined Coltrane's quartet in the company of pianist McCoy Tyner and bassist Jimmy Garrison.

Beginning with the landmark 1961 album *My Favorite Things* and continuing for the next five years, Trane and crew set the jazz world reeling, jettisoning it into the post-bop era that was as revolutionary and influential as the Beatles were in effecting change on the pop side of the platter.

Does it bother Elvin that he's still best known in the Coltrane context? "Not at all. It's simply a point of reference," he says. "The quartet was magic. The whole time we were together we didn't have one rehearsal except if we were recording. We simply hit the stage and played. It was telepathic. We could play for hours and never realize it. It was so intense. I've never experienced such intensity. I can only compare it to what trapeze artists must experience where precision is absolutely essential."

Forty years later and Elvin still recalls the time vividly. "We knew it was special and we all wanted to hug it to ourselves and keep it close to us." But Coltrane was moving fast, making configuration changes that to Elvin's mind upset the chemical balance of the group.

He left Trane's employ and a few years later signed a deal as leader with Blue Note Records. This resulted in a wealth of recordings tracked from 1968 to 1973. (Mosaic Records recently issued the limited edition 8-CD box *The Complete Blue Note Elvin Jones Sessions*.)

Spry and strong, Elvin is excited to be bringing a new edition of his Jazz Machine to San Francisco (two shows on Saturday night with the Brian Blade Fellowship opening and a matinee performance next Sunday). In addition to former Thelonious Monk Competition winners Eric Lewis on piano and Darren Barrett on trumpet, there's saxophonist Antoine Roney and bassist Steve Kirby. They've been fine-tuning their show on the road for close to a year.

So, with this brief respite from touring, does the drummer par excellence get in any practice time in one of the bedrooms of his apartment? Elvin shakes his head and says that when he's home he unplugs. "Besides, I don't practice when I'm not playing," he says. "I'm like an MD who practices when he goes into surgery or a lawyer who practices when he goes to court. When I take to the bandstand, that's my practice."

DOWNBEAT CRITICS POLL DRUMMER OF THE YEAR: THE WISDOM OF ELVIN JONES
1999

After I conversed with Elvin for my San Francisco Chronicle feature profile, there was so much left over from my story that I used his wisdom for my DownBeat article in the occasion of him winning the magazine's critics' poll.

On his ferocious drumming—
"The drums is a sophisticated instrument. You have to know how to hit it consistently to create the dynamics. I guess you could call my style ferocious. But it's really as far from ferocious as you can get. I may hit the drums hard but I also sketch out all the little nuances that occur within a composition. It's all in the stroke. It's not the volume or how many strokes per bar. It's how you make it worth the effort. You don't try to elaborate or do anything fancy. Just keep the time. That's enough."

On mastering your instrument—
"You have to pay attention and study and play as well as you possibly can. You don't do it to satisfy anybody else but yourself. I started playing the drums when I was 13 and in the 7th grade. I learned how to read and be disciplined. I learned how to control the drum sticks. 60 years later and I'm still learning how to do that. You never stop learning and those first lessons are still vividly there."

On practice—
"I don't practice when I'm not playing. I'm like an MD who practices when he goes into surgery or a lawyer who practices when he goes to court. When I take to the bandstand, that's my practice. When I'm home I need the peace and quiet. I need the time away from the drums so I can think objectively about the music."

On keeping in shape—
"I've been thinking about that. This is the first time I have ever verbalized this: I probably run a marathon when I work every week and complete a decathlon two or three times a year. That's how much exercise I get when I perform."

On being prepared for anything to happen on stage (re: John McLaughlin calling in sick, turning a trio gig with Joey DeFrancesco into a duo date at Marciac Jazz Festival 1999)—
"Especially when playing with great artists like John or Trane or Miles or J.J. [Johnson], you're there because they trust you to perform as an artist. When John was ill, he wasn't there physically but his spirit certainly was. We played as if he was right there, only he didn't take a solo. You don't play less; you play better. You're not only playing for yourself and the benefit of the audience, but also as a tribute to the artist."

On the drumming confraternity—
"We're friends and family in a broad sense. We come together to give each other moral support. When I wasn't out running around on tour with Trane, I'd be in town checking out Buddy Rich, Louie Bellson and Max Roach playing. I'd go to a show and there would be 15 other drummers standing around like magnets. We like each other and respect each other. I remember several years ago when I was playing at Ronnie Scott's in London. I looked into the audience, and Buddy and Louie were right there in the center. It was great to see them."

On the drumming vibe in his apartment building on Central Park West on the Upper West Side of Manhattan—
"I've been here 29 years. Max Roach lives here too. He's been here maybe ten years longer than me. He moved here when he was married to Abbey Lincoln. And Art Blakey used to live in this building."

On aspiring to be a drummer—
"One of the first things to learn is breath control. A drummer uses the same discipline for breath control as a horn player. That's how you relax. It's also best for a young drummer to recognize that this is your work, this is your life. You've got to find

things out for yourself and not be afraid to take on difficult challenges. In addition, you have to listen. Sometimes that's hard when the amplifiers are blasting. I know a drummer who puts cotton in his ears to filter out the blare. He hears on another level what everyone else is hearing at the high decibel level. I prefer to play acoustic. When an engineer sets up the stage, I tell him to go easy on the monitors for me."

On leading a band—
"Fortunately my wife Keiko is the best accountant I've ever met. Even before I get anywhere near the music, she makes sure the contracts are precise and the requirements precisely stated. As band leader, I'm responsible for the guys in my group as well as their families, so I treat them accordingly. I want to make sure the fundamentals are secure so they can sustain motivation for excellence and play their hearts out."

On maintaining a long marriage (re: his 34 years with his wife and manager Keiko)—
"Don't talk back. She's the boss. Make no mistake about it. If you don't believe it, try going without a few meals. I can boil a mean hot dog now and then, but that's about it as far as my cooking repertoire."

On career longevity—
"Grapefruit juice."

On retirement at the age of 72—
"What? You can't stop working. That's ridiculous. Age has nothing to do with it. If you're healthy, why not keep playing?"

On friendship—
"I like giving rib-cracking hugs."

Wynton Marsalis—
The Empire at the Crossroads

Wynton Marsalis is inarguably the world's most recognized jazz artist and has been the artistic director of the music's premiere showcase organization, Jazz at Lincoln Center since 1987.

During his almost two-decade rule-of-the-roost at Columbia where he enjoyed carte blanche treatment, the prolific Wynton garnered several jazz and classical Grammy nominations and victories (he was the first and only musician to win a Grammy in both categories, a feat he accomplished twice) and won critical plaudits for a handful of discs, including Black Codes (From the Underground) *recorded in 1985 while still a youngster and ten years later the Pulitzer Prize-winning extended work* Blood on the Fields.

My personal connection with Wynton started in June 2003 when I visited him in the studio as he worked on The Magic Hour, *his first album in several years and his first after leaving Columbia.*

This is the writer's version of the article that appeared in DownBeat *in April 2004.*

NEXT CHAPTER
2004

IN THE SUMMER STUDIO

It's the Wynton Marsalis you rarely see. He's dressed casually—wire-rim glasses, an untucked blue shirt, jeans and gray-white running shoes—not in his routine Brooks Brothers *GQ* duds. Looking relaxed in the spacious Right Track recording studio in New York, he and pianist Eric Lewis, bassist Carlos Henriquez and drummer Ali Jackson, huddle as if they could be discussing strategy for an upcoming four-on-four basketball game.

But this is playtime of a different sort: rhythm talk in preparation for take 14 of a new Wynton composition, "Free to Be," a buoyant freedom song with a sunny bounce and syncopated skip.

While composing the piece, Wynton mixed in a potpourri of rhythms derived from nursery rhymes, Appalachian fiddle tunes and straight-up blues. Today, the tune swings (no surprise, because that is, after all, the trumpeter's mantra), but he's seeking precision. In the control room, he listens to the playback and opens the discussion again, first by encouraging his rhythm section, then pinpointing intervals where the time lags. He smiles and taps his hand on a table, snaps his fingers to illustrate what's required.

After "rushing the rhythm" on the next two takes, the quartet cruises into take 17 with renewed energy. Wynton sails into his solo of curved and clipped phrasings and energizes the band with a roller-coaster squeal and a series of trumpet exclamations. The support team clicks in with sweet thunder and dense tumbles. The group breaks, listens to the playback and grooves to the beat with smiles of satisfaction.

These two days in the studio in June makes for eight tracks, including two vocal numbers, one sung by Bobby McFerrin, the other by Dianne Reeves. It all adds up to Wynton's Blue Note Records debut, *The Magic Hour*—remarkably his first small-ensemble recording in five years. With a full set of catchy melodies and a compelling suite that features sprightly surprises around every bend, the album marks a dynamic new chapter in the recording life of the jazz maestro.

According to Blue Note, the negotiations to sign Wynton took nearly two years. The label's new marquee artist was welcomed by president Bruce Lundvall who had signed the teenage trumpet phenom to Columbia Records two decades earlier when he served as that label's general manager. At the time of his latest Blue Note coup, Bruce tells me, "I believe that Wynton is on the cusp of an innovative new creative period musically. Blue Note will share a pivotal contributing role in the next phase of his already astounding career."

Yet in a phone conversation, Wynton hastens to disagree with the assessment of his new boss. "*The Magic Hour* is just a continuation of what I've been doing all along," he says. "I'm just stating my basic proposition about jazz music with my quartet. Cusp? No. Innovation? No. All my music comes from the same source. I don't go through periods. From my very first album to *All Rise*, my goal has always been to affirm jazz. Blues and swing. Written and improvised. I keep going in the same direction, exploring the different music within the language of jazz."

Did Wynton feel that Blue Note offered him a new start? "I respect Bruce and how much he loves jazz and what he's done for jazz and the musicians," he says. "At Blue Note there are a lot of people who are serious about jazz."

Wynton says he never had a problem at Columbia Records because Sony Music president Don Ienner was always straightforward and easy to talk to. "I respect him, though we didn't always agree," he says. "But it was time to leave. It wasn't acrimonious or ugly. Just a different time for different things." He pauses, then stresses, "But in no way is being at Blue Note a rebirth."

AT BLUE NOTE

In December 2003, Wynton and I meet for an extended conversation, this time in a conference room at Blue Note Records. The rendezvous had been planned two months prior as the only available slot on Wynton's hectic schedule. It's late in the afternoon three days before Christmas, and Wynton, clad in a blue knit dress shirt and dark blazer, is visibly tired.

His youngest son Jasper—the spitting image of his dad—is sitting in a Blue Note office at a computer playing video games. Unlike most elementary school-aged kids who get transfixed by a computer screen, Jasper leaves his seat, smiles, shakes my hand and flashes a shy hello with a meet-and-greet charisma that's part of his DNA. In contrast, the still boyish-faced Wynton seems weighed down and not at all eager to field queries.

Wynton is an enigma of polarity. Depending on the setting, he can be humble or pompous, genial or arrogant, forthcoming or aloof, gracious or fiercely competitive, conciliatory or downright brassy.

Today he just seems exhausted and, given his disdain for the negative press he often receives in jazz magazines, a tad ill-at-ease. At first, Wynton answers questions in his laid-back New Orleans patois with one- and two-sentence responses. He's not at all chatty the way he was the week before while hanging out in dapper attire at the bar at Birdland before accepting his 2004 Musician of the Year award from the Musical America International Directory of the Performing Arts organization.

But he warms up once we dig deeper into talking about band mates ("We're all just like family"), his vision for building Jazz at Lincoln Center and the music itself (the source of all his passion).

What will history say?

Despite all this successes, Wynton also delivered a fair number of weightless albums that neither sold well nor were reviewed favorably. And, while his triumphs have been well noted, he has not recorded a classic or written tunes that are coveted by contemporaries and young upstarts looking to cover new material.

One wonders, is Wynton destined to be a secondary figure in jazz history books a hundred years from now? An Antonio Salieri to the Mozarts of the era? A hard-working jazz statesman and mover-and-shaker who built a presenting empire in New York, but never fully realized his potential as a top-flight composer?

Some of his most suspect releases arrived in one year: 1999, the centennial of one of his main heroes, Duke Ellington. That's when Marsalis had the audacity to shove out a total of 15 albums, including so-so "standard time" homages to Thelonious Monk and Jelly Roll Morton, a fine extended work inspired by Duke (*Big Train*), classical CDs of film scores and dance commissions and an excessive seven-CD box of live Village Vanguard shows (one for each day of the week, the trumpeter said at release time).

But because of the unprecedented marketplace deluge and marketing missteps, most fans and listeners completely missed the best album of the bunch—perhaps the strongest of his career and the closest he's come yet to approaching classic status. *The Marciac Suite* flew far under the radar screen.

It's a remarkable collection of songs for septet and quintet that Wynton wrote to celebrate a tiny farm town in southwestern France. Marciac not only hosts one of the largest European festivals but also prides itself in being one of Wynton's biggest supporters. It even erected a statue of him in the town square (though it was stashed away in the Marciac jazz museum when I visited in 1999).

The CD was the last to arrive on the shelves and garnered scant notice. It's unfortunate because it features a full package of heartfelt and humor-laden tunes, including the radiant melody "Sunflowers," the most enthralling song Wynton has ever penned. Like the Marciac countryside of rolling sunflower fields, the tune blooms with a riot of color.

JAZZ AT LINCOLN CENTER

After the excesses of 1999, Wynton dug deeper into his other responsibilities, most notably planning and fundraising for the $128 million three-venue home for JALC, which is scheduled to open in 2004 as the centerpiece of the new Time-Warner twin high-rise complex on Columbus Circle. While he has been touring nearly non-stop and recording (*All Rise*, released in 2002 on Sony Classical, was an extended piece for big band, gospel choir and symphony orchestra that took over six months to write), the crux of Wynton's existence in the last few years has been the new New York 100,000-square-foot facility—the first of its kind ever created specifically for jazz.

Seven months before the grand opening in 2004, Wynton and JALC's board of directors had raised $113 million. "That's unprecedented for jazz," he says. "I'm excited by it all because this is something that has never happened." While the burden to make the Frederick P. Rose Hall a reality weighs heavily on his shoulders, he credits the board and the development team for spearheading the fundraising. "I'm just one of many people responsible. I meet with people, make presentations, do concerts and walk people through the new space."

The visionary of the space who drafted the "Ten Fundamentals of the House of Swing" in 1998 to help architect Rafael Viñoly design it, Wynton plays down the pressures involved in its completion. "I love pressure," he says gallantly. "That's never been a problem. The more the better. That's how you see who you are. Anything that's important and requires serious concentration involves pressure. It's like playing a game that you want to win or writing a piece that's difficult. You want to give the extra attention so you don't mess things up."

Wynton likens the project to building one's own house but "to the tenth degree." Despite the challenges, such as creating a space within a new large structure and building broadcast facilities, he says Rose Hall will fulfill JALC's two-fold mission: to present the finest artistry and promote the democratic nature of the music. "We want the best," he says, "and we always want to make the space accessible to the different communities of jazz. We want it to be flexible to accommodate everything, from film to community activities to music with theater. And we will also do opera."

Overarching the entire project is the music itself. In a recent interview, Wynton said, "I just want people to be aware of jazz, to make the music available through recordings and broadcasts, and to produce more jazz musicians who can play. Art can always conquer, if it's available to be heard...[Rose Hall will be] a place to address all aspects of our music, so we don't shut our music away from itself, to suit some reductive, abstract notion of what jazz should be."

Given all the hand shaking and wheeling and dealing to cobble together funds for this enormous project, has this been a distraction from his music? Wynton scoffs at the notion, asserting that he is a jazz artist to the marrow.

LIFE BEYOND THE MUSIC

Wynton admits he's a hard worker. He says that in 1999 he challenged himself to work every single day of the year. Why? "Just gratitude," he says. "If you're given something, you want to know, what do I really have? At the end of the year, I knew I could do it. It was a great exercise. I felt exhilarated. Tired? Yeah, but my impulse was all about gratitude."

Gratitude is one word Wynton keeps returning to in our conversation at Blue Note. It's his way of saying how lucky and blessed he is to be in his position of authority and notoriety. Yet it seems at times like he also uses the word to cloak any semblance of ego-motivation and self-aggrandizement.

Though his detractors often feel he's hell-bent on reducing jazz to museum music in the name of protecting jazz's heritage, Wynton contends he's not on any kind of mission. "I'm just doing what I have the abilities to do," he says. "I'm grateful for all the opportunities I've had, for the musicians I play with, for the fan base, for the way we're treated all around the world. Look at Marciac. You can't campaign to be treated like that. It's gratitude."

When told that the word driven could easily be substituted for his every utterance of gratitude, Wynton admits that he is compelled, but, again he stresses, not in any exaggerated sense of self-importance. "The music calls me," he says. "I have the gift, the talent to hear it. I get up in the middle of the night because I hear a song and have to write it down. I'm always heeding the call. Whenever I play, I'm heeding it. That's why I've been able to continue to develop and be resilient through all of life's ups and downs."

That hasn't been a cakewalk because Wynton has chosen to wear many hats. He is *the* jazz ambassador who had an inordinate amount of face time on Ken Burns' *Jazz* documentary series; the bandleader of a globetrotting orchestra, a septet and these days a quartet; JALC's artistic director who has the final say on all programming decisions; an educator who has spearheaded an impressive jazz program that includes concerts for children and a middle-school curriculum; and the go-to fundraiser for the new jazz performance venue, which, though he likes to call the space the House That Swing Built, is more accurately dubbed the House That Wynton Built.

At a recent JALC Gala fundraiser concert and dinner, Wynton performed onstage in support of a bevy of women artists, from pianist Marian McPartland to pop diva Diana Ross, then glad-handed the crowd later. He made the rounds, from table to table, shaking hands and posing for photos. I caught up with him as he was being ushered to the next stop. Do you really like doing this, I asked him. He grinned and said, "I'll do whatever it takes to educate the kids."

In 1999, Wynton Marsalis Enterprises earned $980,024; in 2000, $725,000; in 2001, $627,500; in 2002, $713,500. The slimmer sums after 1999 could be chalked up to the downturn in the economy, but that's still not a bad payday, especially considering he's back on salary with a record label (reportedly for a 40–60 profit split in his favor). He also generates income from endorsements, such as Movado watches, which recently ran a full-page ad in *The New Yorker* with four shots of Wynton mugging for the camera with his trumpet.

He's paid well for his services at JALC with an estimated annual salary of $1.4 million.

It could well be that he's the highest paid musician in jazz history.

Given his speech before the National Press Club last fall where he articulately stumped for increased funding for arts programs in schools, maybe Wynton could even consider politics. He laughs at the mention and shakes his head. "Oh, no," he says, citing the scrutiny his private life would undergo. "I'd have to admit to too much."

TRUMPET RECOGNITION

At Birdland before his Musical America award presentation, photographer Enid Farber gave Wynton a photograph she snapped of him with President Bill Clinton after they both appeared on a recent jazz panel. It looked like Bill was giving Wynton some fatherly advice. What were they talking about? Wynton smiled broadly and said, "Let's just say we weren't talking about jazz. We were finishing up a conversation we had begun right after he got caught."

One of the Marsalis hats that gets short shrift in the press is his trumpet playing. He says he doesn't miss winning jazz magazine critics polls like he did when he was an upstart. But the fact is, judging by his technique and delivery, today he should consistently be at the top of the heap. In his early days, many of his live performances were perfunctory. Now, on any given night, they can be transcendent.

Jeff Levenson, who worked as an exec at Columbia during the end of the trumpeter's reign there, says, "Wynton is an awesome musician who can play anything he wants at will. He has such a compelling command of his instrument that he can summon any emotion, transmit it through his trumpet and reach an audience."

Last April at the Jazz Standard, upstart alto saxophonist Greg Osby joined Wynton on stage for the first time in a quintet led by Ali Jackson. While the chemistry was lacking in the first set, the front-line pair cut loose at one point with Wynton blowing fiery lines that were met by Greg's equally speedy low-toned sax runs. "It was a great pairing," Greg said afterward. "We prodded each other into areas we don't normally go. Wynton has such a strong personality that you can get drawn into his vortex. He embodies the bravado that great jazz trumpeters should possess."

Another area in which Wynton has come under attack has been his perceived narrowness of vision for Jazz at Lincoln Center's programming. However, in recent years, the booking has become more adventurous, with evenings devoted to Brazilian jazz, tango, last fall's Steve Lacy–Martial Solal showcase and most recently a celebration of Ornette Coleman's avant-leaning music featuring Dewey Redman as the Lincoln Center Jazz Orchestra's guest. Part of that can be attributed to veteran jazz impresario Todd Barkan, who has been serving as JALC's artistic administrator for the past three years. He works closely with Wynton on the booking.

"I honestly didn't know what to expect when Wynton hired me, but it's worked out extremely well," Todd says. "We're very much a team. We alert each other to music that we end up booking here. Wynton loves to swing, but he's like Duke, who ranged far and wide. Wynton has a much broader appreciation of jazz harmonically and rhythmically than a lot of people realize or give him credit for."

THE MUSIC

Given the demands Wynton has every day, how does he ever manage to fully invest himself in the music? "Busy? Yeah, but writing is part of the being busy," he says. "It's my passion. You do it. You don't find the time to do it. You do it." He contends the songs on *The Magic Hour* weren't hard to write and didn't take much time. "*All Rise*, with all the horns and the complex forms took six months. Then you figure in the time it takes to distill the information to your band mates."

Wynton says that the ditty McFerrin sings, "Baby, I Love You," was a tune that came to him while talking on the phone to a friend. He developed a bridge later and Bobby finessed the words. As for his manifesto "The Feeling of Jazz," sung exquisitely by Dianne, he wrote that in a hotel in Europe after performing at a jazz festival where there was a dearth of jazz acts. "The music wasn't bad," he says, not willing to name names. "In fact, it was good. But it wasn't jazz."

The longest track on the album is the suite-like title tune, which Wynton says started with the concept of playing a "diminished melody against an augmented chord base." Again, he claims, the composing went quickly. "After doing this for so many years, your experience kicks in. It's like the fiddle influence in 'Free to Be.' I studied fiddle music years ago for four months when I was writing a piece for the New York City Ballet. I absorbed it then." He pauses, and then adds with a wide smile, "I love old country fiddle music."

On the surface it appears the Wynton machine is well-oiled and operating at optimum capacity. Yet, could all the peripheral duties of his jazz life impede his creativity? Could it be keeping him from crafting that classic album that has eluded him?

He dodges the questions, just like, well, a politician. "All that I do is my art," he says. "All the things I do deal with my music. I'm very natural and honest in everything I do. I don't have to make deals. That's how I've been able to maintain my integrity all these years in the music business. I don't have any aspiration to be liked or vilified. All I can do is develop the gifts that I've been given, whether it's teaching or fundraising or writing."

But in the long run? "I do the things that I can do and what I can't do I don't do," says Wynton. "For example, I don't write film music. I've tried but I can't do that. If you're good at rebounding, shooting jumpers and giving out assists, why not do all of them? Even if you're a big man and you can dribble, you should do that too. Don't let someone tell you you can't do them all if you're good at them."

If there's one topic that Wynton has no patience for, it's the allegations made by some insiders at Columbia that he helped sink the jazz ship there with his deluge of CDs (the Columbia Jazz imprint that issued masterpieces by Miles, Mingus and Monk ceased to exist in 2000).

Why did he issue so many poor-selling albums in 1999?

"Like I said, it's just gratitude," he says. "I said a prayer every morning that year. I wanted to put out all the music I had at that time. Plus it was a nine-year and those are very important because you're going in to a new time. I came to New York in 1979 and here it was 1999. It's important to make a statement of intent in a nine-year. It's not a question of sales. It's intent."

But why 15 CDs?

"Because I could."

Wasn't he concerned that if sales tanked, heads might roll, including his own brother's? Branford was head of A&R at Columbia at the time. "I had frank conversations with Don Ienner.," he says. "He didn't think it was the most intelligent thing to do. He said that's a lot of records and retail might not want to stock them all. But I had been there for almost 20 years, so Don agreed to release all the albums out of respect for me."

Suggesting that he contributed to Columbia Jazz's demise infuriates Wynton. "That's totally off the wall," he says. "You're putting two things together that aren't related. People can suggest anything. They can suggest that you're a mass murderer just because some people got killed and you lived nearby."

Some of Wynton's critics even go as far as speculating that he was deliberately shooting Branford in the foot by undermining his A&R position. Sibling rivalry? Contention over their diverse definitions of what constitutes jazz? Wynton bristles. "Let me explain this to you, man," he angrily says. "That's so far from anything that's true. First thing, my brother taught me how to talk. We're brothers. We have disagreements, but he's my brother and I love him because he's my brother. To suggest that I would do that amount of work to mess with my brother is beyond absurd."

Wynton says he's got material for eight more albums right now. Does he think Blue Note would release them en masse? "Yes, in 20 years," he says.

Blue Note exec Tom Evered disagrees. "Releasing that many CDs at one time is the past," he says. "The topography of the retail world has changed. You have to be much more strategic today to get positioned in the market."

Tom admits that he was hesitant when Blue Note was negotiating with Wynton. But he says, "Honestly, it's been nothing but a pleasure working with Wynton. And the new record is smoking. That was clinched at IAJE [International Association for Jazz

Educators conference] when we were playing it at our booth. People kept stopping and asking, 'Who is this?'"

Certainly Blue Note inherited a much more mature and diplomatic musician than the Wynton of the '80s when he was known for his brashness that polarized opinion about him. He recalls those times well, especially how he alienated some jazz elders. "That's part of growing up," he says. "You can't be a puppet. You have your voice. I remember I was 20 or 21 and doing an interview and I was just firing. I was being honest about how I felt, but I rubbed people the wrong way. Everybody was saying, you shouldn't have said all that. But Dizzy [Gillespie] told me, no, what you were saying is true. But he warned me to be ready for the return."

Legendary jazz bassist Ron Carter recalls the teenaged Wynton who took leave from Art Blakey's band to record Herbie Hancock's *Quartet* album in 1981 with him and Tony Williams. "Wynton was eager and very curious," Ron says. "He wasn't brash because the music was so demanding. Plus he understood that he couldn't be on the top in this band. In fact, he seemed to be surprised at the respect we all had for each other and how we all saw the music as being number one. That might have been his first awareness of that level of commitment."

While Ron hasn't had much contact with Wynton in recent years, he feels that he's been placed in a difficult position. "Wynton's been seen as the savior of jazz," Ron says. "But if that were true, there'd be more jazz labels and clubs and concerts. But that's not his fault. People have tagged him. People either love him or hate him. If you say negative things about him, you're seen as Wynton bashing, and if express positive things, you're seen as kissing ass. But I say, why don't people just let Wynton breathe."

And breathe he will. An insatiable student of jazz, Wynton fully recognizes there's plenty of fresh air ahead. He has a long laundry list of things he wants to learn, including understanding the complexities of Don Redman's big band arrangements, new ways to play on the trumpet that will bring shadings and colors to his ballad performance, achieving expertise in playing technical forms. And, Wynton adds, delving deeper into the music. "It's a never-ending depth. You can never get deep enough. It's broad, but the deeper you go, the sweeter it is."

By jazz standards, Wynton is still young. He's poised, persistent, hungry, driven and haughty enough to keep playing with the kind of abandon that can blow the chaff away. And, who knows, maybe one day he'll even record that masterwork that will complete the big picture.

Joni Mitchell—Stranger in the Strange World of Pop Music

In today's pop music world, more often than not, image trumps talent. Melodies are hook-laden and easily digestible; lyrics are trivial and fluffy; vocals are Pro Tooled to intonation perfection. What passes as a mega-hit one year dissolves into oblivion the next. However, in the midst of all the designed-for-mass-consumption music saturating the broadcasting airwaves and suffocating the digital domain, a handful of musicians who can truly be championed as artists continue to create fine art within the confines of popular music.

Preeminent among them is Joni Mitchell.

Starting out as a folk-rock poet and vocalist who flew onto the pop music scene in the late '60s, Joni bloomed into one of the most adventurous and influential singer-song-writers of the last 40 years, with thousands of musicians, from pop stars like Prince and Shawn Colvin to jazz luminaries like Herbie Hancock and Cassandra Wilson, hailing her as a cultural hero and artistic role model. Joni is a true Renaissance artist who also paints, exhibits, collaborates with a ballet company and has been officially recognized as a poet (the lyrics of her song "Bad Dreams" from her new album Shine *appeared as a poem in a September issue of* The New Yorker *magazine).*

As a musician, throughout her career, Joni has explored a range of stylistic expression, including rock and jazz, while racking up accolades that include induction into the Rock and Roll Hall of Fame (1997) and the Canadian Songwriters Hall of Fame (2007).

SHINE & MORE
2007

In 2007, Joni delivered Shine, *her first album of new material in nearly 10 years, which she tells me is "as serious a work as I've ever done." It could well be her final recording of new studio music given that Joni suffered a debilitating brain aneurysm in 2015 that initially left her unable to speak or walk. She has relearned how to play the guitar and miraculously performed her old songs with singer Brandi Carlile at the 2022 Newport Folk Festival.*

Joni's record company, Hear Records, requested that I interview Joni to provide insight into the making and meaning of Shine. *The following was never fully published*

175

in its entirety, with only bits and pieces of my writing used by her publicity to champion the album.

I expanded on my visit to meet Joni and spent two-plus days with her, talking about a lot more than just Shine. *This represents one of my most memorable experiences as a writer.*

ARRIVING AT JONI'S HOME TURF

In August 2007, I was invited to Joni's home in Sechelt on British Columbia's Sunshine Coast to talk with her about *Shine*. "There is a deep sense of sorrow on this album," Joni tells me. "But we need sorrow for sobriety. It feels like we're all fiddling while America burns. Let's not waste the moment. We're out of balance."

Shine was released by Hear Music, the partnership between Starbucks Entertainment and Concord Music Group. It's a collection of 10 radiant songs that are at once compelling and poignant, exquisite and soulful, sublime and haunting. With the exception of the CD's final track, "If," adapted from Rudyard Kipling's poem of the same name, all the tunes are written by Joni, who said that once she started to compose again, "the dam broke and [the music] began to pour out."

Before *Shine*'s launch, I meet with Joni to talk about her new album in preparation for its release. The initial meeting takes place on August 20, 2007 two-and-a-half hours north of Vancouver at the Ruby Lake Resort & Spa (whose motto is "Where nature is the first expression of art") on British Columbia's Sunshine Coast Highway in Madeira Park, at the top of the Sechelt peninsula. The area is known as the Sunshine Coast for its mild temperatures, frost-free months and sunshine in lieu of coastal fog.

Ruby Lake Resort is run by two brothers, Aldo and Giorgio Cogrossi, born into a rich, aristocratic family from Milan, Italy, and relocated into the Canadian wilderness in 1993 by their parents as a means of "unspoiling" their sons. Aldo was the cook, the nature keeper of the property; he was reserved while Giorgio was anything but. He was a rowdy, funny extrovert who is part Playboy, part thrill seeker that takes him to far-off lands like Bali.

There are cottages, trails, a rainforest spa, a bird sanctuary, an ecological reserve and a lagoon across a walking bridge from Ruby Lake. The hills are steep above the lake, lined with tall firs, with wisps of clouds in the sky at the top. That afternoon three turkey vultures perched in the top branches of a fir tree just across the lake, which was mirror calm.

It is so quiet here and little traffic except when the ferry on occasion arrived further north up the road. Then there'll be a stream of cars that scar the calm. And then there's quiet again.

We meet for dinner—we being a small group of people, including a photographer (James) and his wife (Kate), a person from Joni's Vancouver-based management company (Kathy) and her longtime publicist (Alisse)—in the resort's restaurant, adorned by a 200-year-old alabaster eagle from a castle in Italy and an ancient organ for playing waltzes. Plus, there was the Cogrossi family crest that dates back to 1468.

Joni is a regular here. Even so, tonight's dinner is a special affair, with Chef Aldo cooking up an enormous meal of Northern Italian cuisine consisting of seafood and organic vegetables grown on the resort.

Joni arrives about 45 minutes late and leaves her dog Coco in the car. As soon as the waitress notices she is here, she serves Joni a cappuccino, which is how she usually starts out her evenings here.

She isn't wearing any makeup, and her long blond hair is tied up. She wears a khaki-colored jacket, blue jeans and a light blue blouse. She dresses casually in layers as the temps there dip down into the low sixties. She has silver jewelry on her tanned hands. Hardly a diva making a scene, but also hardly a wallflower. She exudes confidence, and get her going and she can talk and talk. She has strong ideas about her art—painting, poetry and almost as a default her music—and willfully expresses them.

Joni sits to my immediate right. The evening starts out slowly, with Joni seeming a bit nervous. After all, at this table of five, she knows only two people. But soon she engages in a conversation with the photographer about art and her theological perspectives—how the creation myth of Christ was brilliant and offers her more than Buddhism. She reads widely and the material she talks about sounds obscure, though she did point to Catholic theologian/writer Thomas Merton as an important thinker in her worldview.

Then Joni talks about the "crazies" who have showed up on her property either in Bel Air, an affluent residential community in the hills of Los Angeles, or up here. She says, "I've gotten many Jesuses—extroverted crazies, introverted crazies. They tell me that God has spoken to them about seeing me." Her response? She says it ranges from feeling sorry to being scared.

Joni goes out to the car to bring Coco in, then sits in the same chair near the dining room's side door, so she could hold open the door and smoke, which from then on she does throughout the night.

Dinner is served. There's a large platter of fresh garden salad with medallion-shaped mozzarella cheese interspersed with fresh sliced tomatoes; a medley of shellfish, mostly muscles, in a tomato sauce; roasted haddock; and steamed yellow and green squash. We go through two bottles of red wine for the table and another glass of red wine for each of us as the evening continues and Giorgio entertains with his stories.

With Joni in the smoker's chair next to me, she disengages from the roundtable and redirects her conversation to me. We talk on various topics including music for well over an hour—about artistry vs. the pop star and the use-'em-up-and-then-let-'em-go mentality of the record industry. She talks about how she felt that only two of her albums were really hits: *Blue* and *For the Roses*—the latter with the back album photograph of Joni standing naked looking out onto the sea, snapped on her property in the early years of her living in Sechelt "when there was nothing up here."

She owns seventy-plus acres purchased in 1969 and lives in an old stone house native to the property. She was hoping to build a new home that she'd be able to live in year round. She talks about selling her L.A. home, but she says she'd miss her close, dear friends. Perhaps, she says, she could convince them to move up here.

In regards to the new album, Joni talks about the reawakening of her creative muse in music after the ten-year lapse. During that time, she'd been painting. (In 1998, she was quoted as saying, "I'm a painter first, and a musician second," and in 2000, she said, "I have always thought of myself as a painter derailed by circumstance.")

Our conversation on her artistic pursuits continues. She talks about the influence of ballet on her creativity and with a well of enthusiasm details her collaboration with choreographer Jean Grande-Maître of the Alberta Ballet Company—Canada's third largest ballet company—on a ballet of her most provocative music, *The Fiddle and the Drum*.

At the end of the dinner we talk jazz, a subject that she knows well, given her experimental yet controversial jazz-influenced recording history that stretched from 1974's *Court and Spark* through her collaboration with jazz giant Charles Mingus in 1979 to her live double LP *Shadows and Light*, featuring an all-star jazz ensemble comprising guitarist Pat Metheny, keyboard Lyle Mays, saxophonist Michael Brecker, bassist Jaco Pastorius, and drummer/percussionist Don Alias—one of the greatest jazz bands ever assembled by a so-called non-jazz artist.

While her new album isn't a jazz-charged recording per se, she does love talking about her good friends who are marquee jazz heroes who had helped her to find her way while she was searching beyond the ordinary for the right sound, flavor, color, timbre.

When I ask Joni about the jazz artists she has collaborated with during her career, she starts with the iconic saxophonist Wayne Shorter, who she considers a genius. She says, "Once when I was playing with Wayne, I asked him to be on a tune. And he said, 'How can you have this song with all these sus chords?' I said, 'Trust me.' And, you know what, Wayne played it perfectly, taking it on like he does everything."

Another close friend and collaborator, piano maestro Herbie Hancock (who along with Wayne was a member of trumpeter legend Miles Davis's classic '60s quintet), is one of her favorite musicians. They first met in a studio when he was recommended to play the piano on her 1979 *Mingus* album. He had attended Joni's induction into the Canadian Songwriters Hall of Fame in Toronto earlier that year in 2007 and performed at that gala induction ceremony, teaming with Chaka Khan on Joni's hit song, "Help Me."

At the time, Joni says that Herbie had become so immersed in her music that he was recording a jazz-fueled album of her tunes, paying her tribute. Also to be released in 2007, *River: The Joni Letters* had yet to be completed at the time we talk. She hasn't heard the finished recording, but Joni is intrigued by the project and was "dying to hear it." {Note: Herbie's album of Joni's music was awarded the Grammy Album of the Year honors in 2008.]

She also talks about her longtime drummer friend Brian Blade (a member of Wayne's present quartet), who first became a part of her recording team with 1998's *Taming the Tiger*. "We work so beautifully together," she says. "It's all about the intimacy and camaraderie you have with another player."

Joni sums up Brian's playing as saying that "he brings a different kind of spiritual approach. I love him, and I love playing with him." She adds that she also likes Brian's sweetness and his ability to play "black," just a bit behind the beat, whereas bassist, producer and ex-husband Larry Klein plays "white," right on the beat, which had been a frustration she has had with his playing.

After a long night of art talk, the topics wound down to being about animals and birds. She tells a tale about her dog being abducted by a coyote. "Coco went chasing after it," she says. "But the coyote turned around, picked him up by his head and tried to steal him off into the bush. Just as I was ready to go charging after them to save her, Coco came back after escaping." She laughs.

And what about those coyotes that she seems to favor in her songs? "I've always found that I like them and feel close to them," Joni says. Changing the subject, she adds, "One day a long time ago, I heard two crows squabbling across the bay. It was like a wife saying 'I can't cope' and the husband saying, 'Calm down.' So I went to the window and did a crow call. Just then a crow flew at the window within a foot of me before flying right over the roof. I was supposed to be naming my song publishing company at the time, which is why I called it Crazy Crow Music."

Again, Joni laughs, obviously enjoying telling her stories.

I tell her that the next day's conversations about the new album would be done in the spirit of honoring her artistry. We agreed to a 3 p.m. session with my MP3 player running.

But I keep thinking of that period in her career where in some camps she was championed, in others she was derided, and in others she was dismissed and deemed to be a haughty has-been.

As we all leave the restaurant close to 1 a.m., we say our goodbyes. Joni comes across the parking lot and gives me a big hug, and at the outdoor ballet showing the next evening, we sit next to each other.

The next day, I visit her house on the acreage she purchased in 1969. It's a sunny afternoon so we sit outside her old stone house native to the property.

THE A-FRAME HOUSE

Joni's love of art is evidenced the next day at her A-frame-like home adorned with several finished canvases including self-portraits on the wall. "I've copied old Van Goghs I loved," she says, "like the one where he's up against a pale wall with a whirly and watery blue-green background and is in a green suit and has a garnet-red beard. So I put together some of these with words and images, just for myself. I wasn't going to take it into the art world. I know that, and it's just another ugly game. There are some other paintings that I've done that are more like Van Gogh. They're easier to like, but people would probably dismiss them as retro. I can already anticipate the slaps. But I like those paintings, and I want to keep painting that way."

Joni also created a new series of anti-war artwork based on eerie green, bright pink, crimson tinted and dismal gray photos she took of her malfunctioning flat screen television set. "There were pulsating green images on the screen, and I started to take thousands of snapshots of them," she says. "I organized the photos into themes, one of which was assembled into a triptych book on war/torture/revolution."

With 35mm disposable cameras, she shot images of random TV footage of, for example, a sequence of a Busby Berkeley musical washed with tanks lumbering up a street. She eventually had those photos enlarged into prints, which she made into photomontages. "I thought, this is cutting-edge stuff," she says. "I need to bite the bullet and present it." She put together an art show of those 64 large triptychs about the tyranny of wars—specifically, at that time the U.S.'s exploits in both Iraq and Afghanistan—and the personalities behind them. She named it *Green Flag Song*, and it travelled to four cities, premiering in Los Angeles in 2006 and then shown in New York, Toronto and Dublin, Ireland.

Green Flag Song takes a biting political slant much like her recordings from the early '80s where she revealed herself to be an astute social commentator with a particular outspoken beef against rampant consumerism. Still she says, "All these projects, my goal was I thought Charlie Chaplin, Busby Berkley and Groucho [Marx] all knew how to deal with heavy material that people didn't want in a palatable way…They got the message without wanting to slit their wrists. It's like the art of delivering the truth in a manner that was still palatable. It would make you cry but wouldn't make you paranoid."

While preparing for her *Green Flag Song* L.A. art show opening, Joni received a call from Grande-Maitre asking for her blessing on his ballet. Upon hearing what songs he had chosen, Joni says she told him, "Some of those songs feel a little light and fluffy for the times. Lately I've been concentrating on the Iraq War and other human atrocities. If you want to use songs about that, you're going to have to use some of my least popular ones."

Grande-Maitre agreed, which set Joni into motion to become creatively involved in the project. She began to pen lyrics to some of the instrumental tunes she had written to bring a freshness to the musical mix (from *Shine*: "If I Had a Heart," "If" and the "Big Yellow Taxi" redux appeared in the ballet).

She also incorporated some of her photo images into the ballet's set design. Not only did *The Fiddle and the Drum* open to rave international reviews in its February 2007 premiere in Calgary, but it fired up Joni to bring to light her long-awaited new album. "The ballet brought everything together—the poetry, the music, the artwork," she said. "It was the thrill of my life."

The ballet went on a limited tour, including a presentation as part of the extensive Vancouver Winter Olympics entertainment. She also made a film of the ballet, which two nights later we watch in an outdoor amphitheater on a white-sheets screen at Ruby Lake—much to Joni's delight. (A few months later, as a part of her art show in the Little Italy section of New York and the launch of *Shine*, the film was shown in a real theater.)

Despite the fact that she had taken a hiatus from music for nearly a decade, *Shine* ranks among the strongest albums of her legendary career.

"I paint music. I approach music visually in very much the same manner as I paint, layer it on," she says. "You do your preliminary sketch, you build your skeleton, and then you start putting an additional area there…It's like OK, you put your first mark on your canvas and then when you put the second one on, where do you put it? Your eye is drawn to put it to the upper right in the same way you lay your first bed, whatever it might be, a bass part or a drum part, and then your ear is drawn to put a little bit there and not there. It's exactly the same process [as making music]."

SHINE TALK

As to why she decided to sideline herself for the past 10 years, Joni candidly replies, "After I recorded *Taming the Tiger* in 1998, the music business no longer interested me. I didn't like the direction it was going. I didn't feel like I fit any more. I didn't want to do social commentary or romantic writing. I blocked myself. I couldn't think of a theme that I wanted to sing about. Plus, there was no incentive to grow. So, I thought, I'm finished. And that was fine with me because music was beginning to feel like a detour from my painting."

Joni fulfilled her Warner Bros. contract by putting out two orchestral albums on Nonesuch—the first, *Both Sides Now* (2000), comprised of jazz standards; and the second, *Travelogue* (2002), which included newly arranged versions of her old songs. "When I turned *Travelogue* in, I was told by an exec that the label thought what I had done was a work of genius, but they didn't know what to do with it," she says. "So that stuck in my craw—to be told that something is too good."

That dismissal appeared to be the final straw for Joni. She had already abandoned playing both the piano and guitar following *Taming the Tiger*. This latest event convinced her that it might be best to never play music again. "I figured that as long as I'm creating, I don't have to do this job anymore," Joni says. "Besides, I never really cared much for most of the perks in the pop music world anyway."

However, a confluence of experiences in 2005—including her photomontage exhibit *Green Flag Song* and her collaboration with choreographer Jean Grande-Maître of the Alberta Ballet Company—inspired Joni to rethink her decision to quit music for good. While reviewing her songs for a box set of her Geffen Records albums she had recorded in the '80s, she began to reflect on her oeuvre. "As I was listening to my work, I thought that I haven't really finished," she says. "There's a journey going on here that isn't complete. I didn't know where it would culminate, but I knew that I wasn't finished yet as long as I could play with authenticity despite being in the midst of today's look-at-me music business."

Soon after, Joni was approached by Hear Music to participate in its "Artist Choice" series of compilation CDs sold in Starbucks. "The company sent me copies of other artists' lists, but that was at a time when I truly hated music," she says. "I couldn't listen to CDs or the radio. It got to a point where I couldn't remember what I liked about music. But when I was asked to put together a list of 12–14 songs that I loved, that forced me to remember those songs that knocked my socks off."

Joni assumes that some artists phoned their picks in the next day. She took much longer to compile her list of songs that ranged from Billie Holiday and Miles Davis to Chuck Berry and the New Radicals. "This was one of those life-and-death matters," she recalls. "If I can get this right and remember why I loved music so much, I might have another record in me."

That proved to be the initial impetus for Joni to return to her own music. After retreating from her Los Angeles home to her longtime coastline house north of Vancouver in the summer of 2005, Joni felt so grateful to be back to what she's calls her 72-acre "heartbeat" that one night her piano "beckoned for the first time in 10 years," as she writes in *Shine*'s liner notes. "My fingers found these patterns that express what words could not." Over the course of a couple of months, she wrote four new piano melodies, none of which had lyrics.

Because of her association with Starbucks Entertainment (which also licensed a limited reissue of *Blue* that was sold in Starbucks stores), Joni says it was an easy decision to release *Shine* on the newly formed Hear Music label. "We had various offers," she says, "but I figured why not work with people who I've enjoyed a good relationship with. They're actually the people who helped to remind me of what I loved about making music in the first place."

The instrumentation on *Shine* is sparse, with Joni leading the way on piano and guitar and coloring the melodies with organic synthesized tones, ranging from oboe to accordion. She invites soprano saxophonist Bob Sheppard and pedal steel guitarist Greg Leisz to ornament many of the tracks and employs a rhythm section, comprising drummer Brian Blade and bassist Larry Klein, to anchor some of the tunes. Special guests include Brazilian percussionist Paulino Da Costa and James Taylor on acoustic guitar.

While the CD title suggests an upbeat recording, in fact, *Shine* is a reflective album, ripe with critiques on the desecration of the earth, musings on the dangerous state of heartlessness, lamentations on the loss of the holy, sober estimations of rampant greed, and a rumination on the "worshipping [of] our ego" that ultimately leads to the "shock and awe" of war. While the outlook is grim, Joni weaves hope throughout the songs, such as in the end prayer to "make genius of this tragedy unfolding" on "This Place," the buoyant "tackle the beast alone" by the protagonist of the song "Hana" and the entreaty to "let your little light shine" on the redemptive title track.

Joni also re-envisions one of her classic tunes from 1970, "Big Yellow Taxi," performed in joyous, humorous fashion as a momentary pause in the profundity. It arrives midway on *Shine*, she says, to keep the health-of-the-planet theme moving with a light touch after one of the CD's most despairing pieces, "Bad Dreams."

"'Big Yellow Taxi' is meant to leaven in this context," Joni says, "while also reminding listeners that the need to combat the ravaging of our environment is dire." Returning to this tune makes a powerful impact.

"The idea of this song wasn't popular when I first recorded it, and it's not now either," she says. "It's taken people a long time to see that we have to cut back on our electricity, but we won't."

For the new "Big Yellow Taxi" take, Joni takes a different music tack. "I came across a doo-wop pattern and kept going with it," she says. "The chorus sounds like bop. I came up with an arrangement that is very French-circus sounding and uses instrumental sounds, like the accordion, that some people may consider square."

As for the overall impact of *Shine*, Joni holds out hope that the album can raise awareness. "It may be too late," she says. "We may be on course for massive troubles as a species. I'm not imparting knowledge. I'm hoping that I can help people ask questions about how to stop the destruction of the planet."

Joni also found *Shine* to be personally significant. "A lot of this album is about my own growth," she says. "It's about how I'd like to be, about things I'd like to grow to be as I keep developing my values system. It's like the character in my song 'Hana.' I'd like to be more like her: with a lot of discipline, with a lot of high thought."

The experience of Joni returning from recording retirement harked back to what many people call another "lost years" period earlier in her career when she was prolifically recording but her jazz-oriented music was largely falling on deaf ears.

As for the jazz impact on the new album, it's not as pronounced as her earlier experimental period. Yet it is now part of her creative impulses. As Herbie Hancock has noted in general about her music, "I would think jazz musicians would recognize the structure of the chords that Joni uses as being totally unfamiliar, her melodies too. They have notes in them that sound like notes that jazz players would use."

"I paint music. I approach music visually in very much the same manner as I paint, layer it on," she says. "You do your preliminary sketch, you build your skeleton, and then you start putting an additional area there…It's like OK, you put your first mark on your canvas and then when you put the second one on, where do you put it? Your eye is drawn to put it to the upper right in the same way you lay your first bed, whatever it might be, a bass part or a drum part, and then your ear is drawn to put a little bit there and not there. It's exactly the same process [as making music]."

TRACK BY TRACK

Joni is eager to offer mini histories of the songs on *Shine*. We sit on her back porch and talk about the songs that I've already listened to a couple dozen times to prepare for our conversation,

1. "One Week Last Summer" (instrumental)

This was originally titled "Gratitude," and it was the first piece I wrote for this album. I was in my house here, and I was feeling so grateful for this place that I've owned since 1969. I'd written a lot of my songs here—nearly all of *For the Roses* and *Court and Spark*, but that was on a baby grand which proved to be too big for the space. I finally replaced it with a spinet that has an old Wurlitzer five-stop electric keyboard in it.

After 10 years of not playing the piano or my guitar, I sat down at the spinet and this just poured out in the spirit of I'm-so-happy-to-be-here. I was just ripple watching and cleaning my house, watching the shoals change on the sea and the blue heron flying over. It was cheap thrills at a time when nothing in Hollywood made me feel good. I started playing the piano and at first came noodles, a nucleus of sound. Then the dam broke, and it began to pour out.

Later in the studio I added the orchestration. I called my engineer, Dan Marnien, to get me a composer's synthesizer that had good orchestral colors. On past albums I had jobbed out the arrangements, but I wanted to do my own this time. I laid down the meat and potatoes of the tune and then I painted over that, skimming a little color around the notes, going back to my palette to see what colors worked best.

Then I called Bob Sheppard in to play saxophone. This is the only song he plays alto saxophone on. All the others are soprano. It was his decision to play alto, and it was good call.

2. "This Place"

This song is about preventing a catastrophe.

When I first moved to this place, it was rural and the land's function hadn't been designed. It contained the remnants of the logging industry, and most of the people who lived here were poor. No one knew about it. I knew that sometimes a famous person moving in can start a gentrification movement, so I've been very quiet here for 30-plus years. But now, five miles away on the Sunshine Coast, developers are beginning to clear cut areas so the wealthy people can build houses and bring in their yachts. And then we learned that we don't own the mineral rights to our land. A company started poking around, wanting to tear a mountain down for gravel, then build a giant conveyor belt out into the ocean where the gravel would be picked up by huge diesel-powered boats several times a day. The deal ended up falling through, but it still concerns everyone living here.

The song talks about my neighbor, caretaker and friend, Hans, who says, "When I get to heaven, if it is not like this, I'll just hop a cloud and I'm coming back down here..." It ends with the line about having the "genius to save this place." I remember an actor in L.A. telling me once that everyone's a genius. I didn't agree with him, but then I thought, wouldn't it be nice if that were true.

3. "If I Had a Heart"

I spent a couple of years in anger. I had fallen into a place where there was a lot of shaming and blaming, which I believe is the lowest level of evil. It conspires to having a bad heart—a heart poisoned with anger. I did a lot of weeping for what's happening to the earth when I was in my twenties. I could see a lot of things coming. Now I feel kind of inoculated to what people are now just discovering. If they're waking up and seeing it, they're in pain and they're feeling helpless.

This is a lamentation that asks the question, what can we do when we feel feeble, when we feel that things are so out of hand. How can we heal the holy earth? I may feel like a flea on a dinosaur, but I'm still kicking it in the shins.

4. "Hana"

I wish I could remember the name of this great old movie from the '30s that I based this song on. The story is about a woman who literally shows up at a house in the middle of a blizzard. It's set in the Depression and she's selling kitchen utensils door to door. She literally comes in from the cold, sees the dire living situation of this school teacher husband and his wife and kid, and becomes like an angel to them. She offers to be their maid, make their money stretch and get them back on the right track. Hana is a wily, street-wise, Irish woman who has a generous heart but also a hidden motive for being in this town: to visit her illegitimate son who was adopted by a rich family. I identified with her, but she was way ahead of me. She's exemplary in the way she dealt with life.

5. "Bad Dreams"

The chorus line, "Bad dreams are good/In the great plan," came from my grandson, who said this when he was 3-years-old. My daughter, grandson and I went to see the play version of *The Phantom of the Opera*. He was all dressed up and had been really well behaved during the play. But afterwards when we went to a restaurant, he was tired and hungry and started acting up. To try to stop his tantrum, I pointed to the theater across the street where the play had been performed and told him that the Phantom lives in a tunnel under the old house. Basically I was resorting to telling him a black fairy tale to keep him quiet. When he settled down, my daughter said, "It's a wonder sometimes that he doesn't give me bad dreams." He responded by saying, "But Mamma, bad dreams are good in the great plan."

And I said, how do you know that? And he replied that he didn't know. All I know is that this was one of the few profound things people have told me in person. (Another one was a guy telling me once, "Joni, Joni, keep up the divine dissatisfaction, but don't worry.")

The beginning of the song is based on a haiku I had written—the only poetry I had written in ten years:

> The cats are in the flowerbed
> A red hawk rides the sky
> A little dog is chewing on a book of matches.

Well, the little dog didn't fit the melody, but the rest did. So, those two lines and the "If" poem by Rudyard Kipling were the only words I had in my head when I started the album.

It's true there's a sorrow and despair in this song. But it's factual. Rather than make a sad sack out of myself, I figured, let's talk turkey and face facts. It's not that I have a negative view. And I don't want people to think, "Oh, Joni, she's suffering." If people are seeing me confessing to something, they're missing the point of this song. Even though I'm using "I," I'm hoping people won't think this is autobiographical, but that they will see themselves in it. Certainly I see myself in that grocery list of failures—like being selfish, forgetting to be grateful, focusing on the me me me.

As for the superheroes saving the day, children who grow up with those fantasy figures may end up being frustrated by this rough world. Fantasy escape may not necessarily be the best toy for the troubles that lie ahead.

6. "Big Yellow Taxi"

This song ended up in the *Fiddle and the Drum*. It's the only song like it in the ballet and on the album. It's the encore of the ballet, which doesn't usually have one because it's dance. But Jean Grande-Maitre said, "Joni always has encores, so we must have one." I chose to revisit this song and do it so that it has an element of humor in it. I came across a doo-wop pattern and kept going with it. The chorus sounds like bop. I came up with an arrangement that is very French-circus sounding and uses instrumental sounds, like the accordion, that some people may consider square. It works great for the ballet encore—it dances perfect without drums—and on the album, the song keeps the theme going and lightens the feel after "Bad Dreams."

7. "Night of the Iguana"

This is loosely based on the film of the same name [director John Huston's 1964 screen adaptation of Tennessee Williams' play] where Richard Burton plays the role of an alcoholic preacher who loses his church because he was seduced by a woman. But he's not defrocked of his clerical collar. He ends up leading a bus tour to Mexico that stops in a funky, rundown place where once again he has to deal with temptation. The song fits in with the theological/ecological theme of the album.

I added cello and sax and then electric guitar into the mix after I had the tune itself. Then I had Brian Blade come in to hit really hard on his drums, and Larry play out the bass sketch I had written.

8. "Strong and Wrong"

This was one of the last songs written for the album. Originally, I had a different syncopation to the melody. I wrote it instrumentally, like I did with all the other songs on the album. At first, I was going to keep it as an instrumental and use it as a hidden track. There was such a spontaneous beauty to the melody, and I had a hard time getting beyond the "breaking away" phrase I was thinking of when I was looking for lyrics.

The words came to me after seeing a National Geographic documentary on the gnostic gospels where two of the experts agreed that Jesus was easily amused and had a childlike sense of humor. They based that assertion on a passage about Jesus in a black robe laughing his head off at his disciples. Behind the scenes of the show, the two experts ended up getting into a bitter dispute, which spoke to me about what that scene is all about anyway: Jesus seeing his disciples worshipping their own egos. He's laughing at their foolishness.

So, the song is talking about Christianity worshipping egos, like [President George W.] Bush saying that he talked with God last night. I see it as him having a little chat with his ego. Then there are the men loving war, like *Jesus Camp* [the documentary film about the evangelical church summer camp that espouses teaching children to be members of the "army of God"]. It's a militant camp where 3-year-olds are being told to stand up for God. It's terrifying. To me, it's the most nonspiritual warp of Christianity to date.

9. "Shine"

These lyrics were born over a period of time, and the song could have been fourteen minutes long instead of seven. In a sense, "Shine" is reminiscent of that old Sunday School song about letting your light shine. I heard the words of the chorus first, but I didn't know what the song was going to be about.

When I recorded it, I was sick, so a doctor prescribed some penicillin, which I had an allergic reaction to. I was delirious, stressed out, and we worked all night long. I was so delirious that I was playing way back on the beat. The tone of it reminds me of the *Blue* album. I was also very sick when I recorded that.

When I was inducted into the Canadian Songwriters Hall of Fame in Toronto in January 2007, I had demos of the *Shine* songs with me and played them to some friends at a party afterward. James Taylor told me that he had to play on this song. I wasn't sure if anyone could because it was created in such a rare spirit. But James came in anyway and I asked him to play short figures like a saxophone. So you can hear fractions of James' guitar playing here.

10. "If"

My friend called me up and read this Rudyard Kipling poem to me over the phone. As soon as I heard it, it resonated with me, and I wanted to set it to music. I love the opening line: "If you can keep your head/While all about you/People are losing theirs and blaming you." So, I wrote down the words, went to my house in Vancouver and made a song out of it. It's the only song that I wrote up there on the guitar.

The poem is written from a soldier's perspective, so I rewrote some of the poetry. Kipling wrote, "If we can fill the journey/Of a minute/With 60 seconds worth of distance run/Then you'll be a man, my son."

I disagree with him, philosophically speaking, that endurance gives you the inheritance of the earth. My experience tells me that the earth is innocence, with wonder and delight, which is renewable. The blue heron on my property flies overhead, and I'm a 3-year-old. I'm filled with wonder and delight. So I rewrote that part of the poem as "If you can fill the journey/Of a minute/With 60 seconds worth of wonder and delight." Kipling's version is macho; I wanted to get the feminine principle into the poetry.

Jason Moran—Pivots

The most important forward-thinking jazz artist of the past decade, Jason Moran, talks about his creative pivots in this article from 2014.

I first experienced Jason in 1997 when he played with saxophonist Greg Osby—a gig that came without audition. Talk about adventure. I followed him everywhere and any time—from Sweet Basil in the Village to a rare duo show with Greg at Lincoln Center. His debut recording in 1998, Soundtrack to Human Motion, launched a string of brilliant albums for Blue Note.

I Blindfolded him twice for DownBeat—first at an IAJE conference, then at the Orvieto Winter Jazz Festival in Italy. He started his own label, Yes, in 2016 and has recorded eight new projects.

A lot has transpired since my meeting up with Jason in 2014—the year he was appointed the artistic director for jazz at Kennedy Center. More Jason journeys are just around the corner.

JASON MORAN—OTHER WAYS OF OPERATING
2014

Jason Moran runs a harried life, even if he says he hasn't been so busy in the past nine months. In fact, he's been at home base for much of the year. His wife, theatrical mezzo soprano Alicia Hall Moran, who served as understudy and often alternate to Audra MacDonald in the Tony-winning Broadway revival of the Gershwin's *Porgy & Bess* in 2012, went on the road as lead, touring the show nationally.

"So I stayed home, with some exceptions," Jason says. "I've been gestating. Ideas churn when I'm at home in the now. And I've been plugged in, checking out music that I usually miss when I'm on the road, and I beefed up my attendance at the Met [Metropolitan Opera House] by going to seven operas. As a result, I have a lot more to say about spending time outside of the jazz field."

Even though the top-shelf pianist/keyboardist hasn't been touring his trio group Bandwagon or even doing duo dates with Charles Lloyd, Jason has hardly been idle. It's not only difficult to track him down these days because of his myriad projects ranging from serving as a spearhead of the Blue Note Records at 75 series of concerts to his duties as the Kennedy Center's artistic director for jazz, but he's also perched to set into motion another creative, time-consuming task that is guaranteed to make his life even more complex.

In his Riverside Drive sixth-floor apartment in Harlem, Jason is running late, enmeshed in a telephone conversation in the other room on the prospects on that new endeavor.

Meanwhile in the living room, Jason's 6-year-old twin boys are entertaining themselves—coloring, singing to no one in particular and playing a make-believe soccer match with toy players on a small green-felt field laid out on the floor while emulating the World Cup lingo of "Goal!" and "Now, let's go back to the game."

Finally free from his phone chat, Jason tells his kids that he's turned on the TV in his bedroom for them. As they scurry away, he settles in for the conversation. He starts by saying that he's being offered the opportunity of giving musical life to a new film, *Selma*, about the 1965 voting rights marches led by a coalition of black leaders, including Martin Luther King Jr., in Alabama, from Selma to Montgomery.

"I just got the call to do this," he says. He's both excited by the prospects, but also a bit daunted. "I've never done anything like this before."

Scheduled for a limited release on Christmas Day before being released widely on January 9, 2015 (a strategy for the film to be eligible for Oscar nomination candidacy next year), *Selma* is directed by filmmaker Ava DuVernay and produced by a team of A-list backers that includes Brad Pitt and Oprah Winfrey (who also has a part in the film). *Selma* stars an array of actors, from Tom Wilkerson (as President Lyndon B. Johnson) to Common (portraying James Bevel, one of the primary organizers of the marches). Vocalist Ledisi and actor Cuba Gooding Jr. also have roles.

Already filmed and in the postproduction stage, *Selma* promises to be a marquee cinematic deal, which, to Jason, conjures up a mix of both intrigue and trepidation in composing the score. "I know how to make music for a recording, and I know how to work with artists to make live performance art," he says. "But this is a different beast. I don't know anything about the process of what it actually involves to make a film score—financially, physically or emotionally. They give you a budget and then you record all the musical sounds." He shrugs and adds, "We'll see if it works."

Moving forward artistically instead of pining for the past, the 39-year-old Moran, already a seasoned vet—and recipient of a 2010 MacArthur "Genius" Grant—has been in the I-don't-know-if-I-can-do-that challenge zone many times through the course of his career. But he's overcome the odds and sparked his way to new frontiers whether launching a solo career in 1999 after a long-term fruitful band member gig with saxophonist Greg Osby, subbing for Danilo Perez in Wayne Shorter's classic quartet for two nights at Melbourne's jazz festival in 2005, collaborating with visual artist and activist Theaster Gates and a 25-member high school band for a new multimedia piece commissioned by the Chicago Symphony Orchestra (*Looks of a Lot* premiered on May 30 at Symphony Space), or finding the right groove in playing a club date backing pop stylist/vocalist/bassist Meshell Ndegeocello.

HOMAGE TO FATS

In fact, when Jason was commissioned by the Harlem Stage Gatehouse in 2011 to perform an homage to Harlem resident Fats Waller (it's been said that when he died, his ashes were spread around the neighborhood), re-envisioning his music for the new millennium, he sought out Meshell to help him create soulful, urbane, deep-grooved interpretations—translating the jazz tradition into contemporary expression as a dance party.

"Meshell is the person who made the conversation so much more interesting when I asked her if she wanted to work on this with me," Jason says. "And she said, yeah, because she knows who she is. It was magical working with her and getting her support. She knows how to navigate. She knows how to make people feel good, and she also kept me on my toes because I didn't know what to expect."

After a series of delays in a recording studio environment to document the short series of exhilarating May 13 and 14 live shows—in the midst of shuttering the entirety of New York City in 2012, Hurricane Sandy postponed their recording dates in Brooklyn—once again Jason sought Meshell's wisdom for the sessions that have finally been released.

Remarkably Moran's first album as leader since *Ten* in 2010, *All Rise: A Joyful Legacy for Fats Waller*, co-produced for Blue Note Records by Meshell and label president Don Was, delightfully crosses genre distinctions. While jazz-infused and featuring Bandwagon's bassist Tarus Mateen and drummer Nasheet Waits on two tracks, the CD primarily features intoxicating deconstructions of Waller music that fuse hip-hop, funk, house, R&B, soul, rock and Afro-beat.

"I want to know other ways of operating," Jason says. Specifically, he wanted to get dance into the music. One night after performing at Harlem Stage, Jason, Meshell and a few other musicians went cross-town to Lenox Lounge (now closed) and played for a small crowd at 2:30 in the morning. "Someone took a video of that set, and just watching the crowd—the songs became vehicles for dance, to keep bodies gyrating."

"We wanted to get the party feel," says Meshell who charges into the stomp and bump of their version of the Waller classic "The Joint Is Jumping" as well as takes "Ain't Nobody's Business" for a dark and slow ride. "Party was the focus to celebrate and praise Fats who was a hit maker in his time. Jason had a few arrangements in his head, and he asked me to approach the tunes as an MC. I'm comfortable with that quality, so we really did have a party."

"The record doesn't sound like anything my own intuition would take me toward," Jason says. "I told Meshell and Don, I can make a sound and I want you all to put your hand on it. Touch it like you're massaging meat. I told Meshell to molest the music anyway you want to. I like working with her because she has a lot of ideas, and I wanted her to be free with Fats' lyrics. There's no law that says you have to sing all the lyrics of a tune. You can pull some out or use a minimal part of the lyrics and unearth a different narrative. That's what Meshell did with 'Ain't Nobody's Business,' talking about the church on Sunday because she knows Fats' father was a preacher at the Abyssinian Baptist Church in Harlem."

Before starting the initial project, Moran had to come to philosophical grips about delving into the Waller songbook, worrying perhaps that the music was too personal to the one-time Harlem hero. "I kept asking myself, where am I treading on his narrative," he says. "Is it about who he is while not knowing what his life was like? What was he thinking when he performed those tunes? But then you have [filmmaker] David Lynch using Fats' music in *Eraserhead* because he loved the way he sounded. So, why not invite more conversations about him? Why play his music the way that it's always been? My goal was: Does it sound good?"

Key to steering *All Rise* away from a jazz-oriented production was Meshell's request to bring in two of her associates: drummer Charles Haynes (who has been a rhythm ace for many pop acts, from Kanye West to Lady Gaga) and engineer Bob Power (well-known for honing the sonics of classic hip-hop albums by Common, The Roots and A Tribe Called Quest's seminal *Low End Theory*).

Of the former, Meshell says, "Jason wanted the album to be beat-oriented, so I thought of Charles, who I work with a lot. His pop groove is formidable." She adds that he has the facility to elicit movement in a listener. "You can't stand still when Charles plays."

Haynes, who has been working on and off with Meshell since 2006, says she called him and talked about putting Afro-beat into the music. "Jason and I knew each other through mutual friends," he says. "I have a jazz background from when I attended Berklee and worked with artists like Kenny Garrett and Christian McBride. I was playing the local Boston jazz scene, but then the world turned and I went into a different direction: hip-hop and funk. You want some feel-good music, want to dance? That's me. Now, I can find a groove in anything."

Working with Fats Waller tunes, he had to dig in to not only understand the music and its Depression-era setting, but also the person. "When I sat down to play, I understood where it had started and where we were going to be taking it," he says. "Fats played the popular music of his time, the party music. It was the pop of the day. We took it on with an Afro-beat groove and injected the spirit of Fats. Where we took it, I'm sure he's smiling on us now."

Meshell says she's an "engineer junky," and is "in awe of three." Power is one. "People take sonics for granted," she says. "Bob doesn't. The fact that you can make a record on your laptop doesn't mean you should."

Jason was pleased. "Bob did some masterful things," he says. "He would add things and the music would come back to me in waves." He singles out his playful solo piano rendition of Waller's "Handful of Keys," which swings, spins, rushes, turns into unpredictable launches. "Bob took it, and it's as if he flushed it down into a black hole, compressing the middle into nothing." Impressed by pianist Kris Davis' second solo album, *Massive Threads*, Moran wanted "Handful" to sound like the way she did, where the music sounded like it folded in on itself.

"I asked Bob if he could do something like that and sure enough he did," says Jason.

"Meshell brought me in and I knew that she and Jason had been working together," Bob says. "Anytime you bring someone new into a project, it's bound to inject a different lifeblood. I knew of Jason but I wasn't familiar with his playing. I found out soon what a great, complete improvisational musician he is—and not by convention. He's from that generation that grew up listening to hip-hop, playing with loops and of course knowing how to play in a pocket."

As for "Handful of Keys" and Moran's conception of what he sought to achieve outside his wheelhouse, Bob says, "He wanted it to sound like it was folding in on itself. I thought that's a cool challenge, working with different effects but also keeping the music organic and not defiling the sound. That takes time and love. This is what's cool: putting the music out there in the best possible frame."

Bob was particularly impressed by the level of musicianship in the entire band (some of the most phenomenal musicians he's worked with, singling out Mateen's ebullience and enthusiasm and mastery in taking the pockets deep) and the willingness of Jason and Meshell to embark on "an oddly otherworldly bent that carries with it a deep emotional level" in the music. "They did the right thing with Fats Waller's songs. They didn't take it out halfway. They were unfettered by the originals."

Another solo keyboard spot for Jason features his original, "Fats Elegy," where his right hand gently, dreamily plays a dainty melody while he overdubs his left band on a Rhodes that issues bubbly rhythms. The piece is subdued until the dramatic end. "Fats makes me think of things that I feel as a father and husband and a pianist and what my role is in the arts," Jason says. "I'm 39 and he passed away at 39 and thinking how much else he could have written and played. So, I had to play something for him that talks in a simple way about this sadness that I have for a man who was so joyful. I wanted to give something back to him."

Jason's desire to broaden his scope of composition and performance has been augmented by looking outwards, especially by the visual arts. His bookshelf includes several contemporary art books, including *Art: 21—Art in the 21st Century, Vol. 6*. The walls of his house are adorned with art works by friends, including Kara Walker, Whitfield Lovell and Leslie Hewitt. New additions include a piece called "Southpark" by Robert Pruitt (a figure wearing an African mask and sporting a tank top) and a work by William Cordova that connects political figures with musical instruments.

"I know the jazz world incredibly well—the music, the tradition," says Jason, who grew up in Houston in a house with a lot of artwork on the walls and with frequent visits to museums. "But I also spend a lot of time with different artists talking about the creative process which is very different from the way I create. We all improvise but in different ways. We talk about it, and it helps me so that I won't be doing the same thing year after year. I want to make sure I vary my process."

Jason talks a lot with his good friend conceptual artist Glenn Ligon, whose art explores a wide variety of topics, from race to sexuality to identity. "I pass a lot of my ideas through him," says Jason who notes, however, that his wife is his "biggest editor." In the last six months, Jason "jumped into the visual arts world" himself and has representation by the Luhring Augustine Gallery downtown in Chelsea.

"I've been fabricating objects now, like small music boxes," he says. "I'm trying to challenge the ways in which I represent myself. Is it just through jazz clubs, through recorded music? As much as I love that, there are other ways that I'm trying to exercise to see what falls out."

CELEBRATING CHICAGO

This mind-set made it easy for Jason to enlist artist/activist Theaster Gates to bring a unique visual viewpoint to a major performance piece he was commissioned to write by the Chicago Symphony Orchestra for its Symphony Center Presents jazz series.

Jason's twofold goal for the piece: create wonderful music and provide mediation on Chicago's impact as a community—both the positive and negative. "When I got the commission, I was allowed to work with anyone I wanted," Moran says. "I could import people in, but I wanted to use artists in Chicago like Theaster for the piece to be more impactful. What he does is collect stories from his neighborhood in the Southside of Chicago where he grew up. He repurposes objects when buildings like churches and schools are ready to be demolished to use as parts of his pieces. He's also bought abandoned buildings to refurbish for artists' workspaces. So when I explained to him what I wanted the stage to look like, he made a tall structure that I sat on that looked like a high chair combined with a shoeshine stand."

When Jason told Theaster that he needed music stands, he showed him pictures from a variety of bands led by such leaders as Duke Ellington, Chick Webb and Count Basie.

"See what I mean?" Jason asked.

"I got it," Theaster said.

Two days later Theaster returned. "He made these long music stands out of wood from old houses," says Jason. "I just salivated. In fact, we converted one of those stands to be a coffin in the piece. Theaster is an object maker as well as a performance artist—he sings well, knows pacing and how to improvise. I relied on him to have a conversation about how to put this piece together. We didn't talk about music. We tried to look at the why and what kind of performance this would be."

(After the May 30 premiere of *Looks of a Lot*—the name based on Chicago rapper Lil Durk's quote about a swarm of police cars at a gig he was playing: "Looks a lot of blues"—Jason wrote on his Facebook page: "Theaster Gates works were all across the stage, making the space feel like an old new home.")

During Jason's envisioning period of what the piece would be like, he visited the *DownBeat* office in the Chicago suburbs to look at the magazine's archives as a part of his research. "I realized how valuable the magazine has been historically because it was documenting black music and a culture in America," Jason says. "*DownBeat* was collecting all these stories and housing them over the years. It's major, just like what the Chicago-based Ebony and Jet magazines were doing."

Jason sought to celebrate Chicago: "I wanted to show my deep love for the city," he says. "I have family there and I cherish the free-thinking jazz artists from Chicago like Andrew Hill, Steve Coleman, George Lewis and Henry Threadgill who left their fingerprints all over my brain. I also knew that Chicago is a city that deals with pain consistently, weekly. There's something wrong when you have people who don't mind killing others. You have to make music that looks at that. That's my job: to look at it head on."

As a result of seeing the Kenwood Academy Jazz Band perform at the 2013 Chicago Jazz Festival (on the recommendation of Chicago piano legend Willie Pickens whose daughter Bethany Pickens, also a pianist, was assistant band director), Jason began to think about how fitting it would be to enlist them as his band for the performance. "I could call anyone to play with me, but I thought, wouldn't it be great to work with 25 kids who have no idea who I am and use their energy in this piece," Jason says. "It would totally transform it. I wrote Bethany on the plane on my way home that I think your kids need to be a part of this thing I'm writing. I told her not to tell anyone yet, but my intuition told me that I had to do it."

Jason returned to Chicago on February 20 and met the students, who didn't have a clue as to who he was. But they liked his energy and asked him when he was coming back. He told them soon, and then he told them to make sure they had May 30 free because "you have a gig with me that night at Orchestra Hall at Symphony Center."

He returned to rehearse and even did a May 8 Skype rehearsal with the band on the score that included his arrangement of Chicago trumpeter Roy Eldridge's "Wabash Stomp."

With band director Gerald Powell, the students began to take shape and get ready for the grand show. "You see the kids' strengths," Jason says. "They weren't at a level of close to perfect—playing wrong notes, being out of tune at times—but hey, that's real and so beautiful. We combined all that with the sound and as a band we made beautiful, organic music. It was mega emotional for all of us."

(Other guests, including Bandwagon and Chicago saxophonist Ken Vandermark, contributed to Jason's 90-minute, evening-long opus, which among new originals also references Franz Schubert/Heinrich Heine's anguished, tragic song "Der Doppleganger" and Edward Elgar's "Pomp And Circumstance, March No. 1".)

At the beginning of *Looks of a Lot*, Deborah Rutter, president of the Chicago Symphony Orchestra Association, made the announcement that a Kenwood member was missing. Less than two weeks earlier on May 22 15-year-old guitarist Aaron Rushing was killed by gunfire—another victim of the violence that has plagued

Chicago. Rutter also dedicated the show to another 15-year-older who had also recently been gunned down. The announcement was a poignant reminder to Jason and his band mates that they were playing at the front lines of a societal calamity.

"Unfortunately I never met Aaron," Jason says. "Whenever I was there, he wasn't. But I'd hear kids and directors talk about him. He was going to play that concert. I didn't really have that deep a relationship with the kids because I wasn't there much, but I knew it was rough on them, especially at the point in the piece where each band member plays a drone of notes in meditation as they pass a casket."

Writing in Facebook, Jason reflected on the show: "We all meditated on the impact the city continues to have, in both lightness and darkness…A lot of glory was given. I broke down a few times during the performance, as I had not anticipated the weight of expressing any of these sonic feelings in front of an audience. Fortunately with the warm audience, it was as if we were all holding each other's hands, to help us through each moment…"

Looks of a Lot proved to be a triumphant concert that lit up the audience of 2,000. In the aftermath, does Jason think that was a one-shot deal?

"I'm trying to figure that out now," he says. "Deborah Rutter was hired by the Kennedy Center to be its new president, so we've been talking. The same issue of violence is at work in other cities, so maybe I could do a tour and use kids from other cities. But I would love to take the Kenwood kids with me anywhere I perform this, especially in D.C. This piece was really built by the students there. They were as much a part of the compositional process as I was. I want to honor that because they gave a lot to have the piece come out the way it did."

Astor Piazzolla–
Nuevo Tango Pioneer

For years, Argentine native Astor Piazzolla was widely celebrated in Europe for his creative output. Finally, even Argentina recognized that he was an important artist as a cultural pioneer who challenged the old tango traditions.

But his appreciation in the United States came late in his life. What finally woke people up came in the late 1980s when the maestro recorded for saxophonist Kit Hanrahan's indie label, American Clavé. *The word slowly spread in 1986 when Astor recorded his masterpiece,* Tango: Zero Hour.

However, although distribution of Astor's work was weak, it found its way to aware open ears.

Sadly, his work only came to greater visibility posthumously in 1998 when Nonesuch Records licensed three of Kip's produced albums with Astor for reissue (including Tango: Zero Hour; La Camorra: The Solitude of Passionate Provocation; *and* The Rough Dancer and the Cyclical Night (Tango Apasionado)).

In May 2022, Nonesuch championed Astor again by releasing for the first time Kip's albums in a remastered three-LP/three-CD box set, Astor Piazzolla: The American Clavé Recordings.

After suffering a debilitating stroke two years after our conversation, Astor died the following year at the age of 71. But today his life continues to be honored as a legendary artist who cut across many genres and traditions. His recorded music lives on.

ASTOR PIAZZOLLA–THE POLITICS OF TAMPERING WITH TRADITION
1989

In a 1989 phone interview from Argentina, bandoneón maestro and dynamic composer Astor Piazzolla tells me that when he comes to the San Francisco Bay Area to perform, he and his sextet will express the spirit of nuevo tango in a chamber music-like setting. He'll be presenting newly arranged compositions from his most recent album, the fiery, soulful *Tango: Zero Hour* which he considered to be his greatest record.

It was recorded in Manhattan in 1986 for adventurous jazz avant-ethnic fusion saxophonist Kip Hanrahan's American Clavé Records. Astor also introduces new pieces composed and arranged for two bandoneóns—larger than accordions with a wide wing span and tonal range. First stop: Zellerbach Hall in Berkeley that showcases Astor's turbulent, complex, unpredictable brilliance on May 10.

Astor is the father of nuevo tango, the passionate, brooding contemporary style of tango. It is influenced as much by the shifting melodies and harmonic beauty of modern classical composers and the complex improvisational patterns of jazz as it is by traditional tango.

One of modern music's most extraordinary innovators, Astor says that his tango doesn't fit into the box people typically think of. "I don't write for tango dancing," he says. "But my compositions make you feel like something is walking inside of you when you hear them. You don't dance with your feet, but you dance inside."

He has been quoted as saying that "zero hour" is "an hour of absolute end and absolute beginning."

That so perfectly describes Astor's Zellerbach excursion. In command of the rhythm-fueled bellows of his instrument, he leads his band of improvisers The New Tango Quintet into his demanding compositions of extended harmonies and surprising counterpoints. The tunes are angular and edgy and then romantically soulful. The movement is rapid where the hard driving propelled by the bandoneón swerves into a syncopation of jerky accents. The music changes directions suddenly with intense force amidst the memorable harmonies. His long-time violinist Fernando Suárez Paz plays free zipping sounds in speedy support.

While Astor delves into stormy drama in each number, there's also romance on "Milonga Del Angel" (the calming ballad that erupts into a forceful end) and a whimsical sentiment in pockets, such as on the fast-paced "Milonga Loca" that enlivens with emotion. The crowd erupts into applause at the conclusion of Astor's memorable concert.

After his exhilarating show, I go backstage to meet the master. He is a gentle, diminutive man, eager to smile. He shakes my hands to thank me for my interview with him. His knuckles are arthritically deformed, his fingers curled over. Not pretty, but powerful. He laughs and says, "This is what happens as you play the bandoneón as much as I have throughout my life."

Astor was born in Argentina in 1921 to Italian parents. In 1924 he emigrated with his mother and father to New York City's Little Italy where he learned how to play the bandoneón (the German button accordion—tango's quintessential instrument). But Astor also learned street toughness in poor New York neighborhoods through street fights and sparring matches with soon-to-be professional boxing heroes Rocky Graziano and Jake LaMotta. He also experienced the sidewalk soundscape of Cab Calloway playing in a Harlem club.

Astor moved back to Argentina in 1937, and in 1954 left for Paris to study on a scholarship with the highly regarded composition teacher Nadia Boulanger. As he notes in the following conversation, that experience was life changing.

Fully invigorated, Astor returned to Buenos Aires in 1955 and began his crusade to revolutionize the tango genre, raising the ire of many Argentines unwilling to see their beloved dance and music form undergo the radical avant-garde innovations he explored. After many years of personal and physical persecution in his native land—and even threatened exile at one point— Astor fled his country during the military coup d'état from 1976 to '83. He settled in Italy with strategic visits back home to play with like-minded friends.

Today, back in Buenos Aires, Astor notes in our telephone conversation that his return had everything to do with the ousting of the military dictatorship, which had not taken kindly to the rebellious nature of his nuevo tango. "I don't know of any military leaders in Argentina who love music," he says. "They hate everything that has nothing to do with the military. They don't appreciate the beautiful things in life. You won't see them at concerts or art galleries. They only like to get up at 5 a.m. and give orders. I came back to Argentina after several years because democracy is back."

Our conversion begins.

What is tango and how did tango, as a musical genre, develop?
It started as a low class form of entertainment that evolved out of an African dance rhythm called *milonga*. Tango had very similar origins to jazz. While jazz came out of the disreputable sections of New Orleans, tango music originated in the slums of Buenos Aires at whorehouses where there was a lot of alcohol consumption and a lot of prostitutes and activity between police and gang members.

The dance and music aspects of tango that developed together in the 1890s were expressive, aggressive and very energetic. The dance part of it was considered to be in very bad taste. The Pope even prohibited it. You couldn't get women to dance it. So, these tough guys from the underworld used to dance the tango together.

How does nuevo tango differ from the tango we are familiar with from the dance styles of the '30s?
Today there are three different types of tango. There's the dancing that you see in the Broadway play *Tango Argentina*. That's a style from the 1930s and '40s that has nothing to do with nuevo tango. Then there's the tango where the emphasis is on lyrics and vocals derived from the earlier slum tango. The kind of tango that I play is contemporary tango and is a form of chamber music. It has very little connection to the other two types of tango except that it's based on passion.

How, and when, did you first become involved in tango?
My first exposure came when I was thirteen. I worked with singer-songwriter Carlos Gardel in New York City on some recordings and in film. My father was in love

with his singing, so he pushed me to work with him. I was playing Bach, Chopin, Beethoven and Mozart on my bandoneón. The first tangos I played were with Carlos.

I don't write for tango dancing. Tango fans in Argentina still don't understand what I'm doing. That holds true for other parts of the world where tango is still associated with vulgarity and sexiness. My tango is simply music. That's why I call it nuevo tango to differentiate it from the other forms of tango expression.

Weren't you exposed to tango in your native Argentina as well?

After living in New York from 1924 to 1937, my family moved back to Argentina. I started listening to small groups of tango musicians who were playing an instrumental kind of tango that I loved. That's when I became convinced that there was potential within the tango format to explore new instrumental arrangements. I started imitating the tango orchestras that grew larger. For example, when tango first started at the turn of the century, there was only one bandoneón in the small groups. In the '40s there would be as many as four bandoneóns in a larger tango orchestra. But after a while I got bored with what they were doing because there wasn't tolerance for tampering with the traditional style.

When did you begin to see the potential for nuevo tango?

A turning point for me came in 1954 when I received a scholarship to study with Nadia Boulanger in Paris. I am what I am today thanks to her. Back when I first started to study with her, I was writing contemporary music and symphonies, which she was analyzing. Finally, one day she told me, "This music is very well written, but I don't find Piazzolla in it." She then asked me what kind of music I played because she knew I was making my living by being a musician.

I was very much ashamed to tell Nadia that I was playing tango music. She said, "Oh, that's wonderful. I like tango very much." Then she asked me what my instrument was because she knew I couldn't play the piano very well. Again, I was ashamed to tell her that I played the bandoneón that was considered to be a very low-class instrument in Argentina at the time. Of course, now everyone wants to play it.

Nadia got very excited and asked me to play some of my music. I played eight bars of one of my tango compositions. When she heard that music, she took my two hands and said, "This is Astor Piazzolla. Never leave it. The other music, throw it away!" So, I threw away all the other music I had been writing and focused on writing tangos. And I haven't stopped since that day in 1954.

When I returned to Argentina, I started my war against everybody. It was me against anybody else who didn't understand my music. I began working with complex musical arrangements in my tangos, using counterpoints, fugues and unusual harmonies. The only people who embraced my music were young people and students. I started giving concerts at universities, which helped to inspire young people to listen to tango.

Since tango is considered a national treasure and even sacred to many Argentines, you must have been considered a subversive.

I was definitely seen as a rebel. I like to be called one. I've always liked doing what I'm not supposed to do. As long as people let me compose and perform my nuevo tango, I'm a very happy person. I've had a lot of experience with people wanting me to conform to their expectations. The most common occurrence is people wanting me to play dance tango.

I'm more interested in moving people to think when I play. That's why I got involved in nuevo tango. It's like Beethoven and Bartók. It forces you to listen and think. Nowadays people don't expect to hear dance tango when they come to hear me play. They know I'm doing something different. They come out of love for the music even though it sounds strange to them sometimes. Yet they know that they can hear and feel the pulse of the tango rhythms at the root of my music.

But it wasn't always the case that audiences knew what to expect from your performances. Early on, weren't there some very violent reactions against what you were doing?

My most dramatic experiences trying to play nuevo tango came in the 1960s when my band and I would get calls to play tango dances. Those shows were necessary if we wanted work, but it was tough because people stopped dancing soon after we started to play. They said my work didn't have a strong enough dance rhythm. Plus, that's when I started writing compositions to be played with an electric guitar in the band. People cursed and insulted us. Some were so upset they threatened to beat me up. Fortunately, I was raised in New York where I had learned to fight. It took us four or five years to finally get hired for shows where people would come only to listen.

You've worked with many jazz musicians over the years. How much has jazz influenced nuevo tango?

It's been very important to my experimenting with tango. I always felt that traditional tango music was boring. After listening to musicians like Charlie Parker, Gerry Mulligan and Miles Davis, I began to think of jazz possibilities in tango. The main difference between nuevo tango and jazz is that while jazz relies on a lot of improvisation by the musicians, my tango pieces are ninety-nine percent composed and one percent improvised. What I have learned from jazz is to allow for a great liberty of expression. For example, when I play a melody, I can turn it upside down and inside out so that it takes on the quality of improvisation.

Another important thing I learned from jazz artists was to have fun while performing. I always saw good jazz players enjoying themselves, which was never the case with tango artists. Tango is very dramatic and lonesome music. Sometimes I refer to it as black tango. Even though it will never be happy music, I decided that playing tango was going to be an enjoyable experience for my band and me.

Why is tango so melancholic?

It's dark music because it was the music of Italian, Spanish, French, German, Polish and Jewish immigrants in Argentina. Most of these people had to leave their homes and move to a new country to work. Their music was integrated into tango. Tango has also represented the lower classes in society, the people who have to struggle in life.

The lower class loves tango. There might be some fans in the upper class in Argentina, but you won't find one tango musician here from that social class. All the tango musicians, poets and composers come from the lower Argentine classes.

In the liner notes to your Libertango album, which you recorded in Milan in 1974, you wrote that "the artist who has no desire to experiment, to feel new sensations, is a dead artist." Fifteen years later, are you still experimenting with tango?

My goals are to keep my tango important, to go on experimenting, to make new innovations, to amaze my audience as well as myself. Last year when I toured the States with my quintet, my music and arrangements were very romantic. Now my music sounds religious. The music is composed for two bandoneóns. The bandoneón originated from the organ and harmonium, both of which are important church instruments. When I write for both bandoneóns, I try to make them sound like an organ or harmonium, which creates a religious sound in the middle.

The most beautiful thing about being an artist is being understood. The most terrible experience is when people who do something different are not understood. They insult you and won't let you work. I don't write for people to like me. What's most important is when my fans tell me, "That's good music. Thank you for the passion you put into your performance." In the last twenty years, I've been very fortunate. I think people are finally embracing nuevo tango because it's a new expression. It's a reflection of the new culture of Buenos Aires and the culture of Argentina.

Lou Reed—Ecstasy and Poe

My wife and I often attended the weekend string-quartet performances in the hallway above the Great Hall entry way at the Metropolitan Museum of Art. It was a quiet fall evening in 2001. The crowds had all but disappeared. We spent some time there but then were ready to go home. We looked downstairs at the entry way, and we spotted Lou Reed and his wife Laurie Anderson entering.

I had recently interviewed both Lou and Laurie for the San Francisco Chronicle. I asked my wife if she'd like to meet Laurie, who by the time we got downstairs was in the lobby herself. We went up to her and she greeted us warmly.

We talked a little before I asked her where Lou had gone. "After all these years, he was never a member of the Met," she said. "He's taking care of that now."

Then Lou returned with a suspicious look as if two strangers were interloping on his quiet night out. Laurie calmly settled him down and said, "It's Dan. Remember doing interviews with him?"

Lou smiled and said, "Oh yeah. He's one of the good ones."

Included here are conversations on Lou's latter-day solo studio albums: 2000's Ecstasy and 2003's The Raven. At the time, while still an iconic figure, Lou was not widely covered in his creative journey that he believed was the best work he had ever done.

At age 71, Lou died in 2013 with his partner and wife Laurie Anderson at his bedside in their Amagansett, Long Island home.

INTRODUCTION

A native Northeasterner, I spent all of my writing years in San Francisco and Oakland until moving back East to New York City in 1999 to the realm of Lou's artistic life.

My experience with Lou's music started in early 1969, when my older brother Dave and I went to Two Guys department store on Boston Road in Springfield, Mass., to buy our records of the month. By that time, I was listening to underground radio on late-night AM programs like WDRC's Scene of the Unheard as well as FM stations—whose goldmine the radio industry hadn't yet discovered—especially WMUA, the college station at the University of Massachusetts, Amherst.

I had my short list. Even though the new LPs were on sale at $2.97 a pop, I had a meager budget. One album, not two or three or four. One. I had to choose. On the one hand there was the eponymous debut album by Led Zeppelin (released in January) that was destined to be a hit. On the other hand was the obscure self-titled Velvet Underground *LP (released in March).*

I had already grown AM-radio fatigued by Led Zep's "Communication Breakdown," but was drawn into VU's new sound (quieter and folksier than the band's provocative two earlier albums). I liked the sentiment in "Beginning to See the Light" and was thoroughly intrigued by "Murder Mystery," an epic feast of layers of fast-spoken poetry and sheets of vocals. I took the road less traveled and went with VU. While it didn't knock my socks off right away, soon I swooned. Today it's one of my all-time favorites.

Interesting fact: While Led Zeppelin broke into the top 10 of Billboard's charts, VU never made it into the top 200. But the rock pioneers proved historically to be more seminal in the long run with its rawness and honesty, spawning countless young groups to follow in Lou's challenging world view.

I stood on the sidelines of VU and later began to peruse Lou's solo career, especially the desert-island album Transformer (1972). I missed a lot after that but caught glimpses of him on the San Francisco radio waves ranging from Berlin (1973) to New York (1989). In 1990 I dove back in fully enraptured by Songs for Drella, the tribute to the late Andy Warhol, with Lou reuniting with VU co-founder John Cale (who had left the band by the third Velvet Underground album).

I returned into the Lou fold at the end of the millennium when I made the bold move to relocate from the Bay Area. At that point, I eagerly jumped back into the post-Velvet domain again when Lou launched into what turned out to be his second-to-last solo studio CD Ecstasy—his first recording in four years and one of the best of his career. I scored a very early advance. I dug in and studied his poetry and soundscape. The compelling and richly lyrical Ecstasy showcases Lou writing indelible melodies, crafting the lyrics, fine-tuning the instrumentation and investing his songs with a range of emotion.

ECSTASY—THE HARD WAY

2000

As the editor of Schwann Spectrum, I wrote the spring 2000 cover feature on Lou. With the support of his manager, Annie Ohayon, this was the first of three meetings in his Sister Ray Enterprises office in SoHo over the next few years, from 2000 to 2003. I came prepared each time.

For the Spectrum piece—"The Raw Beauty of the Poet's Dance: Lou Reed Experiences Ecstasy the Hard Way"—we rendezvous at his office on a rainy afternoon. Attired casually in a black T-shirt and dark brown sweater that zips up the front, the trim 57-year-old Reed with short curly brown hair is sitting at his desk. As I set up my tape recorder, he first stares me down as if to intimidate me. But he softens when he realizes that I was paying deep attention to his music—especially his penetrating lyrics.

To Lou's right is a heavy clear glass ashtray wiped clean of cigarette residue and to his left is a round tin of small, dome-shaped, eucalyptus-flavored jujubes he occasionally pops.

Why? To help him finally shake the smoking habit. How long has he been nicotine free? Weeks? Months? Years?

"Four days," Lou replies dryly.

We then talk at length about *Ecstasy*, a raw yet sophisticated 77-minute song cycle where the longing for the transcendence of love is weighed down by mental illness, alienation, ennui, hopelessness, rejection, infidelity. Without a trace of exuberance, Lou expresses how pleased he is with the new disc. "I've been thinking about recording this album for years," he says. "Everything we had we put in there. All my albums have been real attempts to get to that place, but this one really went there, down to the last dot. I wouldn't change a thing. I really love the songs."

Two-thirds of the way through *Ecstasy*, Lou launches into "Like a Possum," inarguably the most gripping—and clocking in at 18 minutes, unquestionably the longest—song of his storied career. It's an abrasive yet subtly exclamatory piece—part anguish, part rapture—with the guitar volume cranked up so powerfully loud and the slow drone-like motion so mesmerizing that the murky flow forces you to stay with Lou for the entirety of his journey.

"Good morning, it's Possum Day/Feel like a possum in every way," Lou intones after the intense three-minute guitar-grinding instrumental open. The greeting is like a dark wake-up call from a disturbed dream into the grime of New York City's "holy morning" where used condoms float off the Hudson River shore, girls with pieced tongues do tricks on the gents in stained shirts and a down-on-his-luck lover laments, "I got a hole in my heart the size of a truck."

Lyrically, the number dwells on similar bleak themes scattered throughout Lou's portfolio of tunes spanning 35 years: the decadence and perversion of modern urban culture where heartbreak goes hand-in-hand with a multitude of moral trials and tumbles. He likens his character to a possum, the ugliest member of the marsupial family known for its ability to feign sleep or death in the face of danger and also, so it seems, one of the most popular species for roadkill.

Yet what sets this song apart from Lou's earlier work is the uncompromisingly in-your-face sonics that that pull you into the drama and won't let go. It's a riveting display of guitar emotion befitting the protagonist who, with the instinct of a survivor, remains "calm as an angel" and somehow manages—"strong and fearless in the outside air"—to be "the only one left standing."

I tell Lou that I consider "Like a Possum" a tour de force.

"Well, at 18 minutes, it better be worth it," says the soft-spoken Lou, who is not only one of the most influential artists in rock history but also a gifted songwriter/bandleader who refuses to rest on his laurels. "I'd been wanting to do something like this song for a very long time where yon totally get immersed into its core. I just needed the right combination of studio musicians, the right sound and the right lyrics. 'Possum' took us away when we performed it in the studio. And every time we listened to it back, it took us away again."

Lou also credits a "new guitar gizmo" invented by a friend for the tune's success. "It's an unbelievable piece of equipment that makes my guitar sound orchestral," he says. "It's thick as if a bunch of instruments are being played. It's an amazing sound."

Ecstasy stands as a prime example of rock elevated to a state of art—where care has been taken every step in the creative process to guarantee quality. Lou notes that they even played the album to listeners unfamiliar with the songs to make sure the lyrics could be heard clearly in the mix.

With so much contrived sonic candy being pushed into the pop market, Lou offers sustenance by using an organic approach to broaching profound matters of the heart with honesty. It's not a new songwriting philosophy, but one which helped put him on the map in the '60s when, bucking the status quo at the time, he penned tunes that bluntly brought up such frowned-upon subjects as transvestitism, hard-core drug use and sexual experimentation.

Lou's recordings over the years featured artistic triumphs as well as such ill-conceived projects as the electronic music experiment *Metal Machine Music* (1975). Despite the fluctuation in success, Lou is considered to be a rock icon. He was inducted into the Rock and Roll Hall of Fame in 1996.

Lou bristles at the icon notion. "I hardly believe I'm in the Hall of Fame," he says flatly. "But an icon? I can't associate with that. I'm just clawing at the ground like everybody else trying to get that great sound."

RETURN TO SOHO

Three months after our first conversation, I'm back again with a fresh copy of *Schwann Spectrum*, but Lou is running late. He's jammed in midtown traffic after a mid-day shoot at CNN ran overtime and has phoned ahead for Dean & Deluca coffee to be waiting for him when he arrives at his Sister Ray Enterprises office in SoHo. He's been squeezing in a lot of appointments lately as he ramps up for the release of *Ecstasy*.

Today, Reed is again visibly upbeat as he enters the high-ceilinged loft space, walks down the hardwood hallway past the framed concert posters and gold records from his Velvet Underground and solo act days, and greets his energetic rat terrier Lola who's eager for a jaunt to the nearby dog run.

Wearing a black leather jacket and pants, Lou sits down at his desk, then quickly jumps up to go into the other room to retrieve a heavy glass ashtray. On the last visit, he was four days into quitting and relying on a tin of eucalyptus-flavored jujubes to get him through the nicotine withdrawal. Today the dome-shaped candies are gone, replaced by a bowl of shelled walnuts. And the cigarettes?

"Failure," Reed says simply, explaining that he was doing fine until he went to Germany in February with theater director Robert Wilson to debut their new Edgar Allen Poe-inspired collaborative project *Poe-try*. "That was the beginning of the end," he says while munching on a walnut. He shakes his head. "Sad to say."

A humorous, meandering conversation ensues, moving from declining eyesight (both of us admitting to cheating on a driver's license eye test) to ankle problems

(Lou breaking his ankle in the '80s when a rotted mobile staircase at a concert broke underneath him) to a shared passion for playing basketball.

"I like to go half court, but we don't play those rough elbow-swinging-to-the-nose kinds of street games," he says, lighting up a cigarette. "Whenever Eddie Vedder's in town, we go one-on-one. He's got a murderous jump shot that he throws like a football. He's really accurate."

When we finally settle into more *Ecstasy* talk, Lou says he's pleased with the initial pre-release response. "Friends like it just fine and some people are particularly impressed by the sound of the recording. It's like, 'How did you do that?'" He notes that even though he's got the rep as a poet (case in point: his new book), he also takes great pride in perfecting the sonic quality of his recordings.

While his patience wears thin with some scribes who insist on asking him to dissect the meaning of his songs, Lou laughs when talking about a conversation he recently had with a young writer from Eastern Europe. "This kid shows up and tells me he thinks the new album is OK, then pulls out a copy of the first Velvet Underground record. He tells me this is what he really likes and asks me to sign it."

Lou shrugs. Even though Velvet Underground is ancient history, the band's legacy lives on. He was a founding member of the avant-rock group (formed in 1965 and befriended by avant-garde artist and filmmaker Andy Warhol), penning tunes that bluntly brought up such frowned-upon subjects as transvestitism, hard-core drug use and sexual experimentation. Lou is often hailed as the godfather of punk.

Born and raised in the New York metropolitan area, Lou defied pop music conventions with the Velvets (a point of inspiration for the likes of Patti Smith and Johnny Rotten) and moved to solo fame, propelled by his 1972 David Bowie-produced album *Transformer* with its radio hit song, "Walk on the Wild Side" (censors at the time had no clue what the word "head" meant in the context of the story) and the achingly beautiful "Perfect Day."

For *Ecstasy*, Lou enlisted Hal Willner to produce. "It was great having Hal in there with us," Lou says while also crediting sound engineer Tim Latham. "I first worked with Hal on his Kurt Weill project several years ago. He's responsible for making things sound right. Tim made it easy. All we musicians had to do was come into the studio and play."

Joining Lou for the bulk of the sessions included his longtime bandmates: bassist Fernando Saunders, drummer Tony Smith and fellow guitarist Mike Rathke. "These guys are great," Lou says. "We've been playing together so long as a band that we know how to work well together. I was incredibly lucky that everyone was available and in New York when we wanted to record."

The tracking took seven weeks, with the entire recording process, including mixing and mastering, three months. Lou says there were issues with a few snags. Of course, it doesn't hurt that the leader and all tthe other principals—and even such guests as jazz trumpeter Steven Bernstein of Sex Mob fame who did the horn section arrangements on a couple of numbers—are from New York.

Lou laughs and says, "I was thinking of putting a little stamp on the back of the CD jacket that reads, 'Made in New York by New Yorkers.'" He laughs again and says that *Ecstasy* is a true Gotham City album. "It's coming from all of this…"—he extends his arms—"…where we all are. It's the good, the bad and everything else in between."

On *Ecstasy*, Lou delivers a compelling and richly melodic collection of tunes that stand as a prime example of rock elevated to a state of art. There are songs stunning in their gravity, such as the crunching "Mystic Child" about a manic depressive ready to unleash his anger in the streets and the hard-driving "Future Farmers of America" (a tune from "Time Walker," another Wilson collaboration) about a futuristic scenario where black farmers enslave whites.

Equally alluring is the eerie "Rock Minuet," performed in a loping triple meter. It opens a window on the sordid street scenes of hatred, violence and "the thrill of the needle and anonymous sex." It features the musical contribution of Reed's wife, performance artist Laurie Anderson. "We wanted a violin part on the tune and it was obvious who to ask," says Lou, who notes they often perform duets in the privacy of their own home and have been floating the idea of working together on a project. "If you want unique, genius support, you have to call Laurie. She listened to the track and came up with an astonishing part that only she could come up with."

The album opens with "Paranoia Key of E," with its fear-obliterates-love theme and stormy bass-filigree guitar prelude. It's drives with a straightahead rock beat and rhythmic horn ornamentation. Like most numbers on the disc, it has an indelible melody and a dark vision leavened by humor. "Catchy, yeah, that's a great word and a nice place to start when describing the album," says Lou who notes that he often finds himself humming one of the melodies.

As for the levity, not the word usually associated with the grim nature of his tunes, Lou adds, "There are funny things flying around all over the place. I mean, I think they're funny, but I don't think everyone gets it. There's a ton of humor." He quotes a section from "Paranoia Key of E," where an indecisive character cracks the joke: "My bedroom is a female zoo/Worse than Clinton in prime time."

On the lovelorn title track delivered in a gently percussive calm teeming with sadness (Ecstasy is actually the name of the woman who got away), Lou compares the loss to an old Ford stripped of its engine, radio and hood and sitting in the street. In his distinctive spoken-word style, he sings with comic gloom, "In its seat sits a box with a note that says, 'Goodbye Charlie, thanks a lot.'"

Lou also cites "Mad," a slow tempo tune with a Memphis soul-like horn arrangement, as another amusing number even though it tells the tale of a guy who's been caught cheating by his lover. Lines include "I know I shouldn't've had someone in our bed, but I was so tired" and "you said you were out of town for the night and I believed in you, I believed you." Lou laughs and says, "You know it really is funny. There are a lot of emotions working at the same time in these songs, not just one. So 'Mad' is a song about aarrggghh, but another part of it is hilarious."

A cursory survey of Lou's book of poetry, *Pass Thru Fire: The Collected Lyrics* (Hyperion)—that includes the lyrics to all of his songs ranging from his VU days to the new album—reveals another frequent theme: dance. Case in point: Lou's classic "Rock 'n' Roll" where Jenny discovers at the age of five to tune in to the airwaves and "dance to the rock 'n' roll station."

"Yeah, when I was putting the book together, I noticed some of those recurring themes too," Lou says with a laugh. "Of course, I was young then. Now it's 'Modern Dance.'" He is referring to one of *Ecstasy*'s gems, a radiant midtempo rocker that's a love song of sorts about how confusing the shifting roles of relationships are and how that oftentimes results in disappointment and the desire to escape. A particularly poignant line in the tune: "Maybe you don't want to be a wife/It's not a life being a wife."

"That's the whole point of the song," Lou says. "It's no accident that's the very last thing you hear at the fade. But I don't want to explain it. Actually, I could, but it would take a couple of hours sitting at a bar over drinks—and I don't drink anymore. Besides, lyrics can mean so many different things and can be taken in so many different ways. But for certain people, that line should be an arrow."

While humor is weaved through the album, there are no laughs in the gripping, part-anguish, part-rapture "Like a Possum." After the raw beauty of the 18-minute tune, Lou inserts a gem-like musical pause: the quietly reflective instrumental "Rouge," a one-minute palate cleanser featuring Laurie. That's followed by the rousing finale, "Big Sky," a surprising upbeat rocker that offers a glimpse of hope after an hour-plus journey through the underbelly of New York City.

"It is hopeful that the album ends there," Lou says. "We didn't want to end with 'Possum,' with the aarrggghh, so it was quite a trick. Then 'Big Sky' came along with its huge sound and its melodies—by God it's amazing, it's anthemic, it's like a symphony. And I knew it was the end."

On "Big Sky" Lou sings happily, "Big sky, holding up the sun/But it can't hold us down anymore." In the song, everything is big, whether it's a huge storm wreaking havoc or an enormous snake offering original sin.

But there's no holding Lou back. He's bursting free from the shackles of the failed relationships he so keenly observes and so passionately sings about. You don't expect this sentiment from an artist so identified with the dysfunctional. However, at heart this is Lou's joy and ultimately his ecstasy.

THE RAVEN

2003

Once again, Lou has people scratching their heads. This week he releases *The Raven*, a double CD of music and spoken word inspired by the dismal world view of wordsmith Edgar Allen Poe. It's his 19th solo album. Four years in the making, the most ambitious project of his oeuvre clocks in at nearly two and a quarter hours and encompasses a broad span of styles (from a lounge show-tune send-up to an apocalyptic furnace blast of electronic music). Co-starring with the rocker are such actors as Willem DaFoe, Steve Buscemi, Amanda Plummer and Elizabeth Ashley in addition to recording luminaries like ex-glam buddy David Bowie, jazz iconoclast Ornette Coleman, gospel greats The Blind Boy of Alabama and performance artist (and paramour) Laurie.

"This could be a career ender!" exclaims the unusually effervescent Lou, leaning back in his desk chair at his Sister Ray Enterprises office in SoHo while the window radiator hisses and the horns on Broadway blare on this cold-snap January day. "But I'll go out on a high note by taking the high road."

Is Lou indeed issuing the "nevermore" proclamation by Poe's black bird of doom? He sighs and concedes, "I expect even less than I normally do, which is not much in the first place. The album is geared for doom. It requires concentration. It's so contrary to everything out there now that I figure this one could well sink." In a soft voice, he whispers, "It's too good," then, in a burst of mock melodrama, he booms, "It's too good for them!"

Lou laughs heartily at his disparaging sentiment toward record companies that he insists have lost touch with serious—and at times comic—art released in a pop music setting. But Poe? Is the 19th century poet and short story writer—whose grotesque fantasies and paranoia continue to capture the imaginations of junior and senior high students everywhere— the protagonist of a 21st century creative endeavor?

"Obviously, I'm fascinated by Edgar," Lou says, then admits, "It is the worst time in the world for something like this to come out, particularly with the record business the way it is." He pauses then takes another swipe at the loss-accruing industry: "But the record companies are essentially getting what they deserve."

However, there is a glint of hope that perhaps *The Raven* may buck the odds and fascinate both serious listeners fed up with vacuous pop and young adults hungry for a new twist. Lou reports that a radio-only edited version of DaFoe reading "The Raven" was met with favorable reviews during Halloween. "It went to number 12 on one alt-rock college station," he reports. "Now, how's that possible?"

"This is a compendium of all the music I've done in my career," he says. "It is the result of everything I've done. There's no way I could have made this when I was twenty or forty. This is the album that sums up all my experiences. I'm very happy with it. It's exactly what I wanted it to be."

After greeting his and Laurie's frisky rat terrier Lola at the door of his high-ceiling loft office, Lou, brown-eyed and brown-tousled hair, settles into his inner sanctum and scarfs down lunch—a delivered egg-white omelet and lox. He leaves the pale green crusts of iceberg lettuce in the tin, peels off his brown flannel shirt so that he's decked out shoulder to cuff in black (T-shirt and leather pants) and explains that he ran late because he was at his Chinese acupuncturist's office. He's been getting stuck with needles and drinking sludgy herbal tea for five weeks in his latest attempt to kick the cigarette habit. He says so far, so good, but shrugs. "We'll see."

An earlier backsliding episode occurred three years ago when Reed was in Germany debuting his *Poe-try* commissioned collaboration with theater director Robert Wilson at the Thalia Theatre. The project reacquainted the native New Yorker, a college lit major, with the American author who also lived in Gotham. In the liner notes to *The Raven*, Reed argues that Poe, with his haunting and terror-stricken tales, is "peculiarly attuned to our new century's heartbeat than he ever was to his own. Obsessions, paranoia, willful acts of self-destruction surround us constantly."

The staging of *Poe-try* featured thirteen songs, an overture and libretto with spoken-word interludes that wove from biographical detail to liberal adaptations of Poe's works including "The Cask of Amontillado," "The Tell-Tale Heart" and "The Pit and the Pendulum." Three-quarters of the production was translated into German, a sticking point with viewers who attended its nine-day run at BAM's Next Wave Festival in Brooklyn in late 2001. But by then, Lou was already at work in retranslating the play into a recording.

Initially the German division of Warner Bros. wanted to make an album of the play itself. But as Lou began to record some guide vocals to set this in motion it became, as he calls it, "a Lou project." Then his label, Warner/Reprise in L.A., heard about it and wanted to release it. Lou says, "My first thought was, do they know what this is going to be?"

The album started small but quickly grew exponentially as Lou rewrote major sections of the play for the recording. He then enlisted his longtime band mates—guitarist Mike Rathke, bassist Fernando Saunders and drummer Tony Smith—and recruited several guest musicians and dramatic readers. In addition to the two-CD set, there will be a single CD issued with a focus on just the songs (in Lou's words, the "petite" version of the "grand mal" Poe attack).

The first CD (Act 1) opens with an anguished rock overture, two readings (DaFoe as young Poe, Buscemi as old Poe), a cello-backed Prologue, then Lou and co. cranking up the rock spirit with the anthemic "Edgar Allen Poe" (with Lou comically wailing the chorus: "These are the stories of Edgar Allen Poe, not exactly the boy next door"). The rest of the disc includes soft-edged tunes, a rocking instrumental, a lengthy rendition of the morbid "The Fall of The House of Usher" (with eerie sound effects), a reworking of "The Raven" and two numbers Lou revisited from old albums, "The Bed" from *Berlin* and "Perfect Day" from *Transformer*.

"These songs both fit," Lou says. "But I also wanted to bring back memories to fans who know my work." As for the poetic license he took with the "mournful chaos" of Poe's works, Lou says, why not? "In Willem's reading of 'The Raven,' he recites the line 'arrogant, dickless liar.' And someone asked me, did Poe really say that? And I replied, 'No, Lou said that in a Poe way.'"

The second CD (Act 2) is the stronger of the pair. The pacing is better, the tunes weave into the mix with more fluidity and the spoken-word sections are more dramatic and conversational, especially in "The Tell-Tale Heart" suite that brims with exclamatory utterances and distorted guitar fury. "Hop Frog" is a brilliant suite, beginning with Bowie singing the straight-up rocking theme (backed by Lou's obliterating guitar) and ending with "Fire Music," a three-minute surge of electronic effects of annihilation.

Lou cites this piece when asked how Poe is relevant to today's world. "Just think of the twin towers, which I saw fall from my loft [in the West Village]. 'Fire Music' was recorded two days after September 11. People ask me my reaction. Words can't describe it. 'Fire Music' does."

While he's been on the record for not listening to his past works after the studio sessions, Lou frequently notes in our conversation that he's listened to *The Raven* several times. When asked about that, he cites "lousy" sound quality on past releases and says, "Why listen to your own stuff anyway?" But with *The Raven*, he's not only proud of the sonics (mastering the music to his high standards) but also of the performances of his Poe troupe.

Is *The Raven* his masterpiece? Lou hints that it may be. "This is a compendium of all the music I've done in my career," he says. "It is the result of everything I've done. There's no way I could have made this earlier in my career. This is the album that sums up all my experiences. I'm very happy with it. It's exactly what I wanted it to be."

A year after *The Raven*, in 2004 Lou went on the road and taped the proceedings for Sire/Reprise that were released as *Animal Serenade* on March 23, 2004. Recorded live at L.A.'s Wiltern Theater, the two-CD collection covers a breadth of historical and stylistic ground. From thrust to caress, the New York bard and his band crunch through four-chord rockers ("Dirty Bvld.") and flow with elegant lyricism through gentle numbers ("Sunday Morning").

The rock icon revisits his gritty Velvet Underground repertoire (a slow-to-burn "Heroin" that's both a rush and a lament) and his last, tragically off-the-radar disc *The Raven* (the hushed "Vanishing Act"). Underneath the gruff/droll, tough-guy demeanor, Lou is a romantic, evidenced by "Tell It to Your Heart." Cellist Jane Scarpantoni excels on her dark-toned, grace-and-fever solo on "Venus in Furs," and primo vocalist Anthony flies high on "Candy Says." Talking to the crowd, Lou says the tune was always too difficult for him to sing. But what's missing from this song's performance is the raw gloom of Lou's distinctive voice and his powerful primal authority.

While Lou did not return with a new full-blown studio recording after *The Raven*, he engaged in two contrasting recording projects. Four years after *The Raven* in 2007, he collaborated with Hal Willner on *Hudson River Wind Meditations*, a new-age meditational journey. Deliberately hushed. He wrote in the liners: "I composed this music for myself as an adjunct to meditation, Tai Chi, bodywork, and as music to play in the background of life—to replace the everyday cacophony with new and ordered sounds of an unpredictable nature."

In 2011, Lou went into the opposite zone in a collaboration with heavy metal rock band Metallica for the album *Lulu*.

Saxophone Summit—
A Holy Jazz Trinity

In what could well be the finest jazz hour of 2004, Gathering of Spirits opens with the triple helixing and tripartite dance of three of today's top jazz saxophonists—Michael Brecker, David Liebman and Joe Lovano. The Saxophone Summit gusts into the swing-no-swagger tune "Alexander the Great," Joe's composition dedicated to the legendary Cleveland tenor saxophonist Joe Alexander who recorded with Tadd Dameron.

There's a playful race, a plenitude of baton passing, and in Michael's words, "a beautiful matrix...a fascinating juxtaposition of sounds, colors and rhythmic approaches." The music unfurls like inspired collaborative poetry—where a poet writes a line of verse on a subject, folds the paper and passes it to the next poet for the next line. When all the lines are unfolded into an accordion-like manuscript, a poem of manifold voices emerges. In the case of Saxophone Summit, it's a holy jazz trinity—three become one.

SAXOPHONE SUMMIT—GATHERING THE SPIRITS WITH JOE LOVANO, DAVE LIEBMAN, AND MICHAEL BRECKER
2004

The day after the Jazz Journalists Associations' Jazz Awards ceremony in June, the three saxophonists meet for a conversation summit at the Hotel Belvedere in New York. They discuss their dynamic brio as a team and their debut CD, the state of jazz in a culture that increasingly celebrates vapidity, and, of course, their guardian angel, John Coltrane.

Gathering of Spirits reveals an earth of song, a sky of improvisation—inspired by the three saxists' patron saint, John Coltrane. Michael, Dave and Joe pay homage to the saxophone god. The CD is as much about dancing together as well as apart, flocking and flying, migration and transcendence. The music demands and rewards attentive listening: the vivant meditation on Trane's "India" where flutes fill the soundscape with celestial birds; Dave's expansive suite "Tricycle" where the journey encompasses dreamy low-sprocket jaunts, traversals through dark detours under turbulent skies, celebratory swirls of fast pedaling; and Michael's 12-minute title track where waves upon waves of brilliant blowing lap, pound, caress the shoreline.

Saxophone Summit traces its origins to 1996 when the three saxophone friends informally banded together to explore the lesser known and controversial music of late-period Coltrane. Gradually each saxophonist contributed originals in the same Trane spirit. They freed up their busy schedules to play Japan, perform at the Red Sea Jazz Festival in Eilat, share a stage at the Montreal Jazz Festival during Joe's week-long invitational series, perform the Meditations suite at Symphony Space in New York under Dave's direction, and play at least a couple of nights every year at Birdland.

The band's first major tour of 14 shows took place last fall in Europe, where the saxophonists were supported by their crack rhythm section of pianist Phil Markowitz, bassist Cecil McBee and drummer Billy Hart. "These cats know what magic means," Dave says. "As we're shifting and shooting off into different directions as soloists, Phil, Cecil and Billy keep feeding us the kind of openness we need."

Joe notes that every night was like a new set of music. "Each show we were inspired by the evening before," he says. "We played different music and used different instruments and really got into the inner forms of the tunes."

Upon return, the Saxophone Summit entered the studio for Telarc Records with Richard Seidel producing. "It was nice to get a record company interested in this kind of music in this day and age," says Dave. "It was complicated because all three of us are already recording for different labels. Plus, this wasn't going to be a light jazz outing. We thought this might be off the map for Telarc, but they were completely cool. They let us do what we wanted."

Joe adds that they didn't shop a tape. "We shopped the project and the personnel," he says. "We probably took Telarc on a little journey with our music. I don't think they knew what they were getting into. They hadn't come to our concerts. But Richard was instrumental in talking it through. We're happy to have a chance to document the group."

The conversation continues.

When you first started playing together as the Saxophone Summit, was it a battle of the saxes, a cutting contest?

Dave: Joe said one night after an early Birdland gig that it was like three quartets. We didn't play so much together then. When Mike soloed, it was the Michael Brecker Quartet; with Joe, it was the Joe Lovano Quartet. But we started to gravitate toward interaction, especially with a piece like "Meditations" that Coltrane purposely wrote to be like a group choir.

Joe: We're more into ensemble playing than jousting. We're playing with each other to create music together. That rarely happened with cats in the early days of saxophone meetings. Yet a lot of the traditional get-in-your-face competitive kind of playing happens naturally, not only among saxes but also between you and the drummer rhythmically, or with the pianist harmonically. But that's about challenging each other to take the music somewhere else.

On the new recording, there are moments like during my tune "Alexander the

Great" where we trade phrases. We do get in each other's face. We try to take what someone just played and complement each other. It's like, "Oh, man, what you just played was beautiful, but, hey, listen to this."

Dave: It's like what Mike and I were a part of in the late '60s and early '70s in the loft scene in New York. It was free jazz with Coltrane's "Ascension" as the model. For hours, cats would play without anyone ever actually soloing. That spirit was a part of our youth.

Michael: There was a lot of fire back then. I remember it with fondness. We did a lot of playing and experimenting together. The loft scene gave us a way to communicate with each other about the kind of music Coltrane was playing. It was a great learning experience. It ended when we all got too busy.

Dave: Musically and socially it was an amazing time. In a way, we're revisiting that spirit.

Joe: Saxophone Summit is influenced by that ensemble approach. For me, Coltrane's recordings like *Meditations, Kula Se Mama, Ascension* and *Live at the Village Vanguard Again* were influential. That way of playing together and calling the spirits as a unit inspired me to want to play, to come to New York and meet with guys like Dave and Mike. I wanted to sit in and challenge myself to be in a situation that went beyond just a song that I studied. A lot of people hide behind the tune they play. From Coltrane and Ornette and Miles, I learned to want to live in the music and in the moment because that's where the most creative things happen.

You certainly complement each other on Trane's "India."

Dave: I always played "India" on flute. During the course of the tour we all picked up flutes in places like Budapest and Turkey. So we developed it as a nice way to break up the saxophone texture. It became a real fun part of our show, an extension of what we do on the saxophones.

Joe: The three flutes have different ranges and tonality. Each one complements the arrangement Dave wrote. We've been exploring this tune since the first time we played together.

Dave: Everyone talks about world music today, but Trane was looking into it back in the early sixties. He was there already.

Michael: The way "India" works is how we project our feelings throughout the recording. We follow the rhythm changes and then get free. Each one of our solos is a send-off into the next.

Joe: Everyone listens to each other. We each bring different colors and tonalities with our instruments, and the music takes on a free and open journey. We're not just playing at the same time. We're playing together within the orchestration of the piece. The way the rhythm section reacts is the key to making each tune a beautiful journey. You can hear that on Mike's tune "Gathering of Spirits," which is an amazing collective improvisation.

215

Then there's Trane's "Peace on Earth," which is really important to our group. Dave brought in a number of beautiful ballads from the later period. But this one is special because of the way we share the melody and the phrases.

Even though Coltrane wrote some incredible music late in his career, why do you think people walked out of his shows?
Dave: A lot of people still don't understand that music.

Joe: He was moving fast.

Dave: It's like why people don't listen to Schoenberg. The music is difficult, complicated.

Joe: Trane's music is sophisticated harmonically and rhythmically. There's a density of sound, whether he was playing in a club or at Philharmonic Hall. It's not for the casual listener.

Michael: It's not entertainment.

Joe: In his later repertoire, Coltrane was moving so quickly he surprised the cats he was playing with. It's different now. Jazz is a big word. There's a variety of sounds and a lot of different influences coming into the music. Back in Trane's day, the core crowd of jazz listeners in New York was made up of artists and intellectuals.

Dave: I think audiences didn't understand Coltrane because many people want to hear what they grew up with and can identify with. They wanted to hear "My Favorite Things." I remember once hearing him play at the Philharmonic. He started out with the Tibetan chant of the dead, the heaviest chant of them all. But then he eventually went into "My Favorite Things" and everyone started applauding. Of course, after the melody and chorus, Coltrane kept going for the next hour and a quarter with all these cats like Pharoah Sanders and Albert Ayler taking over. It was chaotic. That's when people left. He played his signature tune, but even then, he wouldn't give up where he was going. Amazing.

Michael: The night I saw him in Philly, "My Favorite Things" was the encore. It was a free version, but even so it brought the house down.

Joe: You go back and listen to those recordings like *Live at the Village Vanguard Again*, and now it sounds orderly. It all falls into place. You can hear the orchestration of it.

Michael: Coltrane might have had a subtle premonition.

Dave: Yeah, he probably knew he wasn't going to live long. It sounds like he was rushing toward the finale, like Beethoven with last movement of his Ninth Symphony. You hear the music and you know he knows something. You feel it.

If Trane had lived longer, where do you think he would have gone with his music?
Dave: I don't know if he would have continued. I think he was going somewhere else. That's what it sounded like to me.

Joe: We see the picture of his whole recording career. It's defined. It's hard to say where the music might have gone.

Dave: He didn't have to deal with the fusion thing. He could have done orchestral music. Or he could have gone to Africa and played with drummers.

Joe: Look at Monk. He got to a point he didn't pass. No one heard from him for ten years. Coltrane might have done the same thing: get to a certain place and say, "I'm gonna cool for a minute."

Michael: It's incredible, mind-boggling, the amount of playing and recording he did.

Joe: Every time Coltrane took his horn out, he couldn't do anything else but tell the truth. He played from the heart and the soul every time. That's a good lesson: That's what fuels the music beyond the theory.

Today there seems to be a bias against instrumental jazz because it's the vocalists who are selling. This CD requires focused listening. It goes against the grain of our culture that's bombarded with entertainment/infotainment, that encourages multitasking and discourages reflection. As much as I like pop music, it pales in comparison to what you're doing on this CD.

Joe: Jazz is about passion. Nobody told Monk or Miles [Davis] or Bird [Charlie Parker] or Trane to play a certain way. Today jazz has become about marketing and trying to be commercial. What they call jazz today isn't jazz. It's watered down pop music, background music, party music. The concept of jazz—improvisation and creating music on the spot—is something else. We're a fast-food culture looking for cheap thrills. We're a culture where mediocrity is what everyone is reaching for.

Dave: That's what makes what we're doing more important than ever. We have a duty. The older we get the more it's true. Unfortunately the rest of the world is trying to catch up with our cultural mediocrity. We're beacons not because we're special, but because we're attached to a hundred-year-old tradition that started with black culture, came up through the city and has become a melting pot. In this world, we're more important than ever, yet taken for granted.

Michael: Well put. Jazz is not entertainment. It's an art dealing with complicated and subtle things. It's not an easy listen. It takes some degree of education to understand the format of the music and what's going on in a solo. It involves close and open communication among musicians and a lot of trust onstage. That's partially what makes the music so powerful. Every night the music is so spontaneous that it allows the audience to become part of the creative process.

Dave: As far as I'm concerned, the audience is privileged to be a part of a journey with professionals who take the trip every day and know what they're doing. They're lucky to be there, to be around people who have spent their lives communicating in this way. That's what we do. It's important to remember that jazz can be three things: entertaining, artistic and spiritual. The boundaries of the three mix. But as a young cat, you've got to decide on where to draw the line.

Joe: Blurring the lines and putting it all together is the challenge.

How does working on a project like this impact you when you return to your individual groups?

Dave: It's a thrill to hear great cats play on the same stage, on the same instrument no less. You're in the company of greatness. It raises my game and makes me believe more. There's nothing like it for getting the inspiration to go on, to go back to what else you're doing. You're propelled. Plus I don't feel as lonely.

Joe: It's everything to me. Playing together with musicians you're digging and trying to react to is inspiring. That's what you live for in this music—to surround yourself with people to help you reach for another place. Playing with Dave and Mike is a dream for me.

Michael: I take away the sense of possibilities of other things I hadn't thought about. Saxophonists have a tradition of communing together, whether we're playing in sections or just hanging out. This band makes it easier to learn from each other on the spot—things like sound and construction of lines. After playing with Dave and Joe, my vantage point changes, sometimes pretty profoundly. At the end of this last tour, I moved in my playing and the way I think about music. Plus, this rhythm section is very intuitive yet decisive at the same time. When someone makes a leap, the rest go all the way. I try to bring that spirit back to my own groups.

Dave: It's hard to get inspired as you get older. It's one thing to die when you're 40. You don't have to worry about it. But if you're going to live like Picasso or Stravinsky or Coleman Hawkins or Duke, you've got to keep the flame. You do it by keeping true to yourself. That's the major challenge of aging. Being young, no problem. Get old, now let's see what you can do. This group helps all of us in that respect.

Beyond theory and technique, what advice can you give aspiring young saxophonists?

Joe: To study the music. The more you develop your vocabulary and harmonic concepts within the structure, the freer you can be. It's a repertoire approach.

Michael: By repertoire, do you mean the language as well as the tunes?

Joe: Both sides. You need more than just tunes. The more you're involved, the freer you can be to say something.

Dave: You've got to think beyond the box, and the box is whatever you've been practicing. You learn what you practice, then learn how to forget it. In any spiritual pursuit, you never completely forget, but you leave it and think outside the box. That's a big leap that involves faith and fear and loneliness. I looked at what great musicians did, then looked around me at what was going on down on the street. You don't have to go far. You use your imagination, mind and perception and then improvise to find out who you are in relationship to what went before. When you find that picture of yourself, it speaks for itself. It may take ten to twenty years, but you have to be in pursuit of it.

Wayne Shorter—
The Ultimate Jazz Astronaut

My experiences with Wayne took place over a 10-plus year period in the late '90s and the aughts. What follows are my encounters in a multi-universe journey with the genuine Jazz Space Cowboy.

During that decade, I talked with Wayne several times in a variety of settings. In 1999, we had a conversation for the San Francisco Chronicle about the 1+1 album he and Herbie Hancock recorded. That same year we linked up in person backstage where he and Herbie were doing another edition of 1+1 at the Jazz in Marciac festival in southwestern France. In 2005, backstage at Wayne's two-night performance at the Melbourne Umbria Melbourne Jazz Festival, we conversed again for a Q&A column for Billboard. Soon after, for my biography Ron Carter: Finding the Right Notes, I asked Wayne about his experience with the bassist in Miles Davis's classic '60s quintet. We met up again in 2009 in his dressing room at the Panama Jazz Festival for a DownBeat *feature.*

After being the go-to composer for Art Blakey's Jazz Messengers in the late '50s and early '60s, Miles convinced the drummer to let him bring Wayne aboard after trying out several tenor saxophonists—none to his liking. Art let Wayne join Miles in 1964, the same year the saxophonist also signed with Blue Note Records. Concurrent with his Miles gig, he released seven Blue Note albums and eventually eleven albums in 16 years as a leader. (Wayne returned to Blue Note in 2013 with Without a Net, his first recording for Blue Note in more than 30 years in celebration of his 80th birthday.)

After leaving Miles' employ in 1970, Shorter co-founded the seminal fusion band Weather Report with electric Miles alum Joe Zawinul on keyboards and bassist Miroslav Vitous, staying with the ensemble until 1985.

In 2005 for my Billboard conversation, I asked him about the rumors circulating in the last few years that a Weather Report reunion was imminent. Not so, Wayne says. "That would be like starting over again. It would be like asking Mohammed Ali to go back in the ring."

Wayne, who favors playing soprano saxophone later in his career, adds that he'd have to haul out his tenor saxophone again for a Weather Report show. "The tenor is so heavy I'd need a crane to hold it up," he says with a chuckle. "It's a whole different physicality. It's like Miles before he died. He was in his sixties, and of course your bones and your embouchure aren't as strong as when you're in your twenties. But that didn't stop the complaints from people who still expected him to play as fluid as when he was younger."

Writers only rarely hear plaudits for their efforts. But after my Wayne story from my time with him in Panama ran in DownBeat, *one reader wrote to editor Jason Koransky: "Dan Ouellette's feature on Wayne Shorter was one of the greatest articles I've ever read in your magazine. Wayne is such a beautiful soul, one who embodies all of the best aspects of jazz music. Reading his words is every bit as exciting as hearing his music. He'll surely go down in history as one of jazz's greatest musicians as well as one of its greatest thinkers."*

Wayne Shorter died in 2023—the next stage of his journey into the galaxies.

1+1

1999

In 1997 on a warm summer night, I caught Wayne and Herbie delivering a preview of their *1+1* album in the outdoors Lilian Fontaine Garden Theatre at the picturesque Villa Montalvo Arts Center nestled in Saratoga, California. The night was magical. At the back of the amphitheater, in the woods, a chorus of frogs started croaking in tune with the saxophonist and pianist. We were all enrapt in the pair's improvisational epiphanies—except for a crowd of Silicon Valley types who left en masse three-quarters of the way through the show. The puzzled pianist saw the rude rush and jokingly commented, "What? Did we do something wrong?"

Not a thing goes wrong that night. Wayne, then 64, and Herbie, 57, capture the beauty and surprise of their music that evening in what would later become their studio album: *1+1*. When it arrives soon after, the album is championed. Listening to it transports me back to the fleeting beauty of that warm summer night in Northern California.

The pair decides to hit the road to share *1+1* to large crowds, eager to engage in the incandescence.

In 1999, for one of the early *1+1* tour stops, the pair settles into Zellerbach Hall at UC Berkeley. I'm on assignment for a *San Francisco Chronicle* preview feature. I start doing my homework preparing for an interview with either Wayne or Herbie on their upcoming concert.

Even before the first digit registers on the CD player, I know the prospects are promising based on the Montalvo show. In the 1960s, Herbie and Wayne began their shared history as soul mates under the tutelage of Miles Davis in what was arguably the best jazz quintet ever (with bassist Ron Carter and drummer Tony Williams). That rarefied chemistry is vibrantly alive three decades later on this disc. The setting is intimate, the mood reflective, the emotion deep, the sound exquisite.

{Dialing back to February 1997, six months before the Villa Montalvo concert, Wayne and Herbie attend Tony Williams funeral at St. Ignatius Church, 650 Parker

Avenue in San Francisco. He died at the age of 51. They're joined by Ron and trumpeter Wallace Roney to bid farewell to their onetime bandmate. At the mass, the ensemble plays Tony's "Sister Cheryl" not as a performance or as entertainment, but as a prayer, a communal expression of grief. That same purity of spirit, compassion and friendship is present on *1 + 1* as Hancock and Shorter converse together on piano and soprano saxophone. The integrity of performance makes for a quietly captivating listening experience.]

The ten pieces on *1+1* were recorded over a seven-day period in Herbie's living room. None required more than three takes and none was overdubbed. Wayne and Herbie each brought compositions to the sessions, including the saxophonist's "Aung San Suu Kyi" (his soaring tribute to the jailed Burmese pro-democracy leader), and the pianist's moving ballad "Joanna's Theme," which the pair had originally recorded on Wayne's *Native Dancer* album in 1975.

They also collaborated, combining sections of their individual compositions to create the introspective and passionate "Visitor from Nowhere" and "Visitor from Somewhere." The one nonoriginal on the album, "Memory of Enchantment," penned by the 1996 Thelonious Monk Composition winner Michiel Borstlap, gets rendered with wistful allure. Herbie and Wayne break the meditative spell by closing with a delightfully jaunty ride through "Hale-Bopp, Hip-Hop"—referencing the 1997 fascination of Comet Hale-Bopp that was the brightest comet to ever pass by the planet. Remarkably it was clearly visible to the naked eye. Wayne must have been in his spacetime glory.

The new album, *1+1*, in essence, captures two colossal artists in the role of jazz emissaries.

The tour offers me the opportunity to talk to one of the two legends. It's Wayne's turn to have a press conversation about the alchemy at work. "We've been doing this since we were kids," he says. "It's the stuff we love to do. It transcends the record. It doesn't have to be confined to a certain time or a certain place." In other words, expect the unexpected of improvisation-fueled interchanges.

From there, my initial chat with Wayne leaves me a bit bewildered. First, he answers most of my questions by going into an elliptical thought pattern—cryptic parabolas start at one point, swing widely into the stars and then miraculously come back to earth with a soft landing of insight. After I get off the phone with Wayne, I worry that I don't have anything to work with in writing a story given the oblique conversation.

But then after I review my notes and relisten to the audio tape, I realize that in unraveling Wayne's thought process his responses are indeed quite brilliant—and bizarrely wonderful. And I discover that the way he muses on my questions are reflected in the way he expresses himself in his music with tendrils of tenor or soprano saxophone wisdom.

Preferring to talk on a philosophical level rather than discuss the particulars of his concert performances with Herbie, Wayne says, "It's the determination to make music that has longevity. There's a lot more to it than just creating something new. You have to ask the question, what is this music for, what does it mean? When we go on this tour, that's what we'll be reflecting on before we hit the stage."

Wayne sums up the impact of collaborating in a duo setting with Herbie: "Sometimes two ambassadors, so to speak, can make more of a difference than an army of strings and horns." He calls himself and Herbie "the ultimate astronauts."

They both got their flight training in Miles's hand-picked quintet. The leader pushed his youthful collaborators—Wayne, 31; Herbie, 23—to boldly explore with creative spontaneity and collective originality.

In *Miles: The Autobiography*, Miles gushed about the group: "If I was the inspiration and wisdom and link for this band, Tony was the fire, the creative spark; Wayne was the idea person, the conceptualizer of a lot of things we did; and Ron and Herbie were the anchors. I was just the leader who put us all together. Those were all young guys, and although they were learning from me, I was learning from them too."

The rarefied chemistry from the classic quintet is vibrantly alive in Wayne and Herbie's duo. "Life is something, isn't it?" Wayne asks rhetorically when talking about the upcoming Zellerbach show. "It's a great mystery. So, if it is such a great mystery, why not play it? That's what we do. We express the appreciation for the mystery. We'll be celebrating life and people."

How often they will meet together in concert in the future is unpredictable. After their short North American tour concludes, they'll be putting the duo on hold in lieu of other projects. "Herbie is composing music for dancer Mikhail Baryshnikov," Wayne says. "And I'm working on a new orchestral work commissioned by the Detroit Symphony that will debut on January 2 in celebration of the new millennium."

Even as busy as they are, they reunite when they can. Later in 1999, for example, they bring their mesmerizing *1+1* show to the giant tent stage at the Jazz in Marciac summer festival in the remote southwestern region of France. They arrive via a chauffeured van from the airport in Toulouse after traveling through miles and miles of sunflower fields in full bloom. They greet me backstage shortly before starting the show with two Wayne-composed tunes: the meditative "Meridianne—A Wood Sylph" and a buoyant take on "Footprints." They hold the crowd, once again, in an enraptured state.

UMBRIA JAZZ MELBOURNE Q&A

2005

Wayne serves as the leader when soaring into the stratosphere with his acoustic quartet. It becomes a winning combination overnight and continues for the next two decades.

Wayne and I talk during the landslide of his quartet accolades. We focus on his challenging adventures—and his affection for films, especially sci-fi thrillers.

With his band—bassist John Patitucci, drummer Brian Blade and pianist Jason Moran (subbing for regular Danilo Pérez)—Wayne provided the climax of the 11-day international festival. The group performed music from its live CD, *Beyond the Sound Barrier* (released on Verve).

The following is an excerpt of our fascinating conversation during his two-night appearance at last month's Umbria Jazz Melbourne 2005 festival in Australia where was an intrepid astronaut navigating the musical cosmos with improvisational brio.

Backstage after the second evening in Melbourne, Shorter landed on Earth long enough to talk about the current state of the recording industry and his mission in music.

As a jazz artist, do you feel your music is a hard sell for record companies because sales are lower for jazz than for pop?

It's just like Art Blakey used to say: "You can make a billion dollars on Wrigley's spearmint gum, but you can't make any money on jazz?" — and I would add, "on any kind of music that's truly creative."

When you started recording solo in the early '60s, was it like a playground, a place to be free with your music?

It was, in a way. I recorded a lot with Blue Note. The two guys who ran it then were Alfred Lion and Francis Wolfe. They didn't play like the majors. They were recording mavericks. They went against the grain and stuck with it.

Even back then, though, jazz records didn't make lots of money.

If something makes a lot of money, it doesn't make it cool. People worry about missing out on that pot of gold. But what they're really missing out on is their creative process. It's about evolving. It's like that movie "Resident Evil" with Milla Jovovich. Everybody was getting injected with something that made the people feed off each other like "Night of the Living Dead," but it didn't have the same effect with Milla. Her injection didn't work. So these guys were trying to destroy her, because she wasn't mutating to be some kind of war machine. But one guy said not to destroy her because she wasn't mutating, she was evolving.

That's what happens in your live shows. The music evolves.

That's right. We're all evolving. And there's a faith in eternal existence. I try to do that onstage, intimating that there's no such thing as a beginning or end. That's why I don't want to play songs anymore. They're cute and nice. I've learned things that have a beginning and end, but they're artificial. A lot of people give their lives for artificial reasons. It's like, are your thoughts your own or someone else's? It's as if every generation is being hijacked from the cradle, like those [newborn] sea turtles that get hijacked when they try to make their way to the sea. So for us it's a matter of waking up and not being devoured.

So, do you see that happening in the recording industry?
Yes. I don't know a lot of those people in the industry, but I ask the executives I know if they speak out in meetings. And they say, yes but they play with caution.

You know that label Nonesuch? They're doing something. I heard Pat Metheny's new record, *The Way Up*, and I called him up and said, "Pat, now we're talking." Instead of songs that were three-minute tracks for a single, he had "Part 1," "Part 2" and so on.

Joni Mitchell is also on Nonesuch. What is it about her music that attracted you to play on so many of her albums?
She's talking about things in her lyrics, and she's a fighter. She told me that around the time when she recorded *Don Juan's Reckless Daughter* and *Mingus* that someone sent her a letter accusing her of playing a minor second within a chord and how that was destroying the [pop] feeling she was known for. It was like saying she was going over to some other side.

It's like her song "Both Sides Now" that she wrote when she was 20 or 21. It was about an encounter she had with a man and the daughter she had. She recorded it and a record executive said to her, "You know, don't you?" The words struck him on a business side. She said she had to think fast, on her feet, so she said yes. And the executive detailed it out: We get young artists, squeeze the blood out of the stone, then throw them away and get another young artist. That's what the industry is like.

And you agree?
Yes, it's like this record executive who came on *American Idol* one night who said he could see working in the studio with one of the contestants. It was if he was saying, "I'm going to show you how to judge." The inference was that he could make this singer a star, that he could see and guarantee who could be a moneymaker. That's what *American Idol* is about: giving someone all the responsibility to do the thinking, the marketing, the moneymaking, the making of the idol.

What do you see as the role of the artist?
Being the lone voice in the wind. To be on a mission and not be afraid. It's like Bela Lugosi saying, "Do not be afraid." But you're on your own these days. Even the rap guys start off doing their own stuff but then the trap door opens. You don't have many knights or superheroes anymore.

Herbie Hancock is banding together the Headhunters for a few shows. Will you do the same with Weather Report?
No. This coming-back-together stuff doesn't do what the mission is. I need to stick to exactly what I'm doing and Joe Zawinul needs to stick with what he's doing. To get back together is an ambush. It's a nice trap based on financing. There's an underwriting. Like getting the Beatles back together used to be the big deal. But that's looking backwards, and I believe we should move forward.

THE QUIXOTIC JAZZ SAGE GOING INTO THE UNKNOWN: PANAMA

2009

A few years later I was back into the Wayne orbit.

At the Panama Jazz Festival in January 2009, Wayne Shorter, 75, speaks to a rapt audience of young jazz fans and players at a conversation/clinic. "There's no such thing as a short story," he says. "A short story is for marketing purposes only. Beethoven's nine symphonies are all one." He's comfortably sitting in a chair in front of a packed crowd in a large rehearsal room.

This is Wayne's crazy-like-a-fox way of summing up his own wayfaring career as a musician and composer. His quest for truth through song is no one-act play, but rather resembles an epic novel, with its ebb and flow of victory and tragedy. It's also an affirmation that his lifelong passion for composing stretches beyond isolated tunes and albums into something more mystically akin to songlines, the sacred dreamtime music of Australia's Aboriginals.

Attired in a black T-shirt and white suit at his Panama talk, Wayne holds court as a quixotic jazz sage who speaks with a simple clarity at one turn ("Play what you wish for, play a dream") only to morph into a philosophical riddler around the next bend ("A lot of us have been hijacked from the cradle, so we have to break from what we've become attached to already").

With his Buddha smile and mischievous twinkling eyes, Wayne reaches for parabolic metaphors (a sea turtle hatches in the sand and tries to make it to the sea without encountering a predator) and revels in posing rhetorical questions ("How large is the universe? Should we go for all the universe or not? What should it be?"). Anyone who has ever dialogued with him knows that he excels in elliptical discourse, much like he plays his tenor or soprano saxophone—lifting away from the head and launching into an interstellar trek before mysteriously landing calmly back where he started with mystical stardust in tow.

"You need to know that your life is a process," Wayne tells the gathering that is attentive to every word. "No one can put a process into a can or box and sell it. When you're playing music, this is a work in process, a work in progress. If you have a grasp of this, everything you say or write can be a process about always becoming more of who you are. It's more than mastering your instrument. It's the process of mastering your own life so that you'll be playing your life story. You celebrate the incomprehensible phenomenon of life and give it a present: originality."

Takeaway: that's how Wayne's music continues to resonate as well as evolve.

One of his most enduring tunes, "Footprints," first recorded on his 1966 *Adam's Apple* album then eight months later by the Miles Davis Quintet on *Miles Smiles*, has yet to be fully completed. "There's no end-all, be-all version of that piece," Wayne says.

"Music has a way of telling what it needs, where it's going. We like to put handcuffs on music. The music maker can get in the way. The full thrust of the creative process is started and stopped by us. But I won't let that happen."

Wayne's quartet, comprising Danilo Pérez, John Patitucci and Brian Blade, continues to astound with its top-tier expression of intuitive alchemy. Last fall's collaboration with the Imani Winds at the Disney Hall in Los Angeles and Carnegie Hall in New York centered on Wayne's commissioned piece for the new-classical quintet. "Terra Incognita" will likely lead to a new album recorded in the studio in a collaborative setting of the group with the quartet.

In Panama, even though he's not prominently displayed in the festival's ad campaign—featuring photos of Chucho Valdés; Rubén Blades' singer wife Luba Mason; and festival maestro and indigenous hero, Danilo—Wayne is treated as royalty. He is the guest of honor at a cocktail party at the house of U.S. Embassy Deputy Minister David Gilmour where Wayne is greeted by Ambassador Barbara Stephenson who asks him about what he's up to. "I'm going into the unknown," he tells her.

Along with Chucho, Wayne accepts the keys to the city by Panama City mayor Juan Carlos Navarro, who reads a proclamation, then humorously introduces Wayne by saying that he "comes from another galaxy."

Wayne is later toasted by the president of Panama, Martín Erasto Torrijos Espino, at a special luncheon in the presidential palace. He smiles, but with that kind of faraway look that one wonders, what's going on inside his head. He's short on ceremony, but grins and bears it cordially. He'd much rather be back in his hotel room watching a DVD of a classic film—or, as is the case of the final evening of the festival, preparing to go onstage.

At Panama's sold-out 2,500-seat Teatro Anayansi, Wayne and his quartet are in fine form as the leader sketches on his tenor, beginning in a gentle, lyrical searching manner before John and Brian look at each other and agree to start slowly cooking rhythms. Danilo looks at Wayne and pensively stays in the tenor's stark, dreamlike realm where a quiet, Socratic dialogue plays out. There is rhythmic exuberance that is calmed by the horn's call to order as the quartet settles in only to incite again— four moving parts that operate as a collective with an acute sense of listening and expressing. Indeed, Wayne sails on an intergalactic improvisational journey with his bandmates combusting enthusiastically to charge the ride.

As if it were holding its breath, the crowd exhales with applause when the performance is over. It's a standing ovation. Backstage the crew and members of the opening act—Luba, Rubén, bassist Jimmy Haslip, flautist Hubert Laws—watch in a transfixed state as Wayne returns with his soprano saxophone for the encore which flames and calms in peaks of exclamatory rhythms and valleys of pastoral melodies. Several times during the encore, Wayne watches his band, lurches back in mock surprise as group members take over with their own excursions.

Backstage, Wayne smiles when asked about the quartet, his first permanent acoustic group that has the riches of longevity suitable for telepathic communication—onstage and off. "We're putting things together," he says. "We still have a lot to listen to."

While he says that he likes the fact that each member has his own musical life outside his quartet, the comfort he enjoys with the group is palpable. At the presidential palace, he meets up with John and Brian for the first time in Panama with warm hugs. "We call ourselves The Family," he says. "That's what it's like. Whenever we're making plans to tour or perform, we say, 'When is The Family getting together again?'"

After the show in Panama, John comes off the stage wired, exclaiming, "That was killing. That was nasty, nasty, nasty. We played little bits of everything tonight." The bassist, who began playing with Wayne in 1986, says that he's been on the Wayne train longer than the other guys, but notes, "Since this part of the journey, things have really snapped into place. It's resulted in Wayne writing gobs of music motivated by the quartet. I think it was like a new start for him. He wakes up every morning and writes with the band in mind or for orchestra—or for Imani Winds because he wanted to help further their career. He's very motivated—and very giving and generous."

John says that Wayne's musical life up to the formation of the quartet in 2000 was largely in the context of bands, such as Art Blakey's Jazz Messengers, Miles' quintet, Weather Report. It wasn't until the '80s that he began to venture out on his own. "Wayne tells the story about how Miles would say to him, 'You've got to get more exposed,'" John says. "With all the other bands, even with Herbie, he never got to the level of improvisation as with the quartet. So, for him, this still stands as the beginning."

PANAMA: SPACECRAFTS AND CRYSTALS

While talking with Wayne in Panama after his triumphant festival show, he intersperses our conversation with tangential bits and pieces of hearsay, news items and real sci-fi. He's excited.

Wayne finds it very intriguing that scientists recently discovered plumes of methane gas rising from the surface of Mars. The speculation behind the findings is that this may suggest the presence of water and perhaps even evidence of past life on the planet. "Oh, oh, methane on Mars?" Wayne says with a beaming smile. "Now, that's stuff that dreams are made of." (Given that he's a self-proclaimed "sci-fi kind of guy," it's likely that he might be fascinated by the story in the next day's international edition of *The Miami Herald* about researchers at Duke University creating metamaterials that deflect microwaves around a three-dimensional object, thus rendering it invisible.)

Even more out of the ordinary, Wayne excitedly talks about people encountering a huge spacecraft the size of two football stadiums. "I heard this solid," he says. "We can decide to deal with this or not. Two or three people were standing in this open space when this huge spaceship came hovering over them. They started receiving words, and then a huge light came down. One of the people became a channeler who said that the occupants are calibrating the crystals. Apparently, there are five giant crystals, and that the occupants of the spaceship are getting ready for the change. The light went out, and then there were more lights of many colors as if they were showing off with a light show."

Wayne shyly grins, then adds, "I'm going to write music that has all of this in it."

Wayne's most challenging work that he says will bring together "everything" he's been talking and thinking about musically throughout his life—an orchestral work for Renée Fleming—is today being pieced together bar by bar with a 2010 premiere target. "There are eight notes in a scale, but there are so many different combinations," he says. "What I'm doing is pounding at the door of creativity. That takes curiosity and courage to turn the handle and go through it. I want to let people know the door is there."

That "everything" production comes at the prodding of the classical soprano whose story includes a stint as a jazz singer during her college days. "Renée comes to see the band in Vienna," says quartet bassist John Patitucci. "She's intrigued by Wayne as a composer and is very open to collaboration."

Wayne's first contact with Renée came in 1997 after he and Herbie had recorded their *1 + 1* duet album. She wrote him a letter and asked him if he'd consider writing some music for her. Then he saw her perform in Andre Previn's opera of the Tennessee Williams play *A Streetcar Named Desire*. Wayne was impressed not only by Andre's "contemporary, atonal" musical score but also by Renée's vocal prowess.

"Writing music for Renée has presented me with a way to try to put into action a lot of things I've been talking about and wishing for," Wayne says. "I want to have music and voice do something that inspires people to shoot for the impossible outside of themselves. People are looking for a utopia or a perfect tale, but there's a lot of evil stuff going on. I suppose I'm looking for a dream, like Martin Luther King had. I want the music to do that, but the music itself won't be dreamy. Or ethereal. There's going to be a lot of dissonances going on that will seem contrary to dreaming."

Wayne says the music he's creating for the production is "the most chance-taking stuff I've ever written." This is spurred on in part by Renée, who, Wayne notes, has been known for sending material written for her back to the composer.

"Renée doesn't want someone being careful or polite when they write," Wayne says. "She loves a challenge, but it has to be through real, sincere collaborative action. She's open to new things. She's not a victim of protocol. She's not going to fall for the old axioms. She's ready to make room for a new world of vocalists. She wants to speak to the terms of today's events. When we talk, we talk as collaborators, with mutual respect. I consider her family."

Wayne describes his Los Angeles studio which he's eager to return to after the festival. In the space he says that he surrounds himself with score paper, orchestral books and symphonies by other composers ("I want to make sure I don't write something that's already been written"). Also, in the room are stacks of sci-fi, philosophy, fantasy and fairy tale books as well as a huge film encyclopedia (a birthday present). He has a box of pastels should he feel inspired ("You have to remember that before I started playing jazz I was an art major") and usually has the TV turned on to CNN.

He says that so far, the writing has been going slowly. "The orchestral work for Renée is complex," Wayne says. "But I'm aiming for the simplicity in it. I'm attempting to compose a great eternal adventure. While I'm writing, I'm disagreeing with the status quo and trying to express that in music, whether it's in the sequence of the harmonic story or having new melodic content."

He's aware that 2010 is just around the next bend. "That's why I'm writing as fast as I can right now," he says. "But I can stay on one measure for two weeks. Recently I spent the whole day on one note. But one incident in my little room becomes huge when I come upon something. I have to keep going without repeating myself. You write something, and it's electric. The music is telling me something, but how do I get it all down without my horn. I have a keyboard, but I don't play the piano. Sometimes there are three or four things merging, like galaxies crossing through each other, and you have to get it down—and quickly because it can shut off fast. You think you have the answer, but then it's gone."

Wayne is doing his best to explain the zigzags of his creative process, but he grows weary, finding himself at a loss of words beyond saying that what he's working on now is "involved." He's reminded of what Tony Williams used to tell people when they asked him what he was thinking about when he played the drums: "If I could tell you, I wouldn't have to play it."

Bandmate John says that one of Wayne's favorite lines is "There's no end to a composition." He adds: "Wayne wants his writing to be adventurous and not complacent."

Wayne seconds that: "I like to take chances with a lot of imagination." He pauses, smiles and relishes the thought of the experience. "I sit still and imagine, and I think, 'Oh, oh, this looks dangerous.'"

Wayne addresses the criticism he has faced over the years, in particular the response to his orchestral-fusion 1995 album *High Life*. It was ripped to shreds by several jazz critics who accused the saxophonist of selling out artistically.

"People have been telling me my entire life that I couldn't go in certain directions with my music," Wayne says. "You're supposed to make music that's a guarantee for the royalty conveyor belt. That sense of commerciality dictates what should be written, recorded, played and marketed for easy listening."

He adds, "If I had a record company, I would call it Nothing to Lose Records, with Going Down with the Ship Records in parentheses, followed by Never Mind Lifejackets in smaller parentheses and One Way Ticket Only in even smaller parentheses." He laughs. "The ultimate astronaut. That's what we all are."

SNIPPETS

Wayne always flew against the odds. Here are more snippets of wisdom that cross a decade's worth of conversations.

- In a 1990 conversation with pianist Renee Rosnes early in her career recording for Blue Note, she tells me a story about how Wayne enlisted her for an electric band he planned to tour in 1988. She had recently left tenor saxophonist Joe Henderson's band, so Wayne asked her to join up with him. Renee says the only issue was that Wayne insisted that she play electric keyboards not acoustic. Of course, she complied, happily, yet cautiously

    She recalls that one rehearsal of the entire band at his Los Angeles home wasn't proceeding very well. Wayne paused and asked how many people in the room had seen the film *Alien*. None had. He stopped the session and assembled everyone in his home theater to watch the movie. At the moment when the alien's offspring surprisingly erupts from their host's chest, Wayne froze the screen. "This is what I want to have happen with this band each night," he tells his team of explorers. In other words, unpredictability—and awe.

- As for future jazz musicians, Wayne shared a few nuggets of wisdom at the 1999 commencement services at the Berklee College of Music (the Boston school bestowed upon him and rock star David Bowie honorary doctorates): "I told the young people to check out life because the act of appreciation is a foil to instant gratification. Instead of practicing all the time, do things that are real experiences. Go out into the woods or to a movie with your girlfriend or ice skating with your son or daughter. Practice is important, but it shouldn't be church. Life is bigger than your music."

- In 2004, when journalist Michelle Mercer was writing the saxophonist's biography, *Footprints: The Life and Work of Wayne Shorter*, I asked her about her experience with the iconic jazz master. "Wayne has always been elusive, enigmatic and sometimes difficult to approach," she says. "I had to go into the stratosphere with him before getting him to come back to earth." Now, doesn't that sound familiar. "I'm originally from Kansas," Michelle adds, "so it was as if I clicked my heels three times and ended up in Oz with Wayne."

- In 2010, right on time, Wayne composes "Aurora" for Renée Fleming and orchestra that premiered in the opening gala for the St. Louis Symphony Orchestra season. Inspired by the poem "The Rock Cried Out to Us Today" that Maya Angelou wrote for Bill Clinton's inauguration in 1992, "Aurora" was a project Renée and Wayne discussed for over a decade.

- In 2018, Wayne releases the ambitious *Emanon* three-album project of live recordings of his quartet and orchestra. The package also includes a 74-page graphic novel/comic book about a futuristic fantasy.

- In 2021 Wayne debuted *Iphigenia*, the jazz-meets-classical musical opera that he co-created with Esperanza Spalding. It debuted onstage in 2021 and continued to be performed into 2022.

Jimmy Smith—Basking in the B-3

I revved up my old VW Bug in Berkeley and headed to Jimmy's house in Sacramento for this interview. This is my writer's copy before it was published in DownBeat.

HAMMOND B-3 BOMBER JIMMY SMITH TALKS ABOUT HIS JAZZ REVITALIZATION OF THE MONSTER ORGAN
1994

In 1986 at the height of the synthesized keyboard craze, Jimmy Smith prophetically told a Chicago Sun-Times reporter, "It's just a matter of time before this trend turns over, before people get tired of that damn noise and come back to the pure sound of the organ."

Today, with the Hammond B-3's chunky chords and burbling lines in vogue, the 66-year-old living jazz legend is still bristling over the instrument's falling from favor for nearly two decades. Sitting in the backyard patio of his Sacramento, California home, Jimmy, who singlehandedly and explosively thrust the organ into the jazz lexicon in the mid-'50s with his innovative bop stylings, is unashamedly peppering our conversation on the Hammond B-3 renaissance of the '90s with plenty of I-told-you-so's.

"I was saying synthesizers were bullshit back in 1982 when I wrote the monologue for my *Off the Top* album," says Jimmy, who's black coffee to the max with his rapid-fire responses, delightfully caustic wit and vitriol-laced critiques. "Here today and gone tomorrow just like I said then. But the Hammond will last into infinity. Those synthesizer freaks try to get the B-3 sound, but it's too light, too weak. It's a poor copy. When you play a synthesizer..." He searches for the right word, instead clutches his throat and starts a retching motion. He gasps out, "It makes me want to throw up."

Then, animated with messianic zeal, Jimmy expounds on the B-3's virtues, pausing after each attribute to make sure I'm following him. "The Hammond has body...It's got depth...and resonance. It's got clarity...and quality. And you can feel it. It's not so much that you can hear it. It's the feeling that's important. You see, it's like a drummer. You don't want to hear him. You want to feel him. You can have the best drummer in the world, but if he's too loud, he's out of place. With the Hammond, you feel it in your bones."

After his second morning beer, Jimmy's gravelly voice has risen in pitch and his excitability is ready to bubble over in the same way that he erupts into a scintillating organ groove. "Look at my hands," he says. "They're shaking just thinking about playing. Don't talk to me too much about my music cause I get carried away. I go off. I go completely off."

From the sounds of it, that's how Jimmy has always been when it comes to the keyboards. The son of a stride piano-playing father, Jimmy taught himself how to play at an early age in his hometown of Norristown, Pennsylvania where he was born December 8, 1928.

At nine, he performed a boogie-woogie piece on the popular Major Bowes Amateur Hour radio program. Jimmy remembers his winning performance well, laughing as he retells the story of how they just about had to drag him from the stage.

"There I was in a pair of shorts with piano books on the seat underneath me so that I could reach the keys," he says. "Once I got going, I didn't stop. The announcer was saying, 'Ladies and gentlemen, this kid's on fire. He's burning the place up.' While everyone was applauding me, I kept going. My mother, who took me to the show, was off to the side telling me to get off the stage, but I wouldn't leave."

With show business in his bones, a few years later Jimmy was teaming with his father in a song-and-dance act while immersing himself in Art Tatum music and picking up piano pointers hanging out with Bud Powell's kid brother Richie.

"I was at Bud's house every day," recalls Jimmy, who, once wound up on yet another drink, takes great pleasure in recounting the tales of his youth. "He lived in Willow Grove, Pennsylvania, which is about six miles from Norristown. Richie and I'd be there early waiting for Bud to wake up. He'd get his coffee and then go straight to the piano. After a while, he stopped me from coming because I was learning too much. I figured out a couple of his tunes, 'Loco Poco' and 'Glass Enclosure.' I played them for him and I wiped them out. After that he told me to stay home."

Copping licks from Powell came in handy years later when Jimmy, home after serving in the Navy during World War II, was in a Philadelphia club catching a Charlie Parker show. Powell was in Bird's band but failed to show up for the early gig. "Bud was always late," Jimmy says. "This stride piano player Fats Wright was filling in. He saw me in the audience and wanted me to play. I was good enough, but I was scared. Fats started calling, 'Where's little Jimmy Junior?' Well, by then I was under the bar hiding. Finally, they pushed me up there. The first tune was 'Lady Be Good.' My hands were shaking, but after I got into it, I was gone. After the set Bird thanked me and hugged me. Then, who walked in but the Frantic Man himself. He asked Bird, 'Who played? Who played? He's not goin' take my gig.' But Bird just told him, 'Shut up and play.'"

After stints in formal music education at the Halsey Music School (harmony and theory), Hamilton School of Music (upright bass) and Ornstein School (piano and theory), Jimmy joined the R&B band Don Gardner and His Sonotones in the early '50s. But he soon tired of pounding on the piano. "The pianos were always so out of tune it was ridiculous," he says. "Plus, the ivory was so worn out on the keys I was getting blisters from playing on the wood. I knew there was something better for me."

That's when Jimmy made the trip to the Harlem Club in Atlantic City to check out Wild Bill Davis holding court on the organ. "I said that's for me!" says Jimmy in a shout. Then he quieted his voice as if he were reliving the moment and whispers, "When he finished playing, I snuck up on the bandstand to touch the action. It was so soft. I knew I could play it."

Jimmy borrowed money from a loan shark, bought his first Hammond B-3 and set out to teach himself how to play it. His woodshed was a small room in a Philadelphia warehouse. "Nobody was teaching organ then," he says. "I just looked at it and thought, 'Oh, man, this is going to be a job.' But I liked challenges. Right off I realized I had to do something about the pedals because I didn't want to always be looking down at them. So I had an artist from the Ornstein School make me a three-foot by three-foot chart of the pedals that I taped to the wall in front of me. Then I experimented with different stops and draw bars until finally I found the right sound, the Jimmy Smith sound, and the rest is history."

Not only had Jimmy found his voice on the organ, but he revolutionized its use, eclipsing Wild Bill Davis's swing-oriented style and innovatively proving with percolating foot-pedal and left-hand bass lines and lightning-fast, blues-drenched right-hand runs that the Hammond could scorch with bebop intensity.

Influenced as much by the horn playing of Illinois Jacquet, Arnett Cobb, Sonny Stitt, Dexter Gordon, Coleman Hawkins and Gene Ammons as by keyboard players, Jimmy burst into the jazz world with his guitar-drum-organ trio in 1956 when his first two albums, *A New Sound A New Star* and *The Champ*, were released on Blue Note.

After two well-received live trio albums, in 1957 Smith spent three days recording music in several different ensemble configurations, which resulted in five LPs (recently reissued with the tracks in the order they were recorded by Mosaic as *The Complete February 1957 Jimmy Smith Blue Note Sessions*).

Jimmy continued with Blue Note until 1962 (recording thirty discs with his steady drummer Donald Bailey and oftentimes with guitarist Kenny Burrell) when he signed with Verve, where he scored such mammoth hit albums as *Bashin'*, *Organ Grinder Swing* and two dynamic and adventurous LPs with Wes Montgomery and arranger Oliver Nelson. After his contract with Verve ended in 1968, Jimmy recorded throughout the '70s and '80s with such labels as Atlantic, MGM, Mercury, Elektra Musician and his own label Mojo. He also recorded for Milestone, which is where he issued his last three releases before returning to Blue Note for his appropriately-titled, deep-grooving new disc *The Master*, a trio collection highlighted by many of Smith's greatest hits performed live in Japan and featuring guitarist Burrell and drummer Jimmie Smith (no relation).

While Jimmy takes great pride in his collaborations with Montgomery ("We locked from the moment we met"), he gets absolutely exhilarated discussing his longtime association with Burrell. "On the new album, it was like the old days," he says. "We were feeding each other, steady feeding the whole way through. Most guitarists you gotta tell 'em how to play. You know, play a suspension here or make a chord larger there. But not Kenny. He knows what to do. He's a master in his own right. We burnt Japan up when we recorded this album. Everyone was hollering, even the engineers."

Jimmy is visibly excited, tapping his fingers on the table as if he's ready to retreat into his backyard studio near the swimming pool, switch his Hammond on and roar.

When I mention how great he and Burrell sound on "Down By The Riverside" on the Verve *Carnegie Hall Salutes the Jazz Masters* disc, he barks, "What'd I tell you, man. Anytime we play, it's the same thing. We were just having conversations. I feed him and he feeds me, just like I told you. Look out! We bar nobody. It's a marriage, and we're not talking about divorce."

The organ was relegated to miscellaneous status in *DownBeat's* critics polls until 1964 when Jimmy's prowess on the instrument necessitated it getting its own category. The master of the Hammond B-3 has been king since that time, with such players as Jack McDuff, Jimmy McGriff and most recently Joey DeFrancesco—often credited with the organ's current revival—periodically imperiling Jimmy's reign.

What does he think about that? "Most of those guys were my students," he says. "I can remember Jimmy McGriff and Groove Holmes racing over to my house at nine in the morning. They'd be outside arguing. They were crazy. I tried to get them to practice together, but they didn't want to share anything I taught them. Jimmy learned a passage and then go home and hide. He'd lock the doors, pull the shades down, put soundproofing on the windows. They were good friends, but, man, they woke me up every morning."

What does Jimmy think of Joey, who, I remind him, learned his tune "The Sermon" when he was five? "Come on, now, I don't think nothing of his playing," he says. "I taught him from when he was seven until he was fourteen. He's playing Jimmy Smith. He says he's not, but he lies. He's a nice kid, but he can't help but play me."

Tired of this line of questioning, Jimmy switches gears, telling me he has one more story to tell. Calling it his classic, he launches into his tale of the night that such jazz greats as Sonny Rollins, Hank Mobley, Art Blakey, Max Roach and Monk all came to a small club called Jimmy's in New York to hear him shortly after *The Champ* was released.

Recalling it like a young kid describing a treasure, Jimmy gushes, "They thought I was overdubbing on the record because I was playing so fast, so they came to see for themselves. Well, after a while they all started coming up to play. All those horns and Art asking to take Donald Bailey's place. The house was burning. Then Monk walks up to the bandstand, gets behind me and starts playing with me on the organ. Man, that was the most exciting thing that ever happened to me besides being born."

Not all is so rosy, though, complains Jimmy, who's been living the Hammond life for forty years now. He says his legs are getting worn out, his wind is shorter and his blood is thinner. He's still gigging and even doing some recording with Us3 for its upcoming project, but he says he's tired and wishes he had a nest egg tucked away so that he could start contemplating semi-retirement.

All this talk comes shortly before he invites me into his backyard studio—his organ sanctuary—where in the process of demonstrating just how expressive his Hammond B-3 really is, he magically rejuvenates.

In this private session, Jimmy flicks on his organ and huge Leslie speaker, settles in behind the keys and sketches an impromptu piece that starts with soulful musing and ends with passionate eruptions of molten beauty that make the windows shake. Seeing him drift off to a heavenly zone and listening to him purr-growl while playing, I realize how young Jimmy looks. With no noticeable gray hair, a still-trim body and fingers and feet that can still ignite a blaze, he could almost pass for himself, circa 1957.

With the organ vibrations humming deep inside me as he plays, I understand what Jimmy means when he says it's not necessarily what you hear but how it feels. The Hammond may have been down for a spell, but, as Jimmy continues to testify in his shows and on disc, it's not ready to die.

Jimmy's wife Lola who serves as his business manager, says, give the organ master a good Hammond B-3, two Leslie Model 122 speakers, and microphones for both the tops and bottoms of the speakers and he'll deliver the goods—that mellow and rich funky sound he's famous for. She also notes that Jimmy owns a Baldwin piano. In his private practice studio, his Leslie speakers are housed in a cabinet built by Keyboard Products.

As for why he feels the Leslie speakers work so well with the Hammond B-3, Jimmy replies, "Because they have the beef, they have the power. With a 60-watt driver on top and a JBL on the bottom, they can break your ear drums."

Esperanza Spalding—Sings the Melody, Anchors the Rhythm

Esperanza's responded to my early-aughts "The Question Is" column in DownBeat *about the changing technology: "It's sad to see things go more and more digital. I want artwork. I'd like to see LPs return. But once a trend starts it's hard for people to go backwards. It's like evolution, but with technology. A new species is always taking over." Yes, that's been her life as an artist—an appreciation of the past but with an eye on evolutionary adventures. From 2006 to 2010, we conversed about her latest projects as well as her growth as an artist.*

THE EARLY YEARS
2010

At the time of our 2010 conversation, we focused on her third album, Chamber Music Society, that not only became a commercial success but also resulted in her winning the first of many career Grammy Awards. In 2011, she earned the Best New Artist honors—an unprecedented achievement for a jazz artist up against high-profile pop, hip-hop and rock artists—in this case Justin Bieber, Drake, Mumford & Sons, and Florence and the Machine. This is an expansion of that Billboard column.

In 2006, Esperanza Spalding, a rarity who plays acoustic bass while simultaneously singing, was reveling in the freedom to be offbeat. She told me everything was "fucking amazing." She ranged high on the exuberance meter.

The Boston-based native of Portland, Oregon, was in the midst of launching her career a year after graduating from Berklee College of Music.

We spoke in a wide-ranging, humorous conversation while walking the long piazza in Perugia, Italy, at its summer Umbria Jazz Festival where she was performing for three nights in a small theater. She buoyed with moxie-plus, high-octane ebullience, spirited determination and respectful humility in the face of the jazz legacy.

We talked about her first album *Junjo*, an impressive trio date that she produced and arranged. Recorded in April 2005, it was released in 2006 by the Barcelona, Spain-based AYVA Music label. "My music has come so far from when we recorded it," Esperanza said at the time. "It's all been a trip. It seems like every six months my music evolves. As I meet different musicians in new circles, they influence me and change my sound."

In 2007, Umbria creative director Carlo Pagnotta caught her at the Jazz Standard in New York playing in a trio comprising guitarists Romero Lubamba and Russell Malone. "I wanted to have her come to Umbria with them," Pagnotta told me, "but she insisted on bringing her own band."

At the July festival, Esperanza proved to be a revelation to the audiences at the Oratorio Santa Cecilia with her trio of Leo Genovese on piano and Lynden Rochelle on drums. She was a sparkplug who danced with her bass as she scatted and sang through a mixed set of standards (a grooving "Autumn Leaves" and a funky, upbeat take on "Body and Soul") and originals such as "Winter Sun," a samba-tinged tune with a funk-rock beat that she retitled "Summer Sun" for the occasion.

As for the expansive range of her music, she says, "Everyone wonders, why did you go to jazz when you're interested in so much else? For us young jazz musicians, it's how we learn music. It's like reading a sacred text in Greek. So, we study and learn more and more, but our hearts are into a mishmash of different sounds."

At her Umbria performance, Esperanza was as likely to explode into a patch of vocalese as to solo using her bass to sound like a horn. "I can't help it," she says afterwards. "I always try to tone down my dancing with the bass. I think, I must look like an idiot, but then I bust out and can't control it."

Esperanza exuded such over-the-top excitement at the prospects of her present and future that I wondered if she would flame and crash, a victim of flying too close to the jazz sun. But her willingness to play the nonconformity card won her out. "I've always been that way," the young upstart said. "So many people are asleep, but I'm awake."

CHAMBER MUSIC SOCIETY

2010

Today, in 2010, shortly after recording her brilliant *Chamber Music Society* album, Esperanza continues to marvel, but in a much more mature manner, taking it all in stride. For our latest conversation, she requests meeting at Café Reggio in the West Village, her favorite new neighborhood eating space—not for the sake of any kind of upscale vibe but for its funkiness of piped-in opera and classical music, busts of famous musicians, and its claim to fame as brewing the finest cappuccino in the Village.

Esperanza continues to be a spunky spirit, quick to joke and giggle, and utters little squeaks and oohs. Her trademark Afro is pulled back and tucked up in a bun. She still expresses a hip, carefree attitude, whether it's about the brunch that's being served to her or the confirmation she receives by cellphone for getting tickets to the CareFusion New York Jazz Festival show celebrating Herbie Hancock's 70th birthday at Carnegie Hall.

She's quick to share some background on recording her third album, the strings-laden *Chamber Music Society* (on Heads Up International), which she is extremely proud of. It's the next step in the evolution of her promising career.

Esperanza's jazz ascent has been meteoric, based on the small but substantive body of work she's developed so far—with *Junjo* and her impressive 2008 follow-up, *Esperanza*, on Heads Up—and her buzz-worthy marquee performances, including a high-profile appearance at the 10th annual BET Music Awards show on June 27. There she gave it up for lifetime achievement honoree Prince by playing a solo vocal/bass rendering of his "If I Was Your Girlfriend."

Even so, she's in no danger of becoming a meteorite. Instead, she's in full orbit with her own solo endeavors, as well as playing co-starring roles in bands led by Joe Lovano (Us Five) and McCoy Tyner.

While in the studio for her new album, Esperanza could have easily dictated the proceedings, but she is decidedly not a spoiled diva intent on steamrollering what lies ahead. In fact, she is remarkably humble in front of the monumental jazz legacy that she's tapping into to inform her next steps.

Even so, for *Chamber Music Society*, Esperanza insisted on opening with the moody yet playful vocalese tune "Knowledge of Good and Evil." But she met with resistance from her co-producer/co-arranger Gil Goldstein, her management and others who maintained that the leadoff track should be the lyrical beauty "Little Fly," which showcases both her vocals and her bass playing on a William Blake poem she set to music. Even though she was out-voted, she wielded veto power, which she clung to.

"We were having this little argument, and I was saying, this album is an art piece, and I don't want to get obsessed with marketability," says the 25-year-old Esperanza. "Finally, Gil said, 'Espe, is there anyone in the world whose opinion you would accept if we played them the album?' I told him, 'Yes, there's one person, not that it matters, and that's Wayne Shorter. If Wayne agrees with you, I wouldn't argue.'"

Gil says that he was willing to concede to the artist's demand for the first tune (as musician and co-producer, he says, she gets two votes). But nonetheless he contacted Scott Southard, who works at International Music Network, the Boston-based booking agency that represents Esperanza and Shorter. Gil told Southard that they were ready to go into the mastering stage and requested a quick turnaround.

The next day Esperanza received a text message from Southard. "Scott said that he sent Wayne the tapes overnight," she says with a laugh of amazement. "Wayne listened to it, and he agreed with Gil. So, we went with 'Little Fly.'"

Why consult Wayne, whom Esperanza didn't know? "I figured it would be a moot point because there's no way they could get in touch with Wayne Shorter that quickly to settle some stupid dispute," she says. "I figured that I would just win."

But why Wayne and not some other upper-tier jazz master? "He's the voice of music now that I most respect, flat out, in any genre," she says. "It's not only his music, but also his character, his spirit. He's the artist I most admire. He's valid. He's the real thing. He's solid."

When Wayne voiced his opinion, he also requested that Esperanza give him a call. It took her two days to muster up the courage to ring him. They ended up conversing for 45 minutes.

"Wayne talked about music and his perspectives on many, many things," says Esperanza, who took notes that she attached to her refrigerator so she can reference his sage ruminations. "What he talked about was multilayered, multifaceted—everything from his humanistic and spiritual perspectives to his music and career. It was life-changing for me. He shared so openly and freely about everything."

What Esperanza also took away from the conversation was something that, given the unbridled eagerness inherent in her youth, taught her about her own future. "Wayne has so much bubbling enthusiasm to share," she says. "It's something that can pull you forward. I thought, damn, I can do this for the rest of my days, till I'm old and crunchy and can't move. That's the ultimate for me."

THE MASTER PLAN LIST

When we spoke four years ago at Umbria, Esperanza already had a master plan: to play with her musical heroes. She drew up a list, two of whom she had just recently performed with: Richard Bona and Brian Blade. Then she suddenly remembered meeting up with Stanley Clarke.

Regarding her tete-a-tete with Stanley, she burst out, "Oh, I flew to Los Angeles to work on his new album." Without knowing how she could be of use, she blew in from the East Coast on a 5 a.m. flight and arrived on the West Coast at 10, assuming that she would be escorted to her hotel where she could rest up.

"But the driver took me right to Stanley's studio at his house," Esperanza said. "We met and he gave me a piece of music he had written and asked me to write lyrics to it." Stanley told Esperanza that he'd return in a couple of hours.

"Oh, my God, what was I going to do," Esperanza recounted, in a mock panic. "But I just wrote, and then sang the lyrics." The song, "All Over Again," showed up on Stanley's *The Toys of Men*.

After telling the story, she exclaimed, "This is way better than Superman and Spider-Man. I'm playing with musicians I admire, and that's been amazing. Everything's happening right now. It's not been like a big super bang-up, but more what I see as a natural evolution of a musician working hard on her craft and going places as a result."

The remaining three names on her list of six were Wayne (check), Stevie Wonder (check; he asked her to perform his song "I Know You Know" and accompanied her on her tune "Fall In" at a Los Angeles benefit he puts on annually), and Chick Corea. The last collaboration has yet to happen, but today that doesn't matter as much as it did three years ago.

"I've modified my concept of the list," she says. "Now, I realize that you can't want to be with someone. It's like wanting to marry someone you've never met. Music is so intimate, so fragile, so unpredictable. Today I feel like playing with someone because there's something there to explore and the chemistry is there. I adore Chick

Corea's music, his writing. I've listened to his *Inner Space* record so many times that I could sing every part of it. But that doesn't mean that if we worked together there would be the magic and meaning that would be important for our combined energies. So, now, I'm letting go of my lists."

INSPIRATIONS

When I ask her who influenced her as a bass player, she cites Slam Stewart, Dave Holland and Ron Carter, who was guest speaker at Berklee's 2005 commencement and also presented the grads with their degrees. "When Ron gave me mine, he told me to calm down," Esperanza says. "I'm not quite sure why, but I am hyper. I'm sorry to say that so far I haven't heeded his advice."

Even so, Esperanza says she's not interested in "getting a gig" anymore. She's more concerned about what she can offer when opportunities arise. Case in point: her vocal collaboration with Milton Nascimento on the luscious tune "Apple Blossom," from *Chamber Music Society*. Working with another one of her all-time heroes came by serendipity.

Last year, she and her trio were booked to play two dates in Brazil, at São Paulo and Rio, opening for George Benson. On a whim beforehand, she asked her management to send an email to Nascimento to let him know how much she appreciated his music. A month later he responded and let her know he was paying attention to her, especially since she had recorded his tune "Ponta De Areia" on *Esperanza*. They continued a short correspondence of mutual admiration, and that was it—until Esperanza arrived in Brazil.

"I didn't know he was in the audience, but he saw us perform in São Paulo," she says. "He came backstage and we met. And he invited us to a little party at his house when we got to Rio. We thought it was just a get-together, but he had actually thrown the party in our honor because we were visiting. All these musicians came and we all played, drank and hung together. Milton said to me, 'Let's make some music together sometime.' That was super heavy. It was the ultimate to have that offer come from a hero of mine, not through some management plan."

A couple of months later, Esperanza was in a bind over how to sing one of her own *Chamber Music Society* compositions, "Apple Blossom," which tells the story of an aging man who laments the death of his wife. "I wrote the song, but I had never experienced loss like that," she says. "I needed someone else to sing it with me. That's when I thought of Milton. I love the way he phrases English on his version of 'Norwegian Wood.' It's so dark and melancholy. I thought he would be perfect for my song."

Esperanza emailed him, and he replied that he would be in the United States in November and agreed to come to the recording session in Los Angeles. She showed him the rough draft of the song, and the two nailed their gorgeous duet.

"It all happened so organically," says Esperanza. "You can feel the love between us when we sing. It had nothing to do with [the notion of] having to get this big name on the album."

241

DEEP GROOVES WITH MCCOY

The same held true with Esperanza's connection to McCoy Tyner, who the night before our brunch at Café Reggio commanded SummerStage in Central Park as a part of the CareFusion New York fest. It was a free show on a double bill with Stanley, featuring Hiromi. McCoy's band was an all-star quartet including Esperanza, saxophonist Ravi Coltrane and drummer Francisco Mela, an old friend of the bassist who appeared on *Junjo*.

Smiling throughout, Esperanza kept a close eye on McCoy, watching for the dynamics-prone pianist to wind down and rev up again. She played a deep groove, made sure to avoid McCoy's powerful left hand and lulled with balladic lines when she was offered the space to stretch.

Again, Esperanza did no lobbying to perform with McCoy. That took place last December when she joined his quartet for a week's stay at Yoshi's in Oakland. The all-star cast came together outside of her sphere of influence. This Central Park New York appearance was the quartet's first since early January. They jelled again.

After the show backstage, McCoy praised the young bassist. "Esperanza is brilliant," he told me. "She's gifted. She's solid and dependable. She listens to what's going on and complements what I do. Plus, my first impression of her was that she's a very nice person on top of it all."

As for her onstage alertness, McCoy said, "You have to do that if you're looking for inspiration and direction—not only the notes but how you move physically. You listen to the rhythms and watch the body move."

The next morning, Esperanza is speechless—almost. "Anything I could say would not do justice," she says when asked what it's like to play with McCoy.

But hardly ever at a loss for words, Esperanza says that it wasn't a case of intimidation the first time she played with him, but more self-consciousness and even a sense of insecurity. She recalls that the summer before the Yoshi's gig was dreamed up, she and her longtime pianist Leo Genovese had gotten into a total Tyner-zone over the course of two months of gigging.

"So, McCoy was already in the air," she says. "We listened to hours and hours of his music—solo recordings, live albums, quartets. We'd be driving for six hours through Italy and talking about McCoy the whole way. So, when the Yoshi's week came up, I knew all of his music, so I didn't have to prep as much. But, as a bass player, I knew it was going to be difficult because McCoy plays the bass and the drums at the same time on the piano. At first, that was a challenge for me, figuring how I could offer him the most with my bass, but by the end of the week at Yoshi's, I felt less idiotic. We were all totally engaged."

THE NEW ALBUMS

Esperanza has had a love affair with music since she was very young. She was home-schooled for a stretch after a childhood illness and dropped out of the conventional setting of high school to pursue music. She took her GED, enrolled in the music program at Portland State University and entered Berklee on a scholarship thanks to her bass prowess. She graduated a year early in 2005 at the age of 20, and with much fanfare was immediately hired to teach in the bass department there. After Berklee, Esperanza had already established herself as a side player with such notables as Lee Konitz and Patti Austin, as well as a bandleader in her own right. That led to her recording a demo in April 2005 that was picked up by Ayva. A year later *Junjo* was issued in the States.

In regard to her self-titled Heads Up International debut (an imprint of the Concord Music Group), Esperanza upped the ante on her vocals and plowed deep grooves with her bass. It featured a mix-and-match set of funked-up and rocked-out repertoire. It scored top of class, as far as selling the most CDs internationally for a new jazz artist in 2008.

"It's been a natural evolution that musicians going places experience," Esperanza said at the time. "The new album is a crossover date that has the integrity of jazz. Only one song really swings; the rest are very groove-oriented."

Esperanza was produced by Terence Blanchard and featured all of her original compositions except for two standards, including, as she calls it, "a tripped out" "Body and Soul."

Bottom line, she said, "The object is to get young people moving."

After the popularity of *Esperanza*, *Chamber Music Society* is decidedly an album that's coming in from left field. Inspired by the Chamber Music Society of Oregon (in which she played violin for 10 years), Esperanza decided to create a modern image of a chamber group with string trio arrangements complementing her own originals that are infused with pop, folk and jazz. Genovese is on board, as well as drummer Terri Lyne Carrington.

Esperanza credits her Barcelona-based management, Montuno Productions, with giving her free license to pursue her latest musical vision. "They were the first people to approach me when I was just starting," she says. "They loved my music, and I've loved working with them. Sometimes I forget how blessed I am when I think of young artists with managers who are not really on their team. I told Montuno that I was making a decision that might not seem to make much business sense, but they'd just have to respect me."

Esperanza didn't have a fully developed game plan for *Chamber Music Society*. It evolved slowly and came into focus with the help of Goldstein. "I wanted to work with Gil because of his enthusiasm," she says. "This genius master was so into my music that he was willing to go into it and make it better."

Esperanza, says Gil with admiration, is "always reaching for something new every time she performs. She puts a face on every note. She's become more refined as a player. She's going deeper."

Gil explains how he got involved in Esperanza's project: "It's not luck or an accident. It's more like I attract things that are suited to me. I have a distrust of things that are won through politics or positioning, and feel more blessed and in sync when things unfold in an organic way."

Esperanza showed Gil three *Chamber Music Society* pieces she had arranged. He attended an Esperanza show with pianist Adam Goldberg, vocalist Gretchen Parlato and three string players. "It was an early presentation of her chamber music project," he says. "But I didn't know what I could bring to it to make it better. I wasn't sold on the three strings and suggested that we bring in a couple of woodwinds. Espe immediately said no woodwinds. I said we may need some more colors in the music, so we decided to bring in extra singing voices. As it turned out, Espe sang in such a pure way that she sounded like a woodwind."

While she's received a lot of attention for her bass playing (she won this year's *DownBeat* Critics Poll for Rising Star, Acoustic Bass), Esperanza also has improved immensely as a singer, showcased on wordless and lyrical parts throughout *Chamber Music Society*. Early on, she was best known as a terrific bassist in motion to greater heights, but then she began to charge into vocal numbers among the instrumentals.

She's been intent on that, especially on *Chamber Music Society*. Esperanza downplays the notion that she's doing anything new or special as a bassist who also sings. "I never thought about singing," she says. "I didn't really care, because it came easy to me. I always sang when I was a child. In the last couple of years, I decided to cultivate that. But I didn't know what I didn't know. I was singing by ear and not worrying about how it sounded."

Esperanza's first self-taught vocal exercise was singing Michael Brecker's saxophone solo on "The Sorcerer" from his *Directions in Music*. She recorded herself and became dismayed when she played it back. "What I thought was happening was not really happening," she says. "What I was hearing in my head—the timbres, the different sounds, the textures—was not happening. I had to learn how to get that, how to articulate and come to the understanding of the mechanism of the instrument like I have with the bass." She began to listen to and study singers like Betty Carter, Abbey Lincoln and Nnenna Freelon to find out what was lacking in her own vocals.

Gil has seen the progress and goes so far as to say that Esperanza is one of the best jazz singers on the scene today. "She's a real jazz vocalist like Abbey or Betty," he says, then adds, "not like an Ella or Sarah who were more populous. Espe is so versatile, running the gamut from great R&B to Stevie Wonder pop, and sings with the most personality. You hear half a note and you know it's her."

He's also amazed at how she plays bass and sings. "I can't think of another jazz singer who can sing the melody and comp with the bass notes for herself the way she does," Gil says. "It's singing the melody and anchoring the rhythm. The world could collapse around her, or she could be playing with the worst drummer, and she would still protect the rhythm like a soccer goalie."

Parlato, a good friend who has appeared on Esperanza's last two albums (including their show-stopping duet on Antonio Carlos Jobim's "Inutile Paisagem" on *Chamber Music Society*), says that Esperanza's singing has become "profound and versatile." It helps, she says, that Esperanza studied instrumental music first. "She's singing at such an advanced level. She's developed a very unique sound with her tone and texture that immediately hits you. It gives me goose bumps. She's very precise, perfectly in tune and takes big risks. Her dynamics are so wide. She's doing everything the right way. She's causing a scene by just being herself as a total person."

When reminded of her telling me three years ago that wonderful things happen as a byproduct of the natural evolution of a musician who's in motion, Esperanza says, "Yes, it's all about the process. That's getting reaffirmed over and over. The things I forget the quickest are the events. But what I don't forget is being some place and grabbing a chunk of insight from another musician. It kicks my butt into a new direction."

As for the future, Esperanza, who now splits time between Austin, Texas, and New York's Greenwich Village, is already conceptually working on her next album, *Radio Music Society*, which she initially described as a funk, hip-hop, rock excursion.

That's all changed now, as she's been on the road experimenting with the tunes she's written so far. "It's about putting elements of our own music onto the radio," she explains. "It's about playing songs that should be on the radio but haven't been meddled with for the sake of getting on the radio. We've been doing some of these songs live and people are freaking out. They love them." Knowing Esperanza, their shapes are bound to change even more when she and her band hit the studio in November.

The final question of our interview gives Esperanza pause. She's a fluid talker, who moves from topic to topic with gleeful ease. But when asked to describe herself in six words, she stops in her tracks. The wheels are turning, but after long thought, she settles on her phrase. It's not perfect, she says, but it'll do: Striving to achieve full human potential."

It's an excellent summation of what lies ahead—steady and grooving and determined as she goes.

FAST-FORWARD TO A DUO

2023

These days, esperanza uses a lower case spelling of her name.

In 2018, esperanza teamed up in an experimental duo setting with one of jazz's top pianists, Fred Hersch. They spent a week at the Village Vanguard performing no set lists and no game plan beyond creating for the moment. The album documenting the two came out in 2023 as *Alive at the Village Vanguard*. The captivating duo returned to the Vanguard— as holy a jazz venue as there is —for the album lift off and turned in a special week of improvisation gold.

At the second show on Wednesday, January 11, the pair engaged in a buoyant dance through tunes from the jazz canon. But it was all done with a fun force of musical invention. Nothing straightahead, but twisted with ad libs from esperanza and surprising keyboard zings from Fred. They started the show with a rough sketch of what they would duo on, but that was just the bare studs of the house. They built the structure by embellishing it fully and unpredictability. The two exchanged a friendly banter between songs that served as the launch pad for what was to come, including a tune with scat-like wordless vocals that in glee Fred propelled with a piano frenzy.

The pair highlighted the set with the Charlie Parker calypso "Little Suede Shoes" that esperanza proclaimed was a "song of freedom" that just "takes over and becomes dangerous." She finished by expressing her spirited determination: "This is an activation song." Fred and esperanza also scored on the Neal Hefti/Bobby Troup classic, "Girl Talk" that the fearless vocalist critiqued as a part of her improvisation.

Even though the lights came on, the standing ovation crowd and the appreciative duo onstage went back at it for two encores. Couldn't ask for more. The show was sublime in the wonderful Vanguard womb.

ECLECTIC HIGHLIGHTS

- In 2010, we talked about her next album in the works. Released in 2012, *Radio Music Society*, was the Grammy winner for Best Jazz Vocal Album as well as for its track, "City of Roses," awarded Best Arrangement, Instrument and Vocals.
- A decade later in the pandemic year of 2020, esperanza set up shop in Oregon for her Songwrights Apothecary Lab. She describes it as a collective of creatives that "seeks to respectfully dip into the healing seas of music/musicianship/ song, and distill a few grains of piquancy which carry the life-renewing flavor of the unfathomable ocean of human resiliency, then work those grains into new musical forms, to enhance the healing flavors and intentions innate in all works of devoted creatorship.
- In 2021 esperanza released the album *Songwrights Apothecary Lab* that comprised 12 songs of music therapy and neuroscience. It was created and recorded with different musicians in her traveling lab. In 2022, it was awarded the Best Jazz Vocal Album by the Grammys.
- In an eight-year project, esperanza served as the invaluable creative collaborator on Wayne's 2021 opera, *Iphigenia*. She wrote the libretto to go along with Wayne's music and sang the lead.
- In 2022, esperanza, who had been teaching as a part-time professor at Harvard's Music Department, departed the University. She announced in an email that she had communicated with Harvard about a proposal for a "decolonial education" curriculum she would like to implement as a course or initiative. It was denied, so she quit in protest.

Henry Threadgill— Explores the Contrary

In 1997, I spent a day hanging out in Oakland with Henry Threadgill who was in town for a five-night engagement with his Make a Move band at Yoshi's jazz club at Jack London Square. It was a memorable connect for me.

He was a contrary jazz hero then who went on to push the musical boundaries, garnering the 2016 Pulitzer Prize for Music for his album In for a Penny, In for a Pound. Four years later he was recognized as being an NEA Jazz Master. Impressive indeed.

His contrary ways befuddled major record companies, but since 2001 Henry has found his true home at Pi Recordings which embraces the brilliance of his extraordinary music.

HENRY THREADGILL EXPLORES THE CONTRARY BY MAKIN' A MOVE AND CARRYING THE DAY

1998

This is my writer's cut for Stereophile magazine...it has disappeared from its archives. We conversed in my car, over a catfish lunch at Jack London Square and then back at his Lake Merritt hotel.

In 1997, sitting in the passenger seat of my beat-up 1974 Volkswagen Bug, Henry Threadgill reminisces about a 1990 recording session he had almost forgotten about.

"You kidding, it's out?" Henry exclaims when informed that the *Flutistry* CD by Flute Force Four—the flute quartet he co-piloted with James Newton—has finally been released on Italy-based Black Saint Records. "That's great news. I'd love to see what it looks like. That's a lot of hard music, and we had to play it live first at the Verona Festival in Italy. Now, when was that, 1990?"

Henry explains that the midnight-to-dawn rehearsal in the basement of an Italian hotel posed a formidable challenge for the new quartet member Felecia Magdaluyo who was brought in at the eleventh hour for the date. Yet, the foursome's enthusiasm buoys for the final takes.

While we're navigating through the maze of one-way and no-left-turn streets in downtown Oakland en route to a catfish lunch at a waterfront restaurant, I ask the 53-year-old iconoclastic composer/bandleader if the seven-year wait for the release of the flute disc has been frustrating. "No, you just got to let those things go unless you want to punish yourself," he replies with the poise that only a veteran jazz musician who has been raked over the coals by recording industry bigwigs could possess. "It doesn't usually take this long, but you have to understand that these kinds of things are going to happen. You're not in control."

No kidding. The maverick maestro recently received the news that Sony/ Columbia pulled the plug on his contract after three brilliant, but slow-selling CDs—*Carry the Day, Makin' a Move* and *Where's Your Cup?*

In 1994 when the major label signed Henry, prominent trade magazines such as *DownBeat*, *Jazziz* and *Musician* covered the event as a coup for adventurous, free-thinking and free-wheeling music. Steve Berkowitz, at the time Columbia's A&R rep, was quoted as saying that the label was sincere in wanting Henry to be Henry.

In all the feature articles on the singular Henry Threadgill, writers described him as the champion of the unorthodox, the quintessential outsider, outspoken nonconformist, a virtual genre unto himself and one of America's best-kept cultural secrets. Most celebrated the signing yet also wondered how long the experiment would last. As it turned out, not long.

"People in high places at the label should have spoken up," Henry says, with an angry razor edge in his voice. "They knew who I was. This was no fishing expedition. They knew they couldn't suggest to me that I do a Gershwin album. The label got a whole lot of attention for signing me, but I believe they had already made a decision that the deal was dead. When I signed, the divorce papers were already being drafted."

Henry laughs, then growls, "If you've been around as long as I have, you know not to get your expectations up too high," he says. "They cut heads off at record companies, you know, from presidents all the way down the ladder to secretaries and janitors. When I discovered that, I said, wait a minute, Henry, don't be tripping—walking in the door under the title of artist doesn't protect you." He pauses, then grins. "It's a funny business."

Henry knows this well. He's been a lifer in striving for musical originality and artistic integrity—two callings more often than not at odds with the commercial goals of the record industry.

Born in Chicago in 1944, Henry grew up with a diet of diverse music, including Mexican, gospel, European folk and classical. He was playing boogie-woogie piano by the age of six and took up the saxophone in high school. One of his first professional jobs as a musician was playing gospel with traveling church evangelists. He gigged in blues groups, marching bands and ethnic music ensembles playing polka and mariachi. He studied clarinet, piano and composition at the American Conservatory of Music and was a key figure in the Chicago-based AACM (Association for the Advancement of Creative Music) movement of radical jazz in the '60s.

In 1972, Henry founded the trad-to-free trio AIR with bassist Fred Hopkins and drummer Steve McCall (the group was originally formed to bring new life to a batch of Scott Joplin tunes) and re-envisioned the group as New Air in 1982 with Andrew Cyrille eventually doing the drumming chores.

Also during the '80s, Threadgill began to explore more unusual ensemble configurations to give voice to his increasingly complex and wonderfully strange compositions. He formed X-75, which included four bassists, four reeds and a vocalist, and his Sextett (actually a septet) with two drummers and cellist Diedre Murray.

Then came his Very Very Circus ensemble full of tubas, trombones and guitars and, most recently, his Make a Move band. This latest group to be documented on disc may be relatively tame instrument-wise (the leader on alto saxophone and flute, Brandon Ross on electric and classical guitars, Tony Cedars on accordion and harmonium, Stoma Takeishi on 5-string fretless bass and J. T. Lewis on drums). But the Make a Move project displays plenty of Henry's penchant for adventure from a compositional point of view. In other words, don't expect to hear any of the seven classical, world and folk-infused tracks from *Where's Your Cup?*, Henry's 1996 Columbia swan song, on a mainstream jazz radio station anytime soon.

On the disc, Henry shatters the calm and jars the status quo. Attentive listening is required as he and his crew avoid predictable head-solo-head jazz formulas in favor of charting musical journeys that are at once brimming with joy and eerie unsettling.

There are accordion drones, whimsical helixing saxophone and guitar lines, tumultuous drumming, anguished sax screams, lyrical tango-meets-reggae dances. Tempos accelerate, meters shift, timbres bloom and dissolve. While Henry eschews the spotlight in lieu of letting his simpatico band interpret his compositions, the most gripping moment on the CD arrives when he leads his cohorts out onto the serrated edge with lacerating alto saxophone exhalations.

Henry's music is compelling, even when he and his collaborators are playing instruments as seemingly unthreatening as flutes. Case in point: the abovementioned *Flutistry*. The triumphant CD is a feast of flutes, ranging from piccolo flute to bass flute, all of which color the magical soundscapes. The recording features two of Henry's captivatingly lyrical, jarringly harsh, playfully sweeping and ebulliently beautiful compositions. The flute quartet on "T.B.A." sounds like a flock of birds twittering, chirping and warbling, and his "Leap Nosebor" (Paul Robeson spelled backwards), inspired by watching parakeets in a zoo, also takes wing with flute soars and swoops.

UNDERLYING GRAVITY

In the liner notes of his album, *Song Out of My Tree*, recorded in 1993 and released the following year by Black Saint, Henry set out to explain his latest work of art. He opened with a rambling discourse, then finally crystallized his thoughts in what proved to be a poignant statement on the state of jazz: "The underlying gravity is about Song. Very very strong sense of Song. Not song as an excuse to do something else or a pale platform for dead technique...This recording is not an attempt to be retro or stylistic in any certain way."

Henry's manifesto? Move over young lions intent on preserving a jazz canon and make way for a composer revitalizing jazz with a spirit of border-busting adventurism.

That CD is a forward-looking, freedom-loving collection of deeply personal, vibrantly spiritual songs. Only two of the five pieces include a drummer while Henry, content to don the composer's hat and set aside his sax momentarily, bows out of two of the numbers. He experiments with unusual sonic textures, composing for alto and soprano guitars in two pieces (one of which features Ted Daniels on eerie-sounding hunting horns) and on another brilliantly meshing the sounds of two cellos, accordion and harpsichord together.

The tunes ebb and flow with unfolding melodies as well as stretches of quiet instrumentation followed by torrential downpours of notes. "Gateway" undergoes melodic twists and turns and at one juncture erupts into a charged free-for-all where all the instruments speak their languages simultaneously. The bird-like flittering and nibbling by the three guitarists on "Over the River Club" leads to a frenzy of dissonant piano jabs by Myra Milford. The superb "Grief" is a swirling, scratching, wailing descent into the depths of anguish. Only the title tune, with its soulful organ flourishes by Amina Claudine Myers, bluesy guitar lines by Ed Cherry and a ragged alto solo of ecstasy by Henry, consistently maintains a swing and groove. Otherwise, it's brave new territory with surprises around every corner.

"When I write music, I want something powerful to come at people," says Henry, sipping a glass of chardonnay and waiting for his catfish dinner plate to arrive. "And it don't have to fit no categories. How can you deal with a broad range of thoughts and emotions if you stay locked into one road? I open up my music completely. Keep it wide open. I like the idea of engaging the listener by making music that's not passive. I like playing for people who have a broad diet. Otherwise, it's like someone who only eats hot dogs. I think it's ridiculous that people discriminate against a broad spectrum of music, stuff like opera, punk rock, country."

COUNTRY AND WESTERN

After his catfish dinner, we keep conversing. Feisty and opinionated, Henry talks with a strident exuberance. And he loves to tell stories, like the one about getting schooled in country music.

"I discovered something when I was really young," he says. "I had to give myself a whuppin.' I didn't like country and western music, but I found myself in the army stationed in Kansas where there was nothin' but country music, which was called hillbilly back then. Can you imagine that? It was like being put in jail. Every station on the radio, day and night, every bar, every jukebox. Country and western."

He laughs then sings a warble, sing-songy Hank Williams imitation that sounds more like Jimmy Scott: "Did you ever lose a will to live?"

Henry says that he ended up liking country once he stopped fighting the music. "I can dislike something, but I've got to give it a chance," he says. "I can't close the door completely. Otherwise I shut out something that may be valuable for my own music. I can never turn off something because as a composer and artist I've chosen to deal with sound. I can't put limitations on myself. It was the same way with opera. I didn't like it. But at one point opera registered with me, and the heavens opened up. Because I had been limiting myself, look what I was missing. I had to kill my limitations."

One of the major criticisms of Henry's music is that it's too inaccessible to listeners who want tunes that are safe, polite and palatable. It's branded commercially unviable and too challenging for the mainstream.

What's his response to that viewpoint? Henry narrows his eyes and bristles. Once again, the conversation turns to the faceless decision makers of the recording industry. "In America, record companies and radio stations disrespect the faith and intelligence of the audience to be interested in music that doesn't sound the same as everything else," he says. "They think the audience is stupid. I think the audience is hungry for music that stretches. I've seen it when I play shows. I've had people come up to me and say they were surprised by how much they enjoyed my music because they had heard so many negative things about it. That's what I try to accomplish as an artist: engage people to listen and at least give the music a chance."

VERY VERY CIRCUS

Several years ago Henry loaded his Very Very Circus ensemble into a bus and did a cross-country tour. Along the way, the bus stopped in small towns and performed free sets of Henry's exacting music in civic squares and parks.

"You grab people's attention by doing something as audacious as that," he says. "People were curious. They just stood there waiting to see what would happen next. A crowd draws a crowd, so before we knew it we attracted large audiences. And people stayed. Now that's what I was hoping for. They accepted the challenge without even knowing they were being challenged. They were curious enough to check out a style of music they wouldn't have dared to listen to. We just threw it on the table for them. No tickets. No previews. No reviews. Just, all of a sudden, food on the table, which they could taste without feeling threatened. And the people there got engaged. I'm sure not everyone liked it, but some digested it while hopefully others went away feeling a little less scared to listen to something different."

INSPIRATIONAL READING

As a composer, Henry rarely finds his inspiration by listening to music. He's often informed by theater or literature. Sometimes music flows to him by looking at the way light shines through clouds.

What's he been feeding himself on these days? He shrugs his shoulders and curtly says, "Oh, science manuals, the tradition of frogs around the world, butt jokes."

Anything else? "Right now, poetry, lots of poetry. Derek Walcott, Arab poets, a Paris poet, a whole stack of books by poets from India. But it won't end there. It always gets broader than that. But that's how it works with me. Right now, I'm not composing. I'm taking in information. I'm digesting. I don't know how it works, but I don't sit down and create. I'm like a farmer. I have to work the field before it's ready to produce. All this information I'm gathering inside me is like fuel so that when I do write it all comes out at once. I'll write three or four compositions at the same time—music for string quartet, orchestra, Make a Move, pipe organ—the same way I'll read six or seven books at the same time."

LIVING IN INDIA

Nearly four years ago, Henry decided to move to India where he now lives over half the year with his wife and one-year-old daughter in a large Portuguese mansion far out in the countryside. When he's retreated to India, he's almost impossible to reach. He has no telephone. He carries on correspondence with bookers via a fax machine in town.

Living in India has been a major factor in allowing Henry to stretch as a composer. "I don't have to deal with information I don't want coming into my environment," he says. "I know what the telephone, television and the mailbox have done to our lives. It takes a while to get away from all that, but once you do, you start to hear things inside your head that you could have never heard otherwise. That's why I had to get out of the city. There were things inside me that I couldn't get out."

Those sounds inside his head play an important role in Henry's use of unusual combinations of instruments—tubas, French horns, harmonium, violins. "It's like a DNA game," he says. "I have to take the sound apart and figure it out."

Does he listen to music in India? Some, although Henry's not forthcoming about what's in his collection there. What about his equipment? He laughs. "Just a CD player and a tape deck," he says. "You know, musicians have the worst sound systems in the world. I'm just happy that the stuff I have works because half the time it doesn't. I don't have to hear the fine aspects of the music. I just need to hear it and get it to engage me. That's all."

Is he excited about the prospects of any younger jazz musicians? Henry pauses, and then says he's actually been waiting for some truly revolutionary breakthrough in the music. "I'd love to see a group of kids working with radical ideas, but I don't see it," he says. "There are some individuals that I'm impressed by, but no movement, no avant-garde, nothing that I could latch onto and learn from."

Henry does admire the nerve and audacity of Steve Coleman, even though he's not big on everything the young saxophonist has produced. "But Steve's matured so much in the last few years," he says. "Before it seemed like he was playing from his head. Something organic has happened in his life. He's become a whole person in his music."

Henry is also a James Carter fan, though he worries that too much is being made of his extraordinary technical prowess on the saxophone. "That's all surface qualification," he says. "Those things mean nothing to me. But the jazz world makes a big deal about technique because of the Marsalis influence. But to me, technique isn't nothin.' I like James because James likes music."

MAJOR LABELS

In returning to the topic of his own new projects, Henry is forced to take a few more whacks at the record industry. He's frank in his criticisms of major labels not having a strong artistic vision. At one point in our conversation, he becomes so bluntly bold in his assertions that our waiter comes over to our table and asks if everything is all right with the food.

Henry is irked that he didn't hear about his contract termination with Columbia until after he returned from India with a new Make a Move project ready to rehearse. He admits to being disappointed. "I wasn't hurt, but I was dispirited," he says. "Funny thing is, if you came up to me and asked me to make a record, I wouldn't do it. I couldn't do it. I might be tempted because of the money, but recordings just flow out of me without being planned. That's what happened with this new material, which will probably never get recorded now."

Another Henry project that may never be documented on disc is his 21-piece dance band. Based on how he describes it, that orchestra has the potential to make his most "accessible" recording since his delightfully quirky *Too Much Sugar for a Dime*. That CD was produced by producer/bassist Bill Laswell and released in 1993 on his Axiom label distributed by Island (the record company even packaged a promo CD with made-for-radio edits of two of the tunes). Henry's big band includes strings (three cellos, three violins), brass (tubas and trombones), Brandon Ross on guitar, Tony Cedars on accordion, a few vocalists and a large percussion section. The group used to play at SOBs in New York, but now performs almost exclusively in Europe.

"The young people there go crazy for it," Henry says with a satisfied smile on his face. "It's the killingest thing. We play my compositions for the most part. It's music to dance to, funky stuff and everything, but there isn't no formulas. We cover everything."

He says that he wanted to record the group for Columbia, but was told the cost was too prohibitive. "They chickened out," Henry says. "They dropped the ball on that one. But recording that band isn't as important to me as its live life."

He pauses, takes a drag on a cigarette, swigs down some wine and says, "Look, record companies are not that damn important to me. I'm telling you, I wouldn't be disappointed if I didn't make records. As long as I can perform and make a good living at it, I don't have to record. I'm not thinking about how posterity remembers me. I don't care."

HENRY'S PERFORMANCE

At Henry's Make a Move show at Yoshi's two days earlier, the music was powerful and terrifyingly beautiful. The operative word for the evening was intense even though the leader tossed in dollops of humor throughout the captivating, rapturous fifty-minute set. Recordings give only a fleeting glimpse of the Threadgill genius.

His live shows more than confirm his importance as one of the most innovative composers of the late twentieth century. He winces when people call his music jazz, perhaps because he wants to distance his singular form of artistic expression from what gets typically branded as jazz. But to this listener's ears, Henry, along with a precious few other composer-improvisers (Ornette Coleman and Bill Frisell included), represents the future of jazz. In his music, boundaries tumble and freshness prevails.

"My music is constantly evolving," he explains when asked how he approaches his live dates. "It never gets set. It's a work in progress. Otherwise it becomes boring. You have to challenge yourself unless you want to be a stylist. That's never been my ambition. I admire stylists like Tony Bennett, who is one of my favorite people. But that doesn't go with my nature. I keep myself in a constant state of self-review. That's the only way to come up with something different. Once you know the music in a certain way, habits set in."

Henry pauses and reiterates, "Habits. You know habits are funny things. Your muscles begin to do things a certain way without you even thinking about it. You follow this process without using your mind. For me, I have to destroy the process so I can get to something fresh and new."

That doesn't make it easy on his bands. Brandon Ross and Tony Cedars have been playing with Henry long enough that they telepathically communicate with their leader, instantaneously following his lead through the retards, accelerandos and whimsical detours. Henry's rhythm section has less experience playing with him. But he's committed to being the long-suffering instructor and mentor. As we head back to the car after lunch, he talks about his bassist Stomu Takeishi who plays with spirited abandon, wielding his instrument like a sword in a martial arts exercise as he deciphers the master's works.

"Stomu is great; he's one of the greatest finds I've come across in years," says Henry, who met Takeishi through Brandon. "Stomu has learned a lot. I had to knock some corners off him. He was trapped in this shit he learned in music school. I didn't know what to do with him. In fact, I almost gave up on him because he wasn't able to go into depth with my compositions. It was like he was in a cage. I'd tell him, 'Stomu, please don't play that crap. I'd rather you play wrong than play like someone else.' So finally, he got rid of all his influences and started to find his own voice. He said, 'Henry, I didn't know I could ever get here. I'm free.' Now Stomu could get a job with anyone because he plays the bass like no one else."

Henry is pleased. His perseverance in Stomu's case has paid off. He says that sometimes a bandleader can get fooled by quick studies. He's wary of musicians who produce immediate results because in the long run they may not find the deep soul in his music.

I remark that it sounds like he's a patient taskmaster. "You have to be," he replies, as he climbs into the Bug for the ride back to his hotel where a nap awaits him. "You show me a bandleader that has no patience, and I'll show you a person that's not a bandleader."

He pauses, and then adds, "And diplomacy. What about Billy Eckstine and that congregation he had? His guys were out of control. Their tour bus would come to town, and they'd pull out their horns, gamble in the streets, get high, chase women, everything. A white person in those days wouldn't even think of doing that. But here were these black guys. Phew! They were beyond crazy, but Billy reined them in."

DUKE ELLINGTON

Henry's on a roll. "And Duke Ellington. Damn, I don't know how the hell Duke handled the crowd he had," he says. "Cootie Williams was a terror. Ben Webster was trying to be Joe Lewis and knock out everybody in America. And Paul Gonsalves, he'd be so drunk, but when Duke called on him, he played so damn good. That's the way it was with Duke. He'd say, boom, and that band would be sober and full of love. That was one of the most sophisticated units that ever existed, and it was all because of the way Duke handled it."

Hearing Henry the iconoclast melt when talking about Ellington is a great surprise. I ask him if he would have wanted to play in Duke's orchestra. His reply is immediate: "Oh, yeah. Definitely."

Henry then tells me about the time he hung around backstage after an Ellington concert to introduce himself to the bandleader. "That was one of the highlights of my life." he says. "I was in my early twenties. He took me into his dressing room. I told him I loved his music and his orchestra. He asked me if I played, and I told him I did but that I wasn't known. I also told him I was a composer. So, he asked me to sit down at the piano that was always in his dressing rooms and play something for him. I was so nervous I couldn't even play 'Mary Had a Little Lamb.' But he was such a charmer. I was overwhelmed that he paid attention."

If Duke were still alive, would he have liked Henry's music? "Oh, I don't know," he says shyly. "Well, yeah, I think he'd definitely like it."

As strange as it seems, Henry says he's indebted to Duke. "I learned a lot from him—about leading a band, about musicality—but I never set out to imitate Duke's music," he says. "Just like I never emulated anyone I admired. That's why you can't hear their influences in my music. Piss me off once that a critic said my music sounded like Mingus. Kiss my ass. How can you become a great arranger/composer by copying someone else? Only individuals like a Henry Mancini who do it their own way become great. You have to find it on your own. You can't get stuck in someone else's shit and then try to get out of it. It takes years to wrestle yourself free from the grasp of someone's style."

We're sitting outside his hotel with the Beetle engine shut off. Henry's having fun, pumped full of energy while articulating what it takes to be a pioneer in jazz.

"We all have too much to give the world through our own individuality," he says. "It's like researching cancer. If everyone were doing the same studies, we'd never solve the mystery. But someone will have the nerve to strike out on some wild theory. That's what it takes. You have to dare to stand out there all by yourself without a name. You can't care what the market says. You care about your art. You've got to find how to mix these colors for yourself."

McCoy Tyner—Lyrical Thunder

My first introduction to the power and brilliance of McCoy Tyner came in 1993 when he settled into the Emeryville, California new jazz club Kimball's East. It was just a quick shot away from Oakland. McCoy led his dynamic big band with so much swinging authority that swelled through me. You couldn't avoid—or God forbid, talk through the music.

Just a young pianist when he was enlisted by John Coltrane for his classic '60s quartet that lasted from 1960 to 1965, McCoy launched off on his own career, seemingly in constant motion at clubs and in the recording studio. Until his death in 2020, McCoy recorded over 70 albums for such labels as Impulse!, Blue Note, Milestone and finally his own label McCoy Tyner Music.

He was kind and constant. I was at Clinton Studios in New York in 2006, witnessing the piano giant work with such stellar guitarists as Bill Frisell, John Scofield, and a wild card, blues six-stringer Derek Trucks. So in awe of McCoy after working with him, Trucks shyly asked the pianist to sign his guitar. It was a sweet moment.

I met up with McCoy at home during the unique Guitars project that eventually saw the light of day in 2008.

THE LEGENDARY MCCOY TYNER

2007

In 2006, at age 68, the legendary jazz titan McCoy Tyner is enjoying a career resurgence. "That happens sometimes," says the gracious and soft-spoken McCoy about his new directions, while relaxing on the couch of his midtown-Manhattan apartment that he estimates he's lived in for some 15 years.

Sitting in his modest digs with mirrored walls that give the appearance of the one-bedroom apartment being larger than it is and with an electric keyboard that he practices on (with earphones, so as not to disturb his neighbors) near the couch, McCoy says that all the new recording projects is a pleasant surprise. "More or less, they're presented to me," he says. "Then I think about whether it's something that makes sense for me to do. Then we'll see how it goes."

Everything is falling into place. Recently he settled into Clinton Studios in New York for two days of sessions for a new album (a trio date augmented by an eclectic all-star mix of guest guitarists including Derek Trucks and banjo ace Béla Fleck). He's working with a new producer (John Snyder who not only provided the architectural framework for the recording but also designed an innovative DVD supplement). And the date is being financed by a new label (his own McCoy Tyner Music imprint produced and marketed via Half Note Records), under the aegis of new management (one component of the multifaceted Blue Note club franchise).

But, one wonders if perhaps this could be the final act in a storied career that officially launched a half century earlier when at the age of 17 McCoy was enlisted by fellow Philadelphian John Coltrane to join his new band. Judging solely by the almighty pianist's emaciated appearance—his gaunt face and thin frame where once his brawny good looks perfectly matched his muscular, two-fisted percussive attack on the keys—it certainly suggested that this date could well signify McCoy's swan song.

Yet, as has been proven so many times in so many different circumstances, looks can be deceiving. Once McCoy sits on the piano bench at Clinton Studios and plunges into one of Derek Trucks' unlikely song choices, "Greensleeves," he renders the tune with gentle but potent thunder in his left hand and bright lightning in his right. The guitarist bends the melodic notes with his slide, and the simpatico support team of McCoy's old friends, Ron Carter and Jack DeJohnette, not only lay the rhythmic foundation but also surge it. The well-worn traditional song shines anew.

The next track called for by Trucks, the rousing "Slapback Blues," is a McCoy original that he says was so old that he had forgotten how to play it. But he quickly recalls the number as soon as Trucks links his iPod into the studio sound system. On it, McCoy, as if reacquainted with a lost friend, plays emphatically with emotional bursts of upbeat swing and shuffle. Back is the real McCoy, redux, not missing a beat, though he did slip up on following the agreed-upon road map for ending the tune, a minor infraction that upon listening to the playback is undetectable.

Nine months later in June during a weeklong stint at the Blue Note club in New York with such friends as harmonica sage Toots Thielemans and saxophonist Joe Lovano sitting in, McCoy, still thin but full-faced and sporting his trademark short-clipped ponytail, plays with such fervor and explosive force that the maladies of the recent past waned in favor of a new rising. That aurora will officially appear this fall when the first CD of an MTM trilogy will be released. Tentatively titled *Live at Yoshi's*, a dynamic quartet date with Joe, bassist Christian McBride and drummer Jeff "Tain" Watts, recorded live at the Oakland club on New Year's Eve, will usher in the new Tyner era.

It will be followed early next year by the as-yet untitled guitar album (should it be titled *McCoy With Strings* or maybe *McCoy With (Six) Strings*?) and a solo piano-concert CD recorded live at the Herbst Theater during this year's SFJAZZ spring season.

"It's been quite an event," McCoy says. "I've enjoyed my relationship with the Blue Note organization. I've worked in their clubs a lot, so we've been friends. The label blossomed from that. Here you get the intimacy you don't normally get when you're isolated. You have a meeting and talk about a recording. You don't feel remote and feel like you're dealing with a formal institution. You can talk about ideas. You see the people you'll be working with. It's hands on. That really makes a difference."

In his recording career as a leader, McCoy served a couple of tours of duty with Impulse (in the '60s while in Trane's quartet, then later in the '90s when the imprint was reborn by Verve), but broke in fully with his seminal *The Real McCoy* album on Blue Note in 1967. (When told it's the 40th anniversary of that album, McCoy asks incredulously, "Are you kidding me? I've been around that long?").

He pitched camp with Milestone for several years during the '70s and '80s (highlighted by his superb 1987 big band *Uptown/Downtown* album); and most recently recorded for Telarc with such well-regarded discs as *Land of Giants* and *Illuminations*. McCoy returns to the recording mode this time, with, as Half Note executive vice president Jeff Levenson calls it, "full proprietary intent."

Whose idea was it to give his iconic status the MTM brand? McCoy hesitates for a moment, then replies, "You know, I don't know who did, but it's not a bad idea." He pauses, then adds with a laugh, "Come to think of it, it's probably a brilliant idea."

The fresh recording setting set into motion the guitar album that features Derek, which was conceived of by the Blue Note management. "Initially there was talk about getting some smooth jazz players," Snyder recalls, "but I felt that was fraught with potentially deadly results, especially if it was being done for marketing reasons. I believe that could have been shredded by the critics. But if you record with the music in mind, you've taken the high road no matter what people say. That's why I wanted to bring in iconoclastic players to put a lot of colors on the palette and express different points of view." So he enlisted Bela Fleck, Derek, Bill Frisell, John Scofield and the wild card, Marc Ribot.

McCoy thought the idea was "interesting," says Snyder, "and he gave it everything he had. He was totally cooperative with trying anything. It took him out of the usual spot that he's in. It shows new facets in his playing, like what a prism does to sunlight. You hear the Trane influence, the blues, the African influences, his different ways of improvising. It challenged McCoy. It required more of his abilities to be used in various contexts. He rose to the occasion."

As for the assembled guests, Snyder says that to everyone these sessions were a "life-changing event. They came in so anxious, so in awe, but they also brought in their own personalities. I told them, this may be terrifying to you playing with McCoy, but that's not how he's feeling, so relax."

For McCoy, this was only the second time in his career working with guitarists, the first being his 1982 *Looking Out* recording with Trane-worshipping Carlos Santana. "I wrote the tune 'Señor Carlos' for him," says McCoy with a laugh. "It was kind of a punk-rock tune. I enjoyed it. Carlos made me a rocker."

As for the MTM guitar session, McCoy embraced the idea. He hasn't fully explored how the album as a whole sounds (he's yet to listen to the sessions, just as he rarely, if ever, listens to his old albums, unless he's looking for a song he's written but forgotten), but he does remember the challenge of hooking up with the personnel.

"I was very interested to see how the personalities of the guitarists would work together musically with me and Ron and Jack," he says. "I'm the kind of guy who's flexible. I want to see what each guy is bringing to the table and work around that. I'm not going to try to make someone sound like Carlos."

Snyder points out that Ribot's presence was especially stimulating to McCoy, given that the guitarist does not come exclusively from the jazz camp, even though he brilliantly re-envisions the pianist's classic tune, "Passion Dance" with ferocity.

"Marc makes melodies out of the harmonies," Snyder says. "He brought in a couple of tunes to rehearse that McCoy had a difficult time internalizing. It was too much of a thought process. McCoy was a good sport and tried to learn Marc's music, but we thought, why not play free?"

That strategy bears fruit, with three short duo improvisations scattered throughout the disc. "It's amazing," says Snyder. "They play tonally and atonally. McCoy took to that with no hesitation. Hey, he used to play free with Coltrane all the time."

PLAYBOY JAZZ FESTIVAL

Even during the stretch of time that his health was conspicuously a concern, McCoy seemed to be playing stronger than he had in years. During the June 2006 edition of the Playboy Jazz Festival at the Hollywood Bowl, he shared the stage with the Los Angeles-based Lula Washington Dance Theatre, which developed dances based on McCoy's works. While the choreography was more *Flashdance* than Mark Morris, McCoy's dynamics on the keys carried the set. While visibly lean in stature, his invigorating performance spurred on by a powerful left-hand thrust momentarily caught the attention of the notoriously gabby festival goers. It was an impressive demonstration of authoritative jazz talk hushing even the glibbest of crowds.

"I'm a physical player," says McCoy, who doesn't bang or jump on the piano nor show overt physicality other than his left-hand pounding and right-hand flourishes. "I used to watch Thelonious when he played with John, but I didn't copy him. But I was impressed with the sound he got out of the piano, to hear all the intervals he was able to play on the instrument. He was a physical player too. He attacked the instrument to find what he was looking for. He played the piano like a percussion instrument. He figured you've got to strike the piano; otherwise it won't respond."

While developing his own pianistic style, McCoy also came under the influence of another piano strongman, Bud Powell, who had moved to his Philly neighborhood when he was a teenager. "I liked Bud Powell's playing," McCoy says. "He moved around the corner from me into an apartment. I'd see him in the street all the time, and we even got him gigs at this place called Rittenhouse Hall, which was a dancehall where this guy used to book jazz shows. Bud saw me practicing once. I turned around and there he was listening to me. But he didn't say a word. It was a rare occasion when he would respond to things."

Inevitably, even though McCoy has been a distinguished member of the jazz elite apart from his Trane days, the conversation manages to wind its way back to the saxophone god under whom he served. McCoy actually enjoys reflecting back on the legendary quartet he was in with bassist Jimmy Garrison and drummer Elvin Jones.

In Philadelphia, McCoy played rhythm section when touring heavyweights like Sonny Rollins came to town, but it was his friendship with Coltrane through some friends who knew his first wife, Naima, that secured his destiny. "John was like a big brother to me," McCoy recalls. "I was just a teenager and I was put in a position of hanging with older musicians." When reminded that he was still too young to drink, he laughs and says, "Well, you'd never catch me with a beer in my hands."

Another Guardian Angel was Elvin Jones. "Elvin was always looking out for me, making sure no one would bother me," McCoy says. "If he saw something coming down, he'd step up to the plate. You didn't want to mess with him. He was so protective. I loved him. We got along so great in the band. I listened to him; he listened to me. His musical sensitivity was so dynamic that I understood why John chose him."

REIGNING AT YOSHI'S

The Yoshi's connection for McCoy has been strong since he was invited in 1995 to be the first artist to hold forth for two consecutive weeks at the West Coast outpost, which became an annual event. In the first week of his premiere there, McCoy was featured playing for the first time with Michael Brecker, a remarkable summit that yielded Grammy Award-nominated CDs in its wake.

As for the MTM date at Yoshi's, Joe Lovano was thrilled to be playing with McCoy. It was his connect to Trane that offered Lovano insights into his tenor saxophone hero.

"McCoy had a tremendous journey of music through playing with Coltrane," says Lovano." As a result he's come up with an amazing harmonic and rhythmic sense that's all his own. My birthday is December 29, so the week we did at Yoshi's last year was a gift."

Lovano counts himself blessed, having worked with two piano titans in recent years: Hank Jones and McCoy. "They're both very different, yet similar," he says. "They both play rich harmonies and perform with honesty and trust. As for McCoy, his tunes are like beautiful folk songs and village dances. He creates different plateaus in each song. He's not just hitting for the moment. He sustains what he hits into the next section. As a soloist I try to create that on my saxophone."

MCCOY'S HEALTH

As for his health, McCoy is initially reluctant to go into much detail as to why he was momentarily sidelined. He did collapse while in Europe, but he was not hospitalized for an extended period of time. He did take some touring time off, but he's now back to keeping an almost dizzying international schedule.

Was the cause of his sickness exhaustion, as some people were saying? "No, it's what I inherited," says McCoy. "I don't like to talk about it, but hypertension runs in my family—my mother, my brother, my sister, my grandmother. I didn't realize that I had it until it reached a certain point. But I found out quickly. I collapsed somewhere—I don't even remember where—and I didn't know what had gone wrong."

His weight loss? "I was crossing a line there. My face started looking really thin. I was going in a really bad direction."

And now? "I see doctors regularly, and I've got a bag of new tricks," he says, then points to the prescription pills on his keyboard: "I've also got a bag of candies that I eat every day."

How has he managed to keep playing with such fortitude? "Conviction has a lot to do with it," he says. "You're committed to your instrument. It was like Elvin and his drums. He was committed. He and John were my teachers. They both played with that conviction of feeling that this moment doesn't come often and you need to take advantage of it when it's still here."

Sight unseen, you'll hear McCoy playing with increased vitality—and wonder. Seeing him live, however, you worry. However, McCoy is confident that he's on the mend. He may not look burly any longer, but his music is still robust and strapping. As he said in an interview from the mid-'90s, the wellspring of his music in whatever setting—live or in the studio—comes from his heart.

"I don't try to do anything when I'm playing. I just play," McCoy says. "A number of variables make for special performances—the right night, the right kind of venue, the right audience. These are usually spontaneous, unpredictable things."

Frank Zappa—The Last Interview

Shortly after Frank Zappa's death on December 4, 1993, nine months after I visited him, I faxed a note of condolences to Frank's wife Gail. Their daughter Moon Unit was on the 818-PUMPKIN Zappa hotline informing mourners that in lieu of flowers they could send donations in her dad's name to the Office for Intellectual Freedom of the American Library Association or to a favorite environmental cause. For those musicians and listeners financially restricted, Moon suggested, "Just play his music... That will be enough for him."

Nothing could be more appropriate for the iconoclastic genius composer-performer who lost a lengthy battle against prostate cancer, two and a half weeks before his 53rd birthday. The outspoken political critic, sophomoric humorist and crass satirist died at his Laurel Canyon home in the Hollywood Hills on a Saturday evening. He was buried without fanfare in a private ceremony the next day.

A music workaholic, who in his healthier days employed two shifts of recording engineers to keep up with his insatiable energy, Frank was busy up to the end producing the album The Rage and the Fury—The Music of Edgard Varèse *by the European avant-garde orchestra Ensemble Modern and putting the finishing touches on the double-CD* Civilization Phaze III. *His 63rd album and first studio album of new material since 1986, it was due out next year on Barking Pumpkin/Rhino. The latter is a collection of new Synclavier music, including the inspired treasure, "N-Lite: Negative Light/Venice Submerged/New World Order/The Lifestyle You Deserve/Creationism/He Is Risen," combined with previously unreleased, oftentimes frivolous outtakes from 1967's* Lumpy Gravy.

In reflecting on this music, University of Washington theory chair Jonathan W. Bernard said that Civilization Phaze III *is "heavily influenced by Zappa's disenchantment with avant-garde composition and Zappa's acute awareness of his own mortality." He also noted that he believed the final recording was Frank's "last, greatest attempt at being recognized as a composer of serious music."*

MEETING FRANK

1993

The headline of my Tower Pulse! *magazine cover feature on Frank Zappa in the August 1993 issue reads: "20th-century popular music's philosopher-king...has inspired*

263

independence movements in Eastern Europe and lampooned stupidity in the West. Now, he faces his most serious challenge."

This conversation was the last extended interview with Frank. It was assigned by editors at Pulse!, *the official monthly magazine of the mammoth record retailer Tower Records—launched in Sacramento, California in 1960, it went on to have 200 stores internationally before it eventually went bankrupt and closed in 2006. (It meekly reappeared in 2020 as an-ecommerce operation.) My original Frank cover story for* Pulse! *was scaled back for printed-page necessities. I've enclosed the original piece I delivered. The issue was up for the month of August 1993 at the stores before it was replaced the next month with a new cover story.*

TROUBLE EVERY DAY

In early April 1993 three months after being assigned an exclusive interview with Frank, I get the call and I finally make the trip from San Francisco to Los Angeles. I plan to stay in the Southland for five days in case things don't go as planned. Frank's publicist Mark Holdom explains to me that there are some days when Frank is so sick he can't get out of bed. He's in the late stages of prostate cancer. We arrange for the interview to take place on a Tuesday afternoon at 2, but Mark warns me not to be surprised if it has to be postponed. Call ahead, he tells me. I do, and I'm asked if I can come a little later, perhaps at 4? Sure thing. I'm told I'll have an hour.

Traffic is light on the Los Angeles freeways that day as I listen to Frank's music. While driving, I'm intent on the song "Trouble Every Day" from the first Mothers of Invention album, *Freak Out!*, released in 1966. With wailing harmonica and turmoiled bass in the background, Frank's lyrics on "Trouble Every Day" ominously and prophetically tumble out: "It's the same as the nation/Black and white discrimination/...and all that mass stupidity/That seems to grow more every day/Each time you hear some nitwit say/He wants to go and do you in/'Cause the color of your skin/Just don't appeal to him/No matter if it's black or white/Because he's out for blood tonight."

Written by Frank while the Watts riots were escalating out of control one year earlier in 1965, the song is eerily appropriate nearly thirty years later on this warm spring afternoon when the city is once again bracing for the worst—awaiting the outcome of the second Rodney King beating trial. In the first trial in 1992, a jury acquitted four LAPD officers on charges of excessive force even though the brutal pummeling was captured on video. Within hours of the verdict, the Los Angeles racial riots erupted—lasting six days, killing 63 people and injuring 2,383.

This year the federal government is prosecuting a separate civil rights case, with the verdict coming any day.

I get off the Ventura Freeway at Studio City, stop for a burrito because I'm running early and then drive up Laurel Canyon Boulevard into the Hollywood Hills to get to Frank's house. I'm nervous as I ring the bell while a video surveillance monitor is focused on me. Mark lets me in, leads me to the dark, but comfortable viewing room and tells me Frank will be with me shortly.

After waiting a few minutes, Frank slowly enters. Casually dressed in blue sweats, turquoise T-shirt and a loosely fitting gray sweater, he smiles, lights up the first of several Marlboros and shakes my hand. Today, he says, he's feeling OK. He immediately puts me at ease with a calmness and generosity that I was not prepared for from an artist notoriously reputed to eat journalists for lunch.

For the next four hours—in the video room and in his Utility Muffin Research Center studio where he and his assistants daily feast on popcorn—he is animated at times, fervently enjoying himself as we effortlessly interweave musical matters with politics. However, as a consequence of his illness, there are moments when Frank, his dark hair streaked with gray and tied in a tight ponytail, visibly tires as if his batteries have temporarily faded. But then we take off into another area of music and/or politics where he has strong opinions, and he rejuvenates.

Although he's exhausted, his desire to put his house in order is foremost on his mind. Frank is preparing his catalog for posterity and to provide a legacy for his family. After all, the irascible and iconoclastic 52-year-old has outdistanced most of his peers in the business by his unflagging commitment to both adventurous music and social critique.

I tell him about my driving experience with "Trouble Every Day." I ask him, why is the song still so poignantly relevant? Frank fields the question with aplomb. "Nothing has changed," he says. "We have the same racial hatred, the same unwillingness to face the causes of racial unrest. We've had years to examine the causes of the Watts riots, but no one has done anything about it. There were studies and reports and conclusions then, just like there were studies and reports and conclusions reached after last year's riots. There's a certain type of American adolescent behavior that hasn't gotten any better since the sixties."

Frank pauses then adds to his observation: "There's a distinctively American kind of stupidity that never goes away. Scientists believe that the universe is made of hydrogen because they claim it's the most plentiful ingredient. I claim that the most plentiful ingredient is stupidity. There's far more stupidity than hydrogen on a molecule-to-molecule basis."

ACCIDENTAL ROCK ICON

This opens our initial 90-minute conversation. At first it feels daunting to be talking with the legendary and controversial artist who has masterly experimented with an array of genres, including rock, doo-wop, jazz, poo, avant-garde and contemporary classical music. He's a composer of concept albums and a terrific high-charged guitarist. But with the tape on, our talk proceeds comfortably in his dark video-viewing room with a television screen and several rows of video tapes lining the wall in front of us.

"I never had any intention of writing rock music," Frank says while sitting leisurely in his chair with a bright red kilim-like covering. "I always wanted to compose more serious music and have it be performed in concert halls, but I knew no one would play it. So, I figured that if anyone was ever going to hear anything I composed, I'd have to get a band together and play rock music. That's how I got started."

If ever a long-term plan paid off, it has to have been Frank's. His list of official accolades and honors seems limitless. Then there are the more official accolades and honors. Renowned conductor Kent Nogano called him a genius. Czech playwright and former president Václav Havel wanted to make Frank Czechoslovakia's special ambassador to the West on trade, culture and tourism but reluctantly yielded to pressures from the George Bush administration to ditch the idea. Frank won a Grammy in 1987 for his Synclavier-driven *Jazz From Hell* album, and he was chosen to play John Cage's controversial and perhaps most famous piece *4'33"* for the star-studded Cage tribute album, *A Chance Operation*.

He was recently inducted into the Playboy Music Hall of Fame as its 43rd member, and in the year prior to our meeting *Guitar Player* published *Zappa!*, a full-length comprehensive overview of his career. His works have been performed by a number of esteemed 20th-century ensembles. Pierre Boulez commissioned him to score a symphonic work which resulted in the album *The Perfect Stranger: Boulez Conducts Zappa*. The European contemporary music group Ensemble Modern commissioned him to put together a concert's worth of his orchestral works for the Frankfurt Festival in 1992, and in February of this year Lincoln Center in New York City presented an evening of Frank's serious music in its Great Performers series.

Even the cartoon sit-com series *The Simpsons* creator Matt Groening is on record as saying "Frank is my Elvis."

Not bad for a guy who began his musical career as a drummer in a San Diego R&B group called the Ramblers in 1956. Frank jokes, "I played one or two gigs with them, but I wasn't very good so they fired me."

Then he recorded parody and instrumental doo-wop tunes in Cucamonga, California, and leased them to record companies such as Original Sound in Los Angeles in the early '60s. Zappa's first important record as a composer came in 1963 with the classic West Coast doo-wop tune "Memories of El Monte" released under the name The Penguins. But soon after, he launched what he's best known for—leading the charge into the experimental and distinctively weird rock music of the late '60s with his seminal band of renegades and freaks, the inimitable Mothers of Invention.

In the weeks prior to our meeting, I find evidence of Frank Zappa popping up in the strangest of places. In rush hour traffic, I notice old and smudged Zappa for President bumper stickers at the toll booth of the Oakland-San Francisco Bay Bridge. At my neighborhood coffee shop, Royal, on the Oakland-Berkeley line, the crew is blasting *Absolutely Free* out over the sound system at 7:15 a.m.

Whenever I mention to friends and acquaintances that I'm going to interview the brilliant musician and satirist, everyone has a reaction. Nearly everyone refers to him informally as Frank, in a way that suggests an almost familial relationship, and all people wonder if—and hope that—he is winning his fight against prostate cancer.

Some people pass on highly valued old magazine articles and cassettes of interviews with him taped off the local listener-sponsored radio station (Berkeley's KPFA-FM hosted by experimental electronic classical music composer Charles Amirkhanian). Some recount enchanted tales of catching Frank in concert. Others stress how much they appreciated him going to bat for artists everywhere in his well-publicized 1985 appearance before a Senate committee where he vehemently condemned warning stickers on albums proposed by Tipper Gore's Parents Music Resource Center.

An editor friend tells me a Frank story from her college days. When it came time for her calculus final, her young professor told his class not to cram for the exam. Don't stress it, he said, and then recommended preparing for the test by doing the following: go home, get into your bedroom by yourself, play a Frank Zappa album and then go to sleep. My friend only followed half of her teacher's advice. She studied first and then relaxed to Zappa music. She passed the test.

THE EARLY DAYS OF DEFYING THE NORM

While Frank eventually became an artistic icon, his early days barely hinted at this future. During our conversation at his home after my weeks of prep, we start by tracing his first steps into the music world. He reflects back on his formative years during his high school days at Antelope Valley High in Lancaster, a remote Mohave Desert town in California that he refers to as a cultural wasteland.

A fan of R&B singles and composer Edgard Varese's innovative and dissonant early 20th century classical music, Frank was a drummer in the school band where he was even allowed to do a bit of composing and conducting. But that's also where he began to have strong suspicions that he was destined to live a life deviating from the norms of Americana.

He's enjoying talking about those old days. "I had no outlet in music then to express my discontent," he says. "I didn't start writing rock 'n' roll lyrics till I was in my twenties. So, my aggravation with the way things were festered throughout my high school years. I refused to buy into most of what was going on around me because it all seemed so idiotic."

But Frank really gets fired up when he talks about the emphasis the education system of his hometown placed on sports and all their life-support privilege. "The only reason I got training as a musician was because the school needed a marching band at its football games," he says, grimacing. "It was just another tool to support the sports program. I never did enjoy sports. I always thought they smelled bad, and you could rarely hold a conversation with people involved in them. So, I looked at all that and thought that there certainly must be more worthwhile educational investments than new helmets. That really got me thinking how can you take any of this seriously?"

Fortunately for Frank, his stint with the band didn't last long. "I was thrown out for smoking in uniform," he says, while taking a drag from one of the many Marlboros he would smoke that afternoon. "We had to sit in the freezing cold and wear these dorky maroon and gray uniforms and play every time our team scored a touchdown. The brass sounded and the drums rolled. Jesus, it was pathetic. We had to sit in the stands and play vaudeville accompaniment noises to the jocks on the field. So, during a break, I went under the bleachers for a smoke. I got caught and I was kicked out of there. Not just for smoking, but for smoking in uniform."

Frank enjoys telling the story, expressing it like a joke with a burst of sarcasm. When did he realize the potential for satire in his music? "Even before I had this wonderful band called the Mothers, [original Mothers of Invention member] Ray Collins and I used to piddle around in Pomona doing gigs where the two of us did parodies of folk songs," he says. "We sang 'Puff the Magic Dragon' as 'Joe the Puny Greaser,' and we played a perverted version of 'The Streets of Laredo' called 'The Streets of Fontana.'"

Frank and Ray also recorded some goofy novelty tunes like "Ned 'N' Nelda," "The Big Surfer" and "Surf Along With Ned 'N' Nelda." They were influenced by Spike Jones, who specialized in spoof arrangements of popular music. "But our songs were less sophisticated and more stooge-like," Frank says. "We weren't setting out to make any kind of impact on people. We were just doing it for a laugh, to have fun. If it amused someone else, good. If it didn't, who gives a fuck. Nothing I've ever written has been motivated by trying to impact or influence anybody."

THE RISE OF THE MOTHERS

Little did Frank realize how highly influential his music would eventually become in shaping opinions both at home and abroad. Case in point: the first two Mothers of Invention albums, *Freak Out!* in 1966 and *Absolutely Free* in 1967. The former—the first rock double LP and the first recording fueled by an experimental concept approach—purportedly inspired Paul McCartney to begin work on *Sgt. Pepper's Lonely Hearts Club Band.*

Frank's Mothers' debut helped spawn an American subculture of long-haired, irreverent, authority-questioning freaks. Being a freak in Frank's worldview became a badge of honor.

Behind the Iron Curtain, *Absolutely Free* proved to affect an even deeper and more profound response. The lead-off number of the album, "Plastic People," became an underground hit and potent rallying cry for freedom in Czechoslovakia.

Frank is still surprised by it all. "I had no idea that song made the impact it did there," he says. "The album was smuggled into the country within a year of its release. I found out ten years later how powerful the song had become. We were touring heavily in Europe at the time, and a few Czechs had come across the Austrian border to hear our concert in Vienna." Frank talked with them after the show, and they told him that "Plastic People" was responsible for a whole movement of dissidents within Czechoslovakia.

"It wasn't just the song," he says, "but the entire notion of railing against a plastic society was something that was picked up behind the Iron Curtain. It came as a shock to me to find out that there was a group called the Plastic People there and that a cult of followers had grown up around them."

I remark that "Plastic People" is yet another of his compositions that has aged well in its social commentary. "That's especially relevant today in the United States," he says. In the room there's a poster on the wall portraying a Hitler-like image of Ronald Reagan with the words "He has the right to do anything they want" written underneath.

Frank recites a few lines from the song:

"Take a day and walk around
Watch the Nazis run your town
Then go home and check yourself
You think we're singing 'bout someone else."

He pauses to let the effect take hold, shakes his head slowly in disgust, then comments, "There's been an incredible rise in racist and fascist attitudes here, most of them being helped along by the Republican Party. That Republican National Party Convention last summer was just unbelievable. Even the set decor looked like a Nuremburg rally. The amount of hate and spewage that came out of that convention was appalling. Hatemongers like Pat Buchanan and Pat Robertson and the rest of the featured speakers were convinced they were going to win again."

THE CLINTON PRESIDENCY

Next topic: the new administration. After twelve years of Republican leadership, how does he feel about President Clinton? Frank says it's still too early to be overly critical given that the administration has yet to fill all the staff positions in the executive branch, but adds: "Even if Clinton and his people just stood still for the next four years, it would be better than what we had the four previous years under President Nero, which is what Dennis Miller calls Bush."

But Frank goes on to express an early dissatisfaction with the new president. What's upset him the most since Clinton took office is banning of smoking in the White House. "That really disturbs me," he says while taking another drag from a new cigarette. "Give me a fuckin' break. What kind of symbolism is this? It's a social engineering program by the Health Nazis in the White House against people who like tobacco. I wish people would get off this I'm-gonna-live-forever kick and dispel the myth perpetrated by Reagan's evil Surgeon General Dr. Koop, who said that second-hand smoke is the most dangerous thing Americans confront in their everyday lives. This is from the same guy who told us that green monkeys gave us AIDS."

When I say that it sounds like he's on a crusade for smokers, Frank inhales and nods. "I was pleased to note recently that for the first time in the last dozen years, the number of smokers did not decrease last year," he says. "It's remained constant. Now we need to proselytize people to get them to enjoy tobacco more. I like tobacco. I've always loved it. There is a place for tobacco in the human dining experience. It's like wine. It's an appropriate adjunct to food."

Our conversation pauses for a moment.

Frank's daughter Diva, in her early teens, bounces down the stairs, pokes her head into the viewing room where we're talking and announces herself with a bright "Hi, Daddy." She's the youngest of Frank and his wife Gail's four children. (Eldest daughter Moon Unit collaborated with dad on the 1982 novelty tune "Valley Girl" from Frank's *Ship Arriving Too Late to Save a Drowning Witch* album. His sons Dweezil and Ahmet are into the rock biz with the former leading his own band which the latter sings with on occasion.)

"How's little Squeach?" inquires Papa Zappa.

"Squeach is fine, but I don't think that's the name of it," says Diva. "But you can nickname it whatever you want."

Diva bounds back up the stairs while Frank explains their exchange. "We have a new kitten," he says. "It's the runt of the litter. It's adorable. I've been calling it Squeach because that's the noise it makes. Diva wanted to call it Toaster, but I guess she's changed her mind."

Squeach. Toaster. Names that could pop right out of one of Frank's zanier songs that celebrate such quirky characters as Suzy Creamcheese, Mr. Green Genes, Lonesome Cowboy Burt, Billy the Mountain, Big Leg Emma and the Duke of Prunes.

Then there is Frank's fixation on food in his music, ranging from early tunes like "Call Any Vegetable" and "Invocation and Ritual Dance of the Young Pumpkin" to such later music-to-eat-dinner-by albums as *Burnt Weenie Sandwich* and *Lumpy Gravy*. Of course, you also get a wide array of bizarro song titles, including for starters "The Orange County Lumber Truck (Part 1 & 2)," "The Eric Dolphy Memorial Barbeque" and "G-Spot Tornado."

Frank's career catapulted off the ground in the mid-'60s as a result of his wildly experimental and unpredictable band the Mothers of Invention. On Mother's Day 1964, the name The Mothers was coined. The group had evolved from a bar band called the Soul Giants that recruited Frank as a substitute guitarist after their regular guitarist got into a fist fight with another band member.

Soon after, Frank pushed for playing original material, and the rest is outlandishly weird music history. Early Mothers-inspired "freak outs" in Los Angeles made the local authorities nervous, so Frank and crew headed to New York in 1967. There they worked the Garrick Theatre on Bleecker Street as an improv house band performing experimental music with satirical and impromptu slapstick for several months with special sit-in guests, even including Jimi Hendrix on one occasion.

Returning to Los Angeles the following year, Frank and the Mothers formed the nucleus of a musical community. A member of that scene, Pamela Des Barres of the Zappa-discovered GTO's (Girls Together Outrageously), recalls the unorthodox scene.

In the liner notes to the *Zapped* album that served as Warners/Reprise's 1970 promotional sampler for Bizarre/Straight, the labels that Frank was given to promote new freaks, Pamela wrote: "Somehow in some mysterious and mystical way, a little crack formed in the Americana prefab facade that allowed true, far-fetched inspiration to peek, sneak, lead through for an infinitesimal period of time; a drop in the bucket that made a mighty splash. I am proud and honored to have been a part of the streaming baptism of lunacy that attempted to shake, rattle and roll the fictitious foundation of normalcy."

Frank gathered as many bizarre acts as he could find and formed his record companies with the help of his then-manager Herb Cohen. Among Frank's proteges were Tim Buckley, the GTOs (Jeff Beck, Rod Stewart and Ry Cooder performed as part of the supporting cast with Lowell George helping Frank to produce), Alice Cooper (Frank is said to have encouraged Cooper to dress in women's clothes) and, of course, Frank's high school friend Don Van Vliet, aka the great Captain Beefheart.

BEEFHEART TO MOTHERS

Frank remembers Beefheart in the early days carrying his worldly possessions—his art, poetry books and a soprano sax—around in a shopping bag. Frank recorded his dada-esque masterpiece *Trout Mask Replica* for Bizarre in 1969. Produced as an anthropological field recording in Beefheart's house, the album was deemed the year's "most unusual and challenging musical experience" by rock writer Lester Bangs. After a few days of using a portable taping system that recorded the different instruments in various rooms in the house, Frank complied with Van Vliet's paranoid demands that the rest of the sessions take place in a real studio, where all his vocals were captured.

Even though Frank recorded a wealth of albums with the Mothers (including *Cruisin' With Ruben and the Jets* and *Weasels Ripped My Flesh*), he disbanded the group in 1969 not long after they played a series of East Coast dates on a package tour with jazz stars Rahsaan Roland Kirk, Duke Ellington, and Gary Burton. Over the years, Zappa went on to work with a diverse crew of artists ranging from L. Shankar and Jean-Luc Ponty to John Lennon & Yoko Ono and Flo & Eddie (Mark Volman and Howard Kaylan) of the defunct Turtles.

Of all the collaborations and outlandish albums Frank recorded, which performances from his huge catalog of work does he take the most pride in? "Certainly, I enjoy listening to some recordings more than I do others," he says. "I can't stand to hear some of my classic albums because I remember the horrible conditions under which they were recorded. It hurts to listen to them."

WE HAD LOTS OF LAUGHS

Frank holds fond memories of his live shows. "What I like the best doesn't depend so much on the quality of the composition as it does on the memories of how much fun they were to record," he says. "I'm especially thinking of some of the live shows with my 1984 band that were recorded in the *You Can't Do That On Stage Anymore* series. We had lots of laughs."

He adds, "Those recordings may not be the best performances of the best compositions, but when I listen to them I get transported back to the concerts and still laugh at what was happening onstage." For example, he tells me, one night in Seattle, in the middle of the show, his guitarist Ike Willis started to do an imitation of the Lone Ranger, blurting out, "Hi, ho, Silver!"

"I still don't know how and why it happened, but I cracked up every time he did it," Franks says. "It must have been road fatigue. He'd keep yelling that in the most inappropriate places. The whole show was riddled with bad Lone Ranger jokes and me not being able to sing the right words. I enjoyed that night."

Frank continued touring until 1988 when his road band self-destructed before the tour reached most of the planned U.S. dates. The tour, captured on the excellent *The Best Band You Never Heard in Your Life* double CD, could well have been the last time Frank played guitar in concert. Nowadays, he hardly ever plays his guitars. That's surprising given his prowess on the instrument (though he states that he could never lay claim to being a virtuoso) and that he recorded several impressive guitar albums, including the twin-CD *Shut Up 'N Play Yer Guitar*.

A guitar hero who rarely if ever settled for a clichéd riff, Frank learned to play as a kid by swiping blues licks from such R&B greats as Guitar Slim, Johnny "Guitar" Watson (who worked with Frank in the mid-'70s) and Clarence "Gatesmouth" Brown. Citing a lack of motivation to play the guitar these days, Frank spends most of his time composing on his Synclavier 9600, the high-tech digital keyboard and sampling computer.

I'm curious about how Frank—the punster, the satirist, the humorist, the composer—creates. He obliges, harking back to the old days when he was doing a lot of lyric writing.

"I'd write lyrics when I was traveling," he says. "I was on a flight back from Germany when I came up with the idea for the song 'Dumb All Over.' I scrawled out three pages worth of ideas on the plane. I couldn't wait to get into the studio to record it. The reverse of that happened with 'Inca Roads.' I came up with the melody first. I took it as a challenge to find words to go with it. A lot of songs may start with one or two words. You hear a funny expression and away you go. Some lyrics were based on folklore from the band when we were touring. 'Punky's Whips' is an example of an absurd situation that happened to be a true story. All I had to do was find some musical way to dramatize it."

THE CLASSICAL FRANK

Frank had been fascinated with and influenced by such classical composers as Igor Stravinsky, Varese, Boulez and John Cage in addition to having his bands perform arrangements of pieces by Bartók, Ravel, Tchaikovsky and Stravinsky. He notes that most of the material he writes these days are orchestral compositions on his Synclavier. It's plugged into his home studio, the Utility Muffin Research Kitchen, a couple of rooms away from where we're sitting.

Later we spend two and a half hours with two of his trusted studio workers, mix engineer Spencer Chrislu and Synclavier operator Todd Yvega, while they painstakingly sample all the notes on Frank's 97-key Bosendorfer Grand Imperial piano. That's where Frank's newest, soon-to-be-released gem of an album of his dissonant, whimsical and haunting orchestral works, *The Yellow Shark*, is being prepared for release at the end of the year.

Performed in concert in 1992 by the 25-member European contemporary classical music group Ensemble Modern, *The Yellow Shark* is a suite-like collection of new arrangements of such classic pieces as "Dog Breath Variations," "Be-Bop Tango" and "The Girl in the Magnesium Dress" and such new works commissioned for the project as "Get Whitey" and "None of the Above."

EM and its conductor Peter Rundel spent two weeks in 1991 in Los Angeles at Frank's Joe's Garage studio rehearsing the difficult pieces. They then spent another two weeks supervised by the musical-perfectionist composer last summer in preparation for a series of eight concerts in Berlin, Vienna and at the Frankfurt Festival where Frank was one of four featured composers (the others were John Cage, Karlheinz Stockhausen and Alexander Knaifel). The album represents the best performances of each piece from the different concert venues.

Frank, who personally conducted the whirlwind "G-Spot Tornado" on the Frankfurt Festival's opening night, is pleased with the results, but notes, "I was only able to attend the first and third performances in Frankfurt. I got sick and had to fly home."

Did the exuberant audience response to the shows, captured on tape, help ease the pain? "If I hadn't been sick, the experience would have been exhilarating," he says. "Unfortunately, I felt so excruciatingly shitty that it was hard to walk, to just get up onto the stage, to sit, to stand up. You can't really enjoy yourself when you're sick no matter how enthusiastic the audience is."

CANCER CAN BOTHER YOU

I tell Frank the concerns his fans have expressed about his health, then ask him what he thinks about a recent article that quoted a friend of his as saying, "[Frank's] just not going to be bothered by something as stupid as cancer." Frank pauses, then soberly responds, "Well, that's pretty fucking optimistic. Let me tell you. Cancer can bother you. It can just bother you to death. I'm fighting for my life. So far I'm winning."

He laughs, then continues, "I've already beaten the odds. When the cancer was first diagnosed, the doctors didn't give me too long to go. But I've surprised everybody by sticking around this long."

Frank's prostate cancer was detected in 1990, some eight to ten years after it had first developed. Since the cancer was in an advanced stage, it was considered inoperable. He's been forced to undergo a bladder operation as well as radiation therapy. He's reticent to talk more about his illness beyond that he's "doing a whole bunch of other stuff" for therapy.

I ask Frank if his music is a form of therapy. "I don't do it for therapy. I do it because that's what I've always done," he says. "What's your alternative? Stay in bed or work?"

Frank credits his studio staff for making life easier for him as he's working out his musical ideas. "I used to be a night owl, but now I'm usually in bed by six or seven in the evening. It's hard for me to work a real long day anymore," he says. "I'm up at 6:30 in the morning. If I can do a 12-hour shift. Then I feel I'm really doing something. The staff arrives at around 9:30, so that gives me a little time to work by myself before I sit in the studio all day with them."

Frank's illness also aborted his short-lived, but very serious presidential campaign. It also curtailed his plans to develop an international licensing, consulting and social engineering enterprise called Why Not? set up to forge ties between Eastern Bloc and Western businesses.

Frank has big plans. "Take Russia," he says. "Until the Soviet Union folded, we spent fifty years of Cold War cash convincing Americans that we needed to fight against the Evil Empire. Hey, I traveled to Russia five times right when it was on the cusp of glasnost. The place was a fucking disaster area. These people couldn't even deliver milk. The CIA knew that, but why didn't they say the Cold War was for shit and Russia wasn't a threat to us? If we had been working with the Russians to develop what they knew, we all would have been better off. The Russians may not have the money, but they have the brains."

Frank's idea with Why Not? was to work with the co-ops of inventors, helping them to license their inventions of industrial processes and equipment design in the West. "They could have been knee-deep in hard currency if their ideas and prototypes of ideas were linked to the West," he says. "When I got sick, I had to shut down my plans. It's difficult enough for me to travel, but it's no vacation going to Russia. The conditions are grim there. It's hard to find something to eat, the transportation is a nightmare, and since there's no Russian phone book, it's nearly impossible to get in touch with people unless they've given you their telephone number beforehand."

CENSORSHIP

Another illness-related story is the letter Tipper Gore sent to him when she heard he had cancer. Gore was at the helm of the warning sticker controversy that Frank so vehemently opposed. Gore and the Parents Music Resource Center ended up "convincing" many labels to agree to the stickers which Zappa laments as having a "chilling impact" on artists' First Amendment rights.

Throughout the debates on censorship, Frank was pitted as being Gore's arch-rival. "The media likes to give the illusion that Tipper Gore and I are mortal enemies," he says. "That's not a fact. She sent me a sweet letter when she heard I was sick, and I appreciate that. I've said it before in interviews I've done, but somehow that never gets mentioned when they get published."

Frank, who has himself come under attack for being racist and sexist in a number of songs deemed by his critics as being vulgar and crass, personally adopted his own satirical sticker for his homegrown Barking Pumpkin label that reads in part: "Warning/Guarantee: This album contains material which a truly free society would neither fear nor suppress. In some socially retarded areas, religious fanatics and ultra-conservative political organizations violate your First Amendment Rights by attempting to censor rock & roll albums. We feel this is un-Constitutional and un-American. As an alternative to these government-supported programs (designed to keep you docile and ignorant), Barking Pumpkin is pleased to provide stimulating digital audio entertainment for those of you who have outgrown *the ordinary*."

The issue of censorship prompts Frank to again reflect back on twelve years of Republican rule at the White House. "I have a large and devoted audience overseas, but a lot of people in this country don't know that I still exist," he says. "I think that might have something to do with the Republicans, who have never been too thrilled about my existence. I get the feeling that I've been blacklisted in this country. My music doesn't get played on the radio here. And the only time I'm on TV is when someone wants to get a funny comment out of me for the news. I put together a one-hour show for an HBO special called *Does Humor Belong in Music?* It was a live concert from 1984, and no one would touch it in this country. What probably kept it off HBO was some remarks I made about Reagan in the middle of the show. All my video projects have aired in other countries, but not in the United States."

THE POLITICAL SPECTRUM

So where does Frank stand on the political spectrum? Given his harsh critiques of a slew of governmental policies ranging from Pentagon expenditures to care for the homeless, does he consider himself an anarchist?

"If you're referring to an absence of government, I can only see that coming about at that golden point in the development of the human species when we no longer require a government," he says. "Although I resent government, I can't imagine an effectively functioning society without some machinery to make it work—even if it's incompetent machinery—because the species hasn't evolved to the point where it can take care of itself. So, I'm what I call a practical conservative, which means smaller government and lower taxes. What do you call a system that seeks a bigger government and more taxes? Insanity."

In many ways Frank could be a model figure for the rugged individualist of the American myth. For years, he's called his own shots and heartily aired his controversial opinions. In the pre-Mothers' days, he owned his own recording studio, Studio Z, which he bought from Paul Buff who had run the Cucamonga facility as Pal Recording which was where the surf hit "Wipe Out" was recorded.

In the late sixties, based on the commercial success of his first Mothers' albums, he was given a long leash by Warner Bros. Records to sign alternative and avant-garde (read: weird) acts such as Captain Beefheart, Alice Cooper and Tom Waits to his own Bizarre/Straight label. (On the sleeve of the 1970 Bizarre/Straight sampler LP, *Zapped*, Frank and co-owner Herb Cohen wrote, "We make records that are a little different. We present musical and sociological material which the important record companies would probably not allow you to hear. Just what the world needs...another record company.")

Much later in 1989, Frank agreed to have an authorized biography be written by Peter Occhiogrosso. However, Frank red-lighted the draft because he found Occhiogrosso's style too flat and lacking Zappaesque flair. The tell-all project transformed into the compelling and hilarious autobiography *The Real Frank Zappa Book*.

Today, Frank, who has released well over fifty albums over the course of his career, maintains his own publishing rights, records on his own Barking Pumpkin label, runs a mail order and merchandising company called Barfko-Swill and operates the Honker Home Video arm of the Zappa empire. It markets such video releases as his funny *True Story of Frank Zappa's 200 Motels*. He also has a CD rerelease deal set with Rykodisc and has thwarted the efforts of bootleggers by authorizing Rhino Records to release two series of Zappa-approved bootlegs. He even maintains his own hotline message, 818-PUMPKIN, to keep his fans up-to-date on the latest developments of his career.

But Frank downplays the rugged individualist tag. "Well, that's pretty flattering, but it's not completely true," he says. "I have lots of people helping me to call the shots. My wife Gail runs the business end of things and not only does a great job, but likes to do it. I have great confidence in my attorneys, accountants and auditors, the people who do the mechanics of collecting the money. All of my staff are very competent and nice people that I get along with."

ORCHESTRAL MUSIC

However, Frank notes that one area of his business that he exercises strict control over is permission to perform his orchestral material. "You'd be surprised at how many orchestras and chamber groups all over the world play my music every year," he says. "I get requests for scores all the time. But I won't grant permission if I feel there's not enough money budgeted for proper rehearsal time. I'd rather not have the music played than have it performed in a sloppy way."

Frank laughs and says that he gets unusual requests all the time. The most recent came from the president's own U.S. Marine Corps Band in Fairfax, Virginia.

"They want to play 'Dog Breath Variations,'" he says. "It seems a couple of gunnery sergeants in the ensemble are fans. So, we sent them the music. Then there's Jamey Hampton, the choreographer for the dance troupe ISO in Connecticut. He wants permission to choreograph *The Grand Wazoo* album."

Gail joins the conversation in the studio and reminds Frank about yet another strange request, this one from a young filmmaker in upstate New York who wants to use "Elvis Has Just Left the Building" from the *Broadway the Hard Way* album to conclude a mock documentary he's making of current Elvis sightings. Gail shows me the latest in a series of hilarious faxes the filmmaker has sent to Frank, who is amused by such comically self-deprecating lines in the letter as, "If you have read this far, it's time for more groveling. Please, I long for your kind words of YES or NO. Please grant this feeble, meaningless cipher permission, and inspire me to build temples to you and send riches to you—although you are probably as modest as you are wise and would refuse my pathetic offerings."

THE FINAL WORDS

At the agreed-upon interview length of one hour, I let Frank know that my allotted time has elapsed. He says he can take a few more questions.

I ask him about future projects. Frank says that his slate is full. He will continue to dig into his audio archives to issue old material. Case in point, his just-released *Ahead of Their Time* CD of a 1968 Mothers' concert in London. Fourteen members of the BBC Symphony joined the group to provide the Frank-composed musical accompaniment to a play the band members acted out.

Next year Frank promises another CD of unreleased studio cuts called *Lost Episodes*. Then there's a CD of music for modern dance called *Dance Me This* that he's working on. Frank is still in the negotiating stages with the Vienna Festival, which wants to do a stage version next May of *Civilization: Phaze III*. He describes it as an "opera/pantomime/dance/circus performance."

But what Frank is most excited about are a couple of projects he has been discussing with Andreas Mölich-Zebhauser, the business manager for Ensemble Modern, the European ensemble dedicated to promoting the music of modern composers.

They talked during a visit just a couple days earlier. "Andreas told me about an interview Edgard Varèse gave once where he said he envisioned a film to accompany his piece 'Desért.' I had never heard of that before," Frank says. "Varèse said that the images didn't need to relate to the music."

The Ensemble is booked for a concert in Cologne, Germany next year on May 27, 1994. "Andreas thought of the extensive data bank of video images I've collected and got the idea to commission me to do a 22-minute film," Frank says. "The other project we discussed was for May 1995 when the Ensemble would perform an evening dedicated to my theatrical works like 'Billy the Mountain,' 'Gregory Peckory,' 'Penis

Dimension,' and 'Brown Shoes Don't Make It' arranged for classical ensemble. I think it will make for an entertaining evening and an entertaining CD."

For my final query, I reflect on how Frank's music over the span of nearly thirty years has remained fresh, relevant, challenging and on-the-fringe. I was curious to know to what he owed his career longevity.

So opinionated on so many subjects, Frank displays a rare moment of being both humble and at a loss for words. "I don't know how it's happened," he says. "How have I survived? I guess by word of mouth, but I don't know. I got lucky."

ADDENDUM

Yellow Shark was officially released in November 1993, a month before Frank died: In listing the recording as one of his favorite albums, singer Tom Waits said, "The ensemble is awe-inspiring. It is a rich pageant of texture in color. It's the clarity of his perfect madness, and mastery. Frank governs with Elmore James on his left and Stravinsky on his right. Frank reigns and rules with the strangest tools."

FRANK ZAPPA OBITUARY

1993

Francis Vincent Zappa was born in 1940 in Baltimore where his Sicilian-born, Greek-Arab meteorologist father was employed by an arsenal that manufactured poison gas during World War II. The Zappa family eventually settled in Lancaster, California, a Mohave Desert town Frank called a cultural wasteland. Ironically, it was here, during his high school years, that Zappa's interest in outlandish combinations of music bloomed. He formed an R&B group called the Blackouts, he bought Stravinsky and Varèse records, and he played drums in his high school band where he was introduced to twelve-tone music and even allowed to do a bit of composing and conducting.

His breakthrough group Mothers of Invention proved to be short-lived. The debut Mothers record *Freak Out!* was released in 1966. He disbanded the group in 1969. On his own, Frank went on to work on recording a massive catalog with a diverse and ever-changing crew of collaborators and band members including George Duke, Jean-Luc Ponty, L. Shankar, Johnny "Guitar" Watson, the London Symphony Orchestra, Pierre Boulez, Adrian Belew, Steve Vai, Yoko Ono and John Lennon.

Frank adventurously covered a universe of musical terrain, ranging from '50s doo-wop to 20th century classical music by Stravinsky and Bartók. With a lifelong flair for creating genre-jumping, post-modernist music, Frank released albums that folded in several different styles of music, cross-referencing such seemingly disparate domains as classical with reggae and melodic R&B with dissonant avant-garde. He fused it all into a sometimes brilliant, frequently madcap, always spin-on-a-dime concoction of distinct and inimitable Zappaesque music.

A control freak who ultimately trusted only his inner circle of colleagues, friends and family, the irascible Frank found himself at odds with some of the musicians who worked for him that sometimes led to irreconcilable rifts. Yet, for former band members like drummers Terry Bozzio and Chad Wackerman and trombonist Bruce Fowler, working with Frank was not only the most challenging musical experiences they've encountered, but also the most inspiring.

After gigging in San Francisco as a jazz drummer, in 1975 24-year-old Terry headed to Los Angeles and out-finessed 50 other auditioning drummers after Frank's previous drummer Chester Thompson had left to join Weather Report. "It was a musical experience unlike any college," says Terry, who put in a three-year stint with Frank. "His music was so challenging, and he brought out things I never knew I had in me. Plus, it was amazing just being exposed to his intellect, charisma and wit."

Terry speculates that some former group members may not have seen eye-to-eye with Frank because he was such a genius. "I think some guys were jealous of Frank being the kingpin," Terry says. He cites Frank as a role model: "We'd all love to be just like him in our own way. He's an archetype. He put on the red shoes. He did it 18 hours a day every day. He rode that wave. Frank was a strong, uncompromising guy who believed in his artistic principles. He was convinced and lucky enough to have those convictions about himself early enough in his life to follow through on them."

Chad Wackerman, who worked with Zappa from 1981 to 1988, also had to pass a grueling audition that consisted of reading intricate and complex classical notation, polyrhythmically playing in such odd time signatures as 21/16, and then following Frank's guitar lead into Latin, Cajun, reggae and heavy metal grooves. "He pushed everyone who worked for him," Chad recalls. "He'd ask me to play something incredibly complex. When I couldn't do it, he'd get more specific and ask me to play something even more difficult. I couldn't do that either, but as I would try, I'd come to realize I was playing what he had first asked me to play."

Chad remembers his first Zappa tour. "At the airport while we were waiting for our plane, everybody except Frank would be reading or listening to tapes," he says. "He'd have his score paper out and would be writing this incredibly complicated music. He had endless energy. There was no one else like him. Frank was a unique combination of brilliant 20th century composer and great rock guitarist."

Bruce Fowler first joined Frank in 1973 for his *Overnite Sensation* touring band (with Jean-Luc Ponty, George Duke and Ian Underwood) and played with him on and off for the next two decades. Bruce was well-versed in the complex rhythms Frank was compositionally fond of. Brothers Tom and Walt were also part of various Zappa ensembles. "He liked us because we were an orchestral tool for him," Bruce says. "He was always thinking of ways to use us."

Bruce says Frank was a hard task master, putting his bands through hours of practice. "But it was all fun when we did the actual gigs," he says. "Sometimes Frank wouldn't give us the set list until right before the show. But we knew the material so well we could be spontaneous." Bruce notes that Frank stretched musical boundaries for his audiences as well. "He was real proud to bring music to the masses of people who wanted to get freaked out by him. He wanted to play Bartók for those guys."

Frank's propensity to shock and even outrage people with his idiosyncratic music and his bold political views often made him an easy target of critics bent on dismissing his dissenting vote against the status quo.

When we talked last spring, Frank voiced a quiet hurt over the fact that his music rarely gets airplay in the United States.

While his biggest Stateside hits, "Valley Girl" and "Don't Eat the Yellow Snow," were both novelty tunes and a significant portion of his pop-oriented work falls far short of the genius plateau, Frank's importance as a composer and performer promises to be increasingly recognized. In 1969, *DownBeat's* Larry Kart concluded his cover story article on Zappa by prophesying his future relevance: "...There is still the music, and if any of us are around in 20 years, I think we'll be listening to it."

Twenty-four years later, Terry is even bolder in his predictions: "Frank will be the only guy mentioned two hundred years from now when people are discussing the great music of our era."

THE LEGACY PRESERVED
2016

Before Frank died, he gave his spouse Gail specific instructions on what to do with his music. "I'm a professional wife, and I do what I'm told, almost without exception," she explains in our phone conversation. Gail, who can be as feisty and hard-nosed as her husband was, ran the business end of the FZ empire (including Frank's own Barking Pumpkin record imprint and the Barfko Swill video distribution) for several years. "Frank was adamant that I sell the catalog because he wanted me to have my own life. I didn't feel it was important at the time, but now I realize what a genius he was."

Rykodisc, which had issued Zappa's albums in CD format for the first time in the mid '80s, was one of several record labels vying to own the masters of Zappa's works. The family trust maintains the publishing rights as well as the full rights to all of his unreleased classical works, including *Civilization Phaze III*, which was issued on Barking Pumpkin. Gail finally chose Rykodisc in October 1994 based on the integrity of the label and the intention of Ryko president Don Rose to fully commit his company to not only preserve Zappa's music, but also introduce it to new audiences.

While Frank was strong-willed about his career throughout his life, he was equally determined not to let his music be compromised after he died. "It was hard to negotiate with Ryko when I was asking for what Frank wanted," Gail says. "I couldn't change my mind. I didn't have a choice. What was key for Frank was that the label not have the right to change or alter his music in any way. He didn't want to have one of his songs getting remixed into a disco track."

Gail says her husband was vehement about wanting to maintain control over three of his signature guitar tunes, "Watermelon in Easter Hay," "Zoot Allures" and "Black Napkins," so that they wouldn't end up being used someday for a running shoe or beer commercial. "Those were his favorite songs and I still control the masters. Ryko owns them, but I control their licensing. I couldn't live hearing those tunes in any other way than how Frank wanted them to be heard."

But in March 2006, the Warner Music Group acquired the Ryko Corporation for $67.5 million. Six years later in 2012 the Zappa Family Trust parted ways with Ryko/Warner. The trust reacquired Frank's music catalogue with Universal Musical Enterprises taking over the distribution of all of his recordings.

The Zappa Family Trust ended up running into financial troubles. In 2016, it was $6 million in debt and was forced to sell the house and studio. The buyer? Lady Gaga who paid $5.25 million.

Not quite the way Frank envisioned his legacy.

But his music continues to override everything. For those who knew him best, including drummer Terry Bozzio, this is no surprise. "Frank was Mt. Olympus," Terry says, "and we were mere mortals."

About the Author

Dan Ouellette is a New York-based writer, author, journalist, editor, curator, and speaker with an expertise in jazz music as well as "beyond jazz" music including significant archival interviews with Frank Zappa, Lou Reed, Laurie Anderson, Elvis Costello, John Lee Hooker, David Byrne, Esperanza Spalding, Joni Mitchell and others. His jazz highlights include Wayne Shorter. Carla Bley. Abdullah Ibrahim, Henry Threadsgill, Charlie Haden, Keith Jarrett, Jimmy Smith, McCoy Tyner, and others.

Dan travels the world covering music. His explorations include Beijing, Cape Town (South Africa), Melbourne (Australia), Mali, Istanbul, Canada (Vancouver, Montreal, Quebec City), the Mississippi Delta juke joints, Austria, and Italy (Genoa, Perugia and Orvieto).

Dan has served as a project manager, a co-producer of audio/video projects (including between-show content at the Monterey Jazz Festival) and a chronicler of artist conversations in front of a live audience at major jazz festivals including Monterey and North Sea Jazz Festival.

Dan's sizable catalog of recorded interviews from 1985 to present are being archived at California State University, Monterey Bay. He was twice nominated for the Lifetime Achievement in Jazz Journalism honors by the Jazz Journalism Association.

In addition to his Landfill Chronicles chapters on the Medium platform at danouellette.medium.com, Dan has been delivering his monthly column, Jazz & Beyond Intel, at danouellette.net, now in its fifth year. Landfill celebrates the classic past; Jazz & Beyond Intel champions today's rising stars.

Now firmly based in the East End of Long Island, Dan has been actively involved with the Hamptons Jazz Festival, including appearances on the local NPR station WLIW as well as the local cable television station LTV which features a weekly interview program on music. Both are streamable worldwide.

Appendix—Attributions

JOHN ABERCROMBIE

The Moment Looks for You — DownBeat 2012

LAURIE ANDERSON

Laurie Anderson's Honesty — San Francisco Chronicle 2001

CARLA BLEY

At Home with Carla — QWEST.tv & ZEALnyc 2019

DEE DEE BRIDGEWATER

Dee Dee Bridgewater—Finding Her Roots — DownBeat 2007

DAVID BYRNE

Look into the Eyeball — San Franciso Chronicle & Stereophile magazine 2001

Dance Party with Human Hope — DownBeat & ZEALnyc 2017

REGINA CARTER

Taming the Ghost: Regina's Courtship with Paganini's Violin — April 2003 DownBeat cover

Paganini Comes to New York — Unpublished 2004

Regina Sings Ella — DownBeat 2017

ORNETTE COLEMAN

Harmolodic Recording Studio Lift-Off — ZEALnyc 2003

ELVIS COSTELLO

Elvis Costello & Allen Toussaint Seek the Indestructible Beat of New Orleans — DownBeat cover story 2006

Elvis Heads North in Jazz-Fueled Romance and Pain — DownBeat 2003

Elvis Goes Mingus — DownBeat 2003

Introvert Meets Extrovert: Elvis Costelo and Bill Frisell Join Forces — DownBeat 1998

DownBeat Blindfold Test — DownBeat 1994

CHARLIE HADEN

Charlie Sits and Talks	Strings 1995
Charlie's Quartet West with Strings Opens the 1999 San Francisco Jazz Festival	San Francisco Chronicle 1999
The Artistry of the Duo Perfected	QWEST.tv 2018
Charlie Gets DownBeat Blindfolded	DownBeat 1997
Charlie Gets DownBeat Blindfolded—Again	DownBeat 2005

JOHN LEE HOOKER

Young and Fiesty at 80	DownBeat 1997
John Lee's Blues World	Unpublished 1997

FREDDIE HUBBARD

Blindfold Test – Freddie Hubbard	DownBeat 2002

BOBBY HUTCHERSON

Bobby Hutcherson: California Dreaming	DownBeat 2013

ABDULLAH IBRAHIM

Cape Town & Beyond with Duke	DownBeat 2004
Abdullah Ibrahim: A Focus on Spirituality	DownBeat 2019

KEITH JARRETT

Keith Jarrett Reinvents His Approach to the Piano and Looks to Do the Same for His Reputation	DownBeat 2005
Retrograde: Standards Trio—Keith Jarrett Counts His Blessings	DownBeat 1999
Keith Fully Recovers (With Standards Trio)	DownBeat 2001
Standards Trio—Happy 25	DownBeat 2008

ELVIN JONES

Fascinating Rhythm	San Francisco Chronicle, 2000
DownBeat Critics Poll Drummer of the Year: The Wisdom of Elvin Jones	DownBeat 1999

WYNTON MARSALIS

Next Chapter	DownBeat 2004

JONI MITCHELL

Shine & More	Unpublished 2007

JASON MORAN

Jason Moran—Other Ways of Operating   DownBeat 2014

ASTOR PIAZZOLLA

Astor Piazzolla—The Politics of Tampering   The Berkeley Monthly 1989
with Tradition

LOU REED

Ecstasy—The Hard Way   Schwann Spectrum & San Francisco
                                                   Chronicle 2000

The Raven   San Francisco Chronicle 2003

SAXOPHONE SUMMIT

Saxophone Summit—Gathering the Spirits   DownBeat 2004
with Joe Lovano, Dave Liebman, and
Michael Brecker

WAYNE SHORTER

1+1   San Francisco Chronicle 1999

Umbria Jazz Melbourne Q&A   Billboard 2005

The Quixotic Jazz Sage Going into the   DownBeat 2009
Unknown: Panama

JIMMY SMITH

Hammond B-3 Bomber Jimmy Smith Talks   DownBeat 1994
about His Jazz Revitalization of the Monster
Organ

ESPERANZA SPALDING

The Early Years   Billboard, 2010

Chamber Music Society   DownBeat 2010

Fast-Forward to a Duo   Jazz & Beyond Intel 2023

HENRY THREADGILL

Henry Threadgill Explores the Contrary by   Stereophile 1998
Makin' a Move and Carrying the Day

MCCOY TYNER

The Legendary McCoy Tyner   DownBeat 2007

FRANK ZAPPA

Meeting Frank   Tower Pulse! magazine 1993

Frank Zappa Obituary   DownBeat & SOMA magazine 1993

The Legacy Preserved   ZEALnyc 2016

Also from Cymbal Press
CYMBALPRESS.COM

CYMBAL
PRESS

Life in E Flat – The Autobiography of Phil Woods
Book of the Year - Jazz Journalists Association

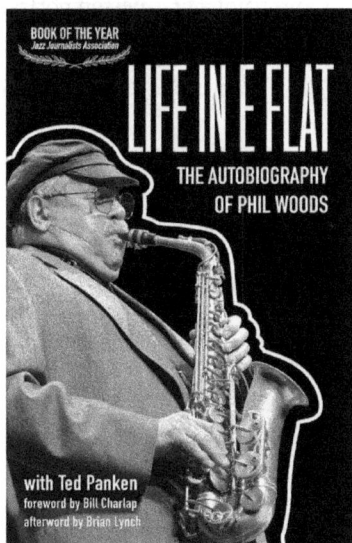

Life in E Flat – The Autobiography of Phil Woods is the life story of the legendary saxophonist, composer, band leader, and National Endowment for the Arts Jazz Master. Look for it in paperback, hardcover, and e-book at cymbalpress.com.

Praise for Life in E Flat

"Life in E-Flat is a gift, a compelling and entertaining memoir by one of the leading alto saxophonists in jazz for 60 years. Phil Woods was a star soloist, influential lead alto player, savvy bandleader, underrated composer-arranger, and consummate studio musician. He was also a charismatic storyteller with a typewriter—literate, funny, insightful, self-aware, with a keen eye and ear for details that reveal character, including his own personal failings. Heroes and colleagues like Charlie Parker, Dizzy Gillespie, Quincy Jones, Benny Carter, and Ben Webster are drawn in quick, astute sketches. Observations about the music business, jazz education, and the vagaries of the jazz life are laced with wisdom and sardonic wit. The book is also an invaluable portrait of world that has vanished: Juilliard at midcentury, the band bus, the bustling post-war bebop academy of the streets, the New York studios of the '60s, the European jazz scene of the early '70s, and the energy and excitement of a remarkable life lived among some of the greatest giants in jazz history."*

—Mark Stryker, author of *Jazz From Detroit*

"Phil Woods's voice on the page is as raw and lyrical and unmistakable as the sound of his alto. If you want to really know about The Life—the true day-to-day of a working jazz musician, with all its agonies and ecstasies and tedium and the ever-exciting challenge of getting paid something like what you're worth for playing your heart out—look no further. *Life in E Flat* pulls no punches and tells no lies."

—James Kaplan, author of *Sinatra: The Chairman, Frank: The Voice* and *Irving Berlin: New York Genius*

Also from Cymbal Press

CYMBALPRESS.COM

Jazz Dialogues with Jon Gordon

Backstage, on the bus, or in the studio, saxophonist Jon Gordon, winner of the prestigious Thelonious Monk International Jazz Saxophone competition, chats with several generations of great musicians. From Jay McShann to Renee Rosnes, *Jazz Dialogues* lets the reader hang out with dozens of jazz artists to learn about their careers, influences, and the dues they've paid. These candid, poignant, and often hilarious conversations paint a first-person portrait of jazz history.

Artists include: Jay McShann, Eddie Locke, Cab Calloway, Maria Schneider, Jan Garbarek, Ken Peplowski, Tim Hagans, Mark Turner, Hank Mobley, Bill Easley, Doc Cheatham, Scott Robinson, Eddie Bert, Phil Woods, Danny Bank, Billy Drummond, Ben Monder, Charles McPherson, Milt Hinton, Ben Riley, Bill Stewart, Art Blakey, Jon-Erik Kellso, Eddie Chamblee, Jimmy Lewis, Chuck Redd, Bill Charlap, McCoy Tyner, Melissa Aldana, Ronnie Mathews, Kevin Hays, Jim McNeely, Steve Wilson, Red Holloway, Barney Kessel, Joe Williams, Quincy Davis, Bob Mintzer, Dick Hyman, Lee Konitz, Leroy Jones, Renee Rosnes, David Sanborn, Gil Evans, Don Sickler, Sean Smith, Sarah Vaughn, Derrick Gardner, Sylvia Cuenca, Harold Mabern, Gene Bertoncini, Mike LeDonne, Essiet Okon Essiet, Bill Mays, and Joe Magnarelli.

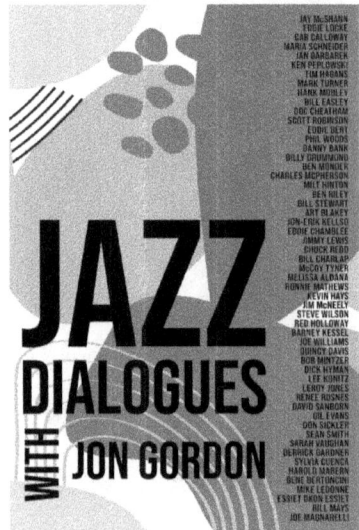

Praise for Jazz Dialogues

"Jazz Dialogues is a rarity among books about jazz: It's a book about people—the individual creators who devote their lives to the making of this profoundly individualistic art. It took a writer who's a first-call musician himself to capture the way jazz artists think and feel, on the bandstand and off. From Cab Calloway and Doc Cheatham to Maria Schneider and Steve Wilson, Jon Gordon brings us face to face, mind to mind, heart to heart, with dozens of fascinating musicians. Like a great player in a jazz band, Gordon knows not only how to play, but how to listen."

—David Hajdu, author of *Lush Life: A Biography of Billy Strayhorn*

Also from Cymbal Press

CYMBALPRESS.COM

Ruminations & Reflections: The Musical Journey of Dave Liebman & Richie Beirach

The Jazz Book of Two Lifetimes

NEA Jazz Master saxophonist Dave Liebman and pianist Richie Beirach have enjoyed a fifty-year friendship on and off the bandstand. They've performed with Miles Davis, Elvin Jones, Stan Getz, Chet Baker, Freddie Hubbard, and their own bands. Ruminations and Reflections takes readers on a rollicking journey through their musical lives. Along the way, they share their views on jazz education, prominent musicians, and musical preparation. Liebman and Beirach pay tribute to their musical mentors, tour their discography, and suggest essential recordings to study. The book's conversational style will engage students, professionals, and music lovers alike.

For Fans of Jazz Masters and Legends

Ruminations and Reflections showcases never before told anecdotes and opinions about musical legends including John Coltrane, Bill Evans, McCoy Tyner, Jack DeJohnette, Wayne Shorter, Michael Brecker, Randy Brecker, Chick Corea, Lee Konitz, Sonny Rollins, Herbie Hancock, and Wynton Marsalis. Jazz fans will delight in the in-depth analysis of over twenty of this duo's best recordings, providing insight and history to this important discography.

Praise for Ruminations & Reflections

"We really don't have an exact name for musicians like Dave and Richie. Across decades of recordings and concerts, their aspirations obliterate the definitions of any single genre. This volume reveals the deep insight and wisdom required to resolve their shared quest for meaning in music. Both are master players who continue to strive for what goes beyond and what lies beneath. Reading their words and following their stories in this wonderful book affirms the feeling that they share on the bandstand as one of the great long-term partnerships in this music." – Pat Metheny

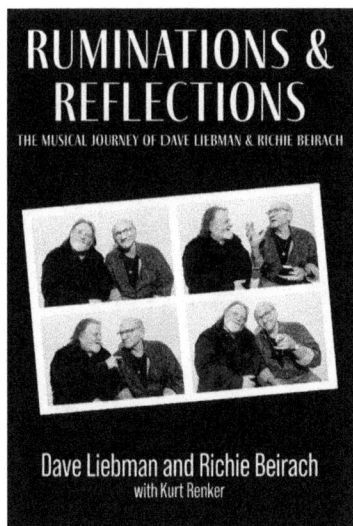

www.ingramcontent.com/pod-product-compliance
Lightning Source LLC
Chambersburg PA
CBHW070342090426
42733CB00009B/1259